The
ULTIMATE
SEARCH
Book

2011 Edition

Worldwide Adoption, Genealogy & Other Search Secrets

by
Lori Carangelo

from the files of
AMERICANS FOR OPEN RECORDS (AmFOR.net)

CLEARFIELD

Copyright © 2011-foreword by Lori Carangelo
Published by Genealogical Publishing Company for
Clearfield Company, Baltimore, Maryland

Previous editions
Library of Congress Cataloging-in-Publication Data
The ultimate search book : worldwide adoption, genealogy, and other search secrets /
[compiled by] Lori Carangelo from the files of Americans for Open Records
(AmFOR). – 2003 ed. rev.
p. cm.

1. Adoptees-Identification-Information services. 2. Adopted children-Information
services. 3. Birthparents-Information services. 4. Missing persons-Information
services. 5. Registers of births, etc.-Information services. 6. Public records-Information
services. 7. Government information. 8. Freedom of information. I. Carangelo, Lori. II.
Americans for Open Records.

1997 and 2000 editions published by Access Press, div. of AmFOR, PO Box 401, Palm Desert, CA 92261-0401
1998 and 1999 by Heritage Quest, PO Box 329, Bountiful, Utah 84011-0329
2002 by Schenkman books Inc. 118 Main St., Rochester, VT 05768

Library of Congress Original Catalog Card Number – 96-86225
Printed in the United States of America

ISBN: 978-0-8063-5515-3

This book is dedicated to all who have had to endure
"impossible" searches for answers to
"Who am I?" and *"Is my child alive and well?"*

`````````````````````

*140 million  Americans Affected by Secrecy of Vital Records—
(half of the United Sates population)

12,000,000
Maternal
Grandparents

12,000,000
Maternal
Grandparents

6,000,000
Birthmothers

6,000,000
Adoptive
Mothers

12,000,000
Maternal
Aunts & Uncles

12,000,000
Maternal
Aunts & Uncles

12,000,000
Paternal
Grandparents

6,000,000
Birthfathers

6,000,000
Adoptive
Fathers

12,000,000
Paternal
Grandparents

12,000,00
Paternal
Aunts & Uncles

12,000,000
Paternal
Aunts & Uncles

7,000,000
Birth Siblings

7,000,000
Birth Siblings

6,000,000
Adoptees
`````````````````````

Disclaimer

It is not the intent of the author, nor Americans For Open Records (AmFOR), nor the publisher, to advocate illegal means to access confidential records or information, nor have we ever done so. Over time, the author has become privy to the ingenuity of both professional investigators and amateur searchers, many of whom are endorsed by referral from Social Services, law enforcement and other groups and individuals, and who, from necessity or desperation, utilized ruses, shortcuts and trade secrets for circumventing roadblocks to gain access to their own wrongfully withheld vital records or information. The inclusion of any group or individual is not intended as an endorsement but is included for informational purposes for the reader to research. AmFOR has never charged fees for its services nor paid fees for information and does not quote fees of private organizations and businesses, nor for state and local agencies that charge fees for disclosure, or confidential intermediaries or searches. Statute sections and procedures, as well as websites and emails cited are deemed reliable prior to publication and may be subject to change. *The Ultimate Search Book* has been an ongoing project with six editions since 1997. We recognize that information may have been inadvertently excluded and invite updates and suggestions for future editions.

Contents

PREFACE

1   **CHAPTER 1: SEARCH BASICS**
     FORTY SEARCH TIPS FOR STARTERS
     Chart (opposite page 1): Selecting Record Types
1   Begin With A List - Discovering Names, Addresses
2   State Department of Motor Vehicles (DMV); Social Security
3   City/ County/ State Records; Courthouse Records; Prisoner Locator;
     Voter Registration; Federal Resources; National Census; Last Name Search
4   First Name/Birth Date/Year Only, Telephone Records/Numbers,
     Got Phone Number/Need Name and Address, Licenses, School Yearbooks/Records;
     Freedom of Information Act (FOIA) and Privacy Act
5   International Soundex Reunion Registry (ISRR)
6   The Birth Certificate - Hospital issued, County issued, State issued
7   The Birth Certificate - Privately issued, Baptismal, Amended;
     Foreign Birth Certificates; The Worldwide Search Network
8   Credit Bureaus
9   Salvation Army, Utility Companies, Employment Checks, Banks,
     Independent Search Firms
10   FBI's NCIC Database, Background Checks, Common Names, Medical Records,
     Physicians, Hospitals, "Life or Death" Search, Military Personnel Records
12   Police Reports, If You Are Denied, Media Access, Passport Service
13   Starting Your Own Search Business
14   Examples: Adoptee's Original and Amended Birth Certificates

15   **CHAPTER 2: MISSING AND RUNAWAY CHILDREN**
15   If a Child Is Missing; Amber Alert/How To Report
16   More Search Tips for Finding Missing or Runaway Children; Black Market Adoption
17   Child Abuse, Runaways, Prevention and Identification, Private Investigators,
     Cyberspace Snatches or Recovers Kids; Children of the Night; Boystown Hotline

19   **CHAPTER 3: FAMILY TREE, GENEALOGY, DEBTOR,**
     CHILD SUPPORT, HEIR, CLASSMATE, OLD LOVE, WAR BUDDY,
     MISSING ADULTS or ANYONE
19   Family Tree and Genealogy; Adoptee's Family Wheel (diagram); Death of Genealogy
20   The Church of Jesus Christ of Latter-Day Saints Family History Centers
21   How to Use the National Archives for Genealogical Research
23   Records Available for Search; Census; Immigration/Naturalization
25   Debtors, Bills, Child Support Matters
25   Classmates, Old Loves, Missing Adults, Anyone
25   To Find an Heir

27   **CHAPTER 4: WITH OR WITHOUT A NAME - FAMILY MEMBERS**
     SEPARATED DUE TO ADOPTION, DIVORCE
     Chart (opposite page 27): 2010 Adoption Disclosure Laws at a Glance (by State)
27   Who Am I?—A Basic Right; Adoption Roadblocks
28   Native American Research Resources; Donor Offspring/Donor Parent Registry
29   With or Without a Name; Starting Point for Adoptees and Parents
30   Request Hospital Record of Birth; Deceased Parent or Adoptee; Adoption File;
     Passport; Foster Care Records; Salvation Army Missing Persons Locator
31   Innovative and Bizarre Search Methods of Adoptees, Parents
33   More Letters From Adoptees and Parents

34   Other Resources for Non-Custodial Parents
35   Questions for Adoptees/Parents to Ask Agency and Court

37   **CHAPTER 5: INTERNET SEARCHES**
37   Search Engines, Websites
43   Example: Adoptee Waiver of Confidentiality: "Birth" Parent Waiver of Confidentiality
44   Example: Sibling Waiver of Confidentiality (CA)
46   Example: Request for Confidential Intermediary (CA)
46   Example: Request to Waive Court Fees (CA)

47   **SEARCHING THE USA**
47   Key to Adoption/Support Group
48   Alabama
49   Alaska
50   Arizona
52   Arkansas
54   California
61   Colorado
64   Connecticut
67   Delaware
68   District of Columbia
71   Florida
74   Georgia
76   Hawaii
78   Idaho
81   Illinois
84   Indiana
87   Iowa
89   Kansas
91   Kentucky
93   Louisiana
95   Maine
97   Maryland
99   Massachusetts
102   Michigan
105   Minnesota
107   Mississippi
108   Missouri
108   Montana
113   Nebraska
115   Nevada
117   New Hampshire
118   New Jersey
120   New Mexico
112   New York
126   North Carolina
128   North Dakota
129   Ohio
129   Oklahoma
133   Oregon
135   Pennsylvania
138   Rhode Island
139   South Carolina
141   South Dakota
142   Tennessee
145   Texas
148   Utah
150   Vermont
152   Virginia

154	Washington
157	West Virginia
159	Wisconsin
161	Wyoming
164	U.S. Possessions and Trust Territories
164	American Samoa
164	Guam
165	Panama Canal Zone
165	Puerto Rico
166	Virgin Islands (St. Croix, St. John, St Thomas)
169	**INTERNATIONAL SEARCHING**
	(Opposite page 169): Example: International Soundex Reunion Registry Form
170	International Search Resources–Consular, Vital Records, Red Cross, Messaging, Registries
171	International Social Services (ISS)
172	Citizenship and Adoption
172	Abducted Children
173	Afghanistan, Albania, Algeria, Angola, Antigua and Barbuda
175	Argentina
176	Armenia
177	Australia:
177	Australian Capital Territory, New South Wales
178	Northern Territory
179	Queensland
180	South Australia
182	Tasmania
183	Victoria
184	Western Territory
185	Austria
186	Azerbaijan, Bahamas
187	Bahrain, Bangladesh, Barbados
188	Belarus, Belgium
189	Belize, Benin, Bermuda
190	Bhutan, Bolivia, Bosnia and Herzegovina
191	Botswana
192	Brazil
193	Brunei, Bulgaria
194	Burkina Faso, Burundi, Cambodia, Cameroon
195	Canada
195	Alberta
196	British Columbia
198	Manitoba
198	New Brunswick.
200	Newfoundland
201	Northwest Territories, Nova Scotia
203	Ontario
206	Prince Edward Island
207	Quebec
209	Saskatchewan
210	Yukon
210	Cape Verde, Cayman Islands
211	Central Africa Republic, Chad, Chile
211	China
212	Hong Kong, Macau, Mongolia
213	Taiwan.
214	Colombia, Comoros, Congo
215	Costa Rica, Croatia, Cuba, Cyprus, Czech Republic
218	Denmark, Djibouti, Dominica
217	Dominican Republic, Ecuador, Egypt, El Salvador

218   Equatorial Guinea, Eritrea, Estonia, Ethiopia
219   Fiji, Finland
221   Gabon, Gambia, Georgia
222   Germany
227   Ghana, Gibraltar, Greece
228   Grenada, Guatemala
229   Guinea, Guinea-Bissau, Guyana, Haiti
230   Hungary
231   Iceland
232   India, Indonesia, Iran
233   Iraq, Ireland, (Republic of)
234   Israel, Italy
236   Ivory Coast, Jamaica, Japan.
237   Jordan, Kazakhstan, Kenya
238   Kiribati, Korea (North and South)
239   Kuwait
240   Kyrgyzstan, Laos, Latvia, Lebanon
241   Lesotho, Liberia, Libya, Liechtenstein
242   Lithuania, Luxembourg, Macedonia
243   Madagascar, Malawi, Malaysia, Maldives, Mali
244   Malta, Marshall Islands, Mauritania, Mauritius
245   Mexico
246   Micronesia - Federated States of Micronesia, Moldava
247   Monaco, Montenegro, Montserrat, Morocco, Mozambique.
248   Myanmar, Namibia, Nauru, Nepal, The Netherlands
249   New Zealand.
259   Nicaragua, Niger, Nigeria
251   Niue, Northern Marina Islands, Norway
252   Oman, Pakistan, Palau, Panama (see also U.S. Possessions: Panama Canal Zone)
253   Papua New Guinea, Paraguay
254   Peru
255   Philippines
256   Poland
258   Portugal, Qatar
259   Romania
261   Russia
262   Rwanda, St. Christopher/Nevis, St. Lucia, St. Vincent and the Grenadines
264   Samoa - Western (See also American Samoa"), San Marino, Sao Tome and Principe, Saudi Arabia
265   Senegal, Serbia, Seychelles
266   Sierra Leone, Singapore, Slovakia
267   Slovenia, Solomon Islands, Somalia, South Africa
268   Spain, Sri Lanka, Sudan, Suriname, Swaziland
269   Sweden, Switzerland
270   Syria, Tajikistan
271   Tanzania, Thailand, Togo, Tonga
272   Trinidad and Tobago, Tunisia, Turkey
273   Turkmenistan, Turks and Caicos Islands, Tuvalu, Uganda
274   Ukraine, United Arab Emirates
274   United Kingdom
274   England and Wales
279   Northern Ireland, Scotland
281   Uruguay, Uzbekistan
282   Vanuatu, Venezuela, Vietnam
284   Yemen, Yugoslavia
286   Zaire, Zambia, Zimbabwe

287-291 **INDEX**
292-294 **ADDENDUM:** State Private Investigator Licensing Boards

"A right is not a right, in America, unless it is enjoyed by all Americans."
—Special Watergate Prosecutor Archibald Cox

Preface

Almost everyone has someone whose absence has left a hole in his or her heart and may like to re-connect with them. In the case of adoptees, the absence is more cruelly shaped by secrecy of records and what is usually their total lack of knowledge about their biological relatives so profoundly connected with their own sense of self, their very identity. "Birth" parents have expressed similar grief from loss of their children to an unknown fate. Over 140,000,000 Americans (half the United States population) have an adoption or relinquishment for adoption in their immediate family[1]. So this 2011 Edition of *The Ultimate Search Book* not only provides "how to" secrets for searching out records and information for finding almost anyone -- a lost love, family member (dead or alive), war buddy, debtor – but also there is heavy emphasis on techniques and resources for adoptee-"birth" family searches. Many of the 765,000 children reported missing each year have been stolen for secret adoption, a multi-billion dollar industry in the United States, where an average private adoption can cost $60,000[2], black market adoptions are up to $80,000[3], and any child can bring $120,000[4] or more for other illicit purposes. Children who have been mass kidnapped from other countries, as during the genocide in Argentina (1976-1983), in Guatemala (2009) and child trafficking amid earthquake devastation and chaos in Haiti (2010), may be legally adopted under U.S. state adoption sealed records laws, as condoned by the U.S. Department of State.[5] That fact has helped make the United States the *"largest market for stolen children in the world,"* according to the United Nations "Rights of the Child" project, while Immigration does not know how many children are taken out of the U.S. for adoption abroad or for other purposes.

Beyond the emotion-charged tabloid depictions of adoptee-parent reunions that resonate with viewers, there is the tedious behind-the-scenes, seemingly magical work of the searchers who made the reunions possible. How do these search experts get past the wall of secrecy and roadblocks to the truth? How do they find someone, often with no prior knowledge of the name? It is these and other questions that *The Ultimate Search Book 2011* answers by providing "how to" search tips and resources, for free or for fee, in every state in the United States and 200 countries, for legally accessing information and for locating anyone – the living as well as one's deceased ancestors. The "insider" search secrets of professional and amateur detectives help discover identities that have been made to "disappear" and perhaps answer questions such as *"Who am I?"* and *"Is my child alive and well?"*

---

1. Using the U.S. government's conservative estimate based on National Council for Adoption (NCFA) pro-sealed records lobby of adoption agencies statistic of "5-10 million adoptees in the U.S.," through 2010, when the National Census counted only "adoptred children" (ignoring decades of adopted adults, unless the respondents counted themselves as "children") and the Mormon Family History Center's definition of "immediate family" as quoted by Abigail VanBuren in the *Los Angeles Times* (5-30-92) as follows: parents, grandparents, aunts, uncles, siblings.
2. Amy Thurston, National Adoption Information Clearinghouse, Washington, DC (anecdotal, 7-16-98).
3. *Los Angeles Times*, June 22, 1996, B-7.
4. Thomas, Gordon, *Enslaved*.
5. 12-92 memo by Peter Pfund, Assistant Legal Adviser, U.S. State Dept., at http://abolishadoption.com/PfundMemo.html

*SELECTING RECORD TYPES

OBJECTIVE : To obtain information about:	RECORD TYPES Look in the Family History Library Catalog, Locality section* for these records types First look for:	Then look for:
Age	Census, Vital Records*, Cemeteries	Military Records, Taxation, Obituaries
Birth date	Vital Records*, Church Records, Bible Records	Cemeteries, Obituaries, Census, Newspapers, Military Records
Birthplace	Vital Records*, Church Records, Census	Newspapers, Obituaries, Military Records
City or parish of foreign birth	Church Records, Genealogy, Biography, Obituaries, Naturalization and Citizenship	Emigration and Immigration, Vital Records*, History
Country of foreign birth	Census, Emigration and Immigration, Naturalization and Citizenship, Vital Records*	Military Records, Church Records, Newspapers, Obituaries
County origins and boundaries	History, Maps	Gazetteers
Death	Vital Records*, Cemeteries, Probate Records, Church Records Obituaries	Newspapers, Military Records, Court Records, Land and Property
Divorce	Court Records, Divorce Records	Newspapers, Vital Records*
Ethnicity	Minorities, Native Races, Societies	Church Records, Emigration and Immigration, Naturalization and Citizenship
Historical background	History, Periodicals, Genealogy	Church History, Minorities
Immigration or emigration date	Emigration and Immigration, Naturalization and Citizenship, Genealogy	Census, Biography, Newspapers, Church Records
Maiden name	Vital Records*, Church Records, Newspapers, Bible Records	Military Records, Cemeteries, Probate Records, Obituaries
Marriage	Vital Records*, Church Records, Census, Newspapers, Bible Records	Biography, Genealogy, Military Records, Probate Records, Land and Property, Nobility
Occupation	Census Directories, Emigration and Immigration, Civil Registration, Occupations, Probate Records	Newspapers, Court Records, Obituaries, Officials and Employees
Parents, children and other family members	Vital Records*, Church Records, Census Probate Records, Obituaries	Bible Records, Newspapers, Emigration and Immigration, Land and Property
Physical description	Military Records, Biography, Court Records	Naturalization and Citizenship, Civil Registration, Church Records, Emigration and Immigration, Genealogy, Newspapers
Place-finding aids	Gazetteers, Maps	Directories, History, Periodicals, Land and Property, Taxation
Place (town) of residence when you know only the state	Census, Genealogy, Military Records, Vital Records*, Church Records, Directories	Biography, Probate Records, History, Land and Property, Taxation
Places family has lived	Census, Land and Property, History	Military Records, Taxation, Obituaries
Previous research (compiled genealogy)	Genealogy, Periodicals, History	Biography, Societies, Nobility
Record-finding aids	Archives and Libraries, Societies, Genealogy	Periodicals
Religion	Church Records, History, Biography, Civil Registration	Bible Records, Cemeteries, Obituaries, Genealogy

*Outside the United States and Canada, see "Civil Registration" instead of "Vital Records"
Note: Also search the Family History Library Catalog (LDS) subject section for key topics in your objective.
(See   "The Church of Jesus Christ of Latter-day Saints" for details)

Chapter1. Search Basics

Forty Search Tips for Starters

1. BEGIN WITH A LIST of all known names, dates, and places. Place this list in a folder so you can add every subsequent bits of information and documents you acquire, no matter how trivial it may seem.

2. KNOW THE NAME? FIRST CHECK THE MOST OBVIOUS. Sometimes the most obvious or easiest means of finding someone is overlooked. If you know the name of the person you seek, examples of free resources are local telephone directories, nationwide address-phone directories on Internet such as http://WhitePages.com (which often includes the person's age or age range, names of others in household and employment information), 411 Directory Assistance operators who may do a computer search by district, or public library Reference librarians can provide instant information without charge. Even if such methods don't produce a listed name and address or phone number, you may find a helpful relative by the same surname. You might find someone who has placed their name and photo/profile and a way to contact them on http://Facebook.com, http://MySpace.com, http://Classmates.com or http://Reunion.com. Sometimes "Googling" the name (by typing the name on the search field at Google.com) ferrets out the person on a website (their own or some other). Add each new lead or document. An all-in-one Internet search resource for addresses, phone numbers, e-mails and reverse lookups is http://SearchGateway.com.

3. DON'T KNOW THE CURRENT NAME OF THE PERSON DUE TO MARRIAGE, DIVORCE OR ADOPTION? In cases of marriage, divorce/remarriage, stepparent adoption and stranger adoption, a woman or child will usually have a name change. If you're adopted and seeking your "birth" family, begin by asking your adopter(s) for whatever information and documents they may have such as the Petition To Adopt, and Final Decree of Adoption. See Chapters 4 and 5 for detailed "how to" search information. There are usually 2 adoption files – the one held by the agency or attorney that handled the adoption and the court's file. The agency's file may have more personal, social information on the parties to an adoption and is usually filed by the adopters' names, while the court file may have only court documents such as the aforementioned Petition and Final Decree. If a public agency adoption, the central office of Social Services in the state where the adoption was finalized will have minimal information but can tell you which branch to contact for further information. See "Questions For Adoptees and Parents to Ask Agency and Court" in Chapter 4. In almost all states in the U.S., an adoptee's original birth certificate is sealed and an "amended" (falsified) birth certificate is issued with the adoptee's changed name and the adopters' names are substituted for the "birth" parents' names as if they were the parents on the date of birth. Other information on the amended birth certificate may be true or omitted (such as name of hospital of birth). Adoption disclosure laws vary from state to state, so one must first know the law in the state where the adoption was finalized. *The Ultimate Search Book* includes the most recent law change in each state as well as procedure and contact information for legally accessing information within the system as well as around the system. (see Examples of Original and Amended Birth Certificates, page 14)

4. HOW TO DISCOVER A CHANGE OF ADDRESS. The fastest resource is usually Internet. If the address you need is not at http://WhitePages.com. or if you find it is not a current address, http://PeopleSearch.com will sell either an inexpensive one-time lookup for all same-name listings (which may include past and current listings for each person by that name, and possibly unlisted phone numbers), or a subscription for a fee. The more information known in advance, such as full name and middle initial, age or age range, last known city/state of residence, the better one's chances of narrowing down listings for more common, identical names. **The United States Postal Service (USPS) no longer offers a form for the purpose of public disclosure of a person's name and address. Neither does the State Department of Motor Vehicles (DMV) in many states such as in California, due to that state's anti-stalking law.** But you can mail a letter in either of two ways to possibly discover the new address: (1) Mail your letter addressed to the person at their last known address and write "Forwarding Order Information Requested" and if the person has filed a change of address within the last sic months, you'll receive your letter back with a yellow label that informs you of the forwarding address; (2) if your letter is returned with a yellow label that says "Forwarding Order Expires, mail a letter addressed to the person sought "c/o" the last known address ("c/o" requires the route carrier to deliver it), and write

"Occupant: Please forward or return if addressee's address not known." If the person now residing there knows the person you seek, they might forward it or return it to you.

5. STATE DEPARTMENT OF MOTOR VEHICLES (DMV). Many State Department of Motor Vehicles (DMV) offices no longer provide a driver's record and/or a messaging service for a fee if the name not to common. However, states that use the Social Security number for driver's license number are: DC, HI, IA, IN, ID, MA, MS, MT/, NV, OK., VA. A non-driver may hold a DMV-issued ID card. A search by a woman's maiden name often produces her current married name. Law Enforcement can run a Driver's License Compact in about 39 states. These records belong to the states, not to the federal government. Texas is the only state that does not notify the state of the old license that the person has obtained a Texas driver's license; so, if it appears that a license has long ago expired and never been renewed and a state abstract does not show any transfer, the subject may be in Texas. Some states may give DMV "address verification" if you give them the date of birth and address. This system is routinely used by auto rental agencies. An investigator using, or posing as, a car rental agent, may offer a bogus address to get the current address. If you know the person's Vehicle Identification Number (VIN) you can obtain information of the vehicle and any transfers of ownership via http://CarFax.com for a one-time fee or multi-use subscription fee...or you can ask a car dealer to "show me the CarFax" as a favor.

6. SOCIAL SECURITY and THE SOCIAL SECURITY NUMBER. Social Security no longer offers a free "Locator Service" by which they would forward your letter if the name is not too common and you have additional identifiers such as date of birth or age.. Local Social Security Administration offices receive about one request a month to locate a missing family member.. .and MAY still comply with certain requests, especially if accompanied by a court order or police report of a missing person.. '
The Social Security number is also a very useful piece of information. Even in states where a driver's license does not share the Social Security number, it is often requested and recorded into the DMV computer. A numeric search can often be run by just knowing the Social Security number. The same is true of auto registration listings. Many states require a person wishing to register a car to provide a Social Security number. A check of the vehicle registration database can often be run this way. Social Security numbers can provide a way to learn about a person's background or to positively identify an adoptee or "birth" parent. The first three digits of a Social Security number are called an area number. Every state is assigned a different set of these area numbers, so you can tell where the person resided when first issued a Social Security Number and you might want to direct your search to that state or have a Collections Agency check their Credit Report which is accessible if the Social Security Number and certain identifiers (such as date of birth and last residence) are known.

SOCIAL SECURITY'S NUMBERING SYSTEM:

416-424 Alabama	010-034 Massachusetts	408-415 Tennessee
574 Alaska	362-386 Michigan	449-467 Texas
526-527 Arizona	468-477 Minnesota	528-529 Utah
429-432 Arkansas	425-428 Mississippi	008-009 Vermont
545-573 California	486-500 Missouri	223-231 Virginia
521-524 Colorado	516-517 Montana	531-539 Washington
040-049 Connecticut	505-508 Nebraska	223-231 West Virginia
221-222 Delaware	530 Nevada	387-399 Wisconsin
577-579 District of Columbia	001-003 New Hampshire	520 Wyoming
261-267 Florida	135-158 New Jersey	
252-260 Georgia	525, 585 New Mexico	ADDITIONS:
575-576 Hawaii	050-134 New York	600-601 Arizona
518-519 Idaho	237-246 North Carolina	602-626 California
318-361 Illinois	501-502 North Dakota	589-595 Florida
303-317 Indiana	268-302 Ohio	587-588 Mississippi
478-485 Iowa	440-448 Oklahoma	585 New Mexico
509-515 Kansas	540-544 Oregon	232 North Carolina
400-407 Kentucky	159-211 Pennsylvania	U.S. POSSESSIONS:
433-439 Louisiana	035-039 Rhode Island	586 American Samoa, Guam
004-007 Maine	247-251 South Carolina	580-584 Puerto Rico
212-220 Maryland	503-504 South Dakota	580 Virgin Islands

Railroad retirees were assigned numbers 700-728, later discontinued. Area 232 was transferred from West Virginia to North Carolina. Southeast Asian refugees were assigned 574, 580, 586 (4/75-11/79). "Retired" Social Security numbers are purchased from the government by private companies that then resell the numbers. The Social Security Death Index lists deceased non-military persons, Korean War, and Vietnam War dead by name and provides their Social Security numbers to assist further research. The Death Index may be searched without fee at Family History Centers of The Church of Jesus Christ of Latter-day Saints or at many major libraries. There are several genealogy websites with versions of the Social Security Death Index (see "Computerized Searches" chapter). You can discover the Social Security Number with just a name (if not too common) and approximate year of birth.

7. CITY/COUNTY/STATE RECORDS can be browsed free or FAXed/mailed for a fee. Public Records include: birth certificates (except those that are sealed due to an adoption), birth indexes in some regions such as in the 5 boroughs of New York City, birth announcements in newspaper back archives (from the newspaper "morgue" or public library), marriage and divorce, voter registrations, property owners, tax assessments, state library archives, church baptismals, the Church of Jesus Christ of Latter-day Saints (Mormon) Family History Center's records, city and suburban white pages and yellow pages (business) directories, address-phone criss-cross directories, school yearbooks, computerized adoption search websites (see Chapter 5), CD-ROM and microfilm databases, and directory assistance telephone operators who may do a computer search by name of the state or telephone district. Other good sources of data include the County Real Estate Index, the local Courthouse Litigation Index and court dockets. To learn who is connected to a property address—even the owner's marital status—you can obtain a copy of the deed from any title company without charge, usually the same day requested. Instant "public records lookups" in many parts of the country can be ordered online for a fee.

8. COURTHOUSE RECORDS are supposed to be public information, but clerks in large cities will refuse you access to some. You will have to call and complain to the local Bar Association or State Attorney's office, or show the clerk's supervisor a Freedom of Information Act (FOIA) written request and ask (with a tape recorder on) on what ground you are denied access. (See Search Tip 17, "Freedom of Information Act and the Privacy Act" in this chapter.)

9. A PRISONER LOCATOR website at http://www.ancestor.com/prison_search.htm, is organized by state in which the person may be incarcerated, and can be searched free but not all state prison systems have computerized such information - California is one example, but you can obtain the prisoner's location (mailing address) by phoning California Department of Corrections' (CDC) records phone number which is on their website. This Prisoner Locator website also has links to County Jail inmate lookups, Sex Offender Registries, Genealogy Data Bases for Prison Records, Old Prison Records in Other Countries, and Civil War Prison Search Engines.

10. VOTER REGISTRATIONS. Voter registrations are public records in County Clerks' offices. You can write for them, but it will take forever. In many areas, they are available on-line.

11. FEDERAL RESOURCES include the Federal Parent Locator (used to access Internal Revenue Service (IRS) records), Social Security, military locator services, National Archives Office of Disclosure, and Immigration and Naturalization Services (INS). Although INS records are not public records, tax accountants routinely and legally tap into certain IRS computer databases. Creative investigators develop sources who may, for a fee or as a favor, furnish a Social Security number. The inside sources risk not only their jobs but imprisonment on charges of conspiracy to obtain confidential information. Do not try to obtain information from me federal government that is not obtainable with a Freedom Of Information Act (FOIA) request, is not a public record, or is classified "confidential" or "secret."

12. THE NATIONAL CENSUS can be used to conduct a search by age. Send for "How the Census Bureau Can Be Used for Genealogical Research" by requesting it from the Superintendent of Documents, U.S. Government Printing Office, Dept. 33, Washington, DC 20402. (See Chapter 3, "Records Available for Search.")

13. LAST NAME SEARCH via Internet, of everyone in the United States with their phone numbers, is available free from public directory listings on Internet or from public libraries or on interlibrary loan on CD-ROM data bases, (see "Computerized Search" chapter for best search engines.)

14. FIRST NAME, BIRTH DATE, OR YEAR ONLY? School yearbooks have been good resources for adoptees and parents who successfully match up non-identifying information with physical characteristics from a description or photo, and the year that the person would have graduated. If the subject is a school-age child, or has a school-age child in a public school, searchers ask the school board office what grade the child of the subject's age would attend. Also try http://Classmates.com . http://Reunions.com , http://Facebook.com, and http://MySpace.com .

15. TELEPHONE RECORDS AND NUMBERS. Public Directory listings at http://WhitePages.com often include the person's phone number and "People Search" sites such as http://Intellius.com will sell you same-name listings which may include unlisted numbers (Caution: the listings may not be current). Private investigators obtain toll records and non-published numbers from service representatives using only name and zip code. The general public is told that operators and service reps do not have access to these numbers. Directory Assistance Operators often give out an address, especially if you state you want to check the address before calling to be sure you have the right party. If the operator refuses, dial back and you'll get a different operator who may. Public libraries also have access to databases compiled from nationwide mailing lists. These give name of individuals or businesses, addresses, and sometimes unlisted telephone numbers. Need a phone number while at an unlabeled home phone or pay phone? Depending on the region, dial (800) MYANI-IS. The recording will state the number you Called from. In AT&T regions using "DETEC," just dial "114." CAUTION: AT&T/GTE changes some codes from week-to-week. This is risky for amateurs. Phone numbers can also be acquired inexpensively from private investigators and subscriber services. A person's phone number also often appears on their Ebay profiles, personal and business checks, and their utility company accounts. TELEPHONE COMPANY CNA (Central Names & Addresses); Private investigators give the phone number to be researched and ask for billing address. Some searchers say, "I'm an installer and am having difficulty accessing Line Assistance ..." Since this is risky for an amateur, ask a "P.I." to assist you.

16. GOT A PHONE NUMBER AND NEED NAME AND ADDRESS? Check http://SearchGateway.com reverse lookups or call the Washington, DC based 1-900-555-MATCH.

17. OCCUPATIONAL AND RECREATIONAL LICENSES AND REGISTRATIONS. Labor unions often will not cooperate with law enforcement. But searchers have been successful in locating people through their labor union by claiming to need to get in touch due to a family emergency. Agencies will provide proof of occupational license with identifying information blackened out. Hunting and Fishing License Records are public records.

18. SCHOOL YEARBOOKS AND RECORDS. Some public libraries stock school yearbooks. Also try http://Classmates.com and http://Reunions.com

19. FREEDOM OF INFORMATION ACT AND THE PRIVACY ACT. Obtain a copy of the *Federal* Freedom of Information Act and the *Federal* Privacy Act from your public library or from your Congressman's district office without charge. Although the two laws were enacted for different purposes, there is some similarity in their provisions. Both the FOIA and the Privacy Act give people the right of access to records held by agencies of the federal government. The FOIA's access rights are given to "any person," but the Privacy Act's access rights are only for the individual who is the subject of the records sought. Some states, like California, have a *State* Freedom of Information Act and *State* Privacy Act pertaining to records held by state agencies; obtain a copy of a *State* Act from your public library or your State Representative. The *Federal* FOIA applies to all records of *federal* agencies. The *Federal* Privacy Act applies only to *federal* agency records in "systems of records" which contain information about an individual and are retrieved by the name or personal identifier. Each law has a different set of fees, time limits, and exemptions from its rights of access. If you request records about yourself under both laws, federal agencies may withhold the records from you only to the extent the records are exempt under both laws. If the information you want pertains to the activities of federal agencies or of another person, you should make your request under the FOIA, which covers all agency records. If the information you want is about yourself and you wish to avoid possible search fees, you should make the request under the Privacy Act which covers most records of agencies that pertain to individuals. Sometimes you can use the FOIA to help you get records about yourself that are not in a Privacy Act "system of records." However, if the records you seek are covered only by the FOIA, you must "reasonably describe" them; and you may be charged search fees. If you are in doubt about which law applies, or which would better suit your needs, refer to both in your request letter. To obtain information about other people, the FOIA contains a very important provision concerning personal privacy: Exemption 6. It protects you from others who may seek information about you, and it may also block you if you seek information about others. The FOIA's Exemption 6 permits an agency to withhold information about individuals if disclosing it would be a "clearly unwarranted invasion of personal privacy." Exemption 6 cannot be used to deny you access to information about yourself, only to deny you information about other persons. (If there is a way to request the information in the name of the person that the information is about, searchers sometimes do this.) To be covered by Exemption 6, the information requested must be (1) about an identifiable individual, (2) an invasion of the individual's privacy if disclosed to others, and (3) "clearly unwarranted" to disclose. Federal and State FOIA and Privacy Acts exempt adoption birth records. This exemption clause is usually vaguely worded, because the law recognizes the adoptee's basic human right to know his own identity and heritage. Yet, no one has yet successfully challenged adoption secrecy laws under FOIA/Privacy Acts because the U.S. Supreme Court simply refuses to hear such cases (*ALMA Society v. Mellon*; *Yesterday's Children*, 1970's; and *Carangelo/AmFOR v. O'Neill/State of CT*, 1989-1993; U.S. District Court of CT). "A Citizen's Guide On Using the Freedom of Information Act and the Privacy Act of 1974" can be purchased from the Superintendent of Documents, U.S. Government Printing Office, Washington, DC 20402. Indicate Stock Number 052-071-00929-9.

20. **INTERNATIONAL SOUNDEX REUNION REGISTRY (ISRR):** This is the largest and oldest free (donation only) registry for "next of kin" searches - whether separated by adoption or for any reason. ISRR was founded by the late Anthony S. Vilardi (b. 1930, d. 2009) and his wife, Emma May Villardi (an adoptee and genealogist, b. 1922, d. 1990). Now (in 2010) ISRR is operated by the ISRR Executive Board of Directors - professionals who, themselves are adoption-affected. ISRR is online at: http://isrr.net . And still located at PO Box 37119, Las Vegas, NV 89137; (775) 882-7755. ISRR receives inquiries from individuals worldwide who complete a simple form and instructions available online at http://www.issr.net.registration.shtml including via referrals from Americans For Open Records (AmFOR). "Soundex" emphasizes phonetic spelling and filing. ISRR first tries to match the pronunciation, then the spelling. Most of the time the input is limited to known date and time of birth, hospital and location, and the requester's name. ISRR's Medic Alert System is available to help adult adoptees and adopters of minor children, receives inquiries from individuals worldwide, and also referrals from search organizations and state agencies. "Soundex" emphasizes the phonetic spelling and filing. ISRR first tries to match the pronunciation before spelling. Most of the time the input is An International Soundex registration form is available online or on request by mail or phone; an example of their form is on page 168, before the International section. To receive a free registration form, send SASE to ISRR, PO Box 2312, Carson City, NV 89702, phone (702) 882-7755 PST. ISRR is a nonprofit organization funded by your donations. On Internet, see http://www.isrr.net .

Dear AmFOR: ... "I have quite a few people that I want to thank for spending the time to send me information or ideas on how to search for my mother. I appreciate everything you did. Luckily for me, the International Soundex Reunion Registry matched my "birth" mother and me on August 24, 1995. I talked with her on the phone that evening and we had a very emotional and special time. We are planning to see each other; she lives in California. We are both very happy and excited for the future. Sincerely, HEIDI B. Cashmere, WA. . . ."

"It is my impression that D.H.H.S. deleted the reference to procedures regarding "opening of records" [in the Model Adoption Bill]. STEPHEN B., Mansfield University, PA."

21. **HIRING A LICENSED PRIVATE INVESTIGATOR.** Times have changed for private detectives. Instead of snapping incriminating photos for divorce cases, most modern "private eyes" earn their fees by serving the business world in security and personnel matters. They are often more effective than police in tracking down runaway or missing children. A missing persons bureau may have 30 cases at a time. A private eye can focus and coordinate the leads for a single client. Tip: If a detective can't find a hard lead within three days s/he may be incompetent, or stalling to run up the bill. Many do not have resources for adoption searches. Before hiring a detective, interview him or her for at least 20 minutes to discuss your needs and how they'd be me. Be sure the detective is licensed and bonded. A bond larger than the minimum bond might be advisable for a broad investigation covering several states or even a foreign country. To make certain the private eye's record is clean, check with the appropriate state division on licensing (See Addendum, State Investigator Licensing Agencies.) Ask the detective for a resume and references. The best detectives usually have ample experience. The best indicator is word-of-mouth: reputations are hard-won in this business.

22. THE BIRTH CERTIFICATE is the foundation document for a person's identity in any country. This book lists the address for the central office of vital records in every state and country as a starting point. A birth certificate acts as a "breeder" document to obtain other information. Adoptees' true, pre-adoption birth certificates have been sealed in court files and exchanged for a falsified version naming the adoptive parents as the "birth" parents and substituting adoptive name for birth name. But even the falsified/amended version contains some true information helpful to a search. For instance, the full certified form may retain the name of the hospital and physician. The date and time of birth is usually always the true date and time. The United States uses a common system of state-issued birth certificate numbers due to an agreement reached among the states years ago, and the falsified version retains the recording numbers of the original birth certificate. A state birth number will not appear on a certificate issued only by a local county registrar. For instance #1-34-75-123456:

> First digit: always a "1" - shows birth in USA;
> Next 2 digits: represents state of birth: "34" is Ohio;
> Next 2 digits: represents year of birth: "75" is born in 1975;
> Last 6 digits: state file number, random sequential number.

County registrars use county registrar file numbers. Any mismatch will alert a Passport Clerk to confiscate the document for possible fraud.

The United States is unique among nations because our birth recording system is highly decentralized and is done on many levels—hospital, county, and state. There are several types of birth records issued in the United States today. In some states, the authorities have attempted to make it more difficult for a "new identity" seeker to obtain state-maintained birth records. But often, in these same states, other types of birth records are equally acceptable, provided they are presented in the proper context.

HOSPITAL BIRTH CERTIFICATES:

Today, most people are born in a hospital, but it certainly is not universal. In some states, over half of all births occurred outside hospitals. When a child is born in a hospital, the attending physician or nurse will fill out a short piece of paper with the time, sex, and type of birth. Later on, after being done in the recovery room, the doctor will fill-out that hospital's standard birth certificate form. Hospital birth certificates will have the name of the hospital, location of the hospital, and some very basic information— the parent's names and ages at the time of the birth, the child's name, sex, and time of birth. No two births are ever recorded at the exact same hour and minute at the same hospital, even if they occurred simultaneously, in order that the time of birth will be the ultimate identifier. At the bottom of the hospital birth certificate are places for signatures of the doctor and witnesses and usually the hospital's own seal. Once this form is completed, a photocopy of it is made and notarized, and the original is given to the parents. At this point, the hospital-generated birth certificate is the only legal record of the child's birth. The hospital will send the notarized photocopy to the county recorder's office later.

LOCAL/COUNTY ISSUED BIRTH CERTIFICATES:

Upon receipt of the notarized copy, the county recorder will enter the birth record into the birth records book and/or computer record, if the county is fully automated, for the county for that month. In some counties, the county recorder will send out a state-issued birth certificate to the parents. In adoptions of newborns, the original birth certificate is withheld from the birth-parents and sent, with the amended version, to the central office of Vital Records at the state capital. Years later when a person attempts to access his own birth certificate from the county office of Vital Records, but is advised he must apply only to the state office at me capital, this is a "dead giveaway" that the person is adopted.

STATE-ISSUED BIRTH CERTIFICATES:

On a monthly or quarterly basis, the county recorder forwards to the central (state) Vital Records Bureau a listing of all births that occurred during that period. So, for a period of months, an infant would not have his birth certificate on file at the central state office. The notarized photocopy of the hospital birth record is usually destroyed by the local registrar once the birth has been entered into the records book or computer. Often there is a delay of up to a month before even the local registrar enters the birth into the records book. Some have reported receiving death certificates recorded prior to birth certificates, when a newborn dies within hours or days of birth. This could indicate that the death certificate was legitimately recorded first; or, it could send up a flag indicating a "baby switch or snatch" with phony death certificate, a common occurrence in the U.S. and Canada in the 1950s and 1960s among physicians who sold babies for black market adoption A Directory of Baby Brokers is found at http://AmFOR.net/BabyBrokers . Almost everyone born in a hospital, therefore, has two birth certificates, each of which has legal status. Some people never get a state-issued birth certificate, and the hospital-issued record is their birth record. Midwives who regularly assist births will have a supply of hospital-type birth certificates and possess their own stamp or embossing tool to certify the document. This is particularly true in rural southern states. This document is given to the parents in the expectation that the parents will take the document to the county and state. Often this does not happen, so most state and federal agencies will accept a hospital-type birth record in lieu of a state-issued birth certificate. However, if someone were to present a freshly-minted birth certificate that does not look as old as the person described in the document, all bureaucrats know that hospitals do not issue duplicate birth certificates and it would be suspect.

PRIVATELY ISSUED "FAMILY RECORD" BIRTH CERTIFICATES

The third type of birth certificate is the privately issued document maintained by individuals. Under certain circumstances, they are acceptable as legal proof of birth. They may be incorporated in a family record book or inside a family Bible. These were, and still are, quite common in rural areas of the Midwest and South. A person can obtain a "delayed birth certificate" from the state years later based on these family records.

RELIGIOUS BAPTISMAL BIRTH CERTIFICATES:

Another type of birth certificate is the religious baptismal certificate. In areas where the Catholic, Episcopal, or other church that practices baptism is very strong, a signed, sealed baptism record is accepted as readily as a state issued document, even by state and federal agencies, as legal proof of birth. Yet the information on certificates is whatever the parents provide. In the case of adoptees, the baptismal birth certificates indicate whatever date and names the adopters provide. AmFOR has frequently dealt with birth and baptismal certificates that have conflicting information about the same person. Therefore, the search should aim for a "match" of other documents, newspaper birth notices, and such.

"AMENDED" ADOPTION BIRTH CERTIFICATES:

Adoptees have an "original" or pre-adoption birth certificate that reflects the true facts of their birth unless their adoption was a "black market" adoption with falsified original records. They also have a falsified/amended (post-adoption) birth certificate; this is usually the one they carry throughout life. When requesting their amended birth certificate, they may be provided either a "short form" or "long form" certified copy. In California, they may also receive a very short, coupon-sized document bearing only the female adopter's maiden name, male adopter's name, child's adoptive name, and birth date. The hospital and physician name is deleted to prevent adoptees from obtaining the hospital record of birth that reveals birth family names. Verify fees before mailing your request and check to avoid delay from returns. Individuals with low income can try requesting a waiver of the fees. The American adoptee is the only citizen prohibited by state law from accessing his/her true birth certificate without court order or special procedures. Courts generally refuse, unless impossible "good cause" is met. Or, if the original birth certificate is released, it is released one time only and is thereafter still considered a "sealed record for life" in most states. AmFOR was informed that some small towns in New England, particularly New Hampshire, still staple the pre-adoption birth certificate to the amended version, so that both versions are unintentionally accessible to public view. In other regions, licensed, card-carrying genealogists are permitted direct access to both original and amended birth certificates as they often appear on computer, side by side.

FOREIGN BIRTH CERTIFICATES:

The Ultimate Search Book-2011 – and *International Vital Record Handbook* (Genealogical Publishing), which includes records request forms worldwide – both update contact info for Vital Records offices worldwide.

23. THE WORLDWIDE SEARCH NETWORK (for free or for fee). Searching involves three aspects – (1) making the decision to search, (2) discovering the name if not known, and (3) locating the person for contact. Americans For Open Records (AmFOR), founded by the author of this book, Lori Carangelo, has been providing free self-help search and support information since 1989, by mail, and for the past two decades via its website at http://AmFOR.net with links to useful information, and to certain individuals and websites that are part of a worldwide search network at http://AmFOR.net/search. The Worldwide Search Network actually consists of thousands of professional, semi-professional, and lay researchers. Most are, themselves, adoption-affected. Licensed detectives often prefer not to jeopardize their licenses by trying to obtain adoption information (even though it is not necessary to open a sealed court record or agency record to do so). The Open Adoption Records Movement in the United States was founded by the late

Jean Paton, an adoptee and former social worker, as result of her 1953 studies on the negative effects of secrecy of records on adoptive families. Today, the Open Records/Search Movement is composed of adoptees, parents, and, increasingly, adopters. Many have found their missing family members; some may never find them due to black market adoptions, yet they assist others. By sharing their own experiences, and perhaps knowledge of where there may be cracks in the system which allows discovery of identities and whereabouts, they can do what seasoned detectives are not equipped to do. Local search and support groups and individuals tend to specialize in their local area or areas in which they are most familiar and have contacts. Some groups or individuals provide only "support" counseling and referrals for search. Some searchers work only on a one-on-one basis while local search-support groups have a sizeable membership, charge a membership fee, require local meeting attendance. and may offer a newsletter subscription. Some have nationwide search capabilities. Many are members of an umbrella organization such as The American Adoption Congress and hold annual national conferences with workshops and speakers as well as other events for which they offer group travel and lodging discounts. Some own original birth indexes from Vital Records offices from which they sell the sought-after names. Birth indexes are not the same as birth certificates. Birth indexes can be either old books or microfilm that cross-reference the adoptee's pre-adoption and post-adoption name and reveal their biological parents' identities. Birth indexes are no longer available to the public in most areas because they reveal adoptive and birth names, but some searchers purchased them, legally, years ago and have been re-selling them to other searchers. **Always include all known names, date of birth and adoption and when mailing or emailing your inquiry to any search organization or individual. By mail, always enclose your SASE to receive a reply by mail.** If you contact a paid searcher, ask for references and call people who have used the searcher so you can hear firsthand if the client completed the search and was satisfied with the service and cost. Ask for a price list or a written quote and written agreement, detailing what you can expect to get for how much, approximately how long it could take, what guarantees, if any records will be furnished to prove you have found the right person, refund policy, whether the price may change, whether the searcher will search for a minor (note: Adoptive parents might obtain a court order preventing your contact until the child is of legal age . You will need to assess the minor's situation in advance and act in the child's best interests and with future relationships of all parties in mind).

Many public Social Services agencies, as well as private adoption agencies and attorneys, have gone into the search business, charging fees for processing registrations for adoptee-parent "matching," and hourly or flat fees for locating parties (despite that these agencies hold the files containing the names withheld). Some greedy agencies charge as much as $100 per hour to provide even non-identifying background information, no matter how sparse. Even if it is true that your mother "was short and in good health" and your father "had brown hair and liked surfing", the information shared with you may be all that was originally collected; or it may be all that the agency, at its discretion under that state's law, is compelled to share with you. In past adoptions, collection of family medical history was not mandatory, was not included in the court file, and may have been "sanitized" by the agency so that adoptive parents would not know of any negative medical history that could discourage them from adopting. So adoptees and "birth" parents prefer to obtain family medical histories by direct contact with each other. When writing to Social Services or other entities for disclosure, it's a good idea to send your letter and required forms by certified, return-receipt mail for easy follow-up.

Dear AmFOR:... "I am writing to express my appreciation to you for providing the informative materials regarding the sealed record in adoption controversy. Given time constraints, I will need to arbitrarily stop my search for information and begin writing the paper soon. "

24. CREDIT BUREAUS. The largest private databases in the nation are run by large, nationwide credit bureaus. Very often, good information can be obtained on a person, when other methods have failed, by tapping into this network. Until recently, these databases were off limits to an investigator. Recent federal government decisions now make some of this information available to the investigator via Heritage Quest, PO Box 329, Bountiful, UT 84011-0329, (800) 760-2455. and subscriber services such as Merlin, Cornerstone and Choice Point (see #28, below). Credit bureau reports contain three types of information. The first is called "header information," the personal data that appears at the top of credit reports. The bottom portion of the credit report contains the recording of any tax liens, bankruptcy, or other financially motivated legal action. Header data is useful for obtaining recent addresses. Landlords and employers can obtain credit reports through a third-party credit reporting service. A common ploy of the searcher using a business name is to claim to be doing a reference check by phone. To tap a credit bureau, you need to have a business for 3 years that is open to the public, a "legitimate reason" to access credit reports, the business subscriber code, or insider resources. Otherwise, to receive complete data on the subject, the subject must agree to release it to you. The largest credit bureau network in the United States is Experian (formerly TRW). Experian has credit files on about 130 million people—nearly half the United States population—and has offices across the U.S. Two other large credit bureaus are Credit Bureau Incorporated (CBI) and TransUnion Credit Bureau. Almost all local credit bureaus are owned by Experian, CBI, or TransUnion, or are affiliated in some way. Equifax Credit Information Services furnishes a combined Experian/Transunion credit report. Other than the federal government, no one has more data than credit bureaus. Experian has employment histories and the best credit reports. TransUnion offers "atlas" search from MetroNet for name, address, and nationwide phone and DMV information. CBI does only credit reports and Social Security traces. All three refuse access to most private investigators despite the fact that CBI is a private investigation agency.

25. THE SALVATION ARMY has a Missing Persons Division in each of four territorial regions. Their national headquarters for maternity home records information is at the Georgia address. below. Their website is at http://salvationarmy-usaeast.org/find/booth_babies.htm

> Eastern Territory Headquarters for CT, DE, ME, MA, NH, NJ, NY, OH, PA, VT, RI
> —120 West 14th St., New York City, NY 10011;
> Central Territory Headquarters for IL, IN, IA, KS, MI, MN, MO, NE, ND, SD, WI
> —2258 Clayborne St., Chicago, IL 60614;
> Southern Territory HQ for AL, AR, FL, GA, KY, LA, MD, MS, NC, OK, SC, TN, TX, VA, DC, WV
> ---1424 NE Expressway, Atlanta, GA 30329:
> Western Territory Headquarters for AK, AZ, CA, CO, HI, ID, MT, NV, NM, OR, UT, WA, WY
> —2780 Lomita Blvd., Torrance, CA 90505.

26. UTILITY COMPANIES. Collections departments of various utility companies legally exchange customer information. But a private investigator who uses the ruse of claiming to be a customer verifying his own billing address, or calling one utility claiming to be skip tracing for the other, is breaking the law and this method of investigation is not advised.

27. EMPLOYMENT CHECKS FOR AN ADDRESS by phone could be accomplished with a straightforward call to a relative of the person being investigated. Private investigators have used the ruse of pretending to be an employer needing an address to forward a W-4, but state have made this illegal and it is not advised.

28. BANKS. Most banks and savings and loan institutions no longer verify a check if you state you've received a check from so-and-so for "x" amount, even if you have the account number, nor will they verify that someone is their account holder without a court order or order to garnish an account to satisfy a judgement debt. Nor do they return your own original cleared check to you with your statement – Under the federal Paperless Banking Law, your original checks are now destroyed after the front and back are scanned. You have to bank online to see and print the scanned images of the cleared check. The back should have the payee's signature (endorsement) and banking information as to date and location where the check was deposited. If, for instance, in case the payee has owed you money but stops making payments, it is important to save the image of any check that was tendered in order to know where the debtor banks so you can get a judgement lien against his account.

29. INDEPENDENT COMMERCIAL SEARCH FIRMS:

> PeopleSearch.com and Intellius.com will sell a name-address-phone# for a fee, not guaranteed
> VOS, Vehicle Operator Service (whole U.S.), PO Box 15334, Sacramento, CA 95813
> Data Search, 3600 American River Drive, Sacramento
> The Nationwide Locator, PO Box 39903. San Antonio, TX 78218. Document searches
>   (courts, corp/real property, DMV, phone. voter registration)
> Executive Search, 29 W. Thomas Rd., Phoenix, AZ 85013, (800) 528-6179; Overnight searches;
>   subscriber access by computer, DMV, courts, real property, national postal locators
> Choice Point, 1000 Alderman Drive, Alphretta, GA 30005

30. FBI'S NATIONAL CRIME INVESTIGATION COMPUTER (NCIC). "Wanteds" and "warrants" can now be purchased legally and inexpensively. Most states cooperate regarding extradictable felony warrants; misdemeanors are rarely shown, however. **Do not try to get NCIC records or any non-public or non-declassified records belonging to the federal government.**

31. BACKGROUND CHECK. A business owner/employer can legitimately request a background check on a "prospective employee" from previous employers to fill in any blank period such as "last known employer."

32. COMMON NAMES. When there are many persons by the same name as the person you are researching, and in the same area, send a postcard to each with your name coded differently on each, asking them to call you. You may get their name and address immediately.

33. "MEDICAL RECORDS, GETTING YOURS" is a booklet detailing laws and your right to your medical records, for a small fee to Health Research Group Publications Manager, 2000 "P" St., NW, #700, Washington, DC 20036. To learn how to correct errors in your medical records, write Medical Information Bureau (MIB), PO Box 105, Essex Station, Boston, MA 02112. California's Health and Safety Code Section 123110 requires that the patient be provided his/her own medical record upon written request (usually a form provided by the physician or hospital, but a letter should also suffice). Not all states have such a law. Check your state's law by using Google.

34. CHECKING OUT PHYSICIANS AND, HOSPITALS (1) To check physician credentials (whether licensed, practicing, living), go to the website for the Medical Board in the state you want to search or call American Medical Association (AMA) (312)464-5000. (2) AMA's informative website is at http://www.ama-assn.org or write American Hospital Association (AHA), 840 N. Lakeshore Blvd., Chicago, IL. For information on hospitals and hospital records; (3) To learn how long medical records are kept by statute in any state, call AMA-Chicago, (312) 787-2672. (4) For license status and actions against a physician, contact the County Medical Society and State Medical Board.

35. "LIFE OR DEATH" SEARCH? See International Soundex (ISRR) Medical Alert (#20, above). Also, volunteers are sometimes available at Terminal Illness Emergency Search (TIES), PO Box 99613, Seattle, WA 98199. Toll free: 1-888-568-8739. E-mail: TIES@absnw.com   If it is in regard to an adoptee, often the social worker who holds the adoption file will drop a name; in California, the social worker risks his/her job doing so.

36. LOCATING MILITARY PERSONNEL AND RECORDS. The Nationwide Locator, PO Box 39903, San Antonio, TX 78218, is a private military searcher. Find a military base at http://www.searchmil.com To find someone in the military, try http://www.GIsearch.com , or addresses below.

> *Dear AmFOR:...* "I would like to know where my father is. I'm not after him for money. I'd just like to get to know him. I think he'd be proud of me. I have already contacted the Navy on this matter. They are searching. Perhaps you can come up with something else. Please do all you can to find the father I've never known. Thank you for your time and consideration . . . JOY I., Chicago, IL."

Requests for information from Military Personnel Records for members and former members of the Armed Forces should include all items listed below. If all items are not known, your request should include the first five items which will aid in the identification of any individual record. All periods of service should be shown, even though information for one period is desired: (1) Full name under which service was performed; (2) Social Security Number; (3) Dates of Service; (4) Date and Place of Birth; (5) Residence of Service Member at time of Entry into Service. If the individual is in a reserve status or completely separated from active duty, the following information in addition to the 5 previous items should be included: (6) Branch of Service; (7) Reserve Status, Branch of Service, and Dates; (8) Last Known Address; (9) Grade or Rank; (10) Name and Address of Service Person's Parents; (11) Organizations with Approximate Dates

Assigned (the most significant ones). One technique to use when little information is known, is to make up some of the information, rather than omit it, and have your request returned for "insufficient information", and see what comes back. The service person may obtain all the information in his/her own record. The person's next-of-kin, if veteran is deceased, and federal offices for official purposes, are authorized to receive certain types of information. Other requesters must obtain written consent from the service person. Fees are determined at the time the records are released.

AIR FORCE:
All reserve members not on extended duty; all retired reservists in a non-pay status: Air Reserve Personnel Center; 3800 York Street, Denver, CO 80205-9998. All active duty personnel; all personnel on a temporary disability retired list (TDRL); general officers in a retired (pay) status: USAF, Military Personnel Center, Military Personnel Records Div., Randolph AFB, TX 78148-9997; (210) 565-2660 (will only confirm in writing.).

ARMY:
Officers separated before July 1,1917; enlisted personnel separated before November 1,1912: National Archives and Records Service, National Archives Building, Washington, DC 20408-0001. All retired personnel; all reserve members (includes retired reservists): Commander, U.S. Army Reserve Personnel Center, 9700 Page Boulevard, St. Louis, MO 63132-5200; all officers on active duty: Commander, U.S. Army Military Personnel Center, Management and Support Division, Officer Records Branch, 200 Stovall St., Alexandria, VA 22332-0400. Enlisted personnel on active duty: Commander, U.S. Army Enlisted Records and Evaluation Center, Fort Benjamin Harrison, IN 46249-5301; (7 03) 325-3732 (will only confirm in writing.).

ARMY NATIONAL GUARD:
All members not on active duty in the U.S. Army; personnel discharged from the National Guard (excludes records of periods of active duty and active duty for training in the U.S. Army): The Adjutant General (of the appropriate state, District of Columbia, or Commonwealth of Puerto Rico). Records for periods of active duty or active duty for training in the U.S. Army for periods ending after December 31,1959; HQ, Dept. of the Army, Office of the Adjutant General, U.S. Army Reserve Components Personnel and Administration Center, 9700 Page Blvd., St. Louis, MO 63132-5200

COASTGUARD:
Enlisted personnel separated less than 6 months; officer personnel separated less than 3 months; all active Coast Guard personnel and members of the Reserves; officer personnel separated before January 1, 1929; Commandant, U.S. Coast Guard, Washington, DC 20221-0001; (202) 267-2229 (will confirm some by phone.).

MARINE CORPS:
Officer personnel on active duty or in reserves; enlisted personnel on active duty or in organized active reserves; all personnel completely separated less than 4 months: Commandant of the Marine Corps, Headquarters, U.S. Marine Corps, Washington, DC 20380-0001; (703) 784-3942 (will confirm by phone.).

NAVY:
Officers on active duty, those separated less than one year, and all officers with rank of admiral; enlisted personnel on active duty and those separated with less than 4 months; active reservists and inactive reservists with 18 or more months remaining in first term of enlistment: Chief of Naval Personnel, Department of the Navy, Washington, DC 20360-0001; (901) 874-3388 + Press 2 (will confirm by phone.).

ALL BRANCHES:
If your request does not pertain to any of the above categories, address an inquiry to: National Personnel Records Center, Att: (Appropriate Branch of Service) Records, 9700 Page Blvd., St. Louis, MO 63132-5200; 314/263-7141. Veteran's Reunions information: VETS, PO Box 901, Columbia. MO 65205: (573) 474-4444. Also: REUNIONS, VFW Magazine, 406 W. 34th St, Ste 523, Kansas City, MO 64111.

WWII VET FATHERS information is available as result of WAR BABES 1988 lawsuit); contact the Dept.of Defense, Pentagon, Washington, DC or The National Archives, Pentagon, Washington, DC (They won't provide street addresses).

TO TRACE A CIVIL WAR SOLDIER:
Confederate Descendants Society, PO Box 233, Athens, AL. 35611; or, Rare Collection, TK Kennedy, PO Box 355, Braddock Heights, MD 21702; and for Union or Confederate soldiers, http://Reunions.com

TO FIND A FEDERAL EMPLOYEE:
The Federal Locator, PO Box 51315, PO Box 51315, Riverside, CA. 92517-2315 (SASE + S5 per inquiry).

DECEASED MILITARY IDENTIFICATION AND RECORD:
The Department of Defense currently maintains a "DNA Specimen Repository" housing 4-5,000 DNA samples by mandatory collection. The goal is to collect 3-5 million DNA samples from U.S. military persons, worldwide, to aid identification of remains in the future, pending a lawsuit by a soldier (Lakofsky) challenging his right to refuse and the potential for genetic discrimination. The Cambridge Statistical Association, Inc., 23 Rocky Knoll, Irvine, CA 97215; (714) 509-9900 (Social Security Index); or Genealogists Inc., Ste. 113, 2031 N. Broad St., Lansdale, PA 19446.

BURIAL INFORMATION, VETERANS IN NATIONAL CEMETERIES:
Director, Cemetery Service (41-A), National Cemetery System, Veteran's Administration, Washington, DC 20420.

PRISONER OF WAR RECORDS:
Andersonville National Historical Site, Rt. 1, Box 85, Andersonville, GA 31711.

37. POLICE REPORTS. Police and sheriff's reports are semi-public records. You are entitled under State Freedom of Information Act (See Chapter 1, item 17 for FOIA) to the "who-what-where-when" concerning any report in which you are named or any investigation in which you are directly involved. You may or may not have access to the actual report, depending on State Government Code Section on disclosure from police records, the particular law enforcement department's policy on disclosure, and the nature and status of the investigation, especially criminal investigations, even if completed. But the court record may glean such information. In general, you will probably obtain access to reports on civil matters as soon as the report has been completed, signed by the officer or deputy, and provided to the Records Division for filing. Criminal investigation and arrest reports, however, can be withheld until after charges are filed and parties are arraigned. Then an attorney can obtain the report. In the meantime, you need to present to the department originating the report your State Freedom of Information Act request, in writing, to at least be told the "who-what-where-when" of the report as it pertains to you. In California arrest reports are available to employers and look-up services.

38. IF YOU ARE DENIED information or access to any government-held record, request the department's written policy which cites the applicable government code on disclosure. Check the county law library, larger public library or college library that has the State Government Codes to see if the policy matches the Code Section referenced; it may not, or the policy may be more vague than the law intended. You should cite this when making your FOIA request. You have the right to know. If you are still denied, you may need an attorney or Legal Aid. If denied a police report, complain higher up. Contact the District Attorney, in writing, by certified, return-receipt mail, to document the situation and to assert your right to amend any report which you feel may be inaccurate. Have your letter filed with the report. If you can't know what the report is about or see it, your due process right may be violated.

39. MEDIA'S ACCESS TO INFORMATION.. A good neutral source of non-legal advice is your local newspaper's investigative news reporter or assignment editor. If there's a good news story, they may help you get the facts you seek.

40. PASSPORT SERVICES AS AN INFORMATION SOURCE. If your immigrant ancestors returned home to visit family. or to bring relatives to America, they might have obtained a U.S. passport. For passports prior to 1906, write to: Diplomatic Records Branch of the National Archives, Washington, DC 20406. Passport applications after 1906. to date, can be located at the Passport Office, U.S. Dept. of State, 1425 K St. NW, Washington, DC 20406. Vital records are kept by state or local registrars in the United States; but if the birth, marriage. divorce, death occurred outside the United States, and the person was a U.S. citizen or his dependent, contact Passport Services, Correspondence Branch, Room 386, U.S. Dept. of State, 1425 K St. NW, Washington, DC 20522-1705. Adoptees might obtain their original birth certificate direct from vital records if needed to apply for a passport (see page 48).

STARTING YOUR OWN SEARCH BUSINESS

While it has always been this author's policy, as " Americans For Open Records (AmFOR)," to not charge fees for what a citizen should have the "right to know," (such as their own true identity, heritage, true records in which they are named, and whether their child is alive and well, adopted or not, and desirous of contact or not), charging reasonable fees for one's actual expenses and time is certainly acceptable.

There are two types of search businesses. One is the result of enjoying doing research and profitably solving cases as one would enjoy satisfaction from solving a puzzle. The other type results from one's deep sense of ethical or moral conviction that "the system" is inadequate to serve the needs of those you can help via your services. This is particularly true in the area of adoption-related search and support services, many of which are also engaged in adoption reform efforts. Reforms don't just happen; they evolve from decades of citizen action, including demonstrating that enabling adoptees and their biological relatives willing to reconnect is as important and as positive as helping to locate any missing child or adult. Today, Social Services Departments charge fees to facilitate locating adoptees and their biological families according to laws and procedures that vary from state to state; the federal government has also put a price on adoption in the form of subsidies and tax breaks. It is not illegal to search for an adoptee or "birth" parent in any state.

There are also two ways to decide whether a search business would be something of interest to you and whether it would be affordable. One way is to complete your own search and/or voluntarily network to assist others who are searching locally or nationwide, as a way to develop resources and practice using techniques described in this book. The other way is to work for a private investigator or attorney in your area to gain experience researching public records and completing "skip traces" and property searches; such work is compensated by either an hourly fee or flat fee per completed search. Become familiar with your local Registrar's and other public records offices and Family History Centers to learn how their computer, microfilm and paper files are accessed, and how they can help you locate someone to settle a civil or criminal matter or to just to help someone connect with a family member or friend from the past.

After acquiring some experience as a searcher or researcher, you will also have a better idea whether you want to specialize or can be flexible enough to accept almost any kind of search assignment, as well as whether you can expect to have sufficient business in your area, whether you can or want to handle searching within the USA and/or internationally, whether you work best independently, or in partnership, or as head of your own organization with the goal of acquiring a large membership and conducting regular meetings, public seminars, producing a newsletter, and/or attracting media attention to promote your business. In any case, the following steps are important to the development and survival of any search business:

TIPS FOR STARTING YOUR OWN SEARCH BUSINESS:

(1) TEST THE LOCAL MARKET. Don't wait for Help Wantedl ads, Find and fill needs of individuals, attorneys, security companies, and others who could use your service. Customize your services to meet your client's needs.

(2) TAKE AN ADULT EDUCATION COURSE or home study in Business, and, if available, in Private Investigation, Business Law, or Criminal Justice.

(3) FILE YOUR FICTITIOUS NAME STATEMENT which will be required to open a Business Checking Account, and check whether there's a BUSINESS LICENSE is required to operate as a "home business" in your county – Often a license is not required, but in your line of work be sure to be "legal."

(4) BUY A COMPUTER for online searches; a portable laptop or notebook enables lookups while at records offices.

(5) SET UP YOUR OWN WEB-SITE to further promote your business.

(6) OBTAIN PRICE LISTS from others engaged in similar businesses and try to maintain competitive rates.

(7) NOTIFY OTHERS THAT YOU EXIST including other searchers with whom you might offer to exchange referrals, newspapers, public and college libraries that you can supply with your flyers or brochures, etc.

(8) KEEP YOUR APPOINTMENT-ADDRESS-PHONE BOOK AT HAND, while at your home- office an when when you're in your car, along with a pen and small lined notepad to jot down leads.

(9) BUILD YOUR REFERENCE LIBRARY. *The Ultimate Search Book 2011 Edition* provides "how to" infor- mation along with valuable resources not found in any other book. *International Vital Records Handbook* published by Genealogical Publishing Company (and which contains listings and useable forms for requesting records from Vital Records offices worldwide).

ADOPTEE'S ORIGINAL BIRTH CERTIFICATE

STATE OF CONNECTICUT
DEPARTMENT OF HEALTH SERVICES
Vital Records Section
Hartford, Connecticut, 06106

(RECORD OF PATERNITY
VS-119A (Rev. 8/88)

COMPLETE IN BLACK INK

PART I: Parents must furnish the following information with items 2,17 and 19 as it relates to those at the time of the birth of this child. The information will be used to prepare the new certificate of birth.

CHILD'S NAME

1. FULL NAME: RICHARD THOMAS WILLIAM CUBBAGE

2. DATE OF BIRTH: 1945

FATHER: JON W. CUBBAGE

3. BIRTHPLACE: Goleta, California

4. RACE: White

MOTHER: LORRAINE CARANGELO

201 Augur Street, Hamden, Connecticut
P.O. Box 401, Palm Desert, CA. 92261

New Haven, Conn.

PART III

CHIEF'S PERSONAL DATA
RICHARD MAROTTI
Male   December 17, 1968   New Haven, Connecticut

NATURAL FATHER'S DATA: Anthony P. Marotti
NATURAL MOTHER'S DATA: Lorraine Carangelo

Sworn to and subscribed to before me at _____, CA
this ___ day of _____ 19 88

(SEAL)
OFFICIAL SEAL
BARBARA COULSON
NOTARY PUBLIC - CALIFORNIA
PRINCIPAL OFFICE IN
RIVERSIDE COUNTY
My Commission Expires 5-24-90

NOTARY PUBLIC
Commission Expires 5-24-90

ADOPTEE'S "AMENDED" BIRTH CERTIFICATE

CONNECTICUT STATE DEPARTMENT OF HEALTH
Public Health Statistics Section — Hartford, Connecticut 06115, U. S. A.

Certificate of Birth

46563

Place of Birth: New Haven, Connecticut
Hospital of Saint Raphael
35 Sylvan Avenue

Name: William Arthur Schafrick
Male   December 17, 1968

FATHER OF CHILD
White   Connecticut   29
Landscaper

MOTHER OF CHILD
Lola Edna Fuller
White   Meriden, Connecticut   21
35 Sylvan Avenue
Meriden, Connecticut

George A. Bonner, M.D.   December 16, 1968
111 Sherman Avenue, New Haven, Connecticut

THE CERTIFICATE RECEIVED FOR RECORD ON December 23, 1968

Gaetano Messina

I certify that this is a true transcript of the information in this office.

Michael V. Lynch, Registrar
Carol Longobardi, Deputy Registrar
Maria DeGaetano, Ass't Registrar

Dated at New Haven, Connecticut, U.S.A., this 27 day of NOVEMBER, 1996

NOT VALID WITHOUT SEAL.

14

Chapter 2. Missing and Runaway Children

Since 1967, the federal government has operated a computerized National Crime Information Center (NCIC), originally used to catch criminals and recover missing property. In 1975, the feds permitted local police to include skimpy information about missing persons. In 1982, Senator Hawkins proposed expanding that service to include listings by blood type, dental records, scars and other details which would help identify missing children. Since 1994, out of 945,000 annual entries into the FBI's NCIC database on missing persons, about 80%, or 765,000, have been missing children. The United Nations Special Rapporteur on abducted Children determined, in the UN's "Rights of the Child" report, that *the United States is the largest market for stolen children in the world.* A child can sell for more than $80,000 for adoption, child sex, or pornography. Law enforcement and child rescue teams urge parents to assemble an ID packet on each child each year (with color photo and fingerprints) and to teach a child to cause a commotion if a stranger grabs him. Tips for abduction prevention include: kids must play and travel in groups, must not be left alone in a car, and must be picked up from school and activities on time. (See also, International section on Abducted Children and Rescue Sources.)

If a Child Is Missing

1. **CALL POLICE FOR "AMBER ALERT" WITHIN 30 MINUTES** from when you first perceive your child to be missing. It is a myth that you have to wait 24 hours before contacting law enforcement. Prompt notification to your local AMBER ALERT system ("America's Missing: Broadcast Emergency Response") has proven to rescue missing children as in the Elizabeth Smart recovery. There were 91 local, regional and statewide AMBER plans credited with recovering 49 children at the time President George Bush signed the "Protect Act 2003" to link all AMBER plans that currently exist. For further information call 1-800-THE LOST.

2. **TO REPORT A MISSING OR RUNAWAY CHILD UNDER AGE 18.** The National Center for Missing and Exploited Children operates a free 24-hour hotline in English and Spanish. To request publications or talk to a live representative, toll-free in U.S., Canada, Mexico: (800) THE-LOST (843-5678); the TDD Line is (800) 826-7653; FAX (703) 235-4067). The line is tape-recorded. National Runaway Switchboard 1-899-621-4000. The Center's address is 669 Prince St., Alexandria, VA 22314. Their website is at http://www.missingkids.com .

3. **TO REPORT A MISSING OR RUNAWAY CHILD POSSIBLY IN CALIFORNIA,** call toll-free to the reporting and information line operated by the Amber Foundation, (800) 541-0777. Amber Foundation's website is at http://www.amberfoundation.lpg.com ; (email from website only) PO Box 565, Pinole, CA 94564 ; (510)-222-9059, or The California Missing Children Clearinghouse website is at http://caag.state.ca.us/bcia2/mups.htm , or call 1-800-222-FIND. California is the largest market for stolen children in the U.S. California Statistics-2000 include the following: Runaways-81,291; Lost--377; Catastrophic (missing after catastrophe)—11; Stranger Abductions—51; Parental/Family Abductions—644; "Unknown Circumstances"—4,489.Total=88,801 (Stats from CA Missing Children Clearinghouse).

4. **LOST CHILD EMERGENCY BROADCAST SYSTEM(EBS) RECOVERY NETWORK** is available via the Lost Children's Public Television Project at http://www.lostchild.net , and http://www.lostchildren.org/ FRAME2.htm They will first verify with local police that the child has been reported missing, then broadcast the child's photo and information to the public, government, and education access channel TV (100 stations) and to a Law Enforcement Television Network (LETN), as well as via 30-second TV commercials, Each program features 50 missing children and utilizes "age progression" photo techniques, with dissemination to member banner websites world wide. email: lostchldren@mailcity.com

5. **TO REPORT A MISSING CHILD OR FOR RECOVERED CHILD THERAPY,** call one of the regional offices of The Adam Walsh Child Resource Center, New York (716) 242-0900; California (714) 558-7812; Florida (407) 848-1900.

6. THE SALVATION ARMY MISSING PERSONS BUREAU will not search for a runaway child, but it is a good resource if you phrase your request as a search for a "close relative." See Chapter 1 for all of the Salvation Army territorial addresses and phone numbers.

More Search Tips for Finding Missing or Runaway Children

1. WHEN REPORTING A MISSING OR RUNAWAY CHILD to Law Enforcement and to the hot lines above, consider whether a non-custodial parent, baby-sitter, relative, or family friend may have taken the child or whether an older child is likely to try to reach a relative or trusted friend who should be alerted to inform you immediately. Photo-posters stating a reward may produce a tipster. The states now have a reciprocal situation under Uniform Custody and Parental Kidnap Prevention Acts. *The Valley Times*, Las Vegas, NV, 6/2/78:

> "'MEAN GENE' GETS HIS BOY . . . Eugene 'Mean Gene' Austin, one of the nation's leading child-snatchers, accomplished the mission which brought him to Las Vegas. Austin snatches small children back from a parent who has kidnapped a youngster from the legal guardians, usually the other spouse.... In 1973, most states would not return a child across state lines to the legal guardian. You could literally take a child out of the home state, in violation of a custody order, and within 24 hours have a new order claiming yourself as the legal guardian in the new state,' said Austin. He has case files where four different people in four states had legal custody of one child ... A Miami child-snatching got national publicity for Austin in 1974 and 4-1/2 months in the Dade County Jail, but resulted in a major push to change the child custody laws. Within two years, approximately 30 states had adopted the Uniform Custody Law. Nevada changed its laws through a Supreme Court ruling in 1972 which is stronger than the Uniform Custody Law, according to Austin."

> *San Diego Tribune*, 2/11/96, page A-3: "Boy's Uncle Held in Kidnap Case... Police arrested the uncle of an 8-year-old boy who was kidnapped early yesterday but returned home nine hours later. Timothy Reine was taken screaming from his bed yesterday morning, apparently part of a custody battle between his parents police said."*Associated Press*, Richmond, VA, 3/31/93 ... "A Missouri woman accused of taking her children at gunpoint from a South Carolina couple who adopted them can't be charged under federal kidnapping law, an appeals court said ... A 4th Circuit Court of Appeals panel ruled 2-1 that the law does not apply to biological parents, even if their rights have been terminated... courts may end a biological parent's right to custody, but it may not alter the parent's identity . .." (This adoption was not finalized until after the kidnapping.)

2. BLACK MARKET ADOPTION. Infants and toddlers may fall prey to kidnappers in illegal adoption rings or to women desperate to have a child. Has anyone recently approached you about adoption or seemed overly interested in the child? Questionable procurement of children for adoption is becoming increasingly common. Adoption is a billion dollar industry in the U.S. Adoption confidentiality statues can cover-up methods of procurement. A new name and birth certificate may hide a child's identity. Search adult adoptees of black market adoptions may find the Directory of Brokers, helpful; the baby brokers are listed, alphabetically by State and Country at http://AmFOR.net/BabyBrokers

> *Dear AmFOR:...* "I have a younger adopted sister. Anna. She wants to find her mother ... I found a hidden letter about a year later. I'LL NEVER FORGET IT! It was from Anna's mother to my mother—'PLEASE, please give me my baby back,' In English ... The mother lived on the Indian reservation and had few modern conveniences. My mother convinced her to let her take the baby home . . .Anna is Cocopa Indian. I desperately need help. Where do I begin ... T.M." [Note: With AmFOR's help, Tammy fond her sister and they had a happy reunion together with Anna's mother.]

> *Omaha World-Herald*, 12/4/94, page 16-B: "IOWA WOMAN, SON REUNITE AFTER 60 YEARS" ... When Marie Vaa tells the story, her eyes glisten as the tears build up. After more than six decades apart, Mrs. Vaa, 78, and her 61-year-old son are reunited. Until this year, the Sioux City woman had not seen her only child. Ray Zachgo, since three days after his birth in 1933 ... Mrs. Vaa says the story began in Sioux City when she was deceived by a man and woman who left town with her newborn infant.. . Had Mrs. Vaa found her son while Fred and Peggy Zachgo were still living, she likely would have sought to prosecute the couple, she said. But things were different back in the 1930's, she said."

3. CHILD ABUSE. Consider whether the child may be hiding from someone in a position of trust and authority, such as a counselor or group leader who could be secretly abusing the child physically, sexually, or emotionally. Runaways also hide from street gangs, drug dealers, parental and school authority, or due to problem relationships, pregnancy, etc.

4. TEEN RUNAWAYS. If a runaway is old enough to possess a driver's license, car, Social Security number, and other ID. and is likely to work at a particular job or has predictable habits, the runaway may be making a paper trail that can be followed and reveal last known addresses, contacts, and any aliases being used. Older, more resourceful teens, may become street survivors for a time, but can fall prey to drug dealers and prostitution. Check rescue shelters in suspect areas.

5. PREVENTION AND IDENTIFICATION OF RECOVERED CHILDREN. Contact your child's school administrator and law enforcement to organize a children's self-defense program if there is none in your local community. Teach your child basic self defense, yourself (such as not permitting strangers to lure a child away, self defense moves that a youngster can successfully use to thwart a 250-pound abductor/molester, etc.) Local police may provide free child ID cards and finger printing services.

There are several websites offering "child safety products," such as an ID card and shoe tag at http://www.safechildcardid.com ; 1-888-485-4696 or write to Safe Card ID Identifier, 4801 East Independence Blvd., Ste 705, Charlotte, NC 28212. As "Child Print ID Kit" is offered to individuals and organizations by your Safe Child. 304 Birch Drive, Lafayette Hill, PA 19444; 1-888-YSC-7232. Their website is at http://www.yoursafechild.com ; email sales@yoursafechild.com ; outside the US, intl@yoursafeshild.com . For search assistance when children are believed to have been taken out of the United States, see the International Section of this book. The Blood Center of New York and the Association for the Advancement of Science have developed a way to use blood and tissue samples to establish family relationship to 99.95% certainty in cases where a child abducted as an infant with no memory of family is recovered from any country, sometimes after many years. Computer-enhanced aging of a photo of a young child can aid Law Enforcement and families still searching for a child who may now be two or more years older. Know where your child's medical records and dental x-rays are.

6. PRIVATE INVESTIGATORS are often more effective than law enforcement in finding missing children because they can devote more time to a particular case and have developed inside resources. Try PI Mall.com.

> *Dear AmFOR:....* "I need your help in locating my 16-year-old granddaughter whom I believe is locked up somewhere in Connecticut, if still alive. . . . Sincerely, GEORGIA H., Portland, OR."

7. CYBERSPACE SNATCHES OR RECOVERS KIDS. Following are excerpted news stories about kids lured via computer; any reform efforts will be arduous. For search resources, see Chapter 5.

> *Los Angeles Times* Wire Service, 6/5/95: "Boy, 15, LURED VIA COMPUTER IS FOUND SAFE". ... A Washington state teenager who ran away from home May 18 after meeting a man on a computer network was found Sunday at the San Francisco airport, police said.. .. The boy's parents say he met a man who goes by the nickname 'Damien Starr' in a gay and lesbian 'chat room' on the computer on-line service America Online.. . . The man ... sent him a bus ticket to San Francisco."

> *Los Angeles Times*, 6/12/95: "GIRL LURED FROM HOME BY E-MAIL IS FOUND IN L.A.... A 13-year-old Kentucky girl, apparently lured away from home by electronic computer message nearly two weeks ago, was taken into protective custody in Los Angeles on Sunday after she contacted authorities . .. The disappearance of Tara and other children has focused attention on the dangers lurking in cyberspace for children with access to computer chat services and e-mail . . . children can be lured into illicit sex or pornography .

8. CHILDREN OF THE NIGHT, http://www.ChildrenOfTheNight.org has, as of 2010, rescued over 10,000 children from prostitution. and offers a variety of services to help them have a good future.

9. BOYSTOWN NATIONAL HOTLINE COUNSELS AND INFORMS. Children under 18 or adults can choose a variety of recorded options or speak with a counselor about problems and programs according to one's situation, toll-free: (800) 448-3000.

10. MORE RESOURCES: Including for American parents of children abducted by a non-American spouse with government complicity:

o America's Stolen Children Network - http://www.StolenChildren.net - for parents of American children abducted by a non-American spouse with government complicity.
o Cybertipline - for past 25 years, for reporting child sexual exploitation or pornogrpahy. 1-800-843-5678 http://www.cybertipline.com
o FindKids.com - http://www.FindKids.com
o Kids Fighting For Kids - nonprofit organization founded by 10 year old Kyle Bunting to help prevent children from being abducted by educating them and others, and to find missing kids: http://www.members.cox.net/shawnpyles
o Missing Children's Web Ring - includes 2,000 websites concerned with missing/abducted kids
o National Center for Missing and Exploited Children - http://www.missingkids.com 1-800-843-5678

11. OFFER A REWARD for information leading to finding the missing child. Money often draws tipsters, but also false leads along with possibly good leads, which are best left to professionals to sort out.

"Everyone on this planet is separated by only six people...but how to find the __right__ six people..."
-from the movie and play, *"Six Degrees of Separation"* by John Guare
and based on the finding that every 6 people share 2 DNA factors in common

Chapter 3. Family Tree, Genealogy, Debtor, Child Support, Heir, Classmate, Old Love, War Buddy– Anyone

Family Tree and Genealogy

So great is our natural "need to know" our " roots," it's not surprising that the Ellis Island website had 8-million visitors in its first 8 hours of existence...and that the average person spends $700 annually of genealogy (according to Elizabeth Bernstein, *Wall Street Journal* columnist in an interview on MSNBC, 6-15-01). A simple genealogy chart begins with known names, dates and places of birth for your self, your parents, their parents, maternal and fraternal relatives and their spouses. Public libraries have helpful genealogy reference sections. Software such as "Family Tree Maker "can help you build your own family history, while Ancestry.com and Reunion.com enable anyone to research and publish their own family tree on Internet so others can add their "branches." But it's discovering the *stories* handed down through the generations, via family members, newsclippings, old letters, photo albums and journals that most fascinate us. According to Attorney Brice M. Claggett (in "Adoption Laws Threaten The Death of Genealogy," in the *National Genealogical Society Newsletter*), **"In another 4 generations or so, about half the ancestry of the American population will be bogus"** because in all states, adoptees' birth records name the adopters as "parents" so their ancestry in public records is bogus. (See Examples of Adoptee's Original and "Amended" Birth Certificates on page 14.)

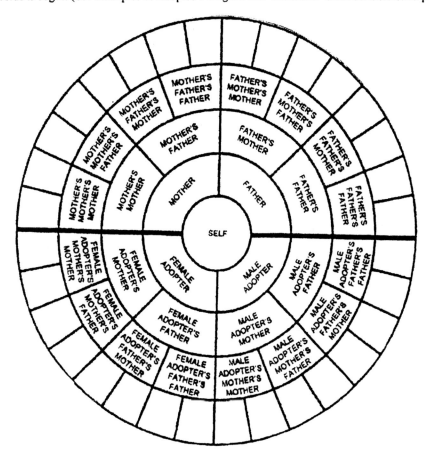

ADOPTEE'S "FAMILY WHEEL"

If you are refused access to public records, submit a written request citing the Freedom Of Information Act (FOIA) and complain to someone higher up. (See Chapter 1 on FOIA.) Tracing early Americans can be tricky. Very few people in Colonial times have three names but may be identified by their occupation without a comma: "John William Carpenter" in 1785 was probably John William, a carpenter. John Henry Taylor may have been John Henry, a tailor. Some wills and deeds were indexed by occupation and name. Many immigrants or their children Americanized their names, particularly movie stars; thus, Benny Kubelsky became Jack Benny, etc.

> *Dear AmFOR*: ". . . How sad that people lack such self-confidence and pride in their heritage that they obliterate their names for the sake of pronunciation. As a Lithuanian-American, I have always had to repeat my name, correct the pronunciation, and put up with myriad nicknames. But, as a result, there are a number of people who know a little bit about my Baltic heritage and appreciate the uniqueness in the spelling of my name. I intend for my children to have Lithuanian names, too. How convenient it would have been to be named Debbie, but I wouldn't change my name for an instant. . . . DIANA P., La Crescenta, CA."

THE CHURCH OF JESUS CHRIST OF LATTER-DAY SAINTS (Mormon) has the largest depository of worldwide genealogical records – over 600 million names, extracted from vital records worldwide. Their genealogy library is headquartered in Salt Lake City, Utah, and Family History Center branches are everywhere. Their records are mostly "more than fifty years old" but include everyone in the United States—not just Mormons—and many foreign births can be researched using their Family History Center or its branches. Neither does the researcher need to be Mormon. Records are microfilmed and on computer. Check ancestral files, census records, and birth records. They have the Social Security Death Index current within the past year, and you don't need to know the Social Security Number if the name is not too common (see also Utah).

To find a Family History Center in your area:
• Call: (800) 346-6044
• Visit the following web site: http://Ancestry.com and http://www.LDS.org

> *Dear AmFOR*: ... "I am writing to you because I am trying to get any information or paperwork I can about finding my "birth" parents. I was looking through some information that the [Church of] Latter-day Saints had. You were among their materials. I am interested in seeing if you can find out whether mine is an open or sealed adoption . . . Sincerely yours, CHERIE T., Olympia, WA."

THE GENEALOGISTS ADDRESS BOOK by Elizabeth Petty Bentley (Genealogical Publishing Co., Inc.) has national and state addresses for archives, libraries, historical societies, genealogical societies, ethnic and religious organizations, and research centers and special resources including adoption and surname registries, newspaper columns, publishers, booksellers, and an index to periodicals and newsletters. There's also a Yellow Pages Directory of Advertisers. The book is available at bookstores and public libraries.

> *Dear AmFOR*:... "I found your address in *The Genealogist's Address Book*. As the President of Family Finders Genealogical Society, I sometimes run into government officials who refuse to open records. For instance, when I went to the local Social Security office in New Bern, NC, and requested the addresses of regional SSA offices, they refused to give them to me. I know this is a violation of the Freedom of Information Act. Fortunately, I found the addresses elsewhere. Any information that my Society or I could use to open more records will be appreciated. Thank you for your help. Sincerely, DAVID B., New Bern, NC."

> *Dear AmFOR*: "... I am writing to ask for information on how to begin the search for the parents of a 21 - year-old man. However, due to special circumstances, he does not wish to actually locate his parents, but to only be able to trace his family tree without their knowledge. He was adopted through Catholic Social Services in Oklahoma City. I am a genealogist and therefore have the knowledge and experience in that area. However, I have never gone looking for family of an adoption. I would appreciate any assistance you can give me ... Sincerely, MRS. MARGARET G., Woodbridge, VA."

Dear AmFOR:... "Thank you very much for your reply ... My grandfather was born at the Des Moines Salvation Army Rescue Home. He was surrendered to and placed by the Iowa Children's Home Society." It is my understanding that sometime around 1963, he searched for and located his mother. She was living in Des Moines, quite near where he himself lived. He never did contact her, why I am not sure ... I wonder if there is something in common, a descendant searching for birth ancestors? I am beginning to feel the 'emptiness' almost as if it were myself. Especially since at times it seems so hopeless. Congratulations on your success! . Your help is greatly appreciated . Sincerely, SHANNON N., Memphis, TN."

How to Use the National Archives for Genealogical Research

The National Archives and its many branches are great resources for the genealogy researcher. The "by-state listings" in this book include the addresses for the archives and its regional branches. The National Archives has custody of millions of records relating to persons who have had dealings with the federal government. The records most useful for genealogical research may contain full information about a person or give little information beyond a name. Searches of the records may be very time-consuming as many records lack name indexes. The National Archives staff is unable to make extensive searches, but, given enough identifying information, will try to find a record about a specific person. Most records, subject to some restrictions or limitations, may be freely consulted in person. Photocopies of most of the records can be purchased for a moderate per-page fee. If you are unable to go to the National Archives, you can hire someone to do research for you. Many paid researchers advertise in genealogical periodicals available in public libraries and bookstores. For records accessed by the National Archives, it is recommended that you move from the smallest to the largest citation element (from the record item to the repository). Citations may differ because internal record group arrangement is based on the organizations structure of the bureaus, departments, and agencies that created the records. Some agencies were organized in more complex structures than others. Citations to records should reflect the hierarchical arrangement of the records as closely as possible. The citation elements to be used (going from the smallest to the largest) are:

RECORD: At the National Archives, a record is a piece of information or an item of information or an item in any physical form (e.g., paper, photographic or motion picture tape, audio tape, computer tape, etc.) that gives information created or received by a government agency in carrying out its duties and functions. Example: letter in a pension application file.

FILE UNIT: A file unit holds the records concerning a transaction, person, case, date, or subject. Example: a pension application file based, on the military service of one veteran; such a file may often contain various record items such as supporting depositions, affidavits, correspondence, etc.

SERIES: A series consists of file units that deal with a particular subject, function, or activity that are related by arrangement, source, use, physical form, or action taken. Example: within pension application files for widows and dependents of sailors for the period 1861-1910, pension applications that were not approved constitute one series while approved applications constitute another series.

SUBGROUP: A subgroup contains two or more series that are related by subject, activity, and source. Example:two services for approved and unapproved pension applications based on sailor's military service for the period 1861-1910 (plus other series of pension applications based on military service in the U.S. Army and the Marine Corps for roughly the same period) form the subgroup known as Civil War and Later Pension Files.

RECORD GROUP: Subgroups are combined into record groups according to the origin of the subgroup material. Most often a record group exists for the records of a bureau or other administrative body of an executive department or for an independent government agency that is equivalent to a bureau in size. Example: the subgroup Civil War and Later Pension Files plus other subgroups constitute Records of the Veterans Administration, Records Group 15.

REPOSITORY: The repository is the institution in which the cited record is kept. Give the name of the institution and the city in which it is located. National Archives repositories in Washington, DC; Suitland, MD; Alexandria, VA; and other locations in the Washington, DC area should be cited as "National Archives, Washington, DC." National Archives field branches should be cited as "National Archives—(name of city) Branch."

National Archives and Records Administration
Seventh and Pennsylvania Ave., NW; Washington, DC 20408
Phone (202) 501-5400; (202) 523-3218; (202) 523-3286
Hours: M-F 8:45AM-4:30PM
Publication: National Archives Calendar of Events (a pictorial calendar of events including genealogical workshops, courses, and presentations).

National Archives and Records Administration
Suitland Reference Branch (NNRR), (4205 Suitland Road, Suitland, MD location); Washington, DC 20409
Phone:(301)763-7410
Hours: M-Sat 8AM-4:15PM
Offers 600.000+ square feet of federal records, more than any other archival entity in the U.S.; Bureau of Land Management 1790-1960 land entry files/homesteads; War Relocation Authority 1940-1945, Japanese Americans interned during WWII; Dept. of State 1906-1925 passports; U.S. District Court for the District of Columbia 1800-1960; and Patent and Trademark Office 1836-1918.

National Archives and Records Administration—Archives II
National Archives at College Park
(8601 Adelphi Road, College Park, MD location), Seventh and Pennsylvania Ave., NW; Washington, DC 20408
Phone:(301)713-6800
Hours: M-F 8:45AM-5PM; Research Rooms M-W 8:45AM-5PM, T, Th, F 8:45AM-9PM; Sat 8:45AM-4:45PM Some records from the Washington, DC and Suitland, MD archives have been transferred to this new facility. There are no genealogical records here. Archives II includes Nixon Presidential Materials, Research Rooms, Center for Electronic Records, Cartographic Reference Branch, Motion Picture, Sound and Video Branch, and Still Picture Branch.

National Archives and Records Administration
National Personnel Records Center (Military Personnel)
9700 Page Ave.; St. Louis, MO 63132-5100
Phone: (314) 538-4261-Army; (314) 538-4243-Air Force;
(314) 538-4141-Navy/Coast Guard/Marine Corps
Hours: M-F 7:30AM-4PM
For records in the National Archives relating to early military service, use NATF Form 26. Request for later personnel should be sent on Form 180.

General Services Administration (GSA) Bureau of Indian Affairs Bureau of Indian Affairs
Civilian Personnel Records Department of Interior Department of the Interior
111 Winnebago Street Muskogee Area Office 1849 "C" Street, NW, St. Louis, MO 63118 Federal Building Washington, DC 20240
125 South Main Street Phone: (202) 343-1334
Has personnel records for the Muskogee, OK 74401 Coast Guard and for Bureau of Land Management most civilian employees Dept. of the Interior terminated after 1909. 1849 "C" Street, NW, Washington, DC 2040
Phone: (202) 343-9435; (202) 343-4152

Records Available for Search

The following records are available from the National Archives and from many major libraries throughout the U.S. These records as well as a host of other records are also available for rental and sale from Heritage Quest, PO Box 329, Bountiful, UT 84011-0329, (800) 760-2455.

POPULATION CENSUS. A Census of the population has been taken every 10 years since 1790. The last Census counted children "natural or adopted", but no Census has counted adoptees. Microfilm copies are available for the 1790-1880 schedules, the surviving fragments of the 1890 schedules, and the 1900-1920 schedules. Practically all of the 1890 census schedules were destroyed by fire in 1921. The remaining entries are for small segments of the populations of Perry County, AL; the District of Columbia; Columbus, GA; Mound Township, IL; Rockford, MN; Jersey City, NJ; Eastchester and Brookhaven Township, NY; Cleveland and Gaston Counties, NC; Cincinnati and Wayne Township, OH; Jefferson Township, SD; and Ellis, Hood, Kauffman, Rusk and Trinity Counties, TX. The 1790-1840 schedules give the names of head of household only; other family members are tallied unnamed by age and sex. For the 1850 and 1860 censuses, separate schedules list slave owners and the age, sex, and color (but not name) of each slave, and county of birth of each free person in a household. Additional information is included with each succeeding census. The published census schedules for 1790 are for Connecticut, Maine, Maryland, Massachusetts, New Hampshire, New York, North Carolina, and Vermont. The schedules for the remaining states—Delaware, Georgia, Kentucky, New Jersey, Tennessee, and Virginia—were burned during the War of 1812. As a substitute, the federal government published names obtained from state censuses and tax lists, thereby listing over half the population of the state in 1790. Helpful in locating specific census entries are the following unpublished indexes in the National Archives Building:

1810 Census — card index for Virginia only;

1880 Census — a microfilm copy of a card index to entries for each household that included a child aged 10 or under;

1890 Census — a card index to the 6,160 names of surviving schedules;

1900 Census — a microfilm copy of an index to heads of families;

1910 Census — a microfilm copy of an index to all heads of families in the following states: Alabama, Arkansas, California, Florida, Georgia, Illinois, Kansas, Kentucky, Louisiana, Michigan, Mississippi, Missouri, North Carolina, Tennessee, Texas, Virginia, and West Virginia. Also available on microfilm are the 1890 schedules of Union veterans and their widows in alphabetical order from Louisiana through Wyoming. Records are available relating to Indians who kept their tribal status, mostly from 1830-1940. They include mainly Cherokee, Chickasaw, Choctaw, and Creek, each of whom moved West during the 1830-46 period. Each entry on these lists usually contains the name of the head of the family, the number of persons in the family by age and sex, a description of property owned before removal with the location of real property, and the dates of departure from the East and arrival in the West. The microfilm rolls of 1885-1940 census rolls show each person in the family by the Indian or English name (or both), age, sex, relationship to head of family, sometimes relationship to other enrolled Indians, and sometimes births and deaths during the year.

Bureau of the Census Department of State
(1201 East Tenth St.—location) **Passport Office,** PO Box 1545, 1111 19th Street, NW, Jeffersonville, IN 47131
Washington, DC 20522-1705
Phone: (812) 285-5314 Phone (202) 647-0518
Hours: M-F 7PM-4:30 PM

NATURALIZATION RECORDS. The Immigration and Naturalization Service has duplicate records of all naturalizations that occurred after September 26, 1906. Inquiries about citizenship granted after that date should be sent to the Service on a form available from INS district offices (addresses of local INS available from local postmasters).

Immigration and Naturalization Service (INS)
FOIA PA UNIT, 425 "I" Street, NW, Washington, DC 20536
Phone: (202)514-3278

SHIP PASSENGER LISTS. Incomplete series of custom passenger lists and immigration passenger lists of ships arriving from abroad at many Atlantic, Pacific, and Gulf Coast ports are available. There are also arrival records for immigration via Canada. Customs passenger lists begin in 1820 and extend to the late 19th century (1890's) for most ports. The immigration passenger lists begin at that time, usually when the customs lists leave off: Baltimore 1820-1948; 1820-1952 indexes; Boston 1820-74; 1883-1943; 1848-91 & 1902-20 indexes; New Orleans 1820- 1945; 1853-1952 indexes; New York 1820-1954; 1820-46 and 1897-1948 indexes; San Francisco 1893-1953; 1893-1934 indexes; Seattle 1899-1957; Canada 1896-1954; 1890-1924 indexes. A customs passenger list normally contains the passenger's name, age, sex, and occupation, country of embarkation, country of destination, and date and circumstances if death occurred during passage. Lists often show place of birth, last residence, name and address of a relative in country of embarkation, and of sponsor with whom they probably lived upon arrival in the USA. The Morton Alien Directory of European Passenger Steamship Arrivals (New York, 1931) lists by year, steamship company, and exact date vessels arrived at ports of New York 1890-1930 and Baltimore, Boston, and Philadelphia 1904-26. This directory is available in some large public and research libraries. For immigration passenger lists . . .

National Archives and Records Administration
FOIA Office, Seventh and Pennsylvania Ave., NW, Washington, DC 20408

VITAL STATISTICS. Records are available of births, marriages, and deaths at U.S. Army facilities, 1884-1912 and some records of births and marriages of U.S. citizens abroad that are registered at Foreign Service posts through 1941 and some deaths through 1949. Requests for information about registrations made less than 75 years ago should be addressed to the Department of State, Washington, DC 20520. Requests for information about earlier registrations should be addressed to the Diplomatic Archives Branch (NNFD), National Archives, Washington, DC 20408. For other original records of birth, marriage, and death, address the inquiry to the Bureau of Vital Statistics, the church, or other appropriate local depository in the appropriate state, county, or city.

GENEALOGY WEBSITES
Genealogy is the third most popular topic on the Internet with more than 170,000 genealogy websites. "Gen Ring" contains over 1600 sites. The largest, most popular genealogy sites are the Mormon LDS Family History Center site at http://familysearch.org has over 600,000 names and "Ancestral Files" databases. Commercial sites such as http://Ancestry.com and http://RootsWeb.com which has the Security Death Index not found on Social Security's website offer limited or extensive free database access, and also sell books, software, research/charting services, coats of arms, etc. Personal family websites, message boards, genealogy columns, newsgroups, directories help one "branch out" in their search for "roots." Here's a sampling:
Afrigenes - http://www.msstate.edu/Archives/History/afrigen
Ancestry Search - http://www.ancestry.com
Australian Genealogy - http://www.vicnet.net.au/~dpsoc
Canadian Genealogy Resources - http://www.iosphere.net/~jholwell/cangene/gene.html
Canada National Archives - http://www.inGeneas.com/free/index.html
Cyndi's List (over 52,000 links, 100 categories) - http://www.cyndrslist.com/
Eastman's Online Genealogical Helper (fee & free) - http://www.everton.com
Family History Center (Mormon LDS) - http://www.familysearch.org
Family Tree Maker's Genealogy Site - http://www.familytreemaker.com
First Name Genealogy Search (unusual first names) - http://www.hypervigilance.com/genlog.firstname.html
Free Family Charts - http://www.onegreatfamily.com
Genconnect - http://www.genconnect.rootsweb.com/usaindex.html
Genealogy BBS - (online messaging bulletin boards) - http://www.genealogy.org/~gbbs
Genealogy Forum (chat) - http://www.rare.on.ca/users/genealogyforum/index.htm
Genealogy Gateway Bookmarks (messages) - http://www.gateway.com/wwwboard/messages/1605.html
Genealogy Mall (commercial ads, library links, Soundex conversion, sites) - http://www.genealogymall.com
GenealNet (surnames before 1850) - http://www.geneat.org
GEN-SHARE Mailing Lists - http://gen_mail_general.html#GEN-SHARE
Government Genealogy Resources - http://www.cooklib.org/gene.html
Helm's Genealogy Toobox (index of 1,000 genealogy web resources) - http://www.genealogy.tbox.com
Heritage Quest (major database supplier and lending library) - http://www.heritagequest.html
Italian Genealogy - http://www.italgen.com
Jewish Genealogy - http://www.jewishgen.org

Map Quest (interactive atlas for finding any place in the world) - http://www.mapquest.com
Nerd World Personal Genealogy Pages A-Z - http://www.nerdworld.com/cgi-bin/subjects
Newfoundland and Labrador Genealogy Resources - http://www.iosphere.net/~jholwell/mlrsh
Roots Web Home Page - http://www.rootsweb.com
Shaking Your Family Tree (column) - http://www.ancestry.com/columns/myra/Shaking_Family_Tree.new.htm
Top Genealogy Sites (also books, search engines) - http://ourworld.compuserve.com/homepages/Strawn/
Treasure Maps (the "how to" site) - http://www.firstct.com/fv/tmaps.html
Soundex Search - http://www.nara.gov/genealogy/soundex/soundex.html
United Kingdom Genealogy - http://www.mirc.co.uk/
US GenWeb - http://www.rootsgenweb.com
U.S. National Archives - http://www.nara.gov
Usenet Genealogy Newsgroups - http://genealogy.usenetway.com
World Genealogy Project - http://www.desneter.com/worldgenweb

Debtors, Bills, and Child Support Matters

Local collections agencies in every city are able to pursue debtors for companies and individuals who are owed money (even child support) and do not charge up-front fees. Most work on contingency, taking 50% of the amount recovered. If you want to attempt collections yourself, you must first make a legal, written demand for payment. Send your letter by certified return-receipt mail. The District Attorney for the county in which child support was incurred can locate deadbeat dads (or deadbeat moms) and have their salaries garnished, liens placed against property, and initiate legal prosecution to enforce court-ordered child support. **In recent years, birth certificates bear the child's Social Security number to establish a child support payment account.** The collections agency should provide the option of removing the negative credit report information if the debt is immediately paid.

Classmates, Old Loves, Missing Adults, Anyone

Is there an old friend from your past with whom you'd like to reconnect, but you don't know where they are? Try techniques described in the "Search Basics" section of this book. Popular websites for connecting include Facebook.com MySpace.com, Reunions.com and Classmates.com. Annually, about 180,000 adults nationwide are reported "missing." Unlike missing children, few resources exist to aid families of missing adults. Here's one: Center for Missing Adults; 2432 West Peoria Ave., Suite 1283; Phoenix, AZ 85029; 1-800-690-FIND.

To Find an Heir

Check the Yellow Pages and classified ads under "Locators" and "Legal Services." Heir searchers also advertise in *Martindale-Hubbell* attorney directory which is also available on Inyternet. "Locators, Inc." is one which has a toll-free number, (800) 395-9131, and offers "free evaluation, references, brochure, fast action, amazing results." As when hiring a detective, check references. "Probate" is the legal determination of validity of a will, by court hearing. The Probate Court for the county in which the deceased maintained "last legal residence" has jurisdiction and requires probate for estates over a certain value (example, "over $60,000"). *The court does not search for heirs.* A Legal Notice about the death and hearing must be published (usually by attorney, administrator, or executor) in a newspaper in the county of last legal residence. Interested parties should follow "Search Basics" tips in this book to locate heirs.

TO START AN HEIR SEARCH BUSINESS, Contact the American Family Records Association, PO Box 15505, Kansas City, MO 64106 on how to start an heir search business. (See Chapter 1, *"Starting Your Own Search Business."*)

UNCLAIMED PROPERTY. To find out if a relative has unclaimed stock certificates, call Stock Search International, (800) 537-4523 toll-free. To find out if a relative has a life insurance policy, write to American Council of Life Insurance Policy Search, 1001 Pennsylvania Ave., Washington, DC 20004.

2010 Adoption Disclosure Laws at a Glance

A=Adoptee; **P**=Parent; **AD**=Adopter; **S**=Birth Sibling; **CI**=Confidential Intermediary; **COO**=Court Order Only; **OBC**=Original Birth Certificate

State	Non-ID	Search Procedures	Records Access
Alabama	A,AD	Passive Registry=P; CI	OBC-A
Alaska	A,AD	Passive Registry=P	OBC-A, at age 18
Arizona	A,AD,P	CI=A.AD	COO
Arkansas	A,AD,P	Passive Registry=A, S, P; CI=A, P : Counseling req.	COO
California	A,AD,P,S	Waiver System=A, P,S	COO
Colorado	A,AD	CI= A, P, S; Passive Registry= A,P	COO/veto post-"99
Connecticut	A,AD,P	CI=A.AD,P ·	COO
Delaware	A,AD,P	Active Registry=A, AD ; P veto	OBC-A, age 21
District of Columbia	No Provisions	No Provisions	COO
Florida	A.AD	Passive Registry=A, AD P; CI=A, P	COO
Georgia	A,AD	Active Registry=A, S; Passive Registry=P	COO
Hawaii	A,AD,P	Active Registry=pre- '91, A; post '91=veto	COO
Idaho	No provisions	Passive Registry=A,S,P	COO
Illinois	A,AD	Passive Registry=A, S, P; CI	COO
Indiana	A,AD,P	CI=A, P; Passive Registry=A ,P (S=restricted)	COO
Iowa	A,AD	Passive Registry=A, P	COO
Kansas	A.AD	Active Registry=OPEN to A age 18	OBC-A, at age 18
Kentucky	A.AD	CI=A, Passive Registry=P, S,AD with consent of P	COO
Louisiana	A,AD	Passive Registry=A pre-'81, A, P with counseling	COO
Maine	A,AD	Passive Registry= A, AD, P	OBC-A pre-6/1/47
Maryland	A,AD,P	Passive Registry= A, P;CI	COO
Massachusetts	A,AD,P	Waiver System=A, P	COO
Michigan	A,AD,P,S	Waiver/Registry/CI=A, P,S	COO
Minnesota	A,AD,P	Active Registry/Waiver=A, P,AD=post"82/P-veto	COO
Mississippi	A,AD	CI=A, P; Registry=post-'94	COO
Missouri	A,AD	Active Registry=A, P w/AD consent pre-'86	COO
Montana	A,AD	Passive Registry=A, P; CI= AD, P veto	OBC=pre '67; COO
Nebraska	A.AD	Waiver/Active Registry=A	OBC-A age 25;P veto
Nevada	AD	Passive Registry, A,P	COO
New Hampshire	A, P	Waiver/Agency-CI=A, P	OBC=A age 18
New Jersey	A	No Provisions	COO
New Mexico	A,AD, P	Passive Registry=A, P	COO
New York	A,P	Active Registry=A,P; CI; Public BirthIndex 5 boroughs	COO
North Carolina	A,AD,P	No Provisions	COO
North Dakota	A,AD	Waiver/Active Registry= A,AD,P,S	COO
Ohio	No Provisions	Passive Registry=A, P, S	OBC-pre1964
Oklahoma	A,AD,.P	Passive Registry=A, P; CI	COO
Oregon	A,AD,P	CI=A,AD,P	OBC=A,age21
Pennsylvania	A,AD CI=A;	Passive Registry=P; Medical Registry	OBC=A, w/P waiver
Rhode Island	A,AD.P	Passive Registry=A, P	COO
South Carolina	A,AD, P	Passive Registry=A, P	COO
South Dakota	A,AD	Passive Registry=A, P	COO
Tennessee	A,AD	Active Registry=A, P	OPEN to A; veto
Texas	A.AD	Passive Registry=A, P	COO
Utah	A,AD,P	Passive Registry=A, P	COO
Vermont	A, AD,P	Waiver at Central Registry=A, P, pre-'86 with consent; veto COO	
Virginia	A.AD	CI=A, P	OBC-A at age 18
Washington	A,AD,P	Passive Registry=A, P ; CI	COO
West Virginia	A,AD	Passive Registry, A,P	COO
Wisconsin	A,AD	Active Registry=A; Passive Registry=P	OBC=A w/ P consent
Wyoming	A.AD	CI; Registry=AD, P	COO

Medical and health information in an adoption file is generally that which was available at time of placement. Only 8 states (AL, IL, KS, MD, MN, MN, MS, WY) allow Adopters to request that the state adoption registry contact "Birth" Parents when additional health information is medically necessary. **As of 2010, only 9 states (AL,AK, DE, KS,NE, NH, OR, TN,VA) provide Original Birth Certificate to adult adoptee on request; in OH,ME,MT,PA.WI access depends on date adoption finalized or Parent Consent;** in all other states and District of Columbia, American Samoa and Puerto Rico, a Court Order is still required and/or require mutual consents/waivers or Confidential Intermediaries. **In the 5 boroughs of New York,** anyone can view Birth Indexes which cross-reference birth and adoptive names, but not elsewhere in New York All states (and American Samoa) now have provisions in statutes that allow access to Non-Identifying information by an Adult Adoptee (at age 18 or older) upon written request, or by an Adopter or Guardian of an Adoptee who is a minor. Non-identifying information depends on availability or social worker discretion, and may include date and place of Adoptee's birth, ages of "Birth" Parents at time of placement, and general physical descriptions, race. ethnicity, religion, family medical history, "Birth" Parents' educational level and occupations at time of adoption, reasons for placement, existence of other children born to each "Birth" Parent. Approximately 15 states allow biological adult **Siblings** of the Adoptee to seek and access Non-identifying information; 36 states allow adult biological **Siblings** to seek and release Identifying information upon mutual consent.

Chapter 4. With or Without a Name - Family Members Separated Due to Adoption/Divorce/Donor Offspring

Private adoption search organizations with over 1-200,000 registrants annually, estimated that 140,000,000 Americans have a "sealed records" adoption in their immediate family ... That's half the United States population. The Open Records Movement believes the present adoption system promotes abortion and deprives all parties of "basic rights."

Who Am I?—A Basic Right

ADOPTION ROADBLOCKS. Adoptee-parent search groups with 1-200,000 registrants have published surveys revealing that 99% of adoptees and parents want to know and be in contact with each other. Yet only 9 states will provide adult adoptees with their true pre-adoption birth certificate upon request, and most states do not permit the biological parent to initiate contact. The "2010 Adoption Laws at a Glance" chart (opposite page) illustrates that non-uniform state laws determine who may know what, depending on accident of place of birth of the adoptee.

> Susan Darke, both an adoptee and relinquishing mother, states the following: *"All my life I have been told, 'If you find her [the mother] it will ruin her life; it will ruin your parents' lives, you'll hurt them so badly.' And, when I talked about knowing the child I had given up, I was told the same thing. At some point I asked, 'Now wait a minute, what is it about knowing me that's going to ruin people's lives?'"*

> Karen Golden, an adopter, reveals her feelings about secrecy in adoption: *"I really believe that openness makes for a healthier child. After all, we strive for openness and honesty in the rest of our lives; why should adoption be the exception? Their need-to-know stems from this lack of honesty and from state laws barring openness."*

Adoptees and parents confront an adversarial adoption system designed to thwart their efforts to locate each other. It has been reported that even when both parties have registered on a state-sponsored, mutual consent voluntary registries, the states may fail to "match" and inform the parties that each has registered and consents to contact. The State usually will not publicize such changes nor solicit waivers of confidentiality. And, when the parties do inquire, they may have to pay fees they can't afford and wait months for a response. Los Angeles County Social Services, for example, takes over a year to respond. When individuals complete searches on their own, some discover each was "registered" with the state for a year or more. What is even sadder is when bureaucratic delay or long searches are completed just after the other party has died. Still, state registries should not be overlooked. They have resulted in reunions for some who do not wish to actively search, or who wish to utilize every means available.

AmFOR has helped tens of thousands of adoptees and their biological parents and siblings to reconnect (without fee), often on referral from Social Services, the Salvation Army Locator Services, The Church of Jesus Christ of Latter-day Saints (Mormon) Family History Centers, court clerks, and private investigators.

> *"Is it any wonder there is difficulty in finding statistics for the number of adoptees who search!? There is a silent majority who search in secret because of such attitudes inflicted by their adopters and society at large. There are those who wait until their adopters die before they fulfill their own needs and desires, because they don't wish to hurt their adopters or deal with the cruel rejection that comes from their lack of understanding . . .* CAROL GUSTAVSON, ADOPTIVE PARENTS FOR OPEN RECORDS (APFOR), Hackettstown, NJ."

Seldom does the adult adoptee know his birth name or his parents' names when beginning the search because this information has been "sealed" and withheld in court and agency files since his adoption. A "sealed" record used to be an envelope sealed with wax and locked in court and agency files. Nowadays, "confidential" files may be in an open, unlocked file drawer, accessible to courthouse employees, but not to the persons named in the documents without court order. Older adoption files may be archived or stored in self-storage or elsewhere. Increasingly, states are permitting destruction of hospital birth records after 21 years or less – which is when most adult adoptees are permitted varying degrees of access to information and may discover the names needed to access their hospital birth records. Adoptees who have always known their identities either were old enough at the time of adoption to remember, or became privy via their adopters, or by discovering adoption papers which sometimes bear names of all parties. Adoptees and parents should ask if there have been law changes in the years relinquishment and placement which may enhance ability to access information and contact.

This chapter, and the *"Searching The USA"* by-state section, and *"International Searching"* by-country section, details how to overcome roadblocks to access "confidential" birth records or information, by knowing how to use the system and how to legally overcome roadblocks imposed by the system. Always ask whether there has been a recent amendment to state law that could be advantageous to your search as adoption laws are the most amended state laws.

NATIVE AMERICAN ADOPTEE SEARCH RESOURCES. The 1978 Indian Child Welfare Act gives special preference in adoptions of Native American children to the child's immediate relatives and tribe. Adult adoptees may find **The Bureau of Indian Affairs** helpful in identifying their tribe and accessing information about their biological families....*the Mexican equivalent* of this U.S. Bureau is the **National Indian Institute**. However, many find the "how to" search information and resources, under the state or country in which the adoption occurred, still essential for locating birth families. While attorneys have been able to open adoption files for some incarcerated adoptees, the following illustrates the problem that even the "civil rights" organization, ACLU, doesn't seem to grasp, perhaps because ACLU has a conflict of interest in that they also represent foster care and adoption agencies:

> July 7, 1992, Letter from Louis Rhodes, Director, American Civil Liberties Union (ACLU), Arizona branch, responding to Wes Bikoff, an adult adoptee wanting to know about his Native American heritage that is sealed In his adoption file: *"Dear Mr. Bikoff, The courts and the legislatures must try to balance the rights of adoptees and the privacy rights of the birth parents....These laws have traditionally had the effect of restricting the rights of American Indians when compared to others' rights.... They do not have greater rights, only different rights."*

> *Dear AmFOR:.... "I know a number of organizations that play on the heart strings of adoptees like me ... For a fee ranging between $650 and $3,000 a full report can be obtained. Is this legal? I am 31-years-old and found out last year I have two siblings. Should this information cost me $650 which I cannot afford? The pedigrees of dogs and cats is easily obtainable, but not adoptees'.. .*
> *Sincerely, WES Bikoff, Scottsdale, AZ.*

Author's Note: Wes found his family three years after he wrote his 1992 letter ... His mother had died five years prior. He located and reunited with his older sister.

DONOR OFFSPRING and DONOR PARENTS. By the early 1990s, about 80,000 women had conceived children by artificial insemination. For children born of sperm/egg donors or surrogates, there is no provision in law at this time, in any state, for disclosure as to the donor's or surrogate's identity and updated medical history. Unregulated for years, some sperm banks purposely mixed sperm from two or more donors so that it would be impossible to determine the biological fathers—usually medical students who were paid—while others maintain records in case the child seeks information via court order. Some unscrupulous doctors used their own sperm to inseminate hundreds of mothers and there have been many KNOWN cases of unknowing donor-created siblings marrying. AmFOR has provided the first totally FREE searchable "DONOR OFFSPRING/PARENT REGISTRY" (for sibling also) online to help them connect according to place and date of the donor procedure and any other known information at http://AmFOR.net/DonorOffspring.html For DNA testing information, call: 1-800-DNA-TYPE.

> *Dear AmFOR:.... "I can't thank you enough for the information ... I am the mother of an only child who, before he passed away, informed me that he had donated sperm over a decade ago at the West Los Angeles Sperm Bank—whose records are closed to me... I would like to locate my biological grand children . . . Sincerely, TOBI S., Encino, CA."*

With or Without a Name-
Starting Point for Adoptees and Parents

To locate an adoptee or "birth" parent, and/or information about them, your starting point is to know the law in the state in which the adoption was finalized. Contact the central office of Social Services in that state to (1) verify that there is a record of a public agency adoption in that state, and (2) verify current state disclosure law and procedure.

SUMMARY OF ADOPTION DISCLOSURE LAW AND PROCEDURE. Adoptees usually have two (2) adoption files - a Court file and a file held by a public or private adoption agency or attorney. Usually the Court file is limited to court documents including the Petition To Adopt and Final Decree of Adoption, while the agency file is more likely to contain the "birth" parents' and adoptee's family social and medical information at the time of relinquishment. Upon finalization of an adoption, the true, original (pre-adoption) birth certificate (which has the birth" parents' names and adoptee's birth name) is withheld from access at the central office of Vital Records and a new, "amended' (falsified) birth certificate indicating the adopters are the "parents" at time of birth is issued as a "certified" copy in all states.

In 2010 only nine (9) states permit ADULT adoptees access to their original birth certificates on request at legal age in the state of birth- they are AL, AL, DE, KS, NE, NH, OR, TN, and VA. In ME, OH, MT, PA and WI, access depends on date adoption was finalized or "birth" parent consent; or states may have mutual consent registries and/or a Confidential Intermediary system; all other states and District of Columbia, access is by Court order only. In recent years, all states were finally compeled by state laws to release "non-identifying" background information to adult adoptees (and in some states to Parents and Siblings of the adoptee) See "2010 Adoption Laws at a Glance" at the beginning of this chapter, and "Questions To Ask" and "The Confidential Intermediary System"at the end of this chapter.

PENALTIES FOR UNAUTHORIZED DISCLOSURE FROM ADOPTION RECORDS vary greatly from state to state. California has the highest fine, $5,000, and considers unauthorized disclosure to be a felony crime punishable by 14 years in prison. This is exceeded only by the former Soviet Union whose vital records are not public records. Idaho fines "up to $100 and/or 30 days." Kentucky and Louisiana will fine $500-$2000 and/or 90 days. In New Hampshire, violating confidentiality of adoption proceedings is a misdemeanor. In some states like Texas, the penalty for telling an adoptee his/her true identity is greater than for unlicensed adoption placement or baby selling. The current Uniform Adoption Act recommends felonizing unauthorized adoption disclosure, and sealing of records "for 99 years."

Search Tips, With or Without a Name
(For families separated by adoption or divorce.)

1. READ CHAPTERS 1 THROUGH 5 OF THIS BOOK. Use the "by-state" or "by-country" resources.

2. REGISTER FREE WITH INTERNATIONAL SOUNDEX REUNION REGISTRY (ISSR), the oldest, largest registry. Send a stamped, self-addressed envelope to receive a registration form. Enclose the form and a tax deductible donation to ISRR. PO Box 2312, Carson City, NV 89701. On Internet: http://www.isrr.net .

3. DON'T KNOW YOUR BIRTH NAME OR YOUR PARENTS' NAMES? Try requesting the hospital Delivery Room Record from a Delivery Room Clerk, as a "Baby Girl/Boy ---" and birth date. Don't say "adoption." Request parents' date or year of birth with non-identifying info from agency / court to determine the year they would have graduated high school and search high school / college year books at public libraries or at http://Classmates.com and http://Reunions.com.

4. REQUEST THE PETITION/FINAL DECREE OF ADOPTION, OR DIVORCE/CUSTODY PAPERS; BROWSE THE PUBLIC COURT DOCKETS. Adoptive parents were given a copy of the adoption papers. If they no longer have them, they can obtain another copy from the court. The court clerk in many areas may obliterate the birth name and birthparents' names with an indelible felt-tip marking pen. Try photocopying the BACK side on a very dark setting to see if impressions will show on reverse side of a typed original. A dab of hairspray on a Q-tip will remove "white-out." Court dockets may reveal names of "birth" parents and adoptive parents at the time the case was heard. This is a public record (not sealed), though sometimes it is withheld).

5. REQUEST COMPLETE HOSPITAL RECORD OF BIRTH for mother and newborn under known names from the Medical Records Department—Request Admissions Record (which can reveal who paid the bill—father?), doctor's and nurse's notes, delivery room record, newborn photo, discharge record. If you are told that the record was "destroyed", it may not be true. In California a hospital may destroy a birth record only after 21 years (Just when an adoptee may request it) or may have old records stored at an inconvenient self-storage facility. Ask the Medical Records Supervisor for the "statistical" or "index" card which is never destroyed; it can reveal the names sought. Determine before-hand whether state law permits you to have your/your mother's/your child's hospital birth record directly or via a physician only.

6. DECEASED PARENT OR ADOPTEE? Cite the following: *Davin v. US Department of Justice*, 60F. 3dl043 (3rd circuit 1995), *"Persons who are deceased have no privacy interest in non-disclosure of their identities, so government should disclose information about them."*

7. LOCATE THE ACTUAL ADOPTION FILE. Although Social Services records all adoptions, the actual file may be stored by a private agency or the attorney that actually facilitated the adoption. That agency or attorney is obligated to provide non-identifying or identifying information under statutory conditions for disclosure.

8. APPLY FOR A PASSPORT AS A RUSE TO OBTAIN ORIGINAL BIRTH CERTIFICATE.
Passport Services requires proof of reason for a year or more delay in issuance or certification of a birth certificate. Adoptees with only an amended birth certificate have reported being able to obtain their original birth certificate directly from Vital Records, on a case-by-case basis, perhaps because Vital Records is approached regarding a "delayed birth certificate" rather than a "sealed record due to adoption." Without their birth name, adoptees can't provide other "proof of adoption.

9. OBTAIN FOSTER CARE RECORDS. Because most children relinquished for adoption are first placed in foster homes pending a home study and court approval of the adoption, and because foster care records are not routinely sealed, adoptees and "birth" parents should tap foster care records and talk with foster parents.

10. CHECK WITH THE SALVATION ARMY MISSING PERSONS LOCATOR SERVICES. They operate in 100 countries. Their services are available to the public under the following guidelines: (1) The inquirer should be searching for a "close relative," such as "mother," but not "birth" mother," because the Salvation Army operated homes for unwed mothers, and it is their policy to maintain confidentiality for these women even though being reunited with offspring was never offered to any birth" mother as an option. If the Salvation Army discovers they have been tricked into looking for birth" parents, they will immediately close the case. Neither can the Salvation Army expend time and money to search for old classmates, sweethearts, wartime buddies, runaway teenagers, or someone who owes you money. (2) The Salvation Army reserves the right to accept or reject any request for search assistance based on reasonableness, feasibility, or notice. (3) The inquirer is asked to forward a non-refundable donation of $25 (check for fee change). (4) The inquirer may obtain information or an inquiry form by contacting the nearest territorial headquarters listed in this book. (See Chapter 1 search tip "The Salvation Army" for addresses)

Innovative and Bizarre Search Methods of Adoptees, Parents

(Desperate actions not advocated and which this book is designed to make unnecessary.)

1. "B.R.", an adult adoptee confined to a wheelchair and unable to gain support of his adopters to seek out his parents, took matters into his own hands. While his adopters were out one day, he cracked open their vault which he believed held his adoption papers. It did. And, the papers contained the names of both his parents.

2. "R.J.", adult adoptee, obtained a copy of his Final Decree of Adoption from the Los Angeles Superior Court Clerk by simply asking for it and paying a small fee. Imagine his disappointment when the clerk, before handing him the copies, took a wide felt-tipped indelible pen and blackened out his birth name and his parents' names, and then photocopied the blackened copy. The Clerk could read what he could not. When he got home with his papers, he tried holding the blackened areas over a light bulb, to no avail. He tried bleach and other chemicals but the chemicals not only lifted the ink, they also further obliterated whatever had been covered up, which is why the clerk made the copy after "blocking out" the names. More determined than ever to discover his roots, R.J. waited until a different Clerk was on duty and again requested a copy of his adoption decree. This time, the clerk blackened the first photocopy but did not recopy the blackened version. This time, using hair spray and cologne, R.J. succeeded in lifting enough black ink from enough letters that he finally had the names he sought.

3. "J.W." had never seen her pre-adoption birth certificate but knew that a copy was kept in a locked file cabinet on an upper floor of a New York skyscraper. No problem. Incredibly, J.W. hired a "human fly" to scale the upper story from the outside ledge of the story beneath under cover of darkness. Pedestrians on the street below looked small as ants from that height. Through an unlocked window, "the fly" entered the file room from the narrow ledge outside, certain that all employees had left work hours before. Within minutes, "the fly" found J.W.'s original birth certificate in so-called "sealed" files ... an unlocked file drawer. J.W. finally had her birth name, "D.S."

4. "S.V", a 30-year-old adoptee with a family of her own, was suddenly more driven than ever to locate her mother. With AmFOR's help, she discovered her mother's identity and date of birth within two weeks from the start of her search. But, she could not locate her. AmFOR put her in touch with a social worker in the county in which S.V. resided. Although the social worker did not have access to adoption files in the county in which S.V. was adopted, the social worker did have the authority, in California, to tap DMV driver's records, using the name and birth date S.V. had provided. Within a few days, S.V. had a current address from her mother's driver's record and was promptly reunited with the woman who had also been searching for S.V. The same social worker risked her job to help many other adoptees to locate their parents because, in California, social workers are prohibited from facilitating contact unless both parties have registered their waivers of confidentiality. In this case, as is typical, the mother did not know of law changes nor the need for filing a waiver to facilitate contact.

5. "B.G." impersonated her own adopter when requesting a copy of her adoption decree. The Clerk asked for ID and questioned why B.G.'s name on her driver's license was different from the adopter's name. B.G. calmly replied that she had remarried and hadn't had an opportunity to change her driver's license, whereupon the clerk handed over the entire so-called "sealed" adoption file in an ordinary file folder from a halfopen file drawer, and B.J. purchased the copies she wanted without problem. As an adoptee, she would have been denied.

6. "C.P." kept her appointment in which her social worker was to disclose non-identifying background information from her adoption file. Sitting very close to the social worker, C.P. was able to glimpse the file's contents long enough to glean her mother's name.

7. Newspaper ads and newspaper birth announcements can attract leads particularly for adoptees and parents. I know many who have been found this way. From Arkansas, an Orthodox Catholic Bishop advertised in Michigan newspapers hoping to locate the daughter he lost to Michigan's adoption system when she was five, before he was a priest. He got a toll-free 800-number and "caller ID." Although he received several calls from young women claiming to be his daughter, he was unconvinced. One woman claimed she was not interested in contact, and others hung up when he

questioned discrepancies. AmFOR was able to follow-up his best lead, matching the adoptee's amended birth certificate with the original birth certificate the father retained for 20 years. Adoptees sometimes find a newspaper birth announcement, naming their parents, was published at the time of their birth. It's rare for adopters to publish a birth or adoption announcement in the newspaper, but it does occur. Some parents found adoptees this way. The newspaper office or the public library can provide old birth announcement pages. Ask for a range of four weeks after date of birth. *Weekly World News*, Omaha, NE, 1/5/93:

> "WOMAN FINDS MOM WITH A NEWSPAPER AD ... A newspaper personals ad has reunited a mother with her daughter—after 40 years. Stunned, Jeannie Hankinson, 60, couldn't believe her eyes when she looked at the ad ... 'My name is Linda, born to Jeannie and Warren in Omaha on 8-7-50 and given up for adoption.' ... Mrs. Hankinson gave up legal rights to her daughter by unwittingly signing an adoption agreement in 1952."

> *Tuscola County Advertiser*, Caro, MI, 8/28/91: "MISSING LINK FOUND ... Kelly Woodruff, 24, of Cass City, was the 'piece of the puzzle' according to her sister Patricia Hacker... the last of eight brothers and sisters to be found. Separated from her family in 1968 at the age of two, Kelly was the youngest of five girls and two boys in the Barnum family. That same year, a brother Mike, sister Mary, and twins Patrick and Patricia were all adopted by different families. Three older sisters went into foster homes ... (Kelly's) desire to search was intensified with the birth of her own daughter, Megan, when she signed release forms to gain information . . . Kelly's father died last June. She will meet her mother soon at a planned reunion."

> *Dear AmFOR*:... "I have been trying to find my mother and brother for over 10 years, since I was 15-years-old ... I think I may have found my father's name in a newspaper birth announcement) from an Ocala Library . Thank you.. LINDA K., Milton, FL."

8. "J.J.", a recovering alcoholic, was referred to AmFOR by the Salvation Army Lodge in Florida where he resided.. His adoption occurred in Connecticut where he was asked to appear in person for counseling and disclosure. J.J. could not afford to go to Connecticut without knowing whether he would find a receptive "birth" mother. At AmFOR's suggestion, J.J. had the Connecticut social worker send his adoption file to a nearby Florida social worker who acted as intermediary to counsel and disclose the desired information. The Florida social worker even put J.J on the phone with his Connecticut mother at government expense. Although his father had died a few years before, he was soon reunited with his large family who invited him to stay at their Connecticut home, saving J.J. some expense of reunion.

9. *CBS True Detectives* (K-Cal, Norwalk/Los Angeles), 3/29/91, Jim Rapsis: "THE CASE OF GRAVE CONCERN:...

> (Iowa). Eight siblings are reunited after having been separated over 50 years by adoption and foster placements. The mother, Martha Bell, died after birth of twins. The father could not afford to raise the new babies. After giving the babies to an orphanage, Mr. Bell later tried to reclaim them when his finances improved, but the twins had already been placed in separate adoptive homes; later the rest of the family was split up. The last missing sister was found via a note in a bottle left by the siblings at the mother's grave site. The reunited siblings erected a tombstone: 'Mother's Love Brought Us Together—8 Little Orphans.'"

10. The Internet helped "L.G." find her son (see Chapter 5, Computerized Searches).

11. Omaha (AP) "OMAHA WOMAN GETS TO MEET BROTHER SEPARATED 62 YEARS AGO:

> An Omaha woman separated as a toddler from her brothers, cried Tuesday as she met one brother for the first time in 62 years. 'It's overwhelming. It's like a dream come true,' Pearl Kuti, 65, said before meeting her older brother, Lou Alonza, 67, of Monroe, Connecticut. . . The family was chosen from about 1,000 entries in a hotel chain's contest to find families and friends for reunions. Homewood Suites Hotels of Memphis, Tennessee, said the reunion was the first of about 200 it plans in cities across the country in the next four years . . . Their mother died of cancer, Alonza said. The two brothers met in the early 1950s after Perez tracked down Alonza by checking with several churches in Connecticut, the brothers said."

Dear AmFOR:... "I am an Illinois adoptee who only recently was able to secure my original birth certificate (a certified copy no less) through 'Bureaucratic Error,' and while I realize this happens once in a million, it makes me support the idea of open records more so than ever before. Beginning with this document, I was able to identify and contact two aunts. My mother died many years ago. In my early search effort the state did nothing and in later contacts with government agencies, refusal was immediate ... MICHAEL O., Chicago, IL."

12. *Omaha World Herald*, 6/19/90, page 22: "FORTY-FIVE YEARS OF SEPARATION END FOR 5 OF 6 SIBLINGS IN FAMILY FROM IOWA "

"Ruthven, Iowa (AP)—Siblings separated for more than 45 years still are searching for their youngest brother to make the family of six complete ... In 1945, the three boys and three girls were taken to an orphanage in Council Bluffs ... In 1949 'our mother remarried, and she came back to the orphanage and got the three older children and, of course, we were gone,' Sally said ... Sally had sent for her birth certificate form the State of Iowa. The state mistakenly sent her the original birth certificate, which had both parents' names, their addresses, and hometowns. The family's last name was Heck, and they were from Council Bluffs, according to Sally ... The next day, the five 'burned up the phone lines' in an attempt to make up for lost time. 'It was worth the phone bill to find out,' Sally said. The five finally got together in April... The five brothers and sisters still are looking for their youngest brother, who was called Thomas Marshall Heck at birth."

13 . *Saginaw News*, 5/17/91: "FOUR SISTERS MEET AFTER 45 YEARS—Michigan Girls Went to Different [Adopters] When Mother Died:
Tampa, FL (AP)—Four Michigan sisters have a lot of catching up to do now that they're reunited 45 years after adoption separated them ... Disterfheft tracked her sisters through newspaper obituaries; Social Security and employment records; and the help of a Michigan support group, Adoption Insight"

More Letters From Adoptees and Parents

Dear AmFOR: ... "I am an adoptee's daughter. My mother and her twin were given up for adoption at birth forty-two years ago. I have written to Sacramento; however, the only response I received was that the files are closed. In order to possibly open the files, I would have to petition the court. I would like to learn about my mother's biological past as well as my own. For medical reasons, I would like this background information as well. I have such information as the biological parents names and the state where they were born ... Thank you for your time and effort... Sincerely, T.R., Nevada City, CA."

Dear AmFOR:... "It would be very nice to get a letter saying that my family has been looking for me too ... I was adopted at birth (2/20/50, Santa Cruz County), given very little information of my birth parents ... My adopters are both dead ... I was raised as an only child and I hated it. I felt there was a stigma about being adopted. There was a greater one about not knowing who my family is. All of this made me feel as though I were from a distant galaxy. I have consistently been met with a great deal of negativity and resistance about finding my family. The older I get the more questions medical professionals ask about my family. Their questions are very frustrating because I don't have any answers ... I have a letter from a doctor to help get my sealed file opened. I just don't know how to write the petition needed to go with it. Maybe you have a copy of a 'petition to open a sealed adoption file' that worked? ... I found your address in a book entitled How To Find Almost Anyone, Anywhere by Norma Tillman. Thank you for your time . . . SUSAN P., Santa Cruz, CA."

Dear AmFOR:... "I am writing on behalf of my wife who was adopted at birth in 1957. She has always known that she was adopted and she has always had a compelling need to know her heritage. She has also had a terrible uncertainty and trepidation which accompanied that need ... I am an attorney, so I can proceed with whatever legal actions are necessary; however, not having done this type of work before, I am probably in need of advice and direction. If you know of an attorney in my area who has experience in this field and could give me some advice regarding court orders, official requests for records, etc., I would appreciate it... Sincerely, R.S.C., Torrance, CA."

just before adoption papers were served to me). About 5 years ago at the start of my search, I called the attorney and asked for a copy of the relinquishment papers, just for my own records. I began the conversation by saying I had no interest in interfering in my son's life (since then he was a minor). Upon my request, the attorney ... got nasty with me, saying he "wouldn't send them." I could not get a word in edgewise and was in tears when I hung up. This attorney's son is a state representative, and according to my M.D., is highly involved in adoptions ... I still don't have a copy and would love one—it certainly wouldn't hurt anyone, since my son and I are developing our relationship now. I don't even know what the state law is on this ... I'd love to receive all possible documentation now that I've found my son. We do have one very nice law that helped my search a lot. Divorce records are available to the public here for the asking—in my son's case, his sterling adopters got a divorce . . . Sincerely, PATTY R., Forest Park, IL."

Dear AmFOR: . . . "You won't believe the progress I have made since I sent you the info about my husband's adoption. First of all we petitioned the Superior Court of L.A. to open the records and it was granted. I sent in the petition July 7, '95 and received the copies of the file Aug. 8, '95. It cost me $17.10 for the copies. Then the next day I received a call from a person I had sent a letter to. It was a sister he didn't know he had. She gave us his father's phone number so I called him. He seems to be happy about us finding him; he's sending pictures and is willing to give us more info on the mother and brother as soon as he digs it out. I cannot believe it happened so fast. I have a lot of great volunteers to thank, including you ... SHARI V., Post Falls, ID."

Dear AmFOR: ... "I am very interested in working with adoptees and parents. I have conducted many different types of investigations, but this will be the first for parent/adoptee searches ... it will be a challenge and I appreciate all the help .. . Sincerely, FRED S., P.I., Daytona Beach Shores, FL."

NON-CUSTODIAL PARENTS, AND CHILDREN SEPARATED BY DIVORCE are also subject to archaic state "confidentiality" laws. If one of the parents remarries, and the new spouse legally adopts the child, the same secrecy is imposed on stepparent adoptions – the child's birth certificate may be altered and is always sealed in the court file. If it's the mother who has remarried, the child us usually given the stepfather's surname. If it is the natural father who has remarried, the adopting stepmother may be listed as the natural mother on the "amended" birth certificate. The same adoption disclosure laws apply as shown on the "2010 Adoption Disclosure Laws at a Glance" chart at the beginning of this chapter, and as detailed in the *"Search the USA"* by-state section, and *"International Searching"* by-country section of this book.

Other Resources for Non-Custodial Parents

(See also Search/Support groups listings under State and International sections.)

CPS Watch, Inc.
168-B Fall Creek Dr.
PO Box 974
Branson, MO 65615-0974
CPS Watch Main Office:
(417) 339-9192
National Hotline: 1-800-CPS-WATCH
http://cpswatch.com

National Maternity Home (800) 637-7974
Reconnection Agency and Birthparent Connection
PO Box 230643
Encinitas, CA 92023

National Adoption Information Clearinghouse
105 30 Rosehaven Street, Suite 400
Fairfax, VA 22030
Mailing Address:
PO Box 1182, Washington, DC 20013-1182
(703) 352-3488; toll free: (888) 352-0075
http://www.calib.com/naic/

National Organization of Women (NOW)
1000 – 16th Street, NW, Suite 700 (HQ)
Washington, DC 20036
(202) 331-0066
http://www.now.org/

Parents Without Partners (HQ)
401 North Michigan Ave., Suite 2200
Chicago, IL 60611
http://www.parentswithoutpartners.org/

Equal Child-Parenting
PO Box 190078
Burton, MI 48519-0078
(810) 694-8123
e-mail: ecpa@tir.com

Questions for Adoptees and Parents
to Ask Agency and Court

QUESTIONS FOR ADOPTEES TO ASK AGENCY AND COURT

1. What was the reason for my relinquishment?
2. What were the ages of my parents?
3. Where were my parents born; where did they reside at the time of my adoption? Were they from same area where I was born?
4. Name of hospital where I was born?
5. What are the nationalities of my parents?
6. Were my grandparents living?
7. Educational background of my parents and grandparents?
8. Occupations and social history of parents and grandparents?
9. Any siblings?
10. Were parents married? Divorced? Previous marriages?
11. Religion of parents?
12. Was I in a foster home? How long? Who were my foster parents?
13. How long between relinquishment & placement?
14. Was my mother in a maternity home? Did she see/hold me? Was she counseled before/after delivery or signing?
15. Color of parents' hair? Eyes? Their height? Weight?
16. Did my parents have brothers, sisters? Ages?
17. Mother's first name and initial?
18. Did she name me? What name?
19. Were my parents active in school activities? What kind?
20. How much did I weigh at birth?
21. Has my mother or any birth family member EVER contacted the agency? Any letters, photos or momentos in my adoption file? Is there any Waiver of Confidentiality in my adoption file?
22. Name of social worker handling my placement?
23. Date adoption was finalized? What court(s) initiating, finalizing?
24. Please provide me a copy of the court proceedings and final decree.
25. Please provide me with all medical information on my birth family.
26. Please place my Waiver of Confidentiality in the agency file.
27. Please contact my parents and inform them my updated Waiver of Confidentiality has been provided to the file.

QUESTIONS FOR PARENTS TO ASK AGENCY AND COURT

1. Regarding the adopter(s): a. what were their ages?
   - b. where were they born?
   - c. what are their nationalities? religion?
   - d. any siblings of adoptive parents?
   - e. length of marriage at time of adoption?
   - f. any previous marriages or divorces?
   - g. other children by birth or adoption?
   - h. deaths in family?
   - i. medical histories, diseases?
   - j. did they own their own home?
   - k. professions, occupations, education?
   - l. where residing at time of adoption?
   - m. where do they now reside?
   - n. reason given for adopting?
2. Regarding the Please provide physical description when last seen by agency, court or attorney.
3. Was child in foster care? How long? Names of foster parents?
4. Date adoption was finalized? What court?
5. Please provide a copy of relinquishment I signed and original birth certificate issued to me.
6. What is the name of the social worker who handled the placement?
7. Has adoptee or adopter(s) contacted agency since adoption?
8. What was and is my child's physical and emotional health?
9. Were the adoptive parents advised to tell child of adoption?
10. What information on me was given to adoptive parents?
11. Please place my Waiver of Confidentiality in the file.
12. What agency/court/attorney will transmit my request for contact to the adoptee or adopter(s)?

THE CONFIDENTIAL INTERMEDIARY (CI) SYSTEM

AmFOR encourages adoptees and parents to do their own searches, if possible, and, ideally, to make their own direct contacts, as no one can adequately deliver the message you've been wishing to communicate all your life. But sometimes this is not feasible, and increasingly, the states have been amending laws by requiring use of a Confidential Intermediary as go-between for contacts between adoptees and their "birth" parents. The CI is not permitted to divulge identifying information unless both parties consent. And the CI's fee is not refundable. In one case, AmFOR persuaded a CI in Washington state to waive her fee for a grandmother (as the adoptee's "birth" mother had died) by providing proof of the grandmother's low income to the court (it never hurts to ask). The CI located the adoptee who was in a different state, and charged only for cost of phone calls. He was glad to have been found. He didn't know where to start searching, nor could he have afforded a CI. But when an incarcerated adoptee requested at least his "non-identifying" information, the nun who headed the Macomb County branch of Catholic Social Services refused to waive her CI fee, while Catholic Social Services in a different county in Michigan had waived the CI fee for an incarcerated adoptee.

States that use the Confidential Intermediary System are: Alabama, which also provides the Original Birth Certificate (OBC) to an adult adoptee, Arizona, Arkansas, Colorado, Connecticut, Delaware (also OBC), Florida, Illinois, Indiana, Kentucky, Maryland, Michigan, Montana, New Hampshire, New York, Oklahoma, Virginia, Washington and Wyoming.

The CI will search for and contact a parent at the request of an adult adoptee, absent the "birth" parent's waiver of confidentiality in the adoption file. In some states, the adoptee's "birth" parent, grandparent or sibling may request a CI also. CIs are supposed to be neutral parties, appointed by and usually responsible to the court of jurisdiction (the court where the adoption was finalized and which holds the adoption file). But also adoption agency social workers can serve as CIs. For a fee (which could be $300-$400 or more) and for a maximum number of hours, a CI will endeavor to locate and contact the party sought. according to the "last known" address and phone number in the court's or agency's (decades old) original adoption file. In a couple states, if the other party is not found, the adoptee may be provided with *identifying* information in order to then conduct their own search (usually by hiring a searcher for an additional fee). Before deciding to hire a CI, it is best to read the state law which may detail time frames, reasonable search efforts and other responsibilities of CIs. Adoption agency case workers are not necessarily "neutral parties" as they have a "conflict of interest." Disclosure of any information is entirely at their discretion rather than by court discretion and some have pocketed fees with no evidence of even minimal services. Fortunately, not all CIs are alike and it would be a good idea to ask a CI their background and what they are willing to provide. Many are adoptees and parents who have become skilled at searching.

Below is a sampling of CIs who may or may not still be the appointed CIs for those states. **There are often several CIs per state, by county. For a *current* list of CIs for the state and county needed, contact the Court, Social Services, or private agency involved.**

AZ- (Pima County), Liza Cappel, stymie54@juno.com
AZ- (Maricopa County/Phoenix), cip@supreme.sp.state.az.us
CO- (Arapaho County), Gordon Kilpatrick, PI), Kilsr@aol.com
CO- (Denver), Mary Kathrens, Time0ut757@aol.com
CO- (Denver), Betty Tyrell, KimTl@juno.com
EL- (Cook County), Gretchen Schulert, macadopt@aol.com
IL- (Williamson County), Darlene Fredman, DFRED41449@aol.com
IN- (Lake County), Kristin Lucas, adoption@mail.icongroup.com
IN- (Grant County), Lori Baxter, smile@comteck.com
IN- (Posey County), Randy Rigg, RandyRigg@netscape.net
MI- (Oakland County), Tina Caudill, caudt@aol.com
MI- (Wayne County/Detroit), Julie Carter, Julesci@aol.com
WA- (King County), Marilyn J. Dean, ISC, marilynjdean@aol.com
WA- (Multmomah County), Darlene Wilson, darlenew@worldaccessnet.com
WA- (Grays Harbor Conty), Rita Zastrow, zastrow@oylynet.com
WA- (Pierce County), Janet Baccus, JanetGB@worldnett.att.net
WA- (Whatcom County), Marlene Smith, marlenesmi@juno.com

Chapter 5. Computerized Searches
Search Engines, Websites, and Emails Helpful for Search

The World Wide Web can be a wonderful information highway to immediate and unlimited information, searchable by subject or "key words" or by the website address (URL) if known. It can help you locate relatives and friends. But also, serial killers and bill collectors alike need only to "Google" your name or Click on http://WhitePages.com, http://411.com, http://Switchboard.com (to name a few) which provide a means to search for an individual's address and phone number in a specific state as well as in "all states" and find not only your own residence address and phone number but also your age, employment, names of others in your household...and even a map to your home! Such "public directory" websites compile personal information, even "unlisted/unpublished" phone numbers that you pay to keep private,, from a variety of databases and sources you'd least suspect. Reverse lookup directories on Internet, such as those at the all-in-one website called "Search Gateway," at http://www.searchgateway.com , enable the searcher to utilize any · of the of multiple search engines to find a street address, phone number, e-mail address, web-site address, or the person's name when only one of these elements is known. They may not always produce the information you seek or the information could be outdated; still, they are useful resources.

The following definitions are from Webster's Dictionary:
   o privacy – *(the state of not being seen by others)*
   o confidentiality – *(unaccountable)*
   o secrecy – *(1- concealment; condition of being secret or hidden; 2- habit of keeping secrets)*

When these terms are used to support "privacy" laws and "confidentiality" policies, against the wishes of the person being "protected," or to withhold a record from the person who is named in the record, one must understand WHO is actually protected or unaccountable. AmFOR's website includes a webpage captioned *"Privacy Hypocrisy,"* at http://AmFOR.net/Privacy, which provides more examples of various companies who sell your personal information which may end up on Internet. While Congress acknowledges that Americans want to keep their private information private, federal and state laws *compel* Americans to disclose their private residence addresses, Social Security numbers, phone records, credit records, medical records, driving records, bankruptcies, criminal records, credit information, property records and much more. Your bank's online banking website and Ebay are but two examples of "secure" websites that not only collect your personal information profile but also unintentionally generate "phishing" emails designed to resemble those sent from your bank or Ebay in order to get you to respond with your personal information and passwords.

Online information providers such as http://PeopleSearch.com or http://Intellius.com. are good sources for finding people – *including you* – for as little as 95-cents per name, although there's no "guarantee" that the "last known"address or phone number is current.

The best general road map is "Librarian's Index to the Internet" http://www.sunsite.berkeley/edu/Internet/Index which includes every subject—even adoptee-parent search help online. For a directory of toll-free "800" numbers, including on adoption topics, try http://www.webshaker.com/directory . An all-in-one website for finding search engines is at http://www.albany.net/allinone/alluser.html . The number of listings or "web results" will vary greatly from the number of exact "matches." For instance, the word "adoption" can bring up 100,000 website listings — which may be focus on either child adoptions or pet adoptions, but also includes tens of thousands of adoptee and parent personal websites concerning their personal stories, views of adoption issues, adoption activism and/or resources for pursuing searches to find adoptees and parents. But the more limiting key words "pet adoption" may bring up only 2,000 "web results" and only 16 "matches." A search for the "National Council For Adoption (NCFA)" website can bring up not only NCFA's home page, but also any other websites mentioning NCFA, such as the listing on Alta Vista's search engine which describes NCFA's *"Adoption Fact Book Page"* covering a broad array of questionable statistics and half-truths." The query "adoptee + birthparents + search" or "post adoption searches" or "reunion registries" may bring up hundreds of the similar or different website listings. So this chapter is intended to save the searcher some time by providing websites offering free information most helpful to specific types of "people searches." Typing an adoptee's birth date on a "reunion registry" site could result in a "match."

ADOPTION SEARCH and SUPPORT WEBSITES

There are five basic types of websites that can assist searching adoptees and parents. They include (1) *"how to"* sites with FAQs (Frequently Asked Questions) and "links" pages; (2) private registries (most are accessed free); (3) search and activism chat rooms or "blogs"; (4) adoptee and parent personal pages (personal stories, views, activism); (5) searcher websites.

(1) "HOW TO" WEBSITES (alphabetically):

AmFOR's Free Search Tips & Links page (U.S., worldwide) - http://AmFOR.net/Search
Canada Adoption Laws - http://nebula.onca/canadopt/
Lost Connections (sample letters, FAQs) - http://www.lostconnections.com/faq/letterj2html
U.S. Adoption Records (Central offices of Social Services, by state) –
     http://www.fosterclub.com/grownups/dhhs/dhhsdirectory.html#anchor4255
U.S. Adoption Laws, By State - http://www.webreflection.com/aiml/uslaws.html
Vital Statistics Online (links for state-held public records) - http://vitalrec.com
Webgator Investigative Resources on the Web - http://www.inil.com/users/dguss/gator9.htm

(2) REUNION REGISTRIES (alphabetically); see also registries listed by state in this chapter and

the 130-by-state registry links at http://members.tripod.com/~jlightkeeper/registries.html
Adoption Search Registry (search large database by birth date) - http://adoptionregistry.com
Adoptees Libery Movement Assn. (ALMA) (registration fee) - http://almasociety.com
Australia Registry - http://www.bensoc.asn.au/parc
Bi-Racial/African-American Registry - http://lilbastard.faithweb.com/biafreg.html
Birth Quest (second largest) - http://www.ReunionRegistry.com
Black Market - http://www.geocities.com/Heartland/Garden/2313/Links.htm
Black Market Adoption E-Mail Support List - http://www.onelist.com/subscribe.cgi/Blackmarketbabies
Butterbox Babies Survivors (Nova Scotia) - http://www3.ns.sympatico.ca/bhartlan/PAGE1.htm
Canada Registry - http://ourworld.compuserve.com/homepages/adoptionregistry
Catholic Adoption Registry ("Relinquished") - http://freeweb.wpdcorp.com/relinquished
Cole Baby Registry (black market adoptees) - http://www.geocities.com/Heartland/Fields/9298/Colebaby.html
D's Search Posts (it's huge & by state) - http://members.aol.com/bmom2amy/SearchPosts.html
Donor Offspring /Parent Registry – http://AmFOR.net/DonorOffspring.html
Find Me (search, registry, maternity home registry, etc.) - http://www.findme-registry.com
First Name & Birth Date Registry - http://www..skylace.net/adoption/g-firstnaes/php3
First Names Registry, Unique - http://www.genealogytoday.com/names/first/unique.html
Italian Adoptees - http://groups.yahoo.com/group/ITALIADOPTION
Hicks Clinic Birth Registry/Silent Legacy (Ohio black market babies) - http://www.hicksclinic.com/
INTERNATIONAL SOUNDEX REUNION REGISTRY (oldest & largest) - http://www.isrr.net
Korea - http://www.geocities.com/Tokyo/Garden/3947; http://www.findparent.or.kr/index_e.htm
Maternity Home Registry - http://www.currala.com or email Curry Wolfe at ccwolfe@worldnet.att.net
Maternity Home Registry, Crittenton 1920's-on - http://www.geociies.com/Heartland/8529/adopt/FCH.html
Maternity Home Registry, Gladney – http://www.gladney.org/html/adopt/post/vol_registry.html
Maternity Home Registry, The Veil - http://www.geocities.com/Heartland/Garden/2313/veilnursery.htm
Montreal Black Market Adoption - http://www.PFTML.org/BMB/inex.html/
New York - Bessie Bernard Black Market Babies - http://www.tallynet.com/perspages/pattyann/bessie.htm
Orphan Trains - http://www.adoptiontriad.org/library/weekly/aa030398.htm/
Scotland - email think@charity.vfree.com
Tennessee Black Market Adoption - http://www.geocities/Heartland/Bluffs/3592/TNBA.html
Twins Reunion Registry, National - http://home.www.geocities.com/Heartland/Acres/9942/twinregform.com/
United Kingdom World Adoption Registry (fees) - http://freespace.virgin.net/jm.kimpton/gentrace/home.htm
Worldwide Profile Registry - http://home.wizard.com/wwprsearch.htm (searchable by previous email,
     alias, birth date, location, real name, occupation/personal interests but low percentage of exact matches)
Worldwide Registry - http://members.xoom.com/wwregistry/birth.html

(3) ADOPTION TOPIC CHAT ROOMS and LINKS (alphabetically):

About.com Adoption Chat - http://www.sitebazer.ne/adoptionworld
Adoption and Family Search Help - http://members.tripod.com/~sumaja/
Adoption Connection - http://www.olywa.net/brouch/adopt.htm; http://www.adoptionconnection.qpg.com
Adoption: Legalized Lies (ALL) - http://www.geocities.com/Heartland/Woods/5027
Adoption Triad Outreach - (6 chat rooms) - http://www.adoptiontriad.org/

Australia's Origins Inc - http://www.angelfire.com/or/originsnsw
Michele's Adoption Site - http://www.seatac.net/adoption/
Missing Peace Adoption - http://www.teleplex.net/deer
R-U-Out-There Adoption Search - http://adoption.virtualove.net
Search - http://directory.netscape.com/Society/issues/Adoption/Support
Sunflower Birthmothers (over 700 members; click on "subscribe") - http://www.bmom.net
Voices of Adoption: Chat-0-Rama - http://www.ibar.com/chat-o-rama/

(4) ADOPTEE and PARENT ACTIVISM SITES (alphabetically):
Abolish Adoption - A Public Information Service Megasite - http://AmFOR.net/AbolishAdoption
Abolish Adoption-Canada – http://abolishadoption/canada
Adoptees, Birthparents for Open Records Nationwide - ABORN - http://ABORN.org
American Adoption Congress (AAC) (membership fee) - http://www.american-adoption-cong.org/
Americans For Open Records (AmFOR) - http://AmFOR.net
Anti-Adoption Ring - http://www.geocities.com/Heartland/Woods/5027/WebRing.html
Bastard Nation (adoptee activism) - http://www.bastards.org
Bay Area relinquishing Birthmothers (BARMA) - http://www.bar.com/unlocking
Concerned United Birthparents (CUB) - http://www.cubirthparents.org
CPS Watch (Abuses by Child Protection Services) - http://www.cpswatch.com
Origins-Australia - http://www.angelfire.com/or/originsnsw
Origins-USA (A legislative inquiry) - http://origins.org

(5) ADOPTION SEARCH & SUPPORT (alphabetically):
Adoption Resource, The (lots of links) - http://www.best.com/~msilva/
Adoption Databases - http://www.skylace.net/adoption/
Australia - Adoption Jigsaw - http://www.bensoc.asn.au/parc
Canada: Parent Finders, The - http://www.bond.nt/~reevej/
Concerned United Birthparents (CUB) - http://www.cubirthparents.org
Credit Checks & DMV Searches (for fee) - http://www.peoplesearch.smarthosting.com
Database American People Finder (not totally accurate) - http://www.databaseamerica.com
Definitive Adoption Links Page - http://webreflection.com/pinkerton
German-born Adoptees' Newsletter, "Geborenor Deutscher"- http://hometown.aol.com/wmlgage/gd/gd.htm
Independent Search Consultants (ISC) (fees) - http://home.mci.net/isc/
International Adoption Search (ASIA) - http://www.webcom/kmc/adoption/faq-3.html#ASIA
International Adoption Search (EUROPE) - http://www.webcom/kmc/adoption/faq-3.html#EUROPE
Irish Adoptees' Page - http://member.aol.com/CODl 8460/IRISHADOPTEES.htnV
Italian Adoptees Search-Support - http://groups.yaho.com/group/ITALIADOPTION
Korean Adoptees' Association (AKA) - (San Francisco): http://www.geocities.com/Tokyo/Garden/3947 ;
(New York): http://www.akaworld.org/ (Minnesota): http://www.mnadoptedkoreans.org/
PI Mall (info brokers, first name search, mailing list, chat) - http://www.pimall.com/
Search Angels (by state; mostly free/"expenses only") - http://members.aol.com/bmom2amy/searchangels.html
State-Specific Search Help - http://members.aol.com/deitrahs
Terminal Illness Emergency Search (volunteers sporadically available) - http://www.ties-search.org/
Vietnam Reunion Planning (Holt Agency; fees) - email reunion@holtintl.org
Volunteer Search Network - http://www.vsn.org
Worldwide Phone Directories - http://www.contractjobs.com/tel/
Yearbook Attic; Yearbook Lady - http://www.geocities.com/Heartland/2236/attic2.html

BY STATE - SEARCH and SUPPORT WEB-SITES,:
AL-Truthseekers (Leah Weslowski) - http://www.Acmeinformation.com/ACME/ACMEInfo.htm
AK-Adoption Triad Outreach-ALASKA - http://www.adoptionoutreach.org/alaska.htm
AZ-Adoption Counseling Home (Dee Davis) - http://www.geocities.com/Heartland/Flats/4507
Arizona Search Association - http://angelfire.com/ntl/cover.html
PACER (Nancy Cerf) - http://mo.com/pacer/
Research Etc. (Kristin Hamilton) - http://www.researchetcinc.com/
Search Co (Dana Vian) - http://www.searchco.com/
SEEK - http://www.seek4you.com.html
AR-Arkansas Adoption Connection (Jenny Kolp) - http://www.arkansasadoption.com
Arkansas Resources - http://members.aol.com/deitrahs/ARKANSAS.html

CA-Adoption Search & Reunion - http://www.adoptionsearcher.com
Adoption Triad Outreach-CALIFORNIA - http://www.adoptiontriad.org/californ.htm
Bay Area Relinquishing Birthmothers (BARMA) (Sheila Ganz) - http://www.bar.com/unlocking
Curry Wolfe (San Diego area search) - http://www.crashers.com/search
Family Find (Judy Alien; Santa Clara Co. search) - http://www.needinfo.com/JulieSearch
Kinship Center (Carol Bishop) - http://www.kinshipcenter.org
PACER (Carrie Buckner) - http://www.pacer-adoption.org
Time Out (Mary Kathrens) - http://www.TimeOut757.aol.com
Triple Hearts - http://www.ubiz.com/triplehearts
CO-Adoption Triad Outreach-COLORADO - http://www.adoptiontraid.org/colorado.htm
CT- Adoption Triad Outreach-CONNECTICUT - http://www.adoptiontriad.org/conn.htm
DE- Delaware Reunion Registry - http://www.geocities.com/dreunion
Finders Keepers Inc (Ginger Farrow) - http://www.finderskeepers.faithwacb.com
DC-Adoptee-Birthparent Support Network - http://www.geocities.com/Heartland/Flats/3666/ABSN.html
AIS (Joanne Small) - http://www.adopteesinsearch.org
Earle Barnes Registry - http://www.MetroReunionRegistry.org
FL- Adoption Triad Outreach-FLORIDA (Sondi Hill) - http://www.adoptiontrais.org
Common Bond (Sonia Gail Davis) - http://www.angelfire.com/flcomonbond/index.htm
Orphan Voyage (Alice Syman) - http://www.geocities.com/orphanvoyage1953/index.html
Research-Reconnect-Reunite (Luanne Pruesner) - http://members.aol.com/LuanneP/adoption.html
Triad (Janice Fruland) - htp://www.virtualnetways.com/triad
GA-Southern Pines Georgia Registry - http://members.wbs.net.homepages/s/o/u/southernpines.html
HI- SEEK (Sue Cook) - http://www.SEEK4you.com/seek.html
ID- Adoption Registry (Gloria Mummery) - http://ourworld.compuserve.com/homepages/adoptionregistry
CUB-Idaho (Bonnie Bis) - http://www.webnations.com/cub
Lois Melina - http://www.raisingadoptedchildren.com
Sheila Gantz - http://www.advancenet/~sgantz
IL- Adoption Blessings - http://www.geocities.com/adoptionblessings/Adoption_Blessings_News.html
Adoption Network - http://www.earthlink.net/~adoptionnetwork
Truthseekers (Barbara Gonyo) - http://www.wbm.com/truthseekers/adoption
IN- Adoption Circle (Pat Alien) - http://www.members.com/akaShawnaL/Group/index.html
Cheri Freeman - http://www.freeyellow.com/ciprogramofin
Indiana Reunion Registry (Bob/Betty Heide) - http://users.mvillage.com/bheide
Reflections (Randy Rigg) - http://www.angelfire.com/in3/Reflections
IA- CUB (Kristi Carman) - http://CUBirthparents.org
Origins Inc. (Jim McDonald) - http://www.originsinc.com
KS- Adoption Concerns Triangle (Marilyn Waugh) - http://adoptionconcernstriangle.freeyellow.com
Wichita Adult Adoptees (Rochelle Harris) - http://locatorsunlimited.com
KY-Locators Unlimited (Linda Cecil) - http://www.KyAdoptions.org
Miracle Search (Paul Brown) - http://www.miracle search.com
LA-Louisiana Adoption Database - http://cust2.iamerica.net/larobnsn/
Southern Lady's Links - http://www.geocities.com/Heartland/Hills/9606/states/louisiana.html
ME-Adoption Resource Center (Mira Bicknell) - http://home.maine.rr.com/mbarc
MD-Adoptee Birthparent Search (T. Mayo) - http://www.geocities.com/Heartland/Flats/3366/ABSN.html
Adoptees In Search (Joanne Small) - http://www.adopteesinearch.org
Linda Evosevich - http://www.search-usa.net
MA-Adoption Connection Inc. (Susan Darke) - http://www.adoptionconnection.qpg.com
TRY-Resource Referral (Ann Henry) - http://www.try.org/
MI- AIM of Michigan (Daryl Royal) - http://www.michigansearching.html
Linda Shipley - http://www.rockroll.net/carol
Michigan Adoption.com - http://www.MichiganAdoption.com
Michigan Searching - http://www.onelist.com/community/MichiganSearching
Moon Mist's Adoptees/Birthparents Site - http://members.tripod.com/~MoonMist69/index.html
Search in Michigan (Susan Armstrong) - http://www.onelist.com/subscribe.cgi/searc
Tina Caudill - http://www.lssm.org
MN-Adoption Triad Outreach-MINNESOTA - http://adoptiontriad.org/minnesot.html
MS-Mississippi Reunion Registry - http://www.geocities.com/Heartland/Bluffs/3592/ms.html
MO-Adoption Triad Outreach-MISSOURI - http://adoptiontriad.org/missouri.html

MT-Adoption Triad Outreach-MONTANA - http://adoptiontriad.org/montana.html
NC-Adoption Triad Outreach-NORTH CAROLINA - http://www.adoptiontriad.org/northcarolina.html
Kinsolving Investigations (Christine Lee-PI) - http://www.kinsolving.com
Tina's NC Adoption Info - http://www.geocities.com/CapitolHill/9606/states/northcarolina.htnl
ND-Adoption Triad Outreach-ND - http://adptiontriad.org/ndakota.htm
NE-Adoption Triad Outreach-NEBRASKA - http://adoptiontriad.org/ne.html
NH-Adoption Triad Outreach-NEW HAMPSHIRE - http://adoptiontroad.org/newhamps.htm
NJ- Connected Hearts - http://community.nj.com/cc/chats
New Jersey Search Resource - http://adoption.miningco.com/msub_nj.htm
OASIS - http://members.tripod.com/BastardGoddess/oasis.html
NM-Rema - http://www.highfiber.com/~rema/index.html
NY-Adoption Crossroads (Joe Soil) - http://www.adoptioncrossroads.org
Angels (Christine Losey) - http://www.geocities.com/sylchi45/angels.htm
Center for Reuniting Families - http://www.familysearch.freeserver.com
Michele L. Tiedman - http://members.aol.com/MLT01/index.html
Mistical-2 - http://members.aol.com/Mistical2/index.html
Priority One Investigations (Richard Gauthier-PI) - http://www.usadetective.com
Tammy Jordan - http://www2.nceye.net.tammy
NV-Adoption Triad Outreach-NEVADA - http://adoptiontriad.org/nevada.html
OH-ABORN - http://ABORN.org
Adoption Network (Betsie Norris) - http://www.adoptionnetwork.org
Ohio Adoption Registry Inc. - http://www.personal.rivers.com/~oburt/adoptee/~sites.htm
OK-Oklahoma Family Search (Sharon Burns) - http://www.oklahoma.com/familysearch
OR-Oregon Adoption Rights Association (OARA) - http://oara.org/12.service.search.html
PA- Adoption Forum - http://www.adoptionforum.org
Ellen Berman - http://www.geocities.com/Hartland/Flats/3666/ENCORE.html
Lisa Frey - http://www.ncentral.com/~lfrey/hwpa.htm
RI- Adoption Triad - http://www.adoptiontriad.org
SC-Carolyn S. Rosemore - http://www.mirabillis.com/1668307
Christine's Place - http://www.geocities.com/SouthBeach/5193
Craig Locating Service - http://hometown.aol.com/craiglocatingser
Janet Davis - http://www.innova.net/~goob/wall.html
SD- Adoption Triad Outreach-SOUTH DAKOTA - http://www.adoptiontraid.org/sdakota.htm
TN-Norma Tillman-PI - http://www.reunion.com
TX-Adoption Knowledge Affiliates (AKA) - http://www.main.org/aka/aka.html
TXCare (Bill Bentzen, ACSW) - http://www.txcare.org
UT- Adoption Triad Outreach-UT - http://adoptiontriad.org/utah.htm
VT- Wendi Whitaker-OSC - http://www.geocities.com/Heartlands/Plains/5016
VA- Adoptee-Birthparent Search (T. Mayo) - http://www.geocities.com/Heartland/Flats/3366/ABSN.html
Sandra Shaw/Tim Morgan - http://www.geocities.com/Heartland/Acres/4713
WA-Reunion Agency (Darlene Wilson/Donna Portuesi) - http://www.reunionagency.org
WARM - http://www.wolfenet.com/~warm
WV-Adoption Triad Outreach-WV - http://adoptiontriad.org/wvirgin.htm
WI- Adoption Triad Outreach-WI - http://adoptiontriad.org/wiscons.htm
ICARE Registry (Mary Wielding) - http://www.icareregistry.com
Wisconsin Search - http://emerald.julnet.com/~icare/
WY-Adoption Triad Outreach-WYOMING - http://adoptiontriad.org/wyoming.htm

BY STATE - HOLDERS OR CONNECTIONS FOR BIRTH INDEXES
(including those searchable by date & either birth or adoptive names, cross referenced)
CA - Colleeen Buckner (for fee), buckner@colusanet.com or therighttoknow@hotmail.com
CA - 1905-1995, - http://searches.rootsweb.com; http://www.vitalsearch-ca.com/gen/_vitals/cabirthm.htm
CA - Adoptee amended names 1904 thru 1991 - Paul Winston Information Services,
    827 Pacific Ave., #178, San Francisco, CA 94133; (415) 956-9817
CA – Pat Bowers – patkb@ix.net
CT - Lucille Shea (fee only if name/person found) - Lucilleshea@prodigy.net
FL- http://www.geocities.com/preston081/publicrecords.html
IN - available from LDS Family History Center Library

KY- (also some CA & OH, for fee) - Caroline Prowser - HUMNGBRD@aol.com
MO - State Dept. of Health sells "all born in state" for about $30 per date searched
OH - Available from city halls by snail mail for about $25
NY - 5 boroughs (Brooklyn, Bronx, Queens, Manhattan, Staten island) indexes available
SD - Pre-1900 (requires year & name) - http://searches.rootsweb.com
TX - ABORN - http://ABORN.org (if Indexes not found online)-
TX - http://www.tdh.texas.gov/bvs/registra/birthidx/birthidx.htm
TX - 1926-1949 & 1950-1995 (requires name & year) - http://searches.rootsweb.com/

MORE DATABASES
RANCH HANDS INDEX - http://searches.rootsweb.com
DEATH INDEXES - http://www.ancestry.com/search or http://ssdi.rootsweb.com
CREDIT REPORTS (for fee) - http://www.ameri.com/121.htm
DMV SEARCHES (fee) - http://www.altrace.com
DMV DRIVER HISTORY RECORDS by Name & DOB are available for fee in
   CO, FL, GA, IL, ME, MN, MT, NH, NM, NY, OH, OK, UT, WA, WI, WY
DMV MESSAGING - In CA & certain other states, public access to DMV records is discontinued due to anti-stalking
   but check your state for a DMV messaging service; names are often cross-referenced if a woman was licensed under both
   maiden and married or remarriage names. You can also get a car's owner and history via http://CARFAX.com for s frr
   or ask your local car dealer to run a CARFAX for free (You'll need the vehicle's VIN number).
DMV ID CARD - If the person does not have a driver's license, DMV may have issued them an ID card
FREE SEARCHABLE PUBLIC RECORDS DATABASE OF ALL KINDS – http://searchsystems.net

BY STATE - SAMPLING OF ADOPTION SEARCHER E-MAILS
(The author recommends http://WhitePages.com and http://Bigfoot.com for looking up changed e-mails, by name)

AL-Leah Weslowski, Leahwes@Acmeinform.com
AZ-Sue Cook, SEEK@prodigy.net
AR-Jenny Kolp, kolp@ipa.net
CA-Colleeen Buckner, buckner@colusqnet.com
CT-Lucille Shea, Lucilleshea@prodigy.net
DC-Earle Barnes, ebarnes@erols.com
DE-Ginger Farrow, searchde@aol.com
FL-Susan Beckman, Pollock7@aol.com
GA-Jane Hart, Clindsay@aol.com
HI-Sue Cook, SEEK@prodigy.net
ID-Maureen Pirc, MITYMO@aol.com
IL-Judy Moreen, adoption@kwom.com
IN-Bob/Betty Heide, bheide@mvillage.com
IA-Jim McDonald, Jim@originsinc.com
KS-Marilyn Waugh, waugh5@aol.com
KY-Linda Cecil, linda@locatorsunlimited.com
ME-Mina Bicknell, pjens@maine.ir.com
MA-Susan Darke, suedarke@aol.com
MI-Tina Caudill, caudt@aol.com
MO-Sandy Hassler, warrenhassler@hotmail.com
MN-Pat O'Gorman, OGormanResearch@aol.com
MT- info@triad.org
NE-Sandy Rolles, sandyrolles@aol.com
NV-Dori Owen, doriowen@sierra.net

NH-Paul Schibbelhute, pschibbe@aol.com
NJ-Mary Hunt, bgotis@bellatlantic.net
NM-Leonie Boehmer, SallyFile@aol.com
NY-Barbara Ilardo, mistical2@aol.com
NV-Christine Lee-PI, mzchrislee@aol.com
OH-M.Greiner, maddogmarley@worldnett.att.net
OK-Jenny Kolp kolp@ipa.net
OR-D. Wilson, darlenew@worldaccessnet.com
PA-Karen DeLuca, Karen.Deluca@msn.com
RI-Doreen Morin, Doreenjvlorin@brown.edu
SC-Pollie Robinson, JRobin474@aol.com
SD-Carolyn Rosemore, csrts@turtlecreek.net
TN-Denny Glad, dglad@bellsouth.net
TX-Linda Strength, srchgrl@wt.net
UT-Charotte Staten, cstaten@netword.com
VT-Mary Lighthall, mlight@accessvt.com
VA-Joann Jewell-ISC, searchline@aol.com
WA-D. Wilson, darlenew@worldaccessnet.com
WV-Loretta Hopson, legacies92@aol.com
WI-Mary Weilding, mary@icareregsirty.com
WY- info@adoptiontriad.org

MISCELLANEOUS PEOPLE-SEARCH WEBSITES
Classmates - http://www.classmates.com , http://reunions.com
Find Anyone—(lots of links by record type) - http://www.informational.com/dirt.htm
Missing Children Worldwide - http://caag.state.ca.us/bcia2/oth_mc.htm
Prisoner Locator - http://www.corrections.com/links/viewlinks.asp?Cat=20
Who Me? - http://who-mc.com

EXAMPLE: ADOPTEE WAIVER OF CONFIDENTIALITY

Dated: _____

TO: (Address it to Child and Family Services or similar public adoption agency, or to private adoption agency or attorney, where adoption was finalized and adoption file is held)

REF: Adoptive Name: _____

Birth Name (if known) _____   Date of Birth _____

Adoptive Parent(s) full names _____

"Birth" Parents' Name(s) (if known) _____

Date (at least Year) of Placement & Finalization (if known) _____

RE: NOTICE AND WAIVER OF CONFIDENTIALITY - TO ALL CONCERNED

I, _____, hereby formally request that this Notice and of my Waiver of Confidentiality not guaranteed to me by any laws or agencies in the state of _____ and/or copies hereof be immediately placed in all records and files pertaining to my above-referenced adoption. This Waiver of Confidentiality applies to all court records, hospital and other records of birth and medical history, and anything that may be considered to be identifying information. I also hereby request non-identifying information as permitted by state law, including whether any letters or waivers are in my file.

The effects of this Waiver extend only to my _____ "birth" parent(s), _____ "birth" sibling(s), and/or their legal representatives. The following information may be released in full to the aforementioned parties: My name in full, my current address, phone number (shown below) and all of my medical records that may be in file.

This Waiver gives my full and legal permission to release my present identity and contact information as shown below and this letter is to remain in effect unless and until formally revoked by me in writing.

Please acknowledge receipt of my Waiver of Confidentiality in writing for my record.

Thank you.

_____
(Signature)

_____
(Printed Name in Full)

_____
(Current Address)

_____
(Current Phone Number)

EXAMPLE: "BIRTH" PARENT WAIVER OF CONFIDENTIALITY

Dated: _____

TO: (Address it to Child and Family Services or similar public adoption agency, or to private adoption agency or attorney, where adoption was finalized and adoption file is held)

REF: My Name in full: _____

Relinquished Child's Name at birth _____

Child's Date and Place of Birth _____

Relinquished/Placed for Adoption (on or about): _____

RE: NOTICE AND WAIVER OF CONFIDENTIALITY - TO ALL CONCERNED

I, _____, hereby formally request that this Notice and of my Waiver of Confidentiality not guaranteed to me by any laws or agencies in the state of _____ and/or copies hereof be immediately placed in all records and files pertaining to my above-referenced adoption. This Waiver of Confidentiality applies to all court records, hospital and other records of birth and medical history, and anything that may ve considered to be identifying information. I hereby also request non-identifying information about my relinquished child and would like to know whether there is any correspondence in the record intended for me or for my relinquished child.

The effects of this Waiver extend only to my "birth" child and/or my "birth" child's legal representatives. The following information may be released in full to the aforementioned parties: My name in full, my current address and phone number (shown below), any and all medical records that may be in file.

This Waiver gives my full and legal permission to release my present identity and contact information as shown below and this letter is to remain in effect unless and until formally revoked by me in writing.

Please acknowledge receipt of my Waiver of Confidentiality in writing for my record.

Thank you,

_____
(Signature)

_____
(Printed Name in Full)

_____
(Current Address)

_____
(Current Phone Number)

WAIVER OF RIGHTS TO CONFIDENTIALITY FOR SIBLINGS

INSTRUCTIONS:

1. Please complete entire form.

2. **This form must be witnessed by a representative of the California Department of Social Services (CDSS) or a California (CA) adoption agency licensed by the CDSS, or notarized by a Notary Public.*** If the signing of this form is witnessed by the CDSS or a California licensed adoption agency representative, photo identification of the person signing must be obtained and noted on this form. **THIS FORM WILL BE RETURNED TO YOU IF IT IS NOT WITNESSED OR NOTARIZED.**

3. The waiver may be sent directly to the CA licensed adoption agency which handled the adoption, if known, or to the CDSS' Central Office: CDSS, Adoptions Support Unit, 744 P Street, M.S. 3-31, Sacramento, CA, 95814. If the adoption was an agency adoption, the waiver will be returned to you with the name and address of the adoption agency that handled the adoption so that you may send it directly to that adoption agency for processing.

DESIGNATE ONE - I AM THE:

☐ **ADOPTEE (age 18 or older)**

☐ **SIBLING (age 18 or older)** Attach copy of birth certificate

☐ **STEP-SIBLING (age 18 or older)** Attach copy of birth certificate **AND** copy of marriage certificate or divorce decree for marriage between birth parent and step-parent.

PART A.   *To be completed by adoptee/sibling signing consent*

☐ ADULT ADOPTEE:

By signing this form, I voluntarily and knowingly waive my rights to the confidentiality of personal information known or contained in the files of the CDSS or the CA licensed adoption agency and give my consent to the CDSS or the CA licensed adoption agency to disclose my name and address to my sibling so he/she may contact me.

☐ ADULT SIBLING:

By signing this form, I voluntarily and knowingly waive my rights to the confidentiality of personal information known or contained in the files of the CDSS or the CA licensed adoption agency and give my consent to the CDSS or the CA licensed adoption agency to disclose my name and address to my adopted sibling so that he/she may contact me.

I realize that both of the designated persons must sign a Waiver before the CDSS or the CA licensed adoption agency may disclose identifying information and that signing this Waiver does not necessarily ensure that a contact will be made. The sibling must also comply with all other provisions of Family Code Section 9205.

I certify that to the best of my knowledge, I am an adoptee or sibling of an adoptee. I understand that I should keep the CDSS or the CA licensed adoption agency informed of my current name, address, and phone number in writing.

I understand that I have the right to revoke this waiver at any time by notifying the CDSS or the CA licensed adoption agency in writing.

I understand that if the CDSS or the CA licensed adoption agency has not received a Waiver from each designated person, I may file a petition in the Superior Court to appoint a confidential intermediary to search for the other party to attempt to obtain a Waiver.

NAME (PLEASE PRINT)	BIRTHDATE	OTHER NAME(S) BY WHICH ADOPTEE/SIBLING HAS BEEN KNOWN	
STREET ADDRESS	CITY	STATE	ZIP CODE	TELEPHONE NUMBER ( )
SIGNATURE		DATE	

PART B.   *To be completed by a representative of the CDSS or a CA licensed adoption agency. If Part B or C is completed, do not complete Part D.*

SIGNATURE OF THE CDSS OR A CA LICENSED ADOPTION AGENCY REPRESENTATIVE   DATE   TELEPHONE NUMBER ( )

AGENCY/DEPARTMENT NAME   ADDRESS

IDENTIFICATION OF ADULT ADOPTEE OR ADULT SIBLING (SPECIFY, I.E., DRIVER'S LICENSE, PASSPORT, ETC.)

PART C. ☐ *Check if notarized signature has been previously submitted to the CDSS or a CA licensed adoption agency.*

PART D.   *To be completed by a Notary Public ONLY if Part B or C is not completed.*

State of _____)
)
County of _____)

On _____ before me, _____ , a Notary Public,

personally appeared _____ ,proved to me on the basis of satisfactory evidence to be
                              NAME OF ADULT ADOPTEE/ADOPTEE'S SIBLING

the person whose name is subscribed to the within instrument and acknowledged to me that he/she executed the same in his/her authorized capacity, and that by his/her signature on the instrument the person, or the entity upon behalf of which the person acted, executed the instrument.

I certify under PENALTY OF PERJURY under the laws of the State of California that the foregoing paragraph is true and correct.

WITNESS my hand and official seal.

_____ (Seal)
Signature

Definition of Notary Public: A Notary Public is a public officer authorized by law to certify documents and to confirm your identity. Notaries may be located at most banks and credit unions or listed in the yellow pages of your local phone directory.

AD 904A (3-08)   **SEE REVERSE SIDE**

EXAMPLE: SIBLING WAIVER OF CONFIDENTIALITY (CA)

FW-001   **Request to Waive Court Fees**

If you are getting public benefits, are a low-income person, or do not have enough income to pay for household's basic needs and your court fees, you may use this form to ask the court to waive all or part of your court fees. The court may order you to answer questions about your finances. If the court waives the fees, you may still have to pay later if:

- You cannot give the court proof of your eligibility,
- Your financial situation improves during this case, or
- You settle your civil case for **$10,000** or more. The trial court that waives your fees will have a lien on any such settlement in the amount of the waived fees and costs. The court may also charge you any collection costs.

Clerk stamps date here when form is filed.

Fill in court name and street address:

Fill in case number and name:

Case Number:

Case Name:

(1) **Your Information** *(person asking the court to waive the fees):*
Name: _____
Street or mailing address: _____
City: _____ State: _____ Zip: _____
Phone number: _____

(2) **Your Job,** if you have one *(job title):* _____
Name of employer: _____
Employer's address: _____

(3) **Your lawyer,** if you have one *(name, firm or affiliation, address, phone number, and State Bar number):*
_____
_____

  a. The lawyer has agreed to advance all or a portion of your fees or costs *(check one):* Yes☐ No ☐
  b. *(If yes, your lawyer must sign here)* Lawyer's signature: _____
    If your lawyer is not providing legal-aid type services based on your low income, you may have to go to a hearing to explain why you are asking the court to waive the fees.

(4) **What court's fees or costs are you asking to be waived?**
  ☐ Superior Court (See *Information Sheet on Waiver of Superior Court Fees and Costs* (form FW-001-INFO).)
  ☐ Supreme Court, Court of Appeal, or Appellate Division of Superior Court (See *Information Sheet on Waiver of Appellate Court Fees and Costs* (form APP-015/FW-015-INFO).)

(5) **Why are you asking the court to waive your court fees?**
  a. ☐ I receive *(check all that apply):* ☐ Medi-Cal ☐ Food Stamps ☐ SSI ☐ SSP ☐ County Relief/General Assistance ☐ IHSS (In-Home Supportive Services) ☐ CalWORKS or Tribal TANF (Tribal Temporary Assistance for Needy Families) ☐ CAPI (Cash Assistance Program for Aged, Blind and Disabled)
  b. ☐ My gross monthly household income (before deductions for taxes) is less than the amount listed below. *(If you check 5b you must fill out 7, 8 and 9 on page 2 of this form.)*

Family Size	Family Income	Family Size	Family Income	Family Size	Family Income	
1	$1,128.13	3	$1,907.30	5	$2,686.46	*If more than 6 people at home, add $389.59 for each extra person.*
2	$1,517.71	4	$2,296.88	6	$3,076.05	

  c. ☐ I do not have enough income to pay for my household's basic needs *and* the court fees. I ask the court to *(check one):* ☐ waive all court fees ☐ waive some of the court fees ☐ let me make payments over time (Explain): _____ *(If you check 5c, you must fill out page 2.)*

(6) ☐ Check here if you asked the court to waive your court fees for this case in the last six months.
  (If your previous request is reasonably available, please attach it to this form and check here: ☐ *)*

I declare under penalty of perjury under the laws of the State of California that the information I have provided on this form and all attachments is true and correct.

Date: _____

▶

_____   _____
Print your name here   *Sign here*

Judicial Council of California, www.courtinfo.ca.gov
Revised July 2, 2009, Mandatory Form
Government Code § 68633
Cal. Rules of Court, rules 3.51, 8.26 and 8.818

Request to Waive Court Fees

FW-001, Page 1 of 2

EXAMPLE: REQUEST TO WAIVE COURT FEES (CA)

Request for Appointment of Confidential Intermediary

Clerk stamps date here when form is filed.

Fill in court name and street address:

Superior Court of California, County of

Clerk fills in case number when form is filed.

Case Number:

(1) I am asking the court to appoint a confidential intermediary to help me get contact information for my sibling.
a. My name: _____
b. My address: _____
c. My phone number: _____

(2) a. ☐ The person helping me complete this request for the appointment of a confidential intermediary is:
(1) Name: _____
☐ My attorney (State Bar No. _____) ☐ My guardian ad litem
(2) Address: _____
(3) Phone number: _____
b. ☐ I do not have an attorney or guardian ad litem who is helping me complete this request for the appointment of a confidential intermediary.

(3) ☐ An attorney used to represent me.
a. Name of former attorney: _____
b. Address of attorney: _____
c. Phone number of attorney: _____
d. This attorney used to represent me because: _____

(4) The department or the licensed adoption agency that joined in the adoption petition for:
☐ me
☐ my sibling
a. Name of agency: _____
b. Address: _____
c. Phone number: _____

Judicial Council of California, www.courtinfo.ca.gov
New January 1, 2008, Mandatory Form
Code of Civil Procedure § 373
Family Code § 9205
Cal. Rules of Court, rule 5.410

Request for Appointment of Confidential Intermediary

EXAMPLE: REQUEST FOR CONFIDENTIAL INTERMEDIARY (CA)

Searching the USA

Search Resources in the 50 States, District of Columbia, US Possessions and Territories

---

CODE KEY TO ADOPTION SEARCH & SUPPORT GROUPS

S=Searcher; SG=Support Group; SS=Search and Support; C=Computer Access;
AAC=American Adoption Congress member; ALMA= Adoptees' Liberty Movement Assn;
AmFOR=Americans For Open Records; CUB= Concerned United Birthparents;
ISC=Independent Search Consultant; L-PI=Licensed Private Investigator

Alabama

CENTRAL RECORDS OFFICES

Vital Records		State (St), County (Co),
To Verify Fees		Birth (B), Death (D),
(rec = recorded message)		Marriage (M), Divorce (DV)
Center for Health Statistics	Accessible?	Indices & Record
PO Box 5625	Basic fee	St-B,D, since 1908;
Montgomery, AL 36103-5418	plus search	St-M,DV since Jan 1936
(334) 206-5418	fee $ 10/hr	Co-M, Probate Judge
www.vitalrecor.com/al.html		Co-B,D.DV Ct Equity Clk

State Archives	Year Adoption	Hospital Records	Legal Notice
Address	Records Closed	Available?	Required?
Dept. of Archives & History	1931	Yes	Unknown
624 Washington Avenue			
Montgomery, AL 36104			

Central Department of Motor Vehicles	National Archives - Southeast Region
Drivers License Division	1557 Saint Joseph Avenue
Certification Section	East Point, GA 30344
PO Box 1471	(404) 763-7477.
Montgomery, AL 36102	Hours: M.W-F 7:30AM-4:30PM Tu 9:30PM
	(Serves AL, GA, FL, KY, MS, NC, SC, TN)

Central Agency	Non-Identifying	Adoption Decree	State
Holding Adoption Records	Info Provided?	From Court	Registry
Family Services (Adoptions)	Yes, by law;	Yes; Probate Court	Yes
50 Ripley Street	Adoptees.		
Montgomery, AL 36130			

ADULT ADOPTEES CAN NOW ACCESS ORIGINAL BIRTH CERTIFICATE ON REQUEST.

Section 26-10-4; records sealed; court order required to release info; AL Code, Title 26, Section 10-4 (1977); allows adult adoptees to access their original birth certificate, but only if birthparent signs consent form; requires disclosing child's social and educational history. Section 26-10-4: adoptive parent and the adoptive child at majority may inspect original birth certificate or adoption records. Section 26-10-9 violation of any provision: Misdemeanor, fine $100 and/or 3 mos. jail. AL Code Section 26-10A-31 (Supp. 1991) mandates disclosure of non-identifying information to adoptees 19 or older; 26-10A-31: disclosure to biological parents. Section 26-10A-31 State Registry at State Department of Human Resources.

ADOPTION SEARCH/SUPPORT GROUPS (see "Key" on page 47)

Leah Weslowski	Loretta Bailey (SS)	Laura Stewart, Adoption Triad
164Maningham	Adoptees for Open Records (AFOR)	Midwest (SG)
Madison, AL 36758	Route 1, Box 725	700 North 9th Street, Suite 204
Leahwes@Acmeinformation.com	Ozark, AL 36360	Opelika, AL 36801
Lynn Davis	Judy Payne	David C. Ansardi
196 Clara Street/PO Box 144	The Adoption Circle	Adoption Thruthseekers
Webb, AL 36321	PO Box 240681	1501 Mountain Lake Road
Lydu007@msn.com	Montgomery, AL 36124	Warrior, AL 35180

Dear AmFOR: ... "I just got your information and yours is the most informative. While in our law library, I met other adoptees researching to locate their parents. I gave them your name and address ... Sincerely, L.ORETTA B. Ozark, AL."

Alaska

CENTRAL RECORDS OFFICES

Vital Records
To Verify Fees
(rec = recorded message).
Department of Health
Bureau of Vital Statistics
PO Box 110675
Juneau, AK 99811-0675
(907) 465-3392 -rec
www.vitalrec.com/ak/html

Accessible?
Immediate
family;
fee $10/hr
Co-DV Sup Ct Clk

State (St), County (Co),
Birth (B), Death (D),
Marriage (M), Divorce (DV)
Indices & Records
St-B,D,.M since 1913;
St-DV since 1950
Co-B ,D,M Co Clerk

State Archives
Address
State Library, History &
Archives, State Office Bldg.
141 Willoughby
Juneau, AK 99801

Year Adoption
Records Closed
Never

Hospital Records
Available?
Yes

Legal Notice
Required?
No

Central Department of Motor Vehicles
Department of Public Safety
Drivers License Section
PO Box 20020
Juneau, AK 99802

Division of Motor Vehicles
5700 Tudor Road
Anchorage, AK 99507

National Archives - Alaska Region
Federal Office Building
654 West Third Avenue, Room 012
Anchorage, AK 99501
Phone (907) 271-2441
Hours: Mon-Fri & 1st Sat: 8AM-4PM
(serves Alaska)

Central Agency
Holding Adoption Records
Family & Youth Services (Adoptions)
PO Box 110630
Juneau, AK 99811-0630
(907) 465-3191

Non-Identifying
Info Provided?
Yes, by law;
Adoptive Parents

Adoption Decree
From Court
Yes; Superior Court

State
Registry
Open
Records
(Adults)

ADULT ADOPTEES (AGE 18) CAN ACCESS ORIGINAL BIRTH CERTIFICATE ON REQUEST.
Section 25-23-150; closed hearings; court order required to release info; original birth certificate disclosure of names and identities of adoptive parent or adopted child may not be permitted without consent of adoptive parent or adopted child over age 14 or by court order. Alaska Statue, Section 18.50.500 (Supp. 1986) allows access to original birth certificate to adult adoptees. No fee stated. Section 18-50-510 provides medical information access to adult adoptee at age 18 and adoptive parent. Section 18-50-500: adopted child may receive a copy of original birth certificate and attached information about addresses of birthparents. Section 18-50-510: adopted child may receive non-identifying info re: birthparents and relatives (physical characteristics, education, medical and social history, etc.) when s/he reaches 18. No penalty for violation stated. Section 18.50.500(a) (Supp. 1991): Birthparent registry for disclosure of identifying information and contact. State Registrar required to attach information to original birth certificate.

ADOPTION SEARCH/SUPPORT GROUPS (see "Key" on page 47)
Jana Tackett/CUB (SG)
7105 Shooreson Circle
Anchorage, AK 99504

Dear AmFOR:... "Please send me all or any information so I can find my son ...

Thank you, SHERRI T., Fairbanks, AK."

Arizona

CENTRAL RECORDS OFFICES

Vital Records
To Verify Fees
(rec = recorded message).
Div. of Vital Records
State Depr. Health Scr.
PO Box 3887
Phoenix, AZ 85030
(602) 364-1300-rec
www.vitalrec.com/az.html

Accessible?
Genealogy
family;
fee

State (St), County (Co),
Birth (B), Death (D),
Marriage (M), Divorce (DV)
Indices & Records
St-B,D, since 1908;
St-M.DV, No index
Co-B,D, pre '09 abstract
Co-M, DV, Sup. Ct. Clerk

State Archives
Address
State Library, Archives &
Records, State Capitol
1700 W Washington Street
Phoenix, AZ 85007

Year Adoption
Records Closed
Unknown

Hospital Records
Available?
Difficult

Legal Notice
Required?
Usually

Department of Motor Vehicles
Motor Vehicles Division
Drivers Licenses
1801 West Jefferson Street
Phoenix, AZ 85007

National Archives - Pacific Central
Southwest Region
24000 Avila Road, First Floor
Laguna Niguel, CA 92656-6719
(714) 643-4241
Hours: Mon-Fri & 1st Sat: 8AM-4:30PM
(Serves AZ, Southern CA counties and NV)

Central Agency
Holding Adoption Records
Child/Youth/Familes Adoptions
PO Box 6123
Phoenix, AZ 85005

Non-Identifying
Info Provided?
Yes, by law;
All Triad.

Adoption Decree
From Court
Sometimes;
Superior Court

State
Registry
No;
Intermediary
System

(1987) ADOPTION DISCLOSURE STATUTES (INTERMEDIARY SYSTEM)
Section 8-110: any interested party may request that the adopted child be referred to, using fictitious name. Section 8-120: records shall be withheld. Section 8-105; 8-109: fees. Section 8-129; medical information provided to prospective adoptive parent, to adopted child after 18, to adopted child's spouse and/or progeny if adopted child is decreased. Section 8-129: non-identifying information to adoptive parents re: health and genetic history, to adopted child after 18; to adopted child's spouse and/or progeny if adopted child is deceased. Section 8-128 penalty: Class 6 Felony.

ADOPTION SEARCH/SUPPORT GROUPS (see "Key" on page 47)

Sue Cook-ISC
4603 S.Sauk Ave
Seirra Vista, AZ 85659
SEEK@prodigy.net

Scottsdale Adoption Connection
PO Box 2512
Scottsdale, AZ 85251

Jude Guilford
Tucson Adoption Reunion (S.SS)
Tucson, AZ
gogilgoes@yahoo.com

Martha Shideler
Flagstaff Research/Support (SG)
PO Box 1031
Flagstaff, AZ 85002

Kristen Hamilton - PI
8390 E. Via DeVentura
Suite F110-184
Scottsdale, AZ 85258
RSearchEtc@aol.com

Charles Wollen
1402 Bethany Home Road
Phoenix, AZ 85013

50

Dara Brown-Watkins
Search Triad, Inc. (SS)
PO Box 10181
Phoenix, AZ 85064

Brenda Wilson-Hasty
TRACE (SG)
PO Box 1541
Sierra Vista, AZ 84636

Adrienne Ash ISC (S)
3025 E First St
Tucson. AZ 85716
ashdesigns@aol.com

Jody King
Triad
7155EFirestoneDr
Tucson, AZ 85730

Family Counseling Center
301 East Bethany Home Road
Suite C-296
Phoenix, AZ 85012

Joy Pantelis
CUB (SG)
8372 N Sage Place
Tucson, AZ 87504

Karen Tinkham ISC
Search Triad, Inc. (S)
PO Box 1432
Litchfield Park, AZ 85340
k.tink@worldnet.att.net
http://www.searchtriad.org

Jana Martin
Rt 1, Box 31-B, Sp 63
Globe, AZ 85501

Torin Scott
Confidential Intermediary.
1501 West Washington #410
Phoenix, AZ 85007

Kay Gartrell
TRIAD
Box 12806
Tucson, AZ 85732

Jayne Askin
10323 North 104th Way
Scottsdale, AZ 85258
JAskin@aol.com

Sherri Ervin
Past Present Future
1290 W. Shaw Butte Dr.
Peoria, AZ 85245

Dee Davis
Adoption Counseling
1038 East Michigan Ave
Phoenix, AZ 85022

Dear AmFOR:... "I obtained the name and address of your organization form a local historical library. I am currently attempting to obtain information concerning my father from the state of Arizona. They rejected my initial request for a birth certificate, even though I provided all the information that was required per their information phone line. I am concerned that since my parents were divorced and when my mother remarried I was adopted by her new husband, they will not allow me access to my biological father's birth information. I have indicated to them my relationship and that I am just trying to trace family roots. but they requested 'proof of my relationship. I have sent them unofficial hospital birth records,.which are the only I have with my birth name on them. I am not optimistic that this will be satisfactory, and was hoping you might have some pointers you could share with me to help me "crack" the stalemate that seems to exist when a state has such strict rules on privacy and records. I might add that my biological father was born in 1908, so I expect he is no longer living. At what point is a record no longer private, but becomes archival in nature? ... Sincerely, BETH L., Oxford. OH."

Dear AmFOR:... "Would you please send me information regarding your organization? I am a mother and hope that someday my daughter and I will be able to meet again ... Thank you. D.H., Phoenix. AZ."

Dear AmFOR: ... "I received your name along with much other information provided by Kathleen Lawson of the 'Open Heritage Society.' I am a mother dealing with LDS Social Services in Arizona regarding the adoption of my daughter in 1970. It is my fervent desire to provide any information to my daughter that she may be seeking. LDS Social Services allows letters to be placed in their files but states this information is not available to the adoptee. Therefore I am interested in the open records movement in Arizona. Any information you can provide would be greatly appreciated . . . Thank you, PATRICIA M., Las Vegas, NV."

Arkansas

Vital Records		State (St), County (Co),	
To Verify Fees		Birth (B), Death (D),	
(rec = recorded message)		Marriage (M), Divorce (DV)	
Div. of Vital Records	Accessible?	Indices & Records	
4815 W Markham St.	Public;	St-B.D, since Feb. 1914;	
Little Rock, AR 72201	fee	St-M, since 1917, Dv 1923	
(501) 661-2336-rec		Co-B,D,M County Clerk	

State Archives	Year Adoption	Hospital Records	Legal Notice
Address	Records Closed	Available?	Required?
State Library Archives	1935	Difficult	Unknown
One Capitol Mall			
Little Rock, AR 72201			

Central Department of Motor Vehicles
Office of Driver Services
Traffic Violation Unit
PO Box 1272
Little Rock, AR 72203

National Archives - Southwest Region
501 West Felix Street
PO Box 6216
Fort Worth, TX 76115
(817)334-5525
Hours: Mon-Fri: 8AM-4PM, Wed:8AM-9PM
(Serves AR, LA, NM, OK and TX)

Motor Vehicle Division
PO Box 1272
Little Rock, AR 72203

Central Agency	Non-Identifying	Adoption Decree	State
Holding Adoption Records	Info Provided?	From Court	Registry
Child/Family Services (Adoptions)	Yes, by law;	No;	Yes.
Div. Social Services Adoptions	Adoptees.	Probate Court	
PO Box 1437 (Slot 636)			
Little Rock, AR 72203			
(501) 682-1569			

(1985) ADOPTION DISCLOSURE STATUTES (INTERMEDIARY SYSTEM)

Arkansas Statue Annotated Section 56-138 to 56-145 (Supp. 1985) provides Registry System. Conformed to Uniform Adoption Act, per Shephard's Acts 1947. Section 56-211 fees stated. Section 56-145: written health, genetic and social history provided to adoptive parents, adopted child at 18 or adopted child's spouse or progeny over 2 if adopted child is deceased. Section 56-141: in exceptional circumstances, specific papers and records may be inspect by adopted child, adoptive parent or birth parents by court order. Section 56-144: Mutual Consent Voluntary Adoption Registry. Section 56-1221; violation of adoption law Class A Misdemeanor. Section 9-9-505 (Michie 1991) mandates disclosure of non-identifying information.

ADOPTION SEARCH/SUPPORT GROUPS (see "Key" on page 47)

Clorinda Kraiger Arace (S)	Mary Ellen Johnson	Jenny Kolp
AR Adoption Triad (SG)	Orphan Train Heritage (SG)	AR/OK Adoption Connection
8809 Colverhill Rd	Society of America	Route 1, Box 613
Little Rock, AR, 72205	4912 Troutfarm Rd	Roland, OK 74954
	Springdale, AR 72762	kolp@ipa.net

Dear AmFOR:... "The 'Orphan Train Heritage Society of America' (OTHSA) is a national organization with over 600 members. We would like to publish a brief story in the next issue of our newsletter, "CROSSROADS", concerning the open records laws in the U.S. Does your organization have a current list, state-by-state, of the open records laws? ? If so, could you share it with us so we may publish it. Thank you for your help ... Sincerely, PHIL SUTTON, ORPHAN TRAIN HERITAGE SOCIETY OF AMERICA, Route 4, Box 565, Springdale, AR."

Dear AmFOR:... "I am 19 years old I wonder what my real parents have named me? I was adopted when I was four days old, and ever since I've known I was adopted, I have been interested in either finding my real parents or at least finding out about them. One thing that is interesting is that my adoptive mother is also adopted, and so is one of my uncles. They both have never pursued finding their parents, but I would like to. I am not obsessed with the idea, but it would be nice to know. Just to see who they are, see how they live and mostly to ask them "why" they put me up for adoption. We adopted children live with hearing other children complemented on how she or he looks like his or her mother/father. Well, who do we look like? We need to know.

Being adopted is an interesting conversation piece. I've found that people are amazed or don't believe me when I tell them I am adopted. When I explain that my younger sister and I are only 8 months apart, it helps it become more believable. The first question they always ask me is, 'Don't you wonder who your real parents are?' (well, of course.)

One thing that helped me decide to write to you was the article I read in *First* magazine, July 1989 issue, called 'My Daughter's Other Mother.' It is an interesting article. I'm sure it doesn't work out that smoothly or end that happy for everyone, and that is too bad. It think everyone (if they want to) should have a chance to find out who actually brought them into the world ... Sincerely, JENNY B. Little Rock, AR."

Concord Monitor, 7/7/90, page A 10: "TATTOO REUNION" ... Vallejo—When Allison Forciea saw her birth name tattooed across her patient's upper chest she was so shocked she walked away for a moment before asking the toughest question of her life ... George Jensen, Sr., 49, who was seeing an orthopedist for minor ailment, turned out to be Forcieas' father, who had given her up for adoption 28 years ago and had had no word of her until the chance encounter June 5.

Forciea, who was born Edith Josephine, had been told her father was dead and believed he was until she saw the names of his children tattooed across his chest: 'George Jr. and Edie Jo.'

'There's got to be a higher being that's pushed us together. This just doesn't happen by accident,' Jensen said ... Forciea found her biological mother, Lois Payne, in 1985, and has been communicating with her since ... Forciea said she was afraid at the moment she met her father of how he would react. Her anxiety turned to happiness when he turned to her and said, 'If you wouldn't mind, I'd like to get to know you better.'"

California

CENTRAL RECORDS OFFICES

Vital Records
To Verify Fees
(rec = recorded
message)
Registrar, Vital Stats
State Dept. of Health
304 "S" Street
Sacramento, CA 95814
(916) 445-2684-rec
www.vitalrec.com/ca.html

Accessible?
Birth records
restricted

State (St), County (Co),
Birth (B), Death (D),
Marriage (M), Divorce (DV)
Indices & Records
St-B,D,M since 1905
St-DV, final since 1/62
initial since 1/66
Co-B,D,M County Clerk

State Archives Address	Year Adoption Records Closed	Hospital Records Available?	Legal Notice Required?
State Library, Archives CA Section, 914 Capitol Mall Sacramento, CA 95814	1935 (Also, State Archives 1020 "0" St., Sacramento, CA 94237)	Yes	Usually

Central Department of Motor Vehicles
Department of Motor Vehicles
Drivers License
PO Box 944231
Sacramento, CA 94244

Department of Motor Vehicles
PO Box 932328
Sacramento, CA 94232

National Archives • Pacific Southwest Region
24000 Avila Road, First Floor
Laguna Niguel, CA 92656-6719
Phone (714) 643-4241
Hours: Mon-Fri & 1st Sat 8AM-4:30PM
(Serves Arizona, the southern California
counties of Imperial, Kern, Los Angeles,
Orange, Riverside, San Bernardino, San
Diego, San Luis Obispo, Santa Barbara, Ventura)

National Archives - Pacific Sierra Region
1000 Commodore Drive
San Bruno, CA 94066
(415)876-9009
Hours: Mon-Fri 8AM-4PM, Wed 8AM-8PM
(Serves California, except southern California)

Central Agency Holding Adoption Records	Non-Identifying Info Provided?	Adoption Decree From Court	State Registry
Dept. Social Services (Adoptions) Adoptions Branch 744 "P" St., MS 19-73 Sacramento, CA 95814 (916) 324-9084	Yes, if agency adoption; All Triad.	Usually; Superior Court	Yes; Waiver System

(1986/1992) ADOPTION DISCLOSURE STATUTES (REGISTRY AND WAIVER SYSTEM)
Section 226m: closed hearings. Section 227: court order required to release information. CA Civil Code Section 227, 230.6 (1986) provides a Registry System. Section 224r: fees stated. Section 224: written report of adopted child health/ medical background to adoptive parent, adopted child at 18 or marriage; sooner if court decides medical info necessary. Section 224.70 (West Supp. 1992) mandates disclosure of non-identifying info limited to agency-facilitated adoptions. Section 227: identifying info about birthparent by notarized waiver (adoptive parent waiver not required since Jan. 1992). Adoption agency prohibited from soliciting waiver from parties. Unauthorized disclosure from adoption files is punishable by $5,000 fine— highest of any state and/or 6 months in prison per CA Civil Information and Practices

Over 80 of California adoptions are handled by private agencies and attorneys. Attorney David Leavitt, Beverly Hills baby broker, was successfully sued for S8 million for conspiring to help a woman give up her child for adoption against the father's wishes. Effective January 1, 2001, post-adoption and/or kinship agreements are now legally enforceable.

ADOPTION SEARCH/SUPPORT GROUPS Alphabetical by City (see "Key" on page 47)

Beth Snider
The Right to Know (a video)
433 North Palm Avenue
Alhambra,CA91801

Karen Huck
Auburn Adoption Search
10583 Rock View Court
Auburn, CA 95602

Ann Spanel, ISC
Lost and Found (SS S)
4212 Starling Dr
Bakersfield, CA 93309

Norma Gutierrez
4042 Harlan Ave
Baldwin Park, CA 91706
NormaFindu@aol.com

Joe Burger (S C)
516BreckCourt
Benicia, CA 94574
Debbie@Monroeburger.com

Adoptsearch
1940 Los Angeles St.
Berkeley, CA 94707

Janine Baer
Chain of Life-Newsletter
Po Box 8081
Berkeley, CA 94707

Sara Vick
Adoption with Truth (SG)
66 Panoramic Way
Berkeley, CA 94604

People Together (S)
2107 Dwight, #100
Berkeley, CA 97404

Toni Nason
PO Box 2355
Beverly Hills, CA 90213

Beverly Difani
Reconnections of CA
11104 Locust
Bloomington,CA92316

Teresa Butler (SG)
Adoption Triad Support Group
1755 Diamond Mountain Rd
Calistoga, CA 94515

Gina Ricci
Friends Forever
PO Box 2829
Capistrano Beach. CA 92624

Linda Higley
CUB
3018 Avenida Christina
Carlsbad, CA 92009

Ed Noonan/Trudy Helminger (S)
Adoptee-Birth Family Registry
PO Box 803
Carmichael, CA 95608

Peggy Wolfe
TRIAD Support
17701 Avalon Blvd.
Carson. CA 90746

Carol Mogenroth (L-PI)
Worldwide Tracers
PO Box 1309
Chester, CA 96020

Danielle Collins / CUB
14170 Evening View Dr
Chino, CA 91709

CA BIRTH INDEXES:
Colleen Buckner
Triad Ties
PO Box 1178
Colusa, CA 95932
therighttoknow@hotmail.com

Lee Bignall (S)
5460 Concord Blvd. Suite #C-3
Concord. CA 94521

Jane Galbreath
PO Box 743
Corte Madera, CA 94976

Delayn Curtis (ISC)
270 S. Bristol #101-PMB#159
Costa Mesa, CA 92626
delayn1@yahoo.com

Elizabeth Lamb
29282 Revis Rd
Coarsegold,CA93614
Mustang_sally1931@yahoo.com

Coco Brush
ANSWERS
PO Box 337
Diablo, CA 94528
CocoBrush@yahoo.com

California Research
11804 Tristan Drive
Downev CA 90241

Pat Miller
7751 Deacosta St
Downey, CA 90240

Patty Lawrence (SS)
Reconnections of CA
1191 Eastside Rd
El Cajon, CA 92020

Jim Shinn
536 Lenrey Ave
El Centre, CA 92243

C. Currie Wolfe ISC (SS S C)
Adoption Connection of SD
PO BOX 230643
Encinitas, CA 92023

Daniel Millward - PI
The Search Company
1020 Second Street #C
Encinitas, CA 92024

Tracy L. Carlis, PhD
17337 Ventura Blvd., Ste. 104-A
Encino, CA 91316

Jams Bowyer (S)
Sunland Search
2917 Anaheim St.
Escondido, CA 92025

Jo Kuhlman
2134 W Alluvial
Fresno, CA 93711

Carol Longoria ISC
5 Stratford Pl
Gilroy, CA 95020

Susan Bott (SS)
Central Coast Adoption Support
PO Box 8483
Goleta, CA 91202

Kate Burke ISC (S SS C)
Truthseekers
336 Bon Air Center #145
Greenbrae, CA 94904

Cynthia Scares, MS
PO Box 1125
Gridley, CA 95948
Cynthiason@aol.com

Caryn Madansky ISC
Central Coast Adoption Support
1718 Longbranch
Grover City, CA 93433
caryn@surfari.net

Marilyn Miller
South Coast Adoption Research/Support
PO Box 39
Harbor City, CA 90710

Phyllis Ernst ISC (S C)
California Research
PO Box 6058
San Pedro, CA 92615
ClassyPhyl@aol.com

Pat Fox
Family Research & Info Services
19381 Newhaven Lane
Huntington Beach, CA 92646
CDNFoxP@aol.com

Claudia Ropers (S)
PO Box 883
Inverness, CA 94937

Betsy Goodwin
CUB
PO Box 3271
La Mesa, CA 91944

Mimi James
Concerned United Birthparents
La Mirada, CA
mimijames@earthlink.net

Nancy Verrier, MFCC
Psychologist/Reunion Work
919 Village Center, #9
Lafayette, CA 49549

James T (Todd) Kepley, President
California Genealogical Alliance
19765 Grand Ave
Lake Elsinore, CA 92230

Cindy Shacklett
PO Box 1
Lake Forest CA 92630

Donna Caterick
PO Box 1076
Lakeside, CA 92040

Pacer of Marin (SG)
PO Box 826
Larrkspur, CA 94977

Patricia Bowers
Bookworm Research
PO Box 8044
Long Beach, CA 90808

J Nelson
ATM
312 Glendora
Long Beach, CA 90803

Mary Ann Rothschild ISC
AKA Mary Ann Dunkinson
People Finders
840 W 29th St
Long Beach, CA 90805

Jeri Brown, LCSW
5657 Wilshire Blvd, Ste 340
Los Angeles, CA 94063
msjb@earthlink.net

Michael Hirschenson / ENUF
Equality Nationwide for Unwed Fathers
4230 Del Rey Ave, #334
Marina del Rey, CA 90292

Menill C. Hunn
PACER/TRIAD-Birthmothers
204 Hawthorne Avenue
Mill Valley, CA 94941

Don Fordham
PO Box 1702
Monterey, CA 93942

Carol Bishop
Kinship Center (SG)
22 Lower Ragsdale Dr-Ste B
Monterey, CA 93940
cbishop@kinshipcenter.org

Adoptees Research Association
Missing Children Search Service
PO Box 304
Montrose, CA 91020

Christina Frazier
25841 Paseo Pacifico
Moreno Valley, CA 92388

Sandra Lexington
PO Box 212
Mount Herman, CA 95041

Sally Dark, MA MFT
2462 Alvin Street
Mountain View, CA 94043
Sallgen@infolane.com

Tina Peddie
Central Coast Adoption Support
488 Tyros Court
Nipomo, CA 93444
tpeddie@charter.net

56

Jerry Dayton
People Search USA
PO Box 2471
Nevada City, CA 95959

Margaret Poschn
PO Box 1099
North Highlands, CA 95660

Post Adoption Center for
Education & Research (PACER)
30 Lombda Vista
Novato, CA 94947

Bo bCrowe
PACER
PO Box 31146
Oakland, CA 94604

Laura Ingram
PACER
980.55th St.
Oakland, CA 94608
LCingram@aol.com

Mary Kay Eberhart
1835 Casa Linda Cir
Orange, CA 92668

Janice A. Miller
2726 Fay Way
Oroville, CA 95966
janice@cncnet.com

Ronda Slater
Oakland, CA
slaterronda@aol.com

Lorraine Wheeler (AAC)
78-409 Kensington Ave.
Riverside, CA 92517
Lorrwheel@aol.com

Susan Hammond
154 Bryant Street
Palo Alto, CA 94301

Barbara Cohen
555 Middlefield Rd.
Palo Alto, CA 94301
BLCohen@aol.com

Paige Crosby Ouimette, PhD
PACER
220 California Ave., Ste. 120
Palo Alto, CA 94306

Patty Prickett
Suzanne Kauffman ISC (S)
1127 E Del Mar Blvd. #232
Pasadena, CA 91106

Tobi Hanft (S)
Adoption Search & Reunion
PO Box 350
Pine Grove, CA 95665
toby@adoptionsearcher.com

Thada Wachtel
CUB
1420 N White Ave
Pomona, CA 91768

Denice Garcia
SD Adoption Triad Support
13626 Catawba Drive
Poway, CA 92064

Judi Meye CUB(SS)
PO Box 3265
2368 Mt Vernon Pl
Quail Valley, CA 92380

Steve Felix (S)
11 Stirrup Rd.
Rancho Palos Verdes, CA 90275
CaSearcher@aol.com

Attorney Martin Brandfon (ISC)
620 Jefferson Avenue
Redwood City, CA 94063
brandfon@earthlink.net

Pam McIntyre, Eileen Baum
Tnple Hearts Adoption Triangle
PO Box 51082
238 Richland Avenue
TQ3HEARTS@aol.com
bbkfjb@pc.net

Sally Peerbolt
Full Circle (SG)
3230 Layton Ct
Riverside, CA 92503

California Searchin' (S)
1384 Gillpepper Ln
Rohner Park, CA 94928

Vikki Schummer ISC (C AAC)
Research Unlimited
LA County Adoption Search (LACASA)
PO Box 1461
Roseville, CA 95678

Maggie Gunn
PACER
1019 "H" Street #12
Sacramento, CA 95648

Trish McAleer ISC (SS S)
CUB-Vice President
306 Ave Costanso
San Clemente, CA 92672

Betsy Goodwin
CUB (SS)
5224 Caminito Aruba
San Diego, CA 92124

Nancy Hale
Reunite of California
PO Box 7524
San Diego, CA 92167

Jo Rankin
Korean Adoptees Assn. (AKA)
PO Box 87291
San Diego CA 92138
jorankin@juno.com

Ann Wren—ISC
14040 Barrymore Street
San Diego, CA 92129
annwren@aol.com

Amy Jane Cheney (SG)
183 Elsie St
San Francisco, CA 94110
fiama@mindspring.com

Ron Morgan
PACER
238 Richland Ave.
San Francisco, CA 94110
rhyzome@kwom.com

Sheila Ganz (SS)
Bay Area Relinquishing Birth
Mothers
1546 Great Hwy 44
San Francisco, CA 94122
sganz1@hotmail.com

Carrie Buckner
179 Granada Ave.
San Francisco, CA 94112
carriel2@earthlink.net

Julia Alien
1455-E FoxworthyAve #164
San Jose, CA 95118

CUB
1787 Michon Dr
San Jose, CA 95106

Search Finders of California
San Jose. CA
searchfindersofcalifornia.com

Denise Roessle
PACER
50 Tom Court
San Ramon, CA 94583
drmcl@ix.netcom.com

Patricia Sanders
AAC-Conference Dept
20111 Riverside Dr
Santa Ana Heights, CA 92702

Jeanne Paredes
3461 State Street
Sant Barbara, CA 93105

Lesley Gunnels
Open Adoption Group
PO Box 3506
Santa Cruz, CA 95063
ksbroom@hotmail.com

Sandra Marshall
CUB
2925 Fourth St, #15
Santa Monica, CA 90405

Edward M Corpus (L-PI)
Edward Corpus Investigations
1130 Freemont Blvd. SP 105, #113
Seaside, CA 93955

Triad Research (SG)
300 Golden West
Shafter. CA 93262

Gayle Beckstead (ISC)
Adoption Reality
2180 Clover St.
Simi Valley. CA 93065

Nancy Cerf
PACER
PO Box 383
Stinson Beach, CA 94970

Barbara Shaw
11138 AguaVista St. #22
Studio City, CA 91602

Neil Kelly (SG)
Adoptees Identity Discovery
PO Box 2159
Sunnyvale, CA 94087

Cyndi Jacobson
41669 Zinfandel Ave.
Temecula, CA 92591

Tricia Cleland ISC (S C)
Roots
10997 Road 252
Terra Bella, CA 93270
lec9@aol.com

Patty Bybee
Hand-in-Hand (SS C)
63 E. Ave. de las Flores
Thousand Oaks, CA 91360

Mary Anna de Parq Goode (S)
PO Box 5161
Torrance, CA 90510

Peggy Wolff
TRIAD Support
PO Box 172
Torrance, CA 90507

Karen Ybarra
Missing Links
963 North Mahaleb Street
Tulare, CA 93274

Bill Bosen
17842 Irvine Blvd., Ste 202
Tustin. CA 92780

Eva Torres (SG)
Menio Lake Adoption Triad
620 Walnut Ave
Ukiah, CA 95482

Anne Marie Olson
Triple Hearts Adoption Triangle
PO Box 84
Vacaville, CA 95696
TriplHearts@aol.com

Hedy-Lynn Berry
Second Abandonment (SG)
2323 Eastern Canal
Venice, CA 90291

Priscilla Margolin, MA, MFCC
Adoptees-Birthparents Support (SG)
260 Maple Ct - Ste 124
Ventura, CA 93003

Diane Vivianco (SG)
Adoption Reunion Support Group
1115 Sunset Dr
Vista, CA 92083

Alberta Sorenson
Family Search Services
PO Box 3315
Walnut Creek, CA 94598
DickandEmic57@aol.com

Adoption Family Services
7137 Damock Way
West Hills, CA 91307

Mary Jo Rillera
Tri adoption Inc
PURE, Inc.
PO Box 638
Westminster, CA 92683

Ida Knapp (ISC)
5982 Toyon Terrace
Yorba Linda, CA 92886

Dear AmFOR:... "I am an adoptee searching for my mom. I have often wondered about the entire process. I am very happy with the two wonderful people I call Mom and Dad. I have become quite ill the last couple of months. The doctors just don't know what could be causing me so much pain. They have run numerous tests, all resulting in no answers. I am tired of all the pain! I thought that there might be some answers in my background. I don't know what else to do at this point. My parents say as far as they know there is no medical history. Someone has to know something ... I was born at O'Conner Hospital on Dec. 8, 1964 at 7:11 a.m. Please if you can help me, or direct me to someone who can I would really appreciate it... Thank You, JENNIFER S., Los Gatos, CA."

Dear AmFOR:... "I am writing to share my success of finally finding my mother. Amazingly, once I began searching it only took me a matter of two and one half weeks to find her. Fortunately, everything went very smooth for me. I hope that maybe my success can help others ... I began at the hospital I was born at. I sent a letter requesting birth records for a 'baby girl born May 21, 1966,' but no name. In less than a week I had received a reply with my last name . . . but no more information. I called the records department at the hospital, and was told to come in to sign a waiver of release. She said from that point it would take approximately one week. Exactly one week and $24 later I had my mother's full name.

After less than a week, and quite a bit of detective work I had her address. She lives in Redlands, about 40 minutes away from me. The following day, I found her house and panicked. I was with my adopted mother at the time. We went to a nearby restaurant to think and prepare. I decided to go to her door. I wrote on a piece of note paper my name and phone number in case she could not talk or was not there. He was not in; a man answered the door and ... I asked him to give her my number and have her call me. He asked what it was in regards to and I replied that I was a friend of the family, and I was trying to make contact. She did not call that night.

The following morning I was to meet a friend in San Bernardino. I took him past her house. Surprisingly, she was outside talking on the phone... The reunion went wonderfully. There was already an immediate bond between us. We have since spent almost two full weeks together, getting to know one another. We are both quite alike, and I get strength from knowing that she is there for me. She always was there for me.

My mother has almost always lived in the same area I have lived. At one point, she lived in Hemet only about a mile from an old boyfriend of mine. How many times could I have passed her? My mother and I are now in the process of finding my father. I hope it will be as rewarding as finding my mother was for me. Thank you for all of your sound advice and directions to take. I couldn't have done it without your . help. If I can be of help to other adoptees who are searching, let me know. Thank you again! . . . Sincerely, CYNTHIA F., Hemet, CA."

Dear AmFOR: ... "I just talked to my adoptive son and he asked me to write you.. He said you sent him some information on the Quackenbush bill AB 3907. We received our information from the Children's Home Society asking us to help defeat AB 3907. CHS asked the wrong people as we believe our son has a right to know who he is. I typed a letter which I am sending you a copy, and sent one to all twelve Senators on the Appropriations Committee hoping at least one will read it. I am not afraid of what Kevin will find as we raised him with a lot of love, and he did us proud. He is a good person, a good student at school and did well in everything he tried to do. We love him and he knows it. Thank you for the help you have tried to give him . . . TINA D.."

Dear AmFOR:... "Just a few lines to update what is going on now with the search for my sons ... I had a great visit with my youngest son, Russell Lee Howard. Now I am searching (still) for Donald (in Texas), Dana and Michael (in Calif.). I wrote a letter to Department of Social Services, Sacramento. They got back with me when I first wrote them, then I did not hear from them after that. I called them and then they mailed back every thing I mailed to them. They told me to write to: Los Angeles County, Social Services, Adoption Bureau

So I did. After I did not hear from them, I called them. They first said that they had to assign a case worker for my case. OK? I called them back later and the lady told me that there was a 12 to 15 month waiting list. A few days later I got a letter from them saying that they did not have the files. And for me to write Sacramento, again. I can't tell you how hurt I was over this. Then I got mad! I called Sacramento, again. This time a lady talked to me and she said that the files are someplace else, in another town and that she would have to send for them. And that as soon as they came in that she would call me and let me know what she could tell me. This is about 2 weeks or so. Now I am waiting again.

I feel like a Ping Pong ball. I am finding myself feeling down in the dumps a lot. Roger sent me a Christmas card and that is all that I have heard from him. I called him and told him that I got back to Ohio, OK. That was in December. His adopter is in her 70's and I told him that if he did not want to, he did not have to tell her about me. Now I need some info. from him and I want to call him but I am afraid to call him; I think that I just might make him mad at me. Why should I feel like I am walking on eggs?? Please, write or call me any time ... Your friend in Ohio, MARY H., Kettering, OH."

Dear AmFOR:... "I have been referred to you by Mike from International Probate Resource ... You are the beacon of hope I have so desperately been looking for because recently my sister ... and I suffered a grievous tragedy. Our mother died—committed suicide actually.

It is this fact, this realization that plagues me now. I have always drawn comfort from the idea that even though I have no knowledge of my father beyond the age of one, I draw my characteristics more from him than my mother ... One of the enclosed papers is from a data archival service listing presumably all the M.C.'s in the country. The other is the letter I've sent to all of the one's with addresses. No luck there. I do not know my father's Social Security Number... Our mother gone, it would be heavenly if we could gain my father. Thank you very much for any effort and consideration you can give us due to our loss . . . Sincerely, G.M.D.C., San Diego, CA."

Dear AmFOR: . . . "Regrettably, under California law, once an adoption is completed, the record is sealed. Adoption laws prohibit the release of information from adoption records to siblings of adoptees. In addition, California prohibits this Department or a licensed adoption agency from assisting you in searching for your adopted sibling. However, the law does provide for a mutual consent registry whereby this Department or a licensed adoption agency can arrange contact between an adult adoptee (age 21 or older) and his/her sibling(s) if both parties sign a Waiver of Rights to Confidentiality of Adoption Records for siblings form. Sibling waiver forms are provided only upon request, as solic- iting waivers is prohibited.

You can also join a search group or hire a private investigator to assist you in your search for your sibling . . . JAMES W. BROWN, CHIEF, ADOPTIONS BRANCH, DEPT. OF SOCIAL SERVICES, SACRA- MENTO, CA."

Colorado

CENTRAL RECORDS OFFICES

Vital Records
Address & Phone
To Verify Fees
(rec = recorded message).

	Accessible?		
Records/Stats Section	Restricted;		
4300 Cherry Creek So.	fee		
Denver, CO 80220			
(303) 692-2200			
www.vitalrec.com/co.html			

State (St), County (Co),
Birth (B), Death (D)
Marriage (M), Divorce (DV)

Indices & Records
St-B since 1910; D-1900
St-M, Dv not 1940-67
Inq Fwd: Co-B,D,M, Co Clk
Co-Dv, Dist Ct Clerk

State Archives
Address
Div. of Archives, Pub. Records
Dept. of Administration
1313 Sherman St.
Denver, CO 80203

Year Adoption
Records Closed
1942

Hospital Records
Available?
Difficult

Legal Notice
Required?
Usually

Central Department of Motor Vehicles
Department of Revenue
Motor Vehicle Division
Master File Section
140 West Sixth Ave
Denver, CO 80204

Department of Revenue
Motor Vehicle Master Files
140 West Sixth Ave
Denver, CO 80204

National Archives - Rocky Mountain Region
Denver Federal Center, Bldg. 48
PO Box 25307
Denver, CO 80225-0307
(303) 236-0817; (303) 236-9354
Hours: Mon-Fri: 7:30SAM-3:45PM,
Wed: 7:30AM-4:45PM
(Serves Colorado, Montana, North
Dakota, South Dakota, Utah, and Wyoming)

Central Agency
Holding Adoption Records
Dept. Social Services (Adoptions)
1575 Sherman St.
Denver, CO 80203
(303) 866-3796

Non-Identifying
Info Provided?
Yes, by law;
Adoptees.
Adoptive Parents

Adoption Decree
From Court
Sometimes;
Juvenile Court
Denver; District

State
Registry
Yes:
Intermediary
System.
Court all other

(1989) ADOPTION DISCLOSURE STATUTES (INTERMEDIARY SYSTEM)
CO Rev Stat Section 19-5-207 (Supp 1990) mandates disclosure of non-identifying info; Section 19-4-104: court order for identifying info; 19-4-122: closed hearings. 1989: Intermediary System. Section 19-4-100: fees stated. No separate provision for medical info. Section 25-2-113.5: identifying information via Voluntary Adoption Registry to relay info with birthparent consent to adult adopted child. Section 19-4-115: compensation for placing a child is prohibited: Misdemeanor, $100 fine, 90 days in jail.

ADOPTION SEARCH/SUPPORT
GROUPS (see "Key" on page 47)

Gordon Kilpatrick-Pl
Confidential Search Inc.
PO Box 110100
Aurora CO 80049
cbkrenny@jimacomb.com

Maggie Pritchard
Adoptees In Search (AIS)
Parker, CO
meritch0201@msn.com

Mary Burton
Adoptees in Search (SS)
PO Box 24556
Denver, CO 80224
aisdenver@yahoo.com

Sandy Sedentko
9800 W. 34th Drive
Wheat Ridge, CO 80033
cuhdenver@aol.com

Anna McComas
CUB
460 Arapahoe Ave
Boulder, CO 80302

Isabel Caldell
PO Box 1425
Winter Park, CO 80482

Mary Redenius (SS)
CUB-Region 5 Director
2538 Keller Farm Dr.
Boulder, CO 80304

Beth Paddock ISC (S)
Adoptees in Search (AIS)
4631 Carter Trail
Boulder, CO 80301

Nancy Rudeen
Adoptees & Birthparents Together (SS)
5213 Miners Creek Court
Fort Collins, CO 80525
Rudeens@prodigy.net

Carol Schuh
Confiidential Intermediary
PO Box 260460
Lakewood, CO 80226

Susan Williams (S)
Loveland-I/Net Connection
PO Box 6006
Loveland, CO 80537

Sally McCracken
Adoption Crossroads (SS)
150 West Ridge Drive
Woodland Park, CO 80863

Carol Holliday
Adoption Option
2600 South Parker Road #2-230
Aurora, CO 80014

Karen Kottmeier
STAC State Representative
728 Meadow Station Circle
Parker, CO 80134
bobkot@aol.com

Victoria Ransler
CUB (SS)
10511 W 104th Ave.
Broomfield, CO 80020

Julie Pelton (SS)
Search & Support of Denver
805 S Ogden
Denver, CO 80209

Patricia Taylor
CUB (S)
2895 Springdale Lane
Boulder, CO 80303
jtaylr@aol.com

Gay Shockley (S)
Rocky Mountain Origins
PO Box 22692
Denver, CO 80222

Nancy Gumina (S)
80 Fir Lane
Evergreen, CO 80439

Betty Tyrell (S)
PO Box 33937
Northglenn, CO 80013
searchlink@earthlink.net

Ronald J. Nydam, PhD.
Colorado Adoption Dynamics
(Legislative Reform)
4301 E. Amherst, #212
Denver, CO 80222
rjnydam@calvin.edu

Nancy J. Sayeedi
2781 South Kearney
Denver, CO 80222

Mary Leverson
11083 West Mexico Drive
Lakewood, CO 80232

Mary Katherens
4001 South Rifle Ct.
Aurora, CO 80013
timeout757@aol-com

DearAmFOR: ... "I made a phone call to Pat Pascoe's office, and she was good enough to phone me back, this being a toll call: We had a rather good talk, and I think she wants to give help to the adoptee. What holds her up is what holds up most people these days—the 'confidentiality' supplied hang up. I have sent her some material, and will be further helpful, if possible. She sounded like a good person.

I don't know how this hang-up on 'confidentiality,' supplied especially to parents, can be overcome and give adopted people a sense of freedom and responsibility in search, except the time ever comes when we wrestle with the factor of illegitimacy. It is something no one, positively no one will talk about. I looked through the entire program of the AAC in NYC and there was not one whiff of it mentioned ... I have made copies of your one-page legal proposal for sending out to people. I do like it so much. It is designed to make attorneys scratch their heads ... Best wishes to you. I asked Kate Burke why AAC can't be liaison with you. I enclose a few items, and wish to encourage you as I can in what you are doing ... Sincerely, JEAN PATON, (FOUNDER OF THE OPEN RECORDS MOVEMENT, 1953, and ORPHAN VOYAGE), formerly of Cedaredge, CO."

Dear AmFOR:... "In 1976 I gave up a baby boy for adoption and I am interested in having my name on file when or if he decides to find me ... Thank you, M.B., Colorado Springs, CO."

Dear AmFOR:... "I have been trying to get any helpful information on my parents and have had no luck. I was born in Colorado and all the records are closed. I would appreciate any help I could get... Thank you, GREG U., Weskan, KS."

Dear AmFOR: . . . "This letter is to inform you that I have found Greg's mother and contact has been made. She wants to know about him and I am in the process of writing her. She in turn is also going to write to Greg. He has a lot of mixed feelings at this point, but we are relieved that we have found her and not been rejected. I want to thank you for your help and support in the past... Sincerely, JULIE U., Weskan, KS."

Dear AmFOR: . . . "My husband is an adult adoptee in search of his mother. At present, he has a Confidential Intermediary working his case. Any information you can provide to help us through this ordeal and to have our voices heard for Open Records would be greatly appreciated ... Sincerely, K.L.E-S., Colorado Springs, CO."

Dear AmFOR:... "Here I am sending you more information about myself. The only thing my Mom told me was that the nuns said that I had an identical twin sister. If possible I would like to locate her. I am a 41 yr. old Hispanic woman, petite 4 ft. 11 in. tall weigh 122 pounds . . . Please hurry; I have severe high blood pressure, and I had a very serious spine accident in 1980. Thank you for your time and bother ... JOYCE M., La Jara, CO."

Connecticut

CENTRAL RECORDS OFFICES

Connecticut State Dept. of Public Health
State Office of Vital Records
PO Box 304308
Hartford. CT 06134-0308   Accessible?
(860) 509-7700   Genealogy
available from State Office, fee
Requests must be
submitted to town where event occurred.

State (St), County (Co),
Birth (B). Death (D),
Marriage (M). Divorce (DV)
Indices & Records
St-B,D,M since 7/1897
St-Dv since 6/47
  Co-B,D,M Registrar VS
Pre-1897, Town Registrar
www.vitalrec.com/ct.html

State Archives Address	Year Adoption Records Closed	Hospital Records Available?	Legal Notice Required?
Dept. of Archives & Records	1974	Difficult	Sometimes

Connecticut State Library
231 Capitol Ave.
Hartford, CT 06115

Central Department of Motor Vehicles
Department of Motor Vehicles
Copy Record Section
60 State St.
Wethersfield, CT 06102

National Archives - New England Region
380 Trapelo Road
Waltham, MA 02154
(617) 647-8100
  Hours: Mon-Fri & 1st Sat: 8AM-4:30PM
  (Serves CT, ME, MA, NH, RI and VT)

Central Agency Holding Adoption Records	Non-Identifying Info Provided?	Adoption Decree From Court	State Registry
Dept. Children/Youth (Adoptions)	Yes, by law;	Sometimes;	Yes;
505 Hudson Street	Adoptees,	Superior Court	Intermediary
Hartford, CT 06106	Adoptive Parents	Waiver System.	
(860) 550-6463			

(1987/1995) ADOPTION DISCLOSURE STATUTES (REGISTRY, INTERMEDIARY AND WAIVER SYSTEM)
Section 45-68m: locked files. Court order for disclosure of information before adopted child has reached majority for medical reasons. CT SB-1162: Registry System, Oct. 1987. No fees stated. Section 45-68c: information about birthparent to: adoptive parent and adopted child at majority. Adoptees (adult) may go directly to DCYS (Department of Children and Youth Services) for release of identifying information rather than the Court. If information is either denied or excessively delayed, appeals to the Court will result in the appointment of a review panel to recommend action. Bill 1162 passed in October 1987 removed the requirement that adoptive parents be informed (and be given the right to be interviewed) when adult adoptees seek identifying information. DCYS and other agencies are required, too. to maintain letters and waivers actively in a file, and to release identifying information when two parties consent. Birthparents have the right to obtain a copy of non-identifying information (previously, only non-id info about themselves were released). A search must be conducted within 60 days after an adult adoptee requests same.

Section 45-68m: penalty for unauthorized disclosure of info $500 fine and/or 6 mos. jail. Section 45-63c: penalty for violation of adoption provisions $5,000 and/or 1-5 years. Mass black market/gray market-physician assisted adoptions, 1950 to 1990's in Connecticut revealed in *Carangelo/Shafrick v. O'Neill/State of CT*, H-90-21-EBB, filed 1/10/90, U.S. District Court of Connecticut, challenging Constitutionality of falsification/ sealing of birth records as government protected child stealing; U.S. Supreme Court refused to hear. The 1950's-60's black market baby broker, Bessie Bernard, sold babies in New York and Connecticut.

Effective October 1, 1995, the adoption law (Public Act (95-179, House Bill 5486) was amended. The following is a brief overview of the changes to the adoption search law. See also CT General Statutes Sections 45a-744 to 754.

Genetic parents who were party to proceedings for termination of parents' rights may initiate a search for an adult adoptee or adult adoptable person. Putative fathers may initiate a search for the adult adoptee or adoptable person with the written consent of the genetic parent whose parental rights were terminated.

A genetic parent whose parental rights were terminated on or after October 1, 1995 can initiate a search for the adult adoptee without consent of the other genetic parent. Those whose parental rights were terminated before October 1, 1995 must have the consent of the other genetic parent.

Adult biological siblings of adult adoptees or adult adoptable persons may initiate a search for the adult adoptee without written consent of the genetic parents whose parental rights were terminated if such proceedings occurred on or after October 1, 1995. Prior to that date, both genetic parents need to give their consent.

The adult adoptee or adult adoptable person's identifying information may not be released without said individual's informed consent.

All parties entitled to search for adult adoptees or adoptable persons may be charged a reasonable fee to conduct such searches. The Children's Center (Hamden, CT) and other CT adoption agencies have been known to retain fees ($150 or more) without provision of services.

ADOPTION SEARCH/SUPPORT GROUPS (see "Key" on page 47)

Lucille Shea
46 Candlewood Dr.
South Windsor, CT 06074
lucilleshea@prodigy.net

Denise Parent
Adoption Healing (SG)
344 Grovers Ave #3
Bridgeport, CT 06605

Barbara Willie
Adoption Healing (SG)
2 Hadik Pky, #F-2
South Norwalk, CT 06854
bjwillie@aol.com

Birthparent Support Group
55 Old Williamantic Rd.
Columbia, CT 06237

Natalie Oliver
989 Ott Dr.
Chesire, CT 06410

Karen Waggoner
CUB
PO Box 558
Bethel, CT 06801

BIRTH INDEXES:
Jane Servadio
Adoption Healing
PO Box 3119
Milford, CT 06460
janerino@optionline.net

Nancy Sitterly
Adoptees Search Connection
1203 Hill Street
Suffield, CT 06078

Mary Ellen Rodriques
Adoption Crossroads (SG)
956 Broad St.
Stratford, CT 06497

Judy Taylor
AASK(SS.AAC)
8 Homestead Dr.
South Glastonbury, CT 06073
jtaylr@aol.com

Ray Thomas
Genealogist/Searcher
836 Marion Ave.
Plantsville, CT 06479

Dear AmFOR:... "By some weird hunch I ended up in Yale's Sterling Library! I know that my mother was born in 1921 and I have a hunch that she's from the New Haven area—well it seems that the Sterling Library has all the birth announcements for 1921 on microfilm—so I'm sure I'll be going back there as there are only 12 tapes to go through for that year. I'll tell you one thing—you need real strong magnifying glasses!... If I petition the Court will I save my money? She said that it's easier for the child to find the natural birthmother than vice versa ... Love, DEE H., Wallingford, CT."

Dear AmFOR:... "I've been following your story in the New Haven Register. Don't ever give up!... We felt what it must be like for you, especially for Allyson. She wants to so badly find her mother.

Ever since I met her when she was 14 (and now she's 20). . . it's been hard for her to get information. She's been working on it since she turned 18. You see it was even harder because her parents didn't want her to do this, especially her mother. Her mother is very insecure, and has problems, and instead of working with Allyson on it she fought her all the way, until she finally found out herself who to contact, and where to get information. She is now working with some organization that helps people like her, and she's gotten so much information it's just incredible. All she needs now is the woman's name and where she lives . . . Allyson feels that anyone who is adopted wants to know where they are really from and things about themselves .. . You are in my prayers. God works in strange ways . . . L.C., CT."

Dear AmFOR: . . . "My reunion went super well, thank God Almighty! My daughter found the letters I sent to her parents (one for her) and left home. Seems they were not getting along at all and she would have left anyway. So they pushed her away themselves ... I am certainly not 'giving her up' again to make anyone else happy!! Hurrah! . . . Love, MRS. MARY F., Portland, CT."

Dear AmFOR:.. . "Bring in the band! 30 year search is over! Yesterday afternoon was the happiest day in my life. A few weeks ago my adopters received a call from Russ Mercer of CT Dept. of Children & Youth Services. I didn't call him, probably because I was so frustrated ... Anyway, Mr. Mercer called twice to Mr. Rick Fowler; Children's Home Society, Ft. Myers, Florida—the man who made this long search easier to handle. He has friends to help adoptees find their families. I think I would have given up, if it wasn't for Rick's persistence and kindness to me ... It was the best news I have had in 30 years! Mr. Mercer said, 'I have found your mother and she is receptive to contact.' Mr. Mercer said that the reason he was ready to give up on this search because she had changed her name. She didn't like her first name and now goes by her middle name. She remarried;

I have two half siblings, a brother that is 22 and sister that is 25. She had moved several times and lives in a town near where I was raised, about eight miles away! I was real nervous, almost ready to cry, sweaty palms, butterflies in the stomach. He dialed the phone number and walked out of the room. Every ring was a loud heartbeat. . . All of a sudden the other person on the receiver dropped the phone and I heard 'Mom! Mom! John's on the phone!' I'm getting goosebumps again!... I always believed in my heart that she always wanted me to find her! I told everyone this. I feel that adoptees have this special gift, and pray to be prepared for anything in their search ... .A few moments of silence; I heard a soft woman's voice say 'Hello, John." I'm crying right now ... She asked me how I am doing, she told me she never wanted to lose me, she always loved me. I talked to her, my half brother and her husband, who is only 3 years older than me. I'm 30. She is 50. She said a lot in 3-1/2 hours on this call. My ear was sore; I have never been on the phone that long. She told me that she thinks about me all the time ... Many times the phone got quiet. I didn't want to say the wrong things. I wanted this to be a nice and adult talk. Really, I just wanted to hear her voice; my heart was getting restored. She told me something about my heritage. Come to find out that I had a lot of mixes. I said to her, 'Man, I'm a mongrel' (laughing). I joked with her a few times. I can joke in any predicament. I was told by her that she would like to see me as soon as possible. She said she loves me. She said her door is always open for me (boy, that threw me for a loop). Anyway, she will write to me and send pictures. I just have sent her the first one ... I will write back to you once Thank you a lot, Lori, for your support. You have been a true friend! Peace, JOHN J., Salvation Army Lodge, Ft. Meyers, FL."

Dear AmFOR: ... "I am writing to you with my support of your Open Records policy. As a person involved in a family genealogy search, I am having a lot of trouble with 'closed records' in the state of Connecticut. As my entire family was in this state for as far back as it existed, it makes it very hard to obtain the information I need when many of the records are 'confidential.'

I fully support the open records policy on any vital statistics ... Sincerely, MOLLY S., Midland Park, CT."

Delaware

CENTRAL RECORDS OFFICES

Vital Records

Address & Phone		State (St), County (Co),
To Verify Fees		Birth (B), Death (D),
(rec = recorded message)		Marriage (M), Divorce (DV)
Bureau of Vital Stats	Accessible?	Indices & Records
PO Box 637	Restricted;	St-B,D,M since 1861
Dover, DE 19903	fee	St-Dv since 3/32, Inq fwd
(302)744-4549		Co-B,D,M, No Co records
www.vitalrec.com/de.html		Co-Dv, Co Prothonotary

State Archives	Year Adoption	Hospital Records	Legal Notice
Address	Records Closed	Available?	Required?
Dept. of State	Unknown	Unknown	Unknown
Hall of Records			
Dover, DE 19901			

Central Department of Motor Vehicles	National Archives - Mid-Atlantic Region
Motor Vehicles Dept. (Drivers Licenses)	Ninth and Market Streets, Room 1350
PO Box 698	Philadelphia, PA 19107; (215) 597-3000
Dover, DE 19903	(Serves DE, PA, MD, VA, WV; primarily
	genealogical records)

Central Agency	Non-Identifying	Adoption Decree	State
Holding Adoption Records	Info Provided?	From Court	Registry
Children/ Youth/Family (Adoptions)	Yes, but law	Yes;	No.
1825 Faulkland Road	gives agency	Superior,	
Wilmington, DE 19805	discretion.	Orphans Court.	

ADULT ADOPTEES (AGE 21) CAN ACCESS ORIGINAL BIRTH CERTIFICATE ON REQUEST.

DE Code Ann. Tit. B., Section 924: Records sealed; court order required to release info; medical info; blood relative of adoptee, for medical reasons. Gives agency discretion re: non-identifying info. Adult adoptee access to birth certificate unless "birth" parent files contact veto.

ADOPTION SEARCH/SUPPORT GROUPS (see "Key" on page 47)

Ginger Farrow	Trialog	Bob Slaughter
Finders Keepers (HQ)(SS)	2005 Baynard Blvd.	Richer Life
PO Box 748	Wilmington, DE 19802	2400 Baynard Blvd. # 2
Bear, DE 19701		Wilmington, DE 19802
searchde@aol.com	Carolyn S. Hoard	http://RicherLife.net
	STAC State Contact	
Ann Hudson (C)	20 Yeats Dr.	Peggy Bohanan
339 Troon Rd.	New Castle, DE 19720	DE Adoption Reunion Registry
Dover, DE 19901		529 Roberta Ave
		Dover, DE 19901
		degal@dol.com

Dear AmFOR:... "Thank you, thank you for all that great info you sent me. You've given me hope for the first time in 20 years. I won't give up until I find my son! It makes one feel good to find others concerned about 'Human Rights' and doing something about it... Thanks again, Lori, for your quick response and I'm with you all the way ... Sincerely, SUSAN Z., Rehoboth, DE."

District of Columbia

Vital Records To Verify Fees (rec = recorded message)		State (St), County (Co), Birth (B), Death (D), Marriage (M), Divorce (DV)
Dept. Human Resourcs Vital Records Section 825 N. Capit 1 St. NE #1312 Washington, DC 20002 (202)442-9309 www.vitalrec.com/dc.html	Accessible? Restricted; fee	Indices & Records St-B since 1871 ;D-1855 St-M,Dv since 9/16/56 Co-B,M,D; no Co/Civil War Co-M.Dv; no Civil War death records

Marriage Bureau
515 5th St., NW
Washington, DC 20001

Clerk-Superior Court   Records since 9/16/56
for DC-Family Division
500 Indiana Ave., NW
Washington, DC 20001

Clerk-U.S. District Court   Records before 9/16/56
for District of Columbia
Washington, DC 20001

State Archives Address	Year Adoption Records Closed	Hospital Records Available?	Legal Notice Required?
Library of Congress Annex Washington, DC 20540 or District of Columbia Archives 1300 Naylor, NW/Washington, DC 20001	1935	Yes	Seldom

Central Department of Motor Vehicles
Department of Transportation
Bureau of Motor Vehicles
301 "C" St., NW
Washington, DC 20001

National Archives & Administration -
Archives II
The National Archives at College Park
(location: 8601 Adelphi Road, College
Park, MD 20740-6001)
(mailing address: 7th & Pennsylvania Ave.,
NW, Washington, DC 20408
(301)713-6800
Hours: Mon-Fri: 8:45AM-5PM; Research
        Rooms: Mon & Wed: 8:45AM-5PM,
        Tues &Thurs-Fri: 8:45AM-9PM,
        Sat: 8:45AM-4:45PM
(Some records from the Washington, DC/Suitland,
MD archives buildings have been transferred to
Archives II; no genealogy records; includes Nixon
Presidential Materials; Research Rooms; Electronic,
Cartographic, Motion Picture, Sound, Video, Still
Picture Branches.)

Central Agency Holding Adoption Records	Non-Identifying Info. Provided?	Adoption Decree From Court	State Registry
Dept Health/ Human Services/Adoptions 609 "H" St., NE, 3rd Floor Washington, DC 20002	Yes, but law gives court	No; Domestic Relations Court. discretion.	No.

(1988) ADOPTION DISCLOSURE STATUTE

Section 16-311: Records sealed; court order required to release info. DC Code Ann 16-311(1989) gives court discretion re: disclosure of non-identifying info.

ADOPTION SEARCH/SUPPORT GROUPS (see "Key" on page 47)

Alan Talbert (S C)
110 Parkside Dr.
Silver Spring, MD 20910

Kinship, Inc.
232 2nd St., SE
Washington, DC 20003

Earle Barnes/ Metro Reunion Registry
6439 Woodridge Rd.
Alexandria, VA 22312
ebarns@erols.com

Linda Clausen
CUB
PO Box 15258
Chevy Chase, MD 20825
dcmtrocab@aol.com

Joanne W. Small
Adoptees in Search
PO Box 41016
Bethesda, MD 20824
AIS20824@aol.com

Tracy Mayo
ABSN—VA/DC
PO Box 8273
McLean, VA22106
tlmayo@aol.com

Dear AmFOR: ... "I recently read an article in the July edition of FIRST Magazine which listed your organization as one of several working for rights of adoptees. I am in total agreement with the concept of open records for adoptees ... I am a professional fire fighter and I was recently hospitalized for cardiac irregularities following a strenuous fire. In follow-up treatment, my Cardiologist suggest I try to obtain some sort of medical background. I was able to obtain non-identifying data from Catholic Charities in Washington, DC but nothing useful. When I obtained this information, my curiosity increased and I called them back and inquired about obtaining identifying data. They referred me to an Attorney who has done some work with them in the past on similar cases. I contacted this attorney and frankly I cannot afford his terms at this time. In essence, I would be taking at least a $525.00 gamble that parents are still alive or would want a reunion, etc. I was able to find out that my birthmother came from a large family in Pennsylvania and so I know that I must have some aunts, uncles, cousins, etc. I am seeking out this information simply because it is something I have always thought about but did not act on because I felt it might upset my adopters. I would appreciate any information or assistance your agency might be able to give me. I think that I should be able to petition the courts to open my records without representation by an attorney. Thank you in advance . . . Sincerely, MALCOLM A. LIGHTFOOT, Port Neches, TX."

Dear AmFOR: ... "I am a 37 year old adoptee who decided several years ago to search for my "birth" parents. Although mine was not so much a search as it was a game of waiting and being at the mercy of the adoption agency and the Washington, DC Superior Court only to be hopelessly and frustratingly disappointed in the end. I am currently very interested in adoptees' rights in searching for parents. I strongly believe that sealed adoption records are not only unconstitutional but are a government sanctioned and legalized form of discrimination against adoptees. Enclosed are letters which I have sent to each and every member of the House and Senate in Washington, DC expressing my personal views. I would greatly appreciate any information you could give me on becoming involved with your organization. I am specifically interested in legislation at the federal level providing adoptees rights to their sealed adoption records .. . Sincerely, MRS. JULIA D., Herndon, VA."

Dear AmFOR:... "I much appreciate your letter of June 19 and the enclosed materials, which are very interesting. I regret to say I would not be able to represent Melanie Sandoval. The project for NEHGS is taking up all the time I can devote to this issue. To make a proposal to our pro bono committee, I would need to know exactly what she is seeking and what the response has been ... Joseph Doss of this firm will be glad to see Melanie Sandoval if a mutually convenient time can be arranged.

I had my secretary call Ms. Best of Family and Child Services. She was told that the report to Ms. Sandoval had been delayed by Ms. Best's illness but would be sent within a week from now. Possibly this will solve the problem; I hope so ... As you doubtless know, most if not all jurisdictions purport to have procedures through which non-identifying medical information can be made available to adoptees, together with identifying information if the parents' consent. To obtain identifying information for medical reasons without such consent, a convincing case would have to be made that identification is necessary for the medical purpose in question.

While if I were a judge I would probably hold that an adoptee has a constitutionally protected right to obtain identifying information without consent. That argument has been consistently rejected by the courts and I think it unlikely that that will change. Our NEGHS project is moving towards legislative recommendations that are somewhat more modest, though certainly we would not oppose a proposal for completely open records.

One of our principal concerns is that fictitious birth certificates, without any indication that they are such, in a few generations will make it impossible for anyone to trace his/her ancestry through public records with any confidence; even if he has no adopted ancestors, he will have no way of knowing that he doesn't. That is the reason for urging that fictitious certificates be required to have an annotation "amended" or some such word . . . Yours sincerely, BRICE M. CLAGETT, COVINGTON & BURLING, ATTORNEYS, 1201 Pennsylvania Ave., NW, PO Box 7566, Washington, DC 20044."

Florida

CENTRAL RECORDS OFFICES

Vital Records To Verify Fees (rec = recorded message) Dept. of Health Rehab. Div. Health, Bureau of Statistics, PO Box 210 Jacksonville, FL 3 2231 (904) 359-6900-rec www.vitalrec.com/fl.html	Accessible? Public; fee plus search fee	State (St), County (Co), Birth (B), Death (D), Marriage (M), Divorce (DV) Indices & Records St-B since 1865: D-1877 St-B,D most since 1/17 St-M, Dv since 6/6/27 Co-B,D,M,Dv Circuit Court	

State Archives Address Florida State Library Archives & Records RA Graves Bldg. 500 S. Bronough St. Tallahassee, FL 32301	Year Adoption Records Closed 1978	Hospital Records Available? Difficult	Legal Notice Required? Yes

Central Department of Motor Vehicles Driver License Division Department of Highway Safety Neil Kirkham Building 2900Apalachee Parkway Tallahassee, FL 32399	National Archives - Southeast Region 1557 Saint Joseph Ave. East Point, GA 30344 (404) 763-7477 Hours: Mon &Wed-Fri: 7:30AM-4:30PM, Tue 7:30AM-9:30PM (Serves AL, GA, FL, KY, MS, NC, SC. TN)

Central Agency Holding Adoption Records Dept. Child/Families/Adoption 1317WinewoodBlvd, #7 Tallahassee, FL 32399-0700	Non-Identifying Info Provided? Yes, by law; All Triad.	Adoption Decree From Court Sometimes; Circuit Court.	State Registry Yes; Intermediary system.

(1985) ADOPTION DISCLOSURE STATUTES (REGISTRY AND INTERMEDIARY SYSTEM)
Section 63.162: closed hearings; court order required to release info; Florida Statue Annotated Section 63.164 (Supp. 1985) provides a Registry System. Section 63.162: info about medical and social history of birth family shall be made available before adoption becomes final to adoptive parent and to adopted child when s/he reaches majority. Section 63.162: name and identity of birth parent will be disclosed with their consent, if (1) adopted child authorizes, if over 18; (2) adoptive parent authorizes if adoptee is a minor; (3) court order for good cause. Ann Code Section 63.162 (West Supp. 1992) mandates disclosure of non-identifying info. Registry and Intermediary System, since 1985.

ADOPTION SEARCH/SUPPORT GROUPS (see "Key" on page 47)

Alice Syman

Orphan Voyage PO Box 5495 St. Augustine, FL 32085 asyman@aug.com	Pat Jakubek (SG) Adoption Triangle 1301 NW 2nd Ave. Delray Beach, FL 3344	Orphan Voyage-Jacksonville 24409 Moss Creek Lane Ponte Verde, FL 32082
		Kathleen Sokolik
Luanne Pruesner Research, Reconnect, & Reunite 10714WestmontRd Leesburg, FL 34788 luannep@aol.com	Justus/Susan Weinstein (SG) GAIN/Adoptnet 130NW28thSt. Gainesville, FL 32607	STAC State Contact (SS) Adoption Connection of Florida 3100 Hunter Rd. Ft. Lauderdale, FL 33331

Rachel Rivers
Organized Adoption Search Info.
  Service (OASIS) (SS)
PO Box 53-0761
Miami Shores, FL 33153

Cyndy Williams (SG)
Circle of Hope
PO Box 491
Pahokee, FL 22476

Denise Mardenborough (SS)
Adoption Search & Support
1604 Norwood Ln.
Tallahassee, FL 32312

Ruth Collings
Comcerned United Birthparents
museumfan@earthlink.net

Orphan Voyage
13505 SE 100 Ct.
Miami, FL 33176

Nancy Lloyd
Adoption Connection
4730 - 83rd Avenue North
Pinellas Park, FL 33781

Marsha Long - PI
1206 - 38th Avenue
St. Petersburg, FL 33704
search1@juno.com

Alix Perry
13 Wood Ash Lane
Palm Coast, FL 32164

Sandy Musser (SG)
Lifelinks
117 SE 44th Terrace
Cape Coral, FL 33914
mussl03@aol.com

June Lewis
Active Voices in Adoption (SS)
PO Box 24-9052
Coral Gables, FL 33124
adopt@bellsouth.net

Fred R. Saluga
PO Box 7522
Daytona Beach, Fl. 32116

Alvie Davidson
PO Box 509
Kathleen, FL 33849

Joanne Steenbergen (former ALARM)
16208 Marshfield Dr.
Tampa, FL 33624

Marilyn Carver
Birthparent & Adoptee Search
2629 Gordan Bella Avenue
St. Augustine, FL 32086

Birthparent Support Group (SG)
176 Harris St., NE
Ft. Walton Beach, FL 32547

Suzie Kuka (SG)
Adoption Support & Knowledge
11646 NW 19th Dr.
Coral Springs, FL 33071

Tallahassee Adoption Support Group
275 John Knox Rd., #F-104
Tallahassee, FL 32303

Judy Young (SS)
Adoption Search & Support
PO Box 3504
Tallahassee, FL 32315

Molly Johnson, Robert Rooks
Orphan Voyage
134 E. Church St. #2
Jacksonville, FL 32207

Sheila Stanford
Orphan Voyage (SS)
Rt. 1 - Box 244
Waldo, FL 32694

Linda Knotts
Mid-Florida Adoption Reunions (SS)
PO Box 3475
Belleview, FL 32621
Sandi Hill
Greenacres, FL
Circle92@bellsouth.net
Circle92@juno.com

Kathryn Spragg
2605 W. Alcuts Dr.
Beverly Hills, FL 32655

Adoption Consultants, Inc.
9329 SW 170th St.
Miami, FL 33157

Sondi K. Hill
Circle of Hope
3530 Pine Tree Court #A-2
Greenacres, FL 33463
circle92@bellsouth.net

Anne Slagle
ALMA
PO Box 4358
Ft. Lauderdale, FL 33381

Bertie Hunt, 15C
Triad (SS)
3408 Neptune Dr.
Orlando, FL 32804
sherlock315@juno.com

National Search Hotline
PO Box 100444
Palm Bay, FL 32910

Chris Adamac
PACE
1921 Ohio St., NE
Palm Bay, FL 32907

Marguerite Smith (SG)
Adoption Connection
5524-F Lakewood Cir.
Margate, FL 33063

Jay Swearingen
Orphan Voyage (SG)
13906 Pepperell Dr.
Tampa, FL 33624

Janice Finland
TRIAD-Central FL (SS)
2359 Summerfield Rd.
Winter Park, FL 32792
jmfruland@juno.com

Sue Eisman (S)
16552 Offenhaur Rd.
Odessa, FL 33556

Dear AmFOR: . . . "As was discussed per our last phone conversation Senator Weinstock has some reservations regarding your proposal to repeal sealed adoption records laws. She feels that she can not sponsor such a bill at this time but did want to thank you for sharing the information with her . . . Sincerely, WENDY D., LEGISLATIVE ASSISTANT, SENATOR ELEANOR WEINSTOCK, 26th District, The Florida Senate."

DearAmFOR:... "Just a note to let you know I am still here and still working the OASIS puzzle ... Your writings are just fantastic, Lori. When it comes to doing news-script, you have it all in hand. I read your yellow mail-out with much interest and appreciation. You can count OASIS in on your list update ... we are now as we have always been a State of Florida chartered organization, not for profit, and offer self-help information free of charge. If asked to do an entire search, it is generally under $100 which is barely expense money. I fear, Lori, that if we charge a fee for searching, we would be in the poor house. It has and always will be the nature of this work that money is what most adoptees have the least of... self-esteem being the forerunner. With all good wishes to you, always, I am ... Sincerely yours, RACHEL S. RIVERS, ORGANIZED ADOPTION SEARCH INFORMATION SERVICES, INC. (OASIS), PO Box 53-0761, Miami Shores, FL33153."

Dear AmFOR:... "My mother has tried to forget that she was forced to give up a baby due to financial impossibilities. She has done a good job of keeping her secret for approximately 33-38 years and has, therefore, also forgotten facts and dates. However, for some reason she told me now, and is sure the baby was a boy, delivered in the Doctor's office ... Mother is having some heart problems at her age of 79. If you can help us to find this young man, my sisters and I would like to break the news to her gently, if at all. I understand that this information would be hers to choose what to do with; however, we are anxious to know if, perhaps, our brother wants to know us. Has he been looking also?... We anxiously await your reply ... Cordially, MRS. W.J.B., Kenner, LA."

Dear AmFOR:... "In December 1975 I had to give my baby up for adoption, I had gone to Miami, FL to have that child. I can't remember what hospital I had her in: yes I knew what I had, but I was only 18.1 was of age to keep my child but under circumstances, I couldn't. I was hoping you or some other organization can help me find her... I am very anxious to find my daughter. I pray to God you or someone you know can help me. In hope . . . Sincerely, C.C., Wallington, N.J."

Dear AmFOR:... "My husband, Donald Wallace Johnson, III, was adopted over 27 years ago. He has wanted to know, for just as long, who his parents are. It is now more important than ever, for he has a child and he is also having problems with his health. If nothing else, I want my husband to know his medical background, for our son's sake. My husband wants to know his parents to find out why he is the way he is ... Thank you, L.J., Statesville, N.C."

Georgia

CENTRAL RECORDS OFFICES

Vital Records		State (St), County (Co),
To Verify Fees		Birth (B), Death (D),
(rec = recorded message)		Marriage (M), Divorce (DV)
Vital Records, Rm 217H	Accessible?	Indices & Records
Dept of Human Resources	Immediate	St-B since 1919
2600 Skyland Drive	family;	St-M.Dv since 6/9/52
Atlanta, GA 30334	fee	Co-B,D,M Co Ordinary
(404) 679-4701-rec		Co-Dv Sup Ct Clerk
www.vitalrec.com/ga.html		

State Archives	Year Adoption	Hospital Records	Legal Notice
Address	Records Closed	Available?	Required?
Georgia State Library	1935	Difficult	No
301 State Judicial Bldg.			
Capitol Hill Station			
Atlanta, GA 30308			

Central Department of Motor Vehicles	National Archives - Southeast Region
Department of Public Safety	1557 Saint Joseph Ave.
Driver Service Section	East Point, GA 30344
Merit Rating	(404)763-7477
PO Box 1456	
Atlanta, GA 30301	

Central Agency	Non-Identifying	Adoption Decree	State
Holding Adoption Records	Info Provided?	From Court	Registry
Dept. Child/Family/Adoptions	Yes, by law;	Rarely;	Yes;
2 Peachtree St., NW, 13th fl	Adoptee,	Superior Court.	
Atlanta, GA 30308	Adop. Parents		
(404) 657-3458			

(1987) ADOPTION DISCLOSURE STATUTES (REGISTRY SYSTEM)
Section 19-8-18: Records sealed; court order required to release info. No specific provision for medical info. Ann Code Section 19-8-23 (Michic 1991) mandates disclosure of non-identifying info. Birthparent Registry.

ADOPTION SEARCH/SUPPORT GROUPS (see "Key" on page 47)

Georgi Tanis	Rick Derby	Adoption Reunion Registry
Adoption Beginnings (SS)	Home Base (SG)	2 Peachtree St., NW, Ste. 3-323
PO Box 440121	PO Box 624	Atlanta, GA 30303
Kennesaw, GA 30144	Evans, GA 30809	
		Jane Hart
	Peggy Band	AAC
Susan Russell	Families First (SS)	1712 Smithwood Drive
Adoptee Birthparent Connection (SS)	PO Box 7948 - Sta C	Atlanta GA 30357'
Marietta, GA 30062	peggy@familiesfirst.org	clindsay@aol.com
Denise Carroll	Leslie Pate Mackinnon	
Hand In Hand	The Triad Connection	
Lawrenceville, GA	Atlanta, GA	
Mainegirl1998@yahoo.com	lesliepatemackinnon@gmail.com	

Dear AmFOR:... "I was adopted at birth... Both my parents and my adopters did the adoption privately through an attorney. When I contacted the attorney, he told me that he could not help me locate my parents because he had worked for both sides. He also told me that I would have to get a court order to have my files opened. I don't have any idea how to begin this process or who to contact... CAROLINE F., Statesboro, GA."

Dear AmFOR: ... "I am a birthmother currently searching for my daughter. I am registering with all agencies in hopes of making a match. Due to the laws in Georgia I am not allowed access to my daughter's adoption file. Please send me information concerning your agency and how I may become involved in changing legislation to open sealed records. My daughter is eighteen as of March of this year. Thank you so much for your concern in this area and thank you for your help... SHARONE H., Atlanta, GA."

Dear AmFOR: ... "I was adopted in Fulton County, Georgia in October of 1969. My date of birth is March 14, 1969. The agency that handled my adoption was, at that point in time, called the Children's Home of Metropolitan in Atlanta ... I would appreciate any information you could send me . . . Thank you, KENDRA H., Lindale, GA."

Dear AmFOR:... "I want to express my appreciation for your offer to mediate with my mother. I am in deliberation on the specific action I want to take concerning her and will share more of this later. It is truly a difficult and painful experience to know someone who will not acknowledge giving birth to you much less a greeting of sort, after all these years. I can only thank those mothers who have replenished my soul from this grief and who give me the courage to prevail. All of this only reinforces the issue that 'We' need to change the system . . . Personally I believe there is need for a new "National Movement' inherit with the principles that effect the good of all rather than the few . . . Best thoughts to you, RONALD S., Rosewell, GA."

Dear AmFOR: ... "I was adopted in 1959. I have been looking for my mother for two years . . . BARBARA L., Pine Mountain., GA."

Hawaii

Vital Records
To Verify Fees
(rec = recorded message).

State (St), County (Co).
Birth (B), Death (D),Divorce (DV)
Marriage (M), Divorce

Research & Stats	Accessible?	Indices & Records
State Dept. of Health	Restricted;	St-B,D since 1853
PO Box 3378	fee	St-M,Dv since 7/51
Honolulu, HI 96801		Co-B,D Circuit Ct Clerk
(808) 586-4533-rec		
www.vitalrc.com/hi.html		

State Archives	Year Adoption	Hospital Records	Legal Notice
Address	Records Closed	Available?	Required?
State Archives	1968	Yes	Yes
Iolani Palace Grounds			
478 South King St.			
Honolulu, HI 96813			

Central Department of Motor Vehicles
Drivers Licenses
530 So. King St.
Honolulu, HI 96813

National Archives - Pacific Sierra Region
1000 Commodore Dr.
San Bruno, CA 94066
(415) 876-9009
Hours: M-F: 8AM-4PM, W: 8AM-8PM
(Serves CA, except So. CA; HI, NV, except
Clark County; Pacific Ocean area.)

Central Agency	Non-Identifying	Adoption Decree	State
Holding Adoption Records	Info Provided?	From Court	Registry
Dept.Human Services/Adoptions	Yes, by law;	Sometimes;	No;
800 Richards St-Ste. 400	All Triad.	Family Court.	Intermediary
Honolulu, HI 96813		Waiver System	
(808) 586-5704			

(1985) ADOPTION DISCLOSURE STATUTES (INTERMEDIARY AND WAIVER SYSTEM)
Section 578-14; records sealed; court order required to release info. Rev Stat Section 578.14.5 mandates disclosure of non-identifying info.

ADOPTION SEARCH/SUPPORT GROUPS (see "Key" on page 47)

ALMA
58-250 (C) Kam Hwy.
Halieva, HI 96712

Frances Harriman
PO Box 1223
Mountain View, HI 96771

Adoption Circle of Hawaii
Honolulu,HI
adoptioncirclehawaii@hotmail.com

Martha Hulbert, MA, RN
Triad Resources (SG)
55 Niuki Circle
Honolulu, HI 96821

Claudia Glienke ISC
Access Hawaii (SS)
PO Box 1120
Hilo, HI 96721

Robert Filipczak
Family Reconnections
2482-G Cochran Street
Kailua, HI 96734
Hm2Flip@yahoo.com

Erin Castillo
PO Box 61723
Honolulu, HI 96839
Hannigirl@aol.com

Los Angeles Times, 1/4/93, pageA5: "In Hawaii, Hanai Helps to Fill In for the Stork... Waimanalo, Hawaii —Kawehi Kanui was walking slowly, pregnant with her fifth child, when a friend approached. 'Kawehi,' she said, 'I have a question that will test how Hawaiian you are. May I have your baby?' Long before in-vitro fertilization and other high-tech methods of making babies, Hawaiians had their own way to balance the vagaries of nature. Those who were blessed with infants gave them to those who were not, a practice known as "hanai." Unlike Western-style adoption, which usually involves strangers and confidentiality, hanai takes place openly among family and close friends; a child is considered the greatest of gifts. Today, despite renewed celebration of native culture, some Hawaiians express concern this ancient custom may be slipping away . .. Historically, in addition to giving joy to childless couples, hanai cemented relations among families. The youngster kept a family tree alive and helped ensure transmission of cultural knowledge from generation to generation. When their daughter was born, Kawahine Kamakea-Ohelo and her husband, Kalani Ohelo, were struggling in poverty. They respected Kawaikapuokalani Hewett's expertise and fluency in Hawaiian, and decided that he could best raise little Leioheloulaopele.

'People ask me, "How could you give up your baby? She's so beautiful!" Kamakeo-Ohelo said, 'I tell them, we never gave up our baby. We're sharing our baby. And our family got bigger'. . . Judith Jenya Jackman, executive director of Global Children's Organization, which handles adoptions, suggests that hanai holds lessons for everyone involved with children. 'They can learn that children are not personal property,' she said. 'It's important for people, whether they have hanai, natural or adoptive children, to think of these children as temporary gifts in their life, not as possessions.'"

Dear AmFOR:... "The reason I am writing to you concerns the search referral for a lady named Georgia. Martha Hulbert refers all searches to me since she has no interest or knowledge of search ... At this time, there is no charge for my services—only expenses ... Thanks & Aloha, MARY G., Honolulu, HI."

Idaho

Vital Record To Verify Fees (rec = recorded messsage) Bureau of Vital Stats State Dept. of Health/Welfare Statehouse Mall 450 West State St. (208)334-5988 www.vitalrec.com/id.html	Accessible? Restricted; fee	State (St), County (Co), Birth (B), Death (D), Marriage (M), Divorce (DV) Indices & Records St-B.D since 1911 St-M,Dv since 1947 Co-B.D County Recorder

State Archives Address State Historical Society Library/Archives 450 North 4th St. Boise, ID 83702	Year Adoption Records Closed Unknown	Hospital Records Available? Unknown	Legal Notice Required? Unknown

Central Department of Motor Vehicles
Motor Vehicle Division
Drivers License
PO Box 7129
Boise, ID 83707

National Archives - Pacific Northwest Region
6125 Sand Point Way, NE
Seattle, WA 98115
(206) 526-6507
   Hours: M-F: 7:45AM-4PM,: 5-9PM
   (Serves ID, OR, and WA)

Central Agency Holding Adoption Records Div.Family Services/Adoptions PO Box 83720 Boise, ID 83720	Non-Identifying Info Provided? Yes, by law; Adoptee, Adoptive Parents	Adoption Decree From Court Adoptee access to court record on demand; Probate, Magistrate court.	State Registry Yes; Waiver System

(1985) ADOPTION DISCLOSURE STATUTES (REGISTRY AND WAIVER SYSTEM)

Section 16-1511: records sealed; court order required to release info upon motion of adoptive parent or adoptee. Idaho Code Section 39-259A (Supp. 1985) provides a Registry System. No fees stated. No separate medical info provision. Section 39-259A: Registry of adult adoptees who have consented to release of all identifying info about themselves and registry of birthparents who have consented to release identifying info about themselves and to birth siblings who have consented. If a match occurs, the information will be released. Section 16-1506 (3) (Michie Supp 1992) mandates disclosure of non-identifying info.

ADOPTION SEARCH/SUPPORT GROUPS (see "Key" on page 47)

Lots Wight ISC Joyce Krummes ISC Search Finders Of Idaho (SS) 1512 Shenandoah Boise, ID 83712 lowight@msn.com	Lois Melina Adopted Child (SG) PO Box 9362 Moscow, ID 83843	Ann Milward ISC (SS S C) Adoption Support Group PO Box 2316 Ketchum, ID 83340

Maureen Pirc
ICARE Investigations
4348 Maverick Way
Boise, ID 83709
MYTYMO@aol.com

Margaret Sisson
RT 1, Box 19-A
Cataldo, ID 83810

Lavone Morris
PO Box 219
Priest River, ID 83854

Patricia Jones
1311 E Commercial/PO Box 226
Wesler, ID 83672

Patricia Tulles
965 E 14th
Idaho Falls, ID 83401

Nancy Henderson PI - ISC
Henderson Assoc.
1520 17th St.
Boise, ID 83702
Nancyhapi@cs.com

Joan Babel
3400 Beverly St.
Boise, ID 83709

Martha Haumann
3802 Targee
Boise, ID 83705

Jan Cottrell - ISC
6223 West Dorian
Boise, ID 83709
jano25@juno.com

Barbara Cannon
2412 12th Ave.
Lewiston, ID 83654

Paula Davis
Search Light
PO Box 5341
Coeur d'Alene, ID 83814
Tspoonmom@aol.com

Barbara Hodgman (SG)
Triad Endeavors (SS)
PO Box 249
Pinehurst, ID 83850
gonk@nidlink.com

Pat Stewart
Dealing With Adoption
PO Box 691
Bonners Ferry, ID 83805

Nancy A. Campbell
Helping Hands / Healing Hearts
1101 West Emma #E
Coeur d'Alene, ID 83814

Dear AmFOR:... "I would be happy to work with you for a bill introduction next legislative session. The time for introductions has elapsed to develop an awareness or support for the concept this session. I would be interested in a measure to put in place an intermediary to whom requests could be made by those seeking information. Upon request the real parent(s) would be contacted to determine if they wanted to maintain anonymity. If so, that would be respected. If not, the adopted information seeker would be put in touch. That is probably the most extensive measure we would see in Idaho for starters. I would be happy to work on the issue in the interim . . . Sincerely, GAIL BRAY, ASSISTANT DEMOCRATIC LEADER, IDAHO STATE SENATE, Boise, ID."

Dear AmFOR:. . . "I'm a member of "Search Finders" of Idaho. In the packet I received from "Search Finders" was a newsletter written by you.

It really hurts to know how Congress and the advocate of sealed records, "Mr. Pierce", can shrug off someone's need in their personal life. I'm searching for my son. I finally—through the help of Joyce Krummes, Search Finders of Idaho, found out my son was adopted through Ada County. I now intend to go to court and try to find out more information with the help of Search Finders ... If you have any suggestions that I a searching parent can do, please let me know ... Thank you, R.F., Council, ID."

The Idaho Statesman, 1/4/89: "SEARCHING FOR FAMILIES—LOOKING FOR NATURAL PARENTS TURNS INTO LIFE-LONG PURSUIT... At times, Joyce Krummes feels like Sherlock Holmes, sifting through court documents, hospital records and other bits of information to find her man . . . The Boise woman is helping adopted adult children find their parents and to help parents find children they gave up. She will take her effort one step further this month when she hosts the organizational meeting of Search-Finders of Idaho ... A handful of states allow children to obtain their birth certificates when they're 18. Others require waivers from the adoptees, parents and adopters before releasing information, says Lori Carangelo, director of Americans For Open Records... Krummes began with the search for her own mother two years ago after she had her first child... A little more sleuth work and she was talking to her mother, a wealthy yacht saleswoman in the Bahamas. Though they haven't met yet because of the distance between the Bahamas and Boise, Krummes says the search has been worth it."

Dear AmFOR: ... "Twenty years ago my son was taken from me at birth by my parents ... I have the attorneys name that I believe handled this for my parents. I want to see the records. Can you please help me find my son? ... In Christ's love. D.H., Boise, ID."

Dear AmFOR: ... "I was born on December 30, 1969 at Saint Alphonsus Hospital in Boise, ID. The only other thing that I know, is that my father was killed in the Vietnam War, and this is the reason I was given up for adoption, or so I was told. I'm also under the understanding that my biological mother was sixteen years old. I would really like your help in this matter and anything that I need to do, or pay, please contact me. I have faith that you understand my situation and my feelings about it. Thank you very much for your time and response to my letter ... Sincerely, C.D.G., Beaverton, OR. "

Illinois

Vital Records To Verify Fees (rec = recorded message). Office Vital Records	Accessible?	State (St), County (Co). Birth (B), Death (D). Marriage (M), Divorce (DV) Indices & Records
State Dept. Health	Genealogy;	St-B,D since 1/1916
605 W Jefferson St.	fee	St-D since 1962
Springfield, IL 62761		Co-B,D,M Co. Clerk
(217) 782-6553-rec		
www.vitalrec.com/il.html		

State Archives Address	Year Adoption Records Closed	Hospital Records Available?	Legal Notice Required?
Illinois State Archives	1945	From doctor	Yes
State Archives Bldg./Capital Complex			
Springfield, IL 63706			

Central Department of Motor Vehicles
Secretary of State
Driver Services Department
2701 South Dirksen Pkwy.
Springfield, IL 62723

National Archives - Great Lakes Region
7358 South Pulaski Rd.
Chicago, IL 60629
(312) 353-0162
Hours: M& W-F: 8AM-4:15PM.
Tu: 8AM-8:30PM
(Serves IL, IN, MI, MN, OH and WI)

Central Agency Holding Adoption Records	Non-Identifying Info Provided?	Adoption Decree From Court	State Registry
Children/ Family Serv/Adoptions	Yes, by law;	Sometimes;	Yes;
406 E. Monroe -Stn. 225	All Triad.	Circuit Court	Intermediary
Springfield, IL 62706-1498			System
(217) 524-2422			

(1986) ADOPTION DISCLOSURE STATUTES (REGISTRY AND INTERMEDIARY SYSTEM)
Section 1522: the words "illegitimate" or "born out of wedlock" will not be used in records. Records maintained in locked files; court order required to release info. Illinois Statute Title 40 Section 1522.1 (Supp. 1986) provides a Registry System. Section 1522:1: Dept. of Health shall establish a Registry; information shall be supplied where both adoptee over age 21 and birthparent haven consented to release information. Chapter 40, ^|1522-4 (Smith-Hurd Supp., 1992) mandates disclosure of non-identifying info).

ADOPTION SEARCH/SUPPORT GROUPS (see "Key" on page 47)

Karen Saunders
The Lost Connection (SS C)
2661 N. Illinois St., #147
Belleville, IL 62221

Gretchen Schulert
Midwest Adoption Center
3158 S. River Rd. Ste 120
De sPlaines, IL 60018

Sharon B. Keeling
Adoption Search & Support/CUB (SS)
1701 Riverview Dr.
Macomb, IL 61455
sbkreapP@macob.com

Lydia Granda
Adoption Triangle (SS)
512 OneidaSt.
Joliet, IL 60435

Michelle Mattes
Adoption Network(SS)
5070 Highwood Lane
Lake in the Hills, IL 60156

Bonnie Spinazza
222 E Pearsons#602
Chicago, IL 60611

Maggie Ruby
Missing Pieces (SG)
PO Box 7541
Springfield, IL 62791
GEM8450@aol.com

Jody Moreen
Adoptees/Birthparents/
Adoptive Parents Together
729 Zaininger Avenue
Naperville, IL 60563
adoption@kwom.com

Karen Shults
18921 Creekview
Mokena, IL 60448

Bonita Bis
CUB (SS)
835 Ridge Ave., #208
Evanston, IL 60202

Sandy Wisniewski
Family Tree (SG)
PO Box 233
Libertyville, IL 60202

Marlene Anderson
Heritage Finders
1337 Park Dr.
Montgomery, IL 60538

Barb Lollar (SG)
Heritage Finders
20955 S. Canterbury
Shorewood, IL 60436

Mark Sellin
18265 Ada St.
Lansing, IL 60438

Alice Lombard (SS S)
Heritage Finders
1102 Erie St.
Elgin, IL 60123

Cyndi Almada
9462 Bay Colony, 3-N
Des Plaines, IL 60018

Katrina Thomas
Reflections (SS)
1121 Stewart St., Rd
Carmi, IL 62821

Mike Egan ISC
Search Connection
PO Box 2425
Bridgeview, IL 69455
SEARCHCON@ix.netcom.com

Marilyn Strohkirch
Healing Hearts, Inc. (SS)
PO Box 606
Normal, IL 61761
Digger719@aol.com

Hidden Birthright
3241 Saxony Rd.
Springfield, IL 62705

CUB
156 W. Burton Pl.
Chicago, IL 60610

Woody Mitchell
ALMA
PO Box 74
Lebanon, IL 62254

Gloria Mummery
Natl Finders Adoption Registry
PO Box 46094
Chicago, IL 60646

Astrid Steinland
Salvation Army-Missing Persons
Division
10 West Algonquin Road
Des Plaines, IL 60016

Marylee MacDonald
CUB
734 Noyes Street #M-3
Evanston, IL 60201

Sally L. Gantz (AAC)
444 East 2150 North Road
DeLand, IL 61839

Kenneth Abraham
CUB
PO Box 304
Fox Lake, IL 60020

Darlene Fredman
The Locators
210 North Olive
Centerville, IL 62918

Mary Wilkins
Coalition for Truth in Adoption
PO Box 4638
Skokie, IL 60076

Anita Anderson
CUB
1401 East 55th Street #704
Chicago, IL 60615

Beth Duensing - ISC
CUB
PO Box 384
Park Forest, IL 60466
AdoptionTriangle@prodigy.net

Evelyn Eman Delmar, ED
Children Remembered Inc.
PO Box 234
Northbrook, IL 60065
mobiuSavant@gateway.net

Jessie Williams
For Birthmothers By Birthmothers
Chicago, IL
birthmomgroup@hotmail.com

Dear AmFOR:... "I am the facilitator of a mothers support group at Catholic Social Service of Rock Island. Since we are located in Illinois, but on the Iowa/Illinois border, there are women from both states in the group. Thus, we deal with the laws of two states—Illinois being the more liberal law with enforcement of that law being somewhat of a concern ... We are also interested in seeing laws of those states who have an understanding of parents. Any information on laws and/or your group would be appreciated ... Sincerely, LOIS WARNHOLZ, WOMEN-IN-NEED COUNSELOR, CATHOLIC SOCIAL SERVICE OF ROCK ISLAND, 413 NE Monore, PO Box 817, Peoria, IL."

get married, and go to war. This appears to adoptees a highly selective violation of their civil rights ...
Current law eases the situation somewhat because agencies may no longer willfully provide misleading
background information. The State Registry is not publicized, and used by so few it is virtually meaning-
less. Equity for adult adoptees will not occur until they have equal access to their birth records ... Thank
you for your attention . . . Respectfully, MARY JO JACKSON, ADOPTION TRIANGLE, Park Forest,
IL."

Dea rAmFOR:... "You can stop sending me information ... I found my mother and family after 3
weeks of searching on my own. I used my own methods, all legal. We have found a relationship and
everything is great! I have 2 new brothers, a sister and a niece! Thank you for your time, correspondence
and encouragement. . . CHRISTOPHER C., Kankakee, IL."

Dear AmFOR: . . . "I'm looking for my father's real parents. He was born in Springfield, Missouri,
September 22, 1938, flown to Chicago Midway to his adopters. This is all we know. Can you
please respond regarding the process to find any information . . . L.H., La Grange, IL."

Indiana

CENTRAL RECORDS OFFICES

Vital Records
To Verify Fees
(rec = recorded message).
Div. of Vital Records
State Board of Health
6 West Washington Street
Indianapolis, IN 46204
(317) 233-2700
www.vitalrec.com.in.html

Accessible?
Genealogy

State (St), County (Co),
Birth (B), Death (D),
Marriage (M), Divorce (DV)
Indices & Records
St-B since 1/1907
St-D since 1900;
M, since 1958
Co-M.Dv, Court Clerk

State Archives
Address
Indiana State Library (Archives)
140 N. Senate Ave.
Indianapolis, IN 46204

Year Adoption
Records Closed
1935

Hospital Records
Available?
From doctor

Legal Notice
Required?
No

Central Department of Motor Vehicles
Bureau of Motor Vehicles
Driver License
State Office Building
100 N. Senate Ave.
Indianapolis, IN 46204

National Archives - Great Lakes Region
7358 South Pulaski Rd.
Chicago, IL 60629
(312) 353-0162
Hours: Mon & Wed-Fri: 8AM-4:15PM,
Tue: 8AM-8:30PM
(Serves Illinois, Indiana, Michigan, Minnesota,
Ohio and Wisconsin)

Central Agency
Holding Adoption Records
Dept. Family/Children/Adoptions
402 W. Washington St
Indianapolis, IN 46204

Non-Identifying
Info Provided?
Yes, by law.

Adoption Decree
From Court
Sometimes.

State
Registry
Yes;
Intermediary/
Waiver System

(1987) ADOPTION DISCLOSURE STATUTES (REGISTRY, INTERMEDIARY, WAIVER SYSTEM)
Section 31-3-4-25: court order required to release information. Section 31-3-1-2: Report of health statue and medical
history of adopted child and birthparent shall be filed with adoption petition; copy shall be sent to adoptive parent.
Section 31-34-19: unauthorized release of medical info is Class A Misdemeanor "up to $100 and/or 30 days in jail." Ann
Section 31-3-4-14 (Burns 1987 & Supp. 1991) mandates disclosure of non-identifying info. State Registry, Intermediary
System and Waiver System.

ADOPTION SEARCH/SUPPORT GROUPS (see "Key" on page 47)

Betty Heide
Adoptees Identity Doorway (AID)(SS)
Reunion Registry of Indiana (No fees)
PO Box 361
South Bend, IN 46604
bheide@mvillage.com

Randy Rigg
Reflections (SG)
1211 Blueben-y St
Evansville, IN 47710
RandyRigg@mail.com

Alma Baumgartner
STAC State Contact
6131 Maren Dr.
Speedway, IN 46224

Anne Monroe (SG)
Midwest Searching Magazine
PO Box 122
Oakland City, IN 47660

Brad & Sharon Ekdahl (CASA) (S)
Court Appointed Intermediaries
3548 Revere Ct.
Lake Station, IN 46405

Sandi Fest (SS)
Adoption Searching with Love
Spaeth Rd.
Mariah Hill, IN 47558

Cathy Miles (SG)
Double Heritage
332 Briner Rd.
Marion, IN 46953

Pat Allen
Adoption Circle
401 Beechwood Drive
Beech Grove, IN 46107
akaShawnaL@aol.com

Pam Kroskie
Adption triangle (SS)
Bloomington, IN
kroskie5@comcast.net

Martha Barrow ISC
Search for Tomorrow, Inc. (SS)
PO Box 441
New Haven, IN 46774

Judy Johnston
Connected by Adoption (SS)
1817 Woodland Drive
Elkhart, IN 46514

Cheri Freeman
Coping With Adoption
61 Country Farm Road
Peru, IN 46970

Candy Jones
Support of Search (SOS)(SS)
Indiana Adoption Coalition (SS)
PO Box 1292
Kokomo, IN 46903

Sherrie Eldridge
Online Adoption Support Group
All-adoptee@yahoogroups.com

Sue Madden (SG)
Lafayette Adoption Search Service
Organization
(LASSO)
5936 Lookout Dr.
West Lafayette, IN 47906

Karen Bolen/CUB
4501 Farnsworth
Indianapolis, IN 46241

Full Circle
1701 N. Madison, #E-5
Anderson, IN 46901

Nancy Vanderhoose
Greater Love Adoption Decision
(GLAD)
PO Box 9105
Evansville, IN 47710

Phyllis Leedom
Search Committee of Madison County
Historical Society (SS)
PO Box 523
Anderson, IN 46015

Kathy Locke
1330 W Michigan St.
Indianapolis. IN 46206

Christina Wilson
Connected by Adoption
3602 Generations Drive
South Bend, IN 46635

Sally Kelly
504 Glenview Heights Road
New Albany, IN 47150

Diana Emmons (SG)
Common Bond
110 N. Sheridan St.
Kendallville, IN 46755
thunder@locl.net

Darlene/Randi Richardson
Full Circle Adoption
PO Box 22461
Indianapolis, IN 46222

Deb Schmidt
Catholic Charities
315 East Washington Blvd.
Ft. Wayne, IN 46802
Dschmidt@fw.diocese.fwsb.org

Lisa Mattingly (SS)
607 North Line Street
Loogootee, IN 47904

Lori Baxter
Double Heritage
1533 North 500 West
Marion, IN 46952
smile@comteck.com

Ron Elly
LASSO
110 N. 9th St, Ste 102
Layfayette, IN 47904
EllysRE@aol.com

Theresa E. Maxwell
St. Elizabeth's
2500 Churchman Avenue
Indianapolis, IN 46203

Maryanne Duplissey
4515 Omer Place
Evansville, IN 47714

Ruth Fraley
2205 E. 74th St.
Indianapolis, IN 46240
mcfraley@IQuest.net

Kristin T. Lucas
Adoption Triangle (SS)
7361 Wilson Place
Merrillville, IN 46410
adoption@mail.icongrp.com

Athens Daily News/Athens Banner Herald, 10/15/95: "ADOPTEE'S SEARCH FOR HER MOM ENDS ON A HAPPY NOTE . . . Laura McDonald sits on her couch looking through a photo album filled with pictures of her mother, grandparents, two half-brothers and a half-sister. They are faces somewhat similar to hers, but they are also faces of people she has yet to meet—with a few exceptions .. . McDonald and her biological mother, Annis Elizabeth Libby, who lives in Maine, have yet to meet face to face, but they have been in continual contact since McDonald first located her, talking and filling in the blank pages of their lives... McDonald, who is married with two children and runs a home day-care center, began looking for her birthmother about seven months ago when she was diagnosed with cervical cancer. Later, doctors found benign tumors on her colon.

Since she was an adoptee, McDonald could not answer questions about her family's medical history and had no way of knowing what other health problems she could face in the future ... McDonald started her search by writing to the State of Indiana, her birthplace, for her adoption records and other birth information. From that information, McDonald found out she had an older brother, someone she never knew existed. The papers also provided her with one of the biggest clues in her search for her mother.

'On my adoption papers, it had my mother's birthday listed. I think this was an oversight on the part of the file clerk for not marking it out, or maybe she was sympathetic to my cause. I'll never know, but without that birth date, it would've been virtually impossible to have found her,' McDonald said."

Author's Note: Laura completed her search quickly with combined help of AmFOR, telephone/networking support and two Indiana adoptees—Jenny Nash and Jan Conlon—who were Laura's "legs" for records research in Indiana. AmFOR then provided Laura's story to media.

Dear AmFOR: . . . "Enclosed are the forms that you requested concerning the release of adoption information in the state of Indiana. If you need any further information, please let us know and we will try to accommodate you. Good luck in your efforts to help people who are searching for their families . . . Sincerely, JANET R., PROGRAM, POLICY AND FIELD, INDIANA FAMILY & SOCIAL SERVICES ADMINISTRATION, Indianapolis, IN."

Iowa

CENTRAL RECORDS OFFICES

Vital Records To Verify Fees (rec = recorded message). Div. Records & Stats Lucas State Office Bldg. 321 East 12th St., 4th fl. Des Moines, IA 50319 (515)281-4944 www.vitalrec.com/ia.html	**Accessible?** Any relative; fee plus SASE	State (St), County (Co), Birth (B), Death (D), Marriage (M), Divorce (DV) Indices & Records St-B,D since 7/1880 St-M,Dv since 1906 Co-B,D,M inq. fwded.

State Archives Address Iowa Genealogy Library History Bldg., 600 E. Locust Capitol Complex Des Moines, IA 50319	**Year Adoption Records Closed** 1945	**Hospital Records Available?** Difficult	**Legal Notice Required?** No

Central Department of Motor Vehicles Records Section (Drivers License) Park Fair Mall, PO Box 9204 Des Moines, IA 50306	National Archives - Central Plains Region 2312 E. Bannister Rd. Kansas City, MO 64131 (816) 926-6272 Hours: M-F: 8AM-4:30PM, 3rd S 9AM-4PM (Serves IA, KS, MI, NE)

Central Agency Holding Adoption Records Dept. Child/Family/Adoption Hoover State Office Bldg. Des Moines, IA 50319	**Non-Identifying Info Provided?** Yes, by law All Triad.	**Adoption Decree** From Court Always; Probate Superior, County; Post-6/41 adoptees need good cause	**State Registry** Yes; court order opens pre-6/4/41 records

(1987/1991) ADOPTION DISCLOSURE STATUTES (REGISTRY, INTERMEDIARY, WAIVER SYSTEM)
Section 600.16: records are sealed. Court order required to release information. Section 600.16: Medical evidence may be released to save life or to prevent irreparable physical harm to adoptee or adoptee's offspring Section 600.16: identifying may be disclosed to adult adoptee with court order and/or consent affidavit. Section 600.24: non-identifying information is allowed for older records for legitimate research or medical treatment. Report of health status and medical history of adopted child and birthparent shall be filed with adoption petition; copy shall be sent to adoptive parent. Section 31-3-4-7: contents of report. Section 31-34-19: unauthorized release of medical info is Class A Misdemeanor "up to $100 and/or 30 days in jail." Ann Section 31-3-4-14 (Burns 1987 & Supp. 1991) mandates disclosure of non-identifying info. State Registry, Intermediary System and Waiver System.

ADOPTION SEARCH/SUPPORT GROUPS (see "Key" on page 47)

Kristi Carman CUB PO Box 8151 Des Moines, IA 50301 kkc720@aol.com	Jim McDonald (SS, UPI) Origins (SS) 4300 Ashby Ave. Des Moines, IA 50310 Jim@origins.inc.com	Des Moines, IA 50317 Doris Smith Iowa Reunion Registry PO Box 8 Blairsburg, IA 50034
Marianne Lippold (SG) Adoption Experience Route 5, Box 22 Osceola, IA 50213	Bonnie Bis, President CUB National HQ (SS) 200 Walker Street Iowa City, IA 52240	Mary Phipps CUB 790 Lilly Lane Boone, IA 50036

Carol Anderson
CUB V-P (SS)
2415 Lincoln Rd.
Bettendorf, IA 52722

Adoptees Quest (SG)
1513 Buresh
Iowa City, CA 52245

Jean McLaughlin (CUB) (SS)
(STAC State Contact)
1049 36th St.
Des Moines, IA 50311

Judy Wilkins (SS)
Iowa Reunion Registry
130 33rd Ave, SW
Cedar Rapids, IA 52404

Ann Victor (CUB) (SS)
RR 2
Prospect, IA 50859

Adoption Experience Group (SG)
1105 Fremont
Des Moines, IA 50316

Dear AmFOR: ... "I saw your organization in a book entitled Search by Askins ... I am a volunteer worker at the LDS Church Family History Center here in Alamogordo, NM; even though I am not a Mormon I enjoy trying to trace ancestors. I was told by the Lutheran Foundling Home in Fort Dodge, IA that it would take a District Court Order for me to just find out the medical history of my birth parents, and also to find out if I had any brothers or sisters. I have so many allergies that I needed to become a part of MEDIC-ALERT ... HERMAN K., Alamogordo, NM."

Dear AmFOR:... "I'm trying to find my parents. I was adopted at 5 years of age. I have found I was born in Union County in Creston, IA. I have to get a court order to have access to any records or for anybody to look and see if I have any records ... Thank you, DON J., Bedford, IN."

Dear AmFOR:... "I was delighted to have your connections to trace my late husband's family. If I could get back to Iowa, I would personally visit all the court houses in all the towns Judge "M" was presiding. Of course, he came up with the phony delayed birth certificate ... I'm sure because of his position, Superior Court Judge, he felt no one would challenge him ... His wife didn't want to meet the mother and surely didn't want to know anything about her at all. She had a new puppy for Christmas! Sorry if I sound bitter, but one does get that way—in this case the culprit got away leaving no clues! ... DORIS A., Palm Desert, CA."

[Copied to AmFOR:] Dear Mrs. Clary: ... Congratulations on finding your mother ... (1) Crittenton lied to them about circumstances of relinquishment. (2) Crittenton did that to so many people that they were shut down some years ago. The new organization uses the Crittenton name, but tries hard to correct the damage done by the old "home" ... Sincerely, EUGENE AUSTIN, Tilden, NE."

Kansas

	Accessible?	State (St), County (Co), Birth (B), Death (D), Marriage (M), Divorce (DV) Indices & Records
Vital Records To Verify Fees (rec = recorded message). Bureau Reg/Health Stats Dept of Health, Forbes 900 SW Jackson Topeka, KS 66612 (913)296-1400-rec www.vitalrec.com/ks.html	Any relative; fee	St-B.D since 7/1911 St-M since 7/58 Co-M Probate Judge

State Archives Address	Year Adoption Records Closed	Hospital Records Available?	Legal Notice Required?
KS Historical Society Library State House - Third Floor Topeka, KS 66603	Never	Difficult	No

Central Department of Motor Vehicles
Division of Motor Vehicles
Driver Control Bureau
Landon State Office Building
Topeka, KS 66616

National Archives - Central Plains Region
2312 E. Bannister Rd.
Kansas City, MO 64131
(816) 926-6272
Hours: M-F: 8AM-4:30PM, 3rd S: 9AM-4PM
(Serves IA KS, ML NA)

Central Agency Holding Adoption Records	Non-Identifying Info Provided?	Adoption Decree From Court	State Registry
Social/Rehab Services (SRS) Adoptions 915 SW Harrison-5th fl Topeka, KS 66606 (785) 368-8157	Yes, by law. Adoptees.	Sometimes; District Court	Open Records (Adults) Waiver System

ADULT ADOPTEES (AGE 18) CAN ACCESS ORIGINAL BIRTH CERTIFICATE ON REQUEST.

Section 59-2279: locked files; court order required to release info. Kansas Statute Annotated Section 65-2423(a) (1980) allows access to original birth certificate. Section 59-22278a: filed with petition: complete genetic, medical and social history. Section 59-2278a: both non-identifying and identifying info shall be filed with adoption petition. Section 59-2278s: destruction of information about birth parent is Class C Misdemeanor. Ann Section 59-2130 (Supp 1991) mandates disclosure of non-identifying information. KS Stat. ANN. Section 59-2122, adult adoptee access to original birth certificate.

ADOPTION SEARCH/SUPPORT GROUPS (see "Key" on page 47)

Shirley Lytle
Catholic Social Services (SS)
2546 20th St.
Great Bend, KS 67530
Slytle@cpeis.net

Adrienne Wojhowicz
Getting to Know You
1770 South Roosevelt
Wichita, KS 67218
hearts121@aol.com

Paul Brown
Miracle search Network
PO Box 66
Spring Hill, KS 66083
pbrwon@idir.net

Bonnie Ferns (SG)
Reunions Ltd.
1537-D Elm Street
Ottawa, KS 66067

Marilyn Waugh
Adoption Concerns Triangle (ACT)
411 SW Greenwood Ave
Topeka KS 66606
waugh5@cox.net

Rochelle Harris
Wichita Adult Adoptees (SS)
4551 Osage St.
Wichita, KS 62717

Adoption Support Group (SG)
1425 New York St
Lawrence, KS 66044

Gayle Etnire
8216 W 96th Terrace
Overland Park, KS 66212
Gayle@Etnire.com

Dear AmFOR: . . . "Open Records" in Kansas does not mean 'open to the public,' but open to the adult adoptee. Nothing awful has happened since our state provided adult adoptee access in 1951." The Uniform Adoption Act (Law 2722) was intended to provide for disclosures but that section, along with the subsidized adoption program, was never passed. Kansas tries to contact people, if still in Kansas, and assists searchers. The adult adoptee may obtain their original birth certificate from our Dept. of Vital Statistics, IF THE ADOPTION WAS A PUBLIC ADOPTION. IF A PRIVATE AGENCY ADOPTION, their own regulations still govern, though most do assist adoptee searches. Vital statistics has all records, and indications as to whether birth is first, second, etc.; court records are limited but they do have the signed consent form. In Kansas, the adoptee just goes to Vital Statistics with identification and proof of age; he doesn't need to petition the court or agency, unless it's a private agency . . . We're always afraid Bill Pierce's group might come back to Kansas, as they did to oppose our 'open records' law ... PEGGY BAKER/SUSAN LOVETT, DIVISION OF YOUTH SERVICES, Topeka, KS."

Dear AmFOR: . . . "Following our conversation on Friday, February 3, I have checked further into the matter of repeal of sealed adoption record laws. At the present time I can find no records or clue that this item will be addressed during this legislative session. However, I have made a note of your name, organization, etc. and should something come to my attention I will let you know . . . Sincerely, CLARENE WILMS, SECRETARY TO ROY M. EHRLICH, STATE SENATOR, Topeka, KS."

Dear AmFOR: . . . "When I first heard my sister was going to give Misty up I told her I would take her. My sister agreed. The next thing I knew it was all done and Misty elsewhere ... The people who took her live in or near Maiz, Kansas not far from Wichita. I know a 'pro' who could probably find her very quickly but I don't have the funds, so I hope I can find her with the info you gave me. It's hard being in another state ... I will let you know when I find her. Thanks for your help . . . M.H., Sedalia, MO."

Kentucky

CENTRAL RECORDS OFFICES

Vital Records		State (St), County (Co),
To Verify Fees		Birth (B), Death (D),
(rec = recorded message).		Marriage (M), Divorce (DV)
Office Vital Stats	Accessible?	Indices & Records
275 East Main St.	Immediate	St-B,D since 1911
Frankfort, KY 40621	family; fee	St-M, Dv since 7/58
(502) 564-4212		Co-M Probate Judge
www.vitalrec.com/ky.html		

State Archives	Year Adoption	Hospital Records	Legal Notice
Address	Records Closed	Available?	Required?
Kentucky State Library Archives	1940	From doctor	Yes
Public Records Division			
300 Coffee Tree Road, PO Box 537			
Frankfort, KY 40602			

Central Department of Motor Vehicles
Division of Driver Licensing
New State Office Building
Frankfort, KY 40601

National Archives-Southeast Region
1557 Saint Joseph Avenue
East Point, GA 30344
(404) 763-7477
Hours: M&W-F:7:30AM-4:30PM,Tues: 7:30AM-9:30PM
(Serves AL, GA, FL, KY, MI, NC, SC and TN)

Central Agency	Non-Identifying	Adoption Decree	State
Holding Adoption Records	Info Provided?	From Court	Registry
Dept. of Social Services/Adoptions	Yes, by law;	Sometimes;	Yes;
275 E. Main St., 3C-E	Adoptees.	Probate Court	Intermediary
Frankfort, KY 40621			System.
(502) 564-2147			

(1984/1986) ADOPTION DISCLOSURE STATUTES (INTERMEDIARY SYSTEM AND REGISTRY SYSTEM)
Section 199.440: Dept. may authorize destruction of some files. Section 199.570: records are sealed; locked files; court order required to release information. New birth certificate shall be filed with old; old birth certificate shall be stamped "confidential." Kentucky Revised Statute 199-572 (Supp. 1986) provides Intermediary System. 199-575 allows access to original birth certificate. Registry system. Section 199-520: medical info. about birth parent shall be given to adoptive parent before adoption is final. Shall be provided upon request to adoptee at age of majority. Ann Section 199.520 (Michie-Bobbs-Merrill 1991) mandates disclosure of non-identifying info. Section 19.575: (1984 siblings provision): procedure for reuniting adult adoptee with pre-adoptive sibs. Section 199.572: 199.52 (Supp. 1986): identifying information about birthparent and consent to release of identifying information are kept on file and will be released to adoptees at age of majority. Access to original birth certificate via Intermediary System. KY Rev. Stat. 199.590: Violation of Adoption Provisions will result in fine $20-$200 and/or no more than 30 days in prison. Unauthorized disclosure from adoption records—$500-$2000 fine and/or 6 months in prison.

ADOPTION SEARCH/SUPPORT GROUPS (see "Key" on page 47)

Ann Hardy, Nancy Comstock (SG)
Louisville Adoptee Awareness
PO Box 23019
Anchorage, KY 40223

Sherry Szewczvkowski
CUB
9803 Encino Ct.
Louisville KY 40223
SherSzwc@aol.com

Susan Monroe (CUB)
140 Molly St.
Versailles, KY 40383

Linda Cecil ISC (SS S C)
Locators Unlimited
PO Box 1218
Nicholasville, KY 40358

Mary Pounder-Tilllotson (CUB)(SS)
10521 Parkerwood Place
Louisville, KY 40229

Suzanne Graham (SG C)
Adoption Education-Lexington
3408 Freeland Dr.
Lexington, KY 40502
linda@locatorsunlimated.com

Dear AmFOR: . . . "Many thanks for your newsletter. It helps boost us up when things look bleak. Am enclosing our club flyer... Keep up the wonderful work you are doing for the movement. I feel like great strides will be made in the next few years. Found my daughter in 1985 (KY). . . Meanwhile Louisville CUB Branch or mine is available for KY referrals . . . BARBARA C., LOUISVILLE CUB BRANCH SECRETARY, Louisville, KY."

Dear AmFOR: . . . "Thank you for all the articles about fathers. Here's one that might be more important than any you sent me. Louisiana fathers can now get their children if the mother surrenders it, unless he can be proven unfit. If this goes nationwide it will be a major change in our adoption system—about as major as Open Records!... BILL P., ALARM-LA, Ponchatoula, LA."

Dear AmFOR:... "My parents told me I was adopted on my fifth birthday and I've never forgotten it. I must say I've led a rebellious life, thinking no one truly loves me, or wants me. I'm now grown out of that state . . . but I can't go on forever not knowing who they are, what they look like and what medical diseases they may have had. For me, I'm at a stage where I'm growing out of epilepsy for now. I would really appreciate it if I could get some more information and find my real parents ... Sincerely yours, TAMMY S., Radcliffe, KY."

Dear AmFOR:... "My only brother was killed in a car wreck when this boy was only 4 years of age. His mother and father were divorced at this time. Her new husband then adopted the boy ... I don't know how to find him, my parents are getting old and would very much love to see their grandson. I have no money for a lawyer ... Thanks so much, E. C., Beaver Dam, KY."

Dear AmFOR: ... "I have just found my mom. She was very happy to be found. Do you have any information on how to tell my adopters? ... Can I obtain my sealed adoption file and my original birth certificate? . . . Sincerely, MRS. LINDA R., Bottineau, ND."

Dear AmFOR: . . . "My great-great grandmother, Sola Williams, age 5, along with her little brother, whose name is Smith Williams, age 1 or 2, were taken to a poorhouse somewhere in Paintsville, Johnson County, KY. Their mother hid in the bushes across the street to see if anyone would come and get them—well someone did, a lady named Blanche McCarty took Sol and an Uncle Sam Williams took Smith ... There was no adoption papers on them, so that's why I am turning to you for help... Thank you so much . . . RAONA N., Joelton, TN."

Louisiana

CENTRAL RECORDS OFFICES

	Accessible?	State (St), County (Co), Birth (B), Death (D), Marriage (M), Divorce (DV) Indices & Records	
Vital Records To Verify Fees (rec = recorded message). Vital Records Registry Po Box 60630 New Orleans, LA 70160 (504) 219-4500 www.vitalrec.com/la.html	Genealogy; fee	St-B,D since 1914 St-M, Dv since 1946, inq. fwd. Co-M,Dv Court Clerk	
State Archives Address State Archives/Records 3851 Essen Lane PO Box 94125 Baton Rogue, LA 70801	Year Adoption Records Closed 1977	Hospital Records Available? From doctor	Legal Notice Required? No

Central Department of Motor Vehicles
Department of Public Safety
Driver License Division
ODR Section
PO Box 64886
Baton Rogue, LA 70890

Department of Motor Vehicles
PO Box 64886
Baton Rogue, LA 70896

National Archives-Southeast Region
501 W. Felix St.
PO Box 6216
Fort Worth, TX 76115
(817) 334-5525
Hours: Mon-Fri: 8AM-4PM,
    Wed: 8AM-9:PM
(Serves AK, LA, NM, OK and TX)

	Non-Identifying Info Provided?	Adoption Decree From Court	State Registry
Central Agency Holding Adoption Records Dept. Social Services/Adoptions PO Box 3318 Baton Rogue, LA 70801 (225) 342-4006	Some, by law; All Triad.	No; Circuit Court	Yes

(1985) ADOPTION DISCLOSURE STATUTES (REGISTRY SYSTEM)
Section 432: closed hearings; court order required to release information. Section 76 (ht.40): records sealed. Louisiana Revised Statute Annotated Section 40:91 (West Supplement 1985) provides for a Registry System. Section 424.1: fees. Adoption disclosure affidavit of fees and charges paid by petitioner must be filed. Section 422.13: parents who surrender child for adoption must provide written statement of medical history. Copy for records, copy for adoptive parents and adopted child, upon reaching age 18. Father's claim on child recognized. Unauthorized disclosure from adoption records: "up to $500 and/or 90 days in jail, LA Rev. Stat. §9.437 West'76. LA Rev Sta tCh C Art 1188 (West 1991) permits some non-identifying info to be disclosed to adoptee.

ADOPTION SEARCH/SUPPORT GROUPS (see "Key" on page 47)

Jenny Kolp
LA Adoption Connection
1 -Box 613
Roland, OK 74954
Kolp@ipa.net

Johnny Kocurek, Gloria Veillon
Adoption Triad Inc. (SS)
120 Thibodeaux Dr.
Lafayette, LA 70503

Dianne Sercovich
Adoption Connection of Louisiana (SS)
7301 W. Judge Peres, Suite 311
Arabi, LA 70032

Pat Atkins (SS)
Volunteers of America
360 Jordan St.
Shreveport, LA 71101

Mary Ellen Davros (S)
Adoption Triad Network
511 Blue Bell
Port Alien, LA 70605

Laura Delgado (L-PI)
Laura PI
180 Blanche Dr.
Avondale, LA 70094

Mary D. Langhetee
Adoptees/Birthparents Committee (SS)
PO Box 9442
Metairie, LA 70002

Donna Green Robertson
CUB
1384 Cooper
DeQuincey, LA 70633

Anne Sensat
Adoption Search Organization (SS)
8154 Longwood Dr.
Denhan Springs, LA 70726

Linda Woods
Adoptees Birthrights Committee
25 Osborne Avenue
Kenner, LA 70065
linerwoods@aol.com

Adoption Triad Network
PO Box 6175
Lake Charles, LA 70605

Michelle & Stephen Chance
Volunteers of America
4152 Canal St
New Orleans, LA 70019
schance@lcc.net

Dear AmFOR:... "I'm looking for my sister... My mother has always told us that my sister was adopted by strawberry farmers in South LA. Is there anyway that you can help me? . . . Thank you, C.V, Yazoo City, MO."

Dear AmFOR: . . . "While reading the book, *Search: A Handbook for Adoptees and Birthparents,* your organization was brought to my attention ... My adoption took place in Louisiana, specifically in Orleans parish (county) and I have discovered that it is practically impossible to open my records. Ironically, I met someone recently whose adoption took place in California, and his records were made available to him with no opposition . . . Respectfully, JEFFREY B., St. Gabriel, LA."

Dear AmFOR: ... "I was born July 2, 1974 in the Shreveport, LA area. The adoption agency was the National Society of the Volunteers of America . . . My mother was around 16 when she had me. Her father had been a fire fighter at Barksdale AFB, but he died. Her mother was Japanese. My mother, who was the eldest of several children, basically took care of the family. There were a lot of relatives in the area. In fact, my adoptive parents were instructed not to take me on to Barksdale AFB (my adoptive dad is a military officer) because so many people in my family had seen me and would recognize me . .. COLLETTE G., Fairfax, VA."

Dear AmFOR:..." I would like to find out about my parents' medical history before I get married and start to have children and meet them if I could .. . SANDRA B., Grant, LA."

Maine

CENTRAL RECORDS OFFICES

		State (St), County (Co),
Vital Records		Birth (B), Death (D),
To Verify Fees		Marriage (M), Divorce (DV)
(rec = recorded message).		Indices & Records
office of Vital Records	Accessible?	St-B,D since 1/1892
Human Services Bldg.	Public;	St-M, Dv since 1/1892
244 Water Street #11	fee	Co-B,D,M Town Clerk
Augusta, ME 04333		
(207) 287-3181		
www.vitalrec.com/me.html		

State Archives	Year Adoption	Hospital Records	Legal Notice
Address	Records Closed	Available?	Required?
State Library	1953	Yes	Yes
LMA Building			
State House Station #84			
Augusta, ME 04333			

Central Department of Motor Vehicles	National New England Region
Secretary of State	380 Trapelo Rd.
Motor Vehicle Division	Waltham, MA 02154
1 Child St.	(617) 647-8100
August, ME 04330	Hours: M-F& 1st Sat: 8AM-4:30PM
	(Serves CT, ME, MA.NH, RI, VT)

Central Agency	Non-Identifying	Adoption Decree	State
Holding Adoption Records	Info Provided?	From Court	Registry
Dept. Child/Family/Adoptions	Yes, but law	No;	Yes
221 State St.	gives court	District,	
Augusta, ME 04333	discretion;	Juvenile Court;	
(207) 287-5060	All Triad		

ADOPTEES BORN PRE-6/1/47 CAN ACCESS ORIGINAL BIRTH CERTIFICATE ON REQUEST.
Section 534: adoption records separate; court order to release information. Maine Revised Statute Title 22, Section 2706-A (1980) provides for a Registry System. No fees provision stated. Section 2706-A: identifying information; adoption contact files maintained for birth parents and adoptees over 18. Penalties for violations not stated. Rev StatAnn Tit. 19 Section 534 (West Supp 1991) gives courts discretion regarding disclosure of non-identifying info.

ADOPTION SEARCH/SUPPORT GROUPS (see "Key" on page 47)

Barbara Hough	Sandy & Scott Kelly	Brenda Peluso, Mina Bicknell
Search Right, Inc.	7 Bradley St.	Adoption Resource Center (SS)
PO Box 506	Fryburg, ME 04037	PO Box 2793
Yarmouth, ME 04096		South Portland, ME 04116
bhough@worldnet.att.net		
	Adoption Support Group of	Mary Ann Bostwich (SS S)
Michael and Jeannine Dennis	Penobscot Bay (SG)	Adoption Search Consultants
Genealogists	Taylor's Point	36 Grove St
PO Box 253	Tenant's Harbor, ME 04860	Bangor, ME 04401
Oakland, ME 04963		

Liz O'Connor (SS S)
52 Summit Cir.
Westbrook, ME 04092

Chris Conway (SS S)
Adoption Search Consultants
30 Parkway St.
Kennebunk, ME 04043

Becki Schrieber (SS S)
Adoption Search Consultants
7 Ledgewood Rd.
Yarmouth, ME 04860

Sybil Coombs
Solomon's Mothers (SG)
RR3, Box 1050
Wells, ME 04090

Lucy Gagnor (SS S)
Adoption Search Consultants
183 West Shore Rd.
Auburn, ME 04210

Sheriden Robbins
The Adoption Counsel (SS)
34 Winn Rd.
Falmouth, ME 04105

Amy Higgins
STAC State Representative
PO Box 600
Scarborough, ME 04070

Cathy Robishaw
OBC For Me triad Support Group
Portland, ME
crncmr@mvfairpoint.net
www.OBCdorme.org

Dear AmFOR:... "I am seeking information on how to find out if my daughter has ever tried to find me ... I don't know where she is or even if she is alive. I just want to know where to start or if I can do anything. I did not give her up willingly. It was a forced situation . . . Sincerely, B.M.C., Calais, ME."

Dear AmFOR: . . . "I have been assisting a search in the state of Maine, where the laws dictate that all adoptions after 1953 are confidential. Therefore, I had to petition the Probate Court in Augusta, Maine to open the adoption files. At the same time I petitioned the courts, I also sent for a copy of the local newspaper to see if there was any records of births on that day. Although there were two births on that day (both boys), neither was the one that I was looking for. After several weeks the petition to open the adoption records was granted, and the name of the mother was found, as well as her present address and telephone number. I now have one very happy client. I am now in the process of providing a method in which my client and his mother can meet without traumatizing both my client and the mother and her family. The most ironic aspect while conducting this investigation is that both my client his mother lived in the same town for several years . . . Sincerely, RALPH S., L.P.I., Sequor Investigation Agency, Pompano Beach, FL."

Maryland

CENTRAL RECORDS OFFICES

| Vital Records
To Verify Fees
(rec = recorded message).
Div. of Vital Records
State Dept of Health
6550 Registertown Ave.
PO Box 68760
Baltimore,. MD 21215
(410) 764-3038
www.vitalrec.com/md.html | Accessible?
Immediate
family; fee
St-Dv since 1/1961 | State (St), County (Co),
Birth (B), Death (D),
Marriage (M), Divorce (DV)
Indices & Records
St-B,D since 1898
St-M since 6/1951 | |

| State Archives
Address
Maryland State Library
Hall of Records Building
350 Rowe Blvd.
Anapolis, MD 21401 | Year Adoption
Records Closed
1948 | Hospital Records
Available?
Difficult | Legal Notice
Required?
No |

Central Department of Motor Vehicles
Motor Vehicle Administration
6601 Richie Highway, N.E.
Glen Burnie, MD 21062

National Archives-Mid-Atlantic Region
Ninth & Market Streets, Room 1350
Philadelphia, PA 19107
(215) 597-3000
    Hours: Mon-Fri: 8AM-5PM
           2nd Sat: 8AM-4PM
    (Serves Delaware, Pennsylvania, Maryland, Virginia
    and West Virginia; primarily genealogical records)

| Central Agency
Holding Adoption Records
Dept. of Human Services
Adoptions
311 W. Saratoga St.
Baltimore, MD 21201
(410) 767-7713 | Non-Identifying
Info Provided?
Yes, by law;
All Triad, | Adoption Decree
From Court
Sometimes;
pre-1953;
Probate Court | State
Registry
Yes |

(1986) ADOPTION DISCLOSURE STATUTES (REGISTRY SYSTEM)

Section 5-329: court order required to release information. Maryland Family Law Sections 5-4A-01 to 5-41-07 (Supp. 1986) provides for a Registry System. No fees statement. Section 5-329: medical information shall be released with court order if needed for health of individual or blood relative of individual adoptee. Section 5-328: Medical history shall be obtained. Section 5-4A-01: Mutual Consent Voluntary Adoption Registry for birthparent, adoptees and natural siblings. Fam Law Code Ann Section 5-329.1 (Supp 1991) mandates disclosure of non-identifying info.

ADOPTION SEARCH/SUPPORT GROUPS (see "Key" on page 47)

Laurie Lewis (S)
(formerly ALARM)
14914 Nighthawk Ln.
Bowie, MD 20716

Joanne W. Small
PO Box 41016
Adoptees in Search (SS)
A1520824@aol.com

Linda Clausen
CUB (SS)
PO Box 15258
Chevy Chase, MD 20825
lcc9@aol.com

Sharon Price
Adoptee Birthparent Connection
PO Box 115
Rockey Ridge, MD 21778

Carol Setola ISC (S)
PO Box 441
Glenn Dale, MD 20769

Margaret McMorrow (SS)
CUB-Region 2 Director
327 Dogwood Rd.
Millersville, MD 21108
MargyMC@aol.com

Katherine G. Gaeng
Maryland Mutual Consent Registry
311 W. Saratoga St.
Baltimore, MD 21217

Peggy Matthews-Nilsen
STAC-State Contact
4622 Woodfield Rd.
Bethesda,MD20814

Amy Pla
18221 Mehrens Terrace
Oiney, MD 20832

Ronda Barmoy-Wilt
Adoption Search & Support
1427 Church Street
Cumberland, MD 21502

Jean Stewart
Adoptee Birthparent Group
PO Box 6485
Columbia, MD 21045

Earle Barnes
Metro (MD) Registry
6439 Woodbridge Road
Alexandria, VA 22312
ebames@erols.com

Linda Evosevich
4010 Chestnut Road
Baltimore, MD 21220

Marilyn Cramer (S)
PO Box 7052
Silver Spring, MD 20907

Tracy Mayo
(NE Fairfax Co MD Search)
PO Box 8273
McLean, VA 22106
tlmayol@aol.com

Ellen Berman
Encore (E York Co., MD)
683 Hidden Hill Farm Lane
York, PA 17403

Ginger Metzger
Adoption Contact Search
311 W Saratoga St.
Baltimore, MD 21201

Dear AmFOR:... "When I first wrote you, I knew nothing. I didn't even know I was entitled to info from the adoption agency (in my case Montgomery County, MD Social Services). I wrote for non-identifying info in January. By December, I met my aunt and uncle (my mother's sister and brother).
It was brought about through persistence, hard work (trial and error and many hung-up phones and unanswered inquiries) and luck. By traveling to Laurel, Maryland (my birthplace and asking lots of questions at the library and local bars (my bio. mother was a waitress), I found people who knew my mother (physical description—she has a deformed right arm) by the name Annie. My code name at Social Services was Cindy Bosler, so I knew the last name began with a 'B.' I went to several of her old acquaintances' homes and I learned Annie married and moved to Bowie, MD and died ... I called social services ... They said they could only tell me whether or not the name was incorrect, not correct. I asked if Anna Bennington was incorrect. They said no... I received the birth certificate but no death record was on file ... I placed a personal ad 'In Search of Relatives ...'... That evening I received a phone call from my mother's sister—my aunt (I met her 12-4-89). I was as shocked as she was. I tried to bluff my way through as doing a genealogy project. But I couldn't. I called her back and told her the truth. That her sister Anna was my mother. I found out my mother is still alive... I have not met my mother. She denies me. However, I have met her sister, her two living brothers ... In the meantime, I help others search. I believe it's part of my purpose in life. It's meant to be... Keep up the good work! Keep me posted! And let me know what I can do here to help . . . Yours in search, REBECCA W., Hampton, VA."

Massachusetts

CENTRAL RECORDS OFFICES

Vital Records
To Verify Fees
(rec = recorded message).
Registry of Vital Stats
150 Mt. Vernon St., 1st fl..
Dorchester, MA 02125
(617) 740-2600
www.vitalrec.com/ma.html

Accessible?
Public; fee

State (St), County (Co),
Birth (B), Death (D),
Marriage (M), Divorce (DV)
Indices & Records
St-B,D,M since 1841;
St-Dv since 1952
St-B,D Boston since 1848
Co-Dv Probate Ct. regis.
Pre-1901:MA Archives,
220 Morrissey Blvd.,
Boston, MA 02125

State Archives Address	Year Adoption Records Closed	Hospital Records Available?	Legal Notice Required?
State Library Archives 220 Morrissey Blvd., Columbia Pt. Boston, MA 02133	1972	From doctor	Yes

Central Department of Motor Vehicles
Registry of Motor Vehicles
Court Records Section
100 Nashua St.
Boston, MA 02114

National Archives-New England Region
380 Trapelo Rd.
Waltham, MA 02154; (617) 647-8100
Hours: M-F & 1st Sat: 8AM-4:30PM
(Serves CT, ME, MA, NH. RI, VT)

Central Agency Holding Adoption Records	Non-Identifying Info Provided?	Adoption Decree From Court	State Registry
Dept. Social Services/Adoptions 24 Farnsworth St. Boston, MA 02110 (617) 727-0900	Yes, by law; All Triad.	Usually; Domestic Relations	No; Consent & Waiver System

(1986) ADOPTION DISCLOSURE STATUTES (REGISTRY, CONSENT AND WAIVER SYSTEM)
Section 5C: court order required to release information. Files kept separately. Section 6: closed hearings. Massachusetts General Law Chapter 210, Section 5D (West Supp. 1986) allows access to records with consent only (no search or registry). No fees statement. No separate provision concerning medical information. Section 5D: records of non-identifying information about adopted child, birthparent or adoptive parent shall be released to adopted child over age 18, to birthparent or to adoptive parent with consent of required party or parties. Identifying information shall also be released with written consent of the party or parties. Ann Laws Ch. 210 section A (Law Co-op Supp 1992) mandates disclosure of non-identifying info. DSS does not charge fees but every private adoption agency in MA has its own fee schedule.

ADOPTION SEARCH/SUPPORT GROUPS (see "Key" on page 47)

Susan Darke (SS) (AAC)
The Adoption Connection , Inc.
The O'Shea Building
11 Peabody Square, #6
Peabody, MA 1960
suedarke@aol.com

Ann Henry
TRY-Resource Referral (SS)
PO Box 989
Northhampton, MA 01061
try@try.org

Janice Chalifoux (CUB)(SS)
63 Mile Hill Rd.
Boylston, MA 01505

Adoption Community of New England
Westborough, MA
www.adoptioncommunityofne.org

Nancy Noble
Adoption Healing (SG)
PO Box 211
S. Orleans, MA 02662

Carolyn Canfield (S)
Adoption Healing (SG)
44 Wareham Lake Shore Drive
East Wareham, MA 02538
Canoak@capeonramp.com

Libbi Campbell (CUB)(SS)
PO Box 396
Cambridge, MA 02238

Cape Cod Adoption Connection
PO Box 336
Brewster, MA 02631

Jo Devlin
34 Pleasant
Stoneham, MA 02180

Penny Callan Partridge (SG)
PO Box 3193
Amherst, MA 01004

Jack Marvin (AAC-VP)
20 Nagog Hill Rd.
Littleton, MA 01460

CUB
45 Holyoke St.
No.Quincy.MA02171

Deb Schwarz
TIES / PACER
112 Mt. Vernon Street
Boston, MA 02108

Jeffrey LaCure
Adoption Support
9 Martha's Way
Franklin, MA 02038

Susan White
Healing Adoption/Completing Circle
PO Box 684
Bridgewater, MA 02324

Birthmother Support Group
University of Massacusetts
Wilder Hall
Amherst, MA 01003

Joyce Pavao, Ed.D (SG)
Adoption Resource Center
350 Cambridge St.
Cambridge, MA 02041
Kinnect@aol.com

Peabody Times, 04/29/91, front page: "SEARCH FINDS MOTHER AFTER 30 YEARS: Daughter Given Up for Adoption Elects to Uncover Past . . . Peabody—For years after giving up her daughter, Nancy Chipman drove to Middleton to catch glimpses of her growing up. The Marblehead adoption agency kept the location of her daughter, Mary Ellen, a secret, but Chipman thought she had it figured out. At about the time Mary Ellen was adopted, Chipman read a newspaper report of a shower held for a Middleton woman who'd adopted a baby girl. "And I said, 'A-ha, this is where my Mary Ellen is,'" she recalls ... "I checked that house out periodically, to make sure they were keeping up the house, because I thought if they were doing this or doing that, they were taking good care of her." She kept her distance, though, and never introduced herself. Mary Ellen—now Brenda Fernandez, age 30—grew up in West Peabody, in Brookline, N.H. and Quincy. She has never lived in Middleton.

She always knew she was adopted and remembers her childhood as a happy time. Still, Brenda had her own favorite fantasy: 'Queen Elizabeth was my birth mother and she had come over her, had an affair with a sailor and, of course, being the proper English woman, she couldn't keep me. And of course the sailor, he was long gone out to sea.'

She didn't know that her mother spied on a Middleton home or that she would buy her birthday presents every Oct. 15 only to return them to the store a few days later. Four years ago, Fernandez decided she'd had enough of not knowing . . . Unlike many courts, Essex County Superior Court is relatively cooperative in adoption cases, says Fernandez. A judge in Salem unsealed her records after Fernandez petitioned the court . . . 'Essex is one of the few courts that will give you information. Most courts just won't open records,' says Fernandez. "They're sealed and they're protecting the birthmother and they're protecting the adoptee, so they won't open them unless it's a life and death thing where you have a doctor's request. But I was lucky."

The judge 'figured out I wasn't an ax murderer and that I was a reasonably sane person, and she opened my records," she says. They included her original birth certificate, where she lived during the six months before she was adopted and "all the names." ... "I think you have to think about what you want to find and how you're going to deal with what you find, because you go through lots of emotions ....
'We have a relationship to work on,' says Fernandez. 'It's like any relationship—it doesn't end. You work on it, you build on it, and it's an ongoing thing. It's a life-changing thing.' "

Dear AmFOR:... "I have been trying to find out something about my father and mother. I went
to the town hall in the town I was adopted in and tried to get a copy of my adoption certificate. When I
asked for it the whole place came to a halt! A man came to me and quietly asked me to follow him to his
office. I did. He then explained that I couldn't have it without my parents being there with me ... I am an
adult and I can't even get a copy of my birth certificate without my mom being there! I am outraged! I
want this changed... Please send me all you can that would help me. Good luck and God bless ... Thank
you, TAMERA T., Shelburn Falls, MA."

Michigan

CENTRAL RECORDS OFFICES

Vital Records
To Verify Fees
(rec = recorded message).
Vital Records
204 Townsend St., 3rd fl.
Lansing, MI 48909
(517) 335-8666
www.vitalrec.com/mi.html

State (St), County (Co).
Birth (B), Death (D),
Marriage (M), Divorce (DV)
Indices & Records
St-M since 4/1867
St-Dv since 1897
Co-B,D,M,Dv, County Clerk

State Archives Address	Year Adoption Records Closed	Hospital Records Available? From doctor	Legal Notice Required?
State Archives of Michigan MI Bureau of History 717 W. Allegan St. Lansing, MI 48918	1925	From doctor	No

Central Department of Motor Vehicles
Department of State
Bureau of Driver and Vehicle Service
Commercial Look-Up Unit
7064 Crowner Dr.
Lansing, MI 48918

National Archives - Great Lakes Region
7358 South Pulaski Rd.
Chicago, IL 60629; (312)353-0162
Hours: M & W-F: 8AM-4:15PM, Tu: 8AM-8:30PM
(Serves IL, IN, MI, MN, OH and WI)

Central Agency Holding Adoption Records	Non-Identifying Info Provided?	Adoption Decree From Court	State Registry
Family Independence Agency (FIA) PO Box 30037 (Adoptions) Lansing, MI 48909 (517) 335-4652	Yes, by law; All Triad.	Seldom: Probate Court.	Yes; Intermediary System.

(1995) ADOPTION DISCLOSURE STATUTES (INTERMEDIARY SYSTEM, REGISTRY AND WAIVER SYSTEM)
Section 710.67: locked files; court order required to release information. (1990): Medical information when adopted child is 14. Section 710.27/68: birthparent, at release of child, may file a denial of release of identifying information or may consent to release of information, Section 710.68: non-identifying information shall be made available to adoptive parent after placement and to adult adoptee. Section 710.27: intentional destruction of information is a Misdemeanor.

ADOPTION SEARCH/SUPPORT GROUPS (see "Key" on page 47)

Christine M. Soley (S) (SG)
A.I.M./ Court Intermediary
37231 Tall Oak Dr.
Clinton Township, MI 48036
CKSoley@gateway.net

Peg Richer
Adoption Identity Movement (SS)
5767 Liesure South Drive
Kentwood. MI

Elaine Meints (SS)
Adoption Insight (SS)
PO Box 171
Portage, MI 49081
FMEINTS@aol.com

Carol Gray
Kalamazoo Birthparent Support (SG)
PO Box 2183
Portage, MI 49081
cgravbmom@ics.com

Jeanette Abronowitz (SS S)
Adoptees Search for Knowledge
PO Box 762
East Lansing, MI 48823

Tina Caudill /Linda Bevins
Adoption Identity Movement
PO Box 812
Hazel Park, MI 49696
caudt@aol.com
haveshovelwilltravel@comcast
www.michieanscorching.com

Gayle Merkle
Adoptee-Birthparent Support
21700 Northwestern # 1490
Southfield, MI 48075

Elaine Scott (SS S)
Mid-MI Adoption Identity Movement
13623 Podunk
Cedar Springs, MI 49139

Patti VanderBand
Roots and Reunions (SS)
210 Barbeau
Sault Ste. Marie, MI 49783

Adoption Identity Movement
PO Box 812
Hazel Park, MI 49696

Irma Amore
4615 Western Rd., Lot 76
Flint, MI 48506

Linda Wilbur (S)
11960S.LachanceRd
Marion, MI 49665

Eleanor Wilson
5007 Sandlewood
Grand Blanc, MI 48439

Carleen Helgesen
Montevideo Support Group
Montevideo, MI
edgarnortici@yahoo.com

Deanna Rogers
8107 Webster Rd.
Mt. Morris, MI 48458

Randy Ferrari (SS)
Tri-County Genealogical Society
21715 Brittany
Eastpointe, MI 48021

Dave & Linda Cark
2431Roanoake
Ypsilanti, MI 48197

Adoptees Search for Knowledge
4227 S. Belsay Rd.
Burton,MI48519

Paths Reunited
U-Haul 751/50 #56
2720 Burlingame, SW
Wyoming, MI 49509

Lois Plantefaber (S)
Adoption Circle (SG)
Catholic Social Services
4925 Packard
Ann Arbor, MI 48104

Beth Johnson (SS)
Adoption Identity Movement (AIM)
PO Box 72
Ortonville, MI 48462

Christine Bueher ISC
(formerly ALARM)
1270 Grosvenor Way
Palmyra, MI 49268
cabueher@tc3net.com

Karen Mehlberg
Tri-County Genealogy Society
15492 MacArthur
Redford Township, MI 48239

Daniel Wolf
MI Ass. Openness in Adoptn (SG)
3244 Pembroke Drive
Traverse City, MI 49684

Chris Spun- ISC
Adoption Identity Movement (SS)
1602 Cole
Birmingham, MI 48009

Julie Carter
Adoption Connections (SS)
PO Box 293
Cloverdale, MI 49035
Julesci@aol.com

Linda Yellin, MSW, ACSW
Post Reunion Support Group (SG)
27600 Farmington Rd. #101
Farmington Hills, MI 48344

Courtney Marshall
Birthmom's Life By Adoption
Christian Cradle
535 North Clippert #2
Lansing, MI 48912

Marilyn Kay Phillips
Truth in the Adoption Triad (SS)
6634 Gage St.
Gagetown, MI 48735

Jane Carter (SS S C)
Adoption Identity Movement (AIM)
8072 Kingsbury Rd.
Delton, MI 49046

Bob Schafer (SG)(AAC)
Adoption Reform Movement-MI
(ARMM)
95 Whitesbridge Rd.
Belding, MI 48809

Mary Purkal
Adoption Identity Movement (AIM)
PO Box 5414
Traverse City, MI 49596
aimofnorthernmi@hotmail.com

Dave Weaver
Adoption Identity Movement
PO Box 930086
Wixom, MI 48393

Ken Bryson
Adoption Identity Movement (AIM)
PO Box 337
Kalkaska, MI 49646

Patty Packhorn
304 W. Morgan
Battlecreek, MI 49017

Marianne Bach
Adoptee Supp/CSS
117 North Vision
Ann Arbor, MI 48104

Brenda Romanchik
721 Hawthorne Avenue
Royal Oak, MI 48067
brenr@r2press.com

Connie Courtade
Birthmother Support
1152 Scribner
Grand Rapids, MI 49503

Linda Klais (S)
2521 Bowen Rd.
Howell, MI 48843
klais@ismi.net

Jean Waters
APART Ministries
11175 Roberts Road
Stockbridge, MI 49285

103

Susan Armstrong
Search in MI
613 East Sunset Drive
North Muskegon, MI 49445

Mary S. Ahrens/ CUB
524 Westchester
Saginaw, MI 48603

Rosa Schindler
Alliance for Adoptions/Stars of David
7423 Westbury
West Bloomfield, MI 48322

Ann Zsenyuk
PO Box 70
Manchester, MI 48158

Joanne Swanson
Post-Adoption Support Services
North 1194 W. Tie Lake Road
Whitmore, MI 49895

Daryl Royal
A.I.M.
22646 Michigan
Dearborn, MI 48124
droyal@ameritech.net

Mary Louise Foess
Bonding by Blood Unlimited (SS)
5845 Waterman Rd., Rt. 1
Vassar, MI 48768
mlfoess@gmail.com

Flint Journal, 03/26/91: "VOICES OF HIDDEN LIVES RING OUT ON ADOPTION LAW....
on Gaining Access to Records ... Vassar school teacher Mary L. Foess' inability to get information on her
[birth]parents gave her a 'low self esteem' for most of her life. 'I was ashamed of not knowing who I was,'
Foess, 45, told a state house subcommittee hearing on Michigan's adoption law, held Monday in Flint.
Urging open adoption records, Foess said hiding information 'is an immoral thing to do to a human
being.' Adoptees, such as Foess, often must travel a maze of red tape, bureaucratic blocks and an unap-
preciative society to find their identity."

Detroit Free Press, 05/10/92: "FINDING [BIRTH]MOTHER AND SELF... Virginia Dombrowski sifts
through the court documents, letters and journals that litter her kitchen table. Eventually she finds the
faded photograph of the heavy-set woman in spit curls and wire-rimmed glasses who gave her up for
adoption to a Detroit family in 1925 . . . she'll travel to St. John's Cemetery in Jackson to stand by
her [birth] mother's grave for the first time . . . 'I'll regret that I never met her, and I'll expect to feel her
presence. It's not upsetting. Here I was 66 years old and begging a judge to tell me who I was,' she says.
'It felt ridiculous to be protesting at juvenile court at my age.' Catholic Social Services employee
finally gave her the news about her [birth] mother. "She proved my birthmother was deceased, and by
law, she was able to release the information to me," Dombrowski says
. . . 'Some people have told me, 'You're too old to be looking for your mother,'" she says. 'But this is a
civil rights issue. We need to know who we are and where we came from.'"

Detroit Free Press, 8/18/92: "Adoptee's 17-Year Quest Brings Only Dead Ends... The file told Judy that
her mother's heart was dextrocardial—on the right side of her body instead of the left. History tells
Piotrowski that her mother's heart may have been broken, too . . . And that is the driving force of this
interminable journey: There is so much she doesn't know. JUDY ANN CANNON (later JUDY
PIOTROWSKI) was born April 4, 1954, at Herman Kiefer Hospital. If you can help her in her search for
her birthmother, call 278-8096, anytime."

Dear AmFOR:... "Adopters get to live out their role as a parent at the expense of someone else
... I resent the fact that I ended up as a provider of a baby (my only child, too) for a wealthy couple, but
there is nothing I can do but enjoy the relationship I have now with my son and work towards some
reform of the system . . . It was the way of the times. I had had too much to drink and a one-night stand;
four months later my pregnancy was confirmed. I didn't feel right about telling the man; he was just a friend
but also I didn't think he'd believe me. I wanted to keep my baby, and my conviction grew when her son was born.
I begged Social Services, Boston, where I had hidden myself, to let me keep my boy. They granted a three-month
extension, but insisted on proof that I could support the baby.. I couldn't come up with it. So age 24, I took
Polaroids of my infant and said good-bye. In 1960 they wanted babies—healthy, white babies. We had no choice.
Sincerely yours, BARBARA ANDERSON-KARI, Roseville, MI".

Minnesota

CENTRAL RECORDS OFFICES

Vital Records		State (St), County (Co),
To Verify Fees		Birth (B), Death (D),
(rec = recorded message).		Marriage (M), Divorce (DV)
Dept of Health	Accessible?	Indices & Records
Section Vital Stats.	Public	St-B,D since 1/1908
PO Box 64882		St-M since 1958
St. Paul, MN 55164-0882		St-Dv since 1/1970
(651-201-5970		Co-B,D,M,Dv District Court
www.vitalrec.com/mn.html		

State Archives	Year Adoption	Hospital Records	Legal Notice
Address	Records Closed	Available?	Required?
Minnesota Historical	1941	Difficult	No
Society Research Center			
345 Kellogg Blvd., W.			
St. Paul. MN 55101			

Central Department of Motor Vehicles
Department of Public Safety
Driver License Office
State Highway Bldg., Rm. 108
St. Paul, MN 55155

Central Agency	Non-Identifying	Adoption Decree	State
Holding Adoption Records	Info Provided?	From Court	Registry
Dept. Children's Services (Adoptions)	Yes, by law;	Usually;	Yes;
444 Lafayette Rd	All Triad.	Probate Court.	Intermediary
St. Paul. MN 55155			System.
(651) 297-2711			

(1985) ADOPTION DISCLOSURE STATUTES (INTERMEDIARY SYSTEM AND REGISTRY)

Section 259.27: confidential records. Rev. Stat. Section 259.27 (West Sup-. 1992) mandates disclosure of non-identifying information. Section 259.31: closed hearings; court order required in order to release information. Ann Section 259.49 (West Supp. 1985) provides an Intermediary System (provides active search and consent procedure). No fees statement. Section 259.47: Health information given which may affect physical/mental health of genetically-related persons. Section 259.253: parties will be informed when parent or child dies or has terminal illness. Section 259.47: birthparent must file objection to release of identifying information (name and last known address) to adoptee at age 18 who requests identifying information. Within 6 months of request, Department shall try to contact birthparent.

ADOPTION SEARCH/SUPPORT GROUPS (see "Key" on page 47)

Cheryl Rock. Patty O' German (SS)	ALMA	Concerned United Birthparents
MN Reunion Registry/LEAF	7048 Progress Rd.	info@cubbirthparents.org
23247 Lofton Ct., N.	Hugo, MN 55038	
North Scandia, MN 55073		
David Clausen/Univ. MN Walter Library	Sandy Sperazza (SS)	Michele Benson
117 Pleasant Street SE	6429 Mendelssohn Ln.	Duluth Adoptee Support Group
Minneapolis. MN 55455	Edina, MN 55343	mbens525@gmail.com

Dear AmFOR: . . . "We passed a law in 1987 requiring agencies to notify mothers, adopted persons, or adopters of the death of one or the other if the parties have stated they wish to be notified and if they keep the agency file updated with current addresses ... Good luck in your struggle. If there is anything more I can do to help, please let me know... Sincerely, MEG BALE, SOCIAL WORKER, POST-LEGAL ADOPTION SERVICES, CHILDREN'S HOME SOCIETY OF MN, Saint Paul, MN."

Dear AmFOR: ... "I am very happy with my adopters and love them dearly, but I have some questions that only my birthparents can answer. I also have some medical problems and would like to know some background information. Lutheran Social Service, Minneapolis, is the agency I was adopted through in 1970. Last year they wanted $350 to start the process to find my parents. I am a college student and currently don't have the funds. I was born in Henipen County, November 8, 1970. When my adopters came to get me, they also received a small locket. This was to be given to me at their discretion. There is no writing on it... Can you help me? Sincerely, JULIEANN D., Cambridge, MN."

Dear AmFOR: ... "I have been asked to be on a panel discussion in November at a conference on adoption issues being presented by the Bio-Medical Ethics Dept. of the University of Minnesota. I would like to distribute the paper you sent which is entitled, "The Failure of Foster Care and Adoption System." There are some great statistics listed . . . Your friend, SANDY SPERRAZZA, CONCERNED UNITED BIRTHPARENTS, Edina, MN."

Dear AmFOR: ..." I was born in St. Paul, MN on March 17, 1958. I do have the name given to me at birth (there was an error on my adoption papers!), but every attempt I've made to obtain those records results in being told my files are sealed. The other problem I have encountered is that the search fees are way out of my budget (between $600-$1000!) That makes me so angry. Why can't I have access to my records?... Thank you in advance! I'm glad you're there to help!... SUSAN K., Madison, WI."

Mississippi

CENTRAL RECORDS OFFICES

Vital Records
To Verify Fees
(rec = recorded message).

	Accessible?
Vital Records Reg	Restricted
PO Box 1700	fee
Jackson, MS 39216	
(601) 576-7960	
www.vitalrec.com/ms.html	

State (St), County (Co),
Birth (B), Death (D),
Marriage (M), Divorce (DV)
Indices & Records
St-B,D,M since 1/1912
St-Dv since 1/1926
Co-B,D,M Circuit Court
Co-Dv Chancery Clerk

State Archives Address	Year Adoption Records Closed	Hospital Records Available?	Legal Notice Required?
Dept. Archives & History	Unknown	Difficult	No
100 So. State St./PO Box 571			
Jackson, MS 39201			

Central Department of Motor Vehicles
MS Highway Safety (Drivers License)
PO Box 958
Jackson, MS 39215

National Archives-Southeast Region
1557 Saint Joseph Avenue
East Point, GA 30344; (404) 763-7477
Hours: M&W-F:7:30AM-4:30PM, Tu: 7:30AM-9:30PM
(Serves AL, GA, FL, KY, MS, NC, SC and TN)

Central Agency Holding Adoption Records	Non-Identifying Info Provided?	Adoption Decree From Court	State Registry
Dept. Human Services /Adoptions	Yes, by law;	No;	No; Waiver
PO Box 352	Adoptees.	Chancery Court	System.
Jackson, MS 39205			
(601) 359-4996			

(1987) ADOPTION DISCLOSURE STATUTES (WAIVER SYSTEM)
Section 93-17-25: closed hearings; court order required to release information. Section 93-17-27: reference to marital status of birthparent prohibited. Section 93-17-29: docket entries shall not name birthparent or adoptive parent. Section 93-17-3: doctor's certificate must accompany adoption. Rev. Stat. Section 93-17-3 (Supp 1991) mandates disclosure of non-identifying info. No penalties for unauthorized release stated.

ADOPTION SEARCH/SUPPORT GROUPS (see "Key" on page 47)
Lee Sande/Adoption Info. Network (S)
5917 5th St.
Meridian, MS 39307
nleesande@yahoo.com

> *Dear AmFOR:* . . . "Thank you for your quick response. My name at the time of relinquishment, in Mississippi, was Shirley Elaine Wood ... I use Elaine Wood on my driver's license in case my daughter tries to find me ... ELAINE M., McKinney, TX."

> *Dear AmFOR:* ... "Could you help me find my sister? ... I think she was born in Lucidale, MS and was adopted out in Ackerman, MS ... I wonder if I could find out if she is looking for her mother, or if I could find her? . . . Thank you, LYNN B., Chico, TX."

Missouri

CENTRAL RECORDS OFFICES

| Vital Records
To Verify Fees
(rec = recorded message).
Bureau Vital Records
PO Box 570
Jefferson City, MO 65102
(573) 751-6387
www.vitalrec.com/mo.html | Accessible?
Restricted;
fee | State (St), County (Co),
Birth (B), Death (D),
Marriage (M), Divorce (DV)
Indices & Records
St-B,D,M since 1/1912
St-Dv since 1948
Co-M: Deeds Recorder
Co-Dv-Circuit Court | |

| State Archives
Address
State Library
308 E. High St.
PO Box 387
Jefferson City, MO 65101 | Year Adoption
Records Closed
Unknown | Hospital Records
Available?
Unknown | Legal Notice
Required?
Unknown |

Central Department of Motor Vehicles
Department of Driver Licenses
Department of Revenue
301 W. High St.
Jefferson City, MO 65101

National Archives - Central Plains Region
2312 E. Bannister Rd.
Kansas City, MO 64131
(816)926-6272
Hours: M-F: 8AM-4:30PM, 3rd Sat: 9AM-4PM
(Serves IA, KN, MO and NE)

| Central Agency
Holding Adoption Records
Dept. of Social Services
Adoptions/PO Box 88
Jefferson City, MO 65103 | Non-Identifying
Info Provided?
Yes, by law.
Adoptees,
Birthparents | Adoption Decree
From Court
Unknown;
Circuit Court | State
Registry
Yes; Waiver
System |

(1987) ADOPTION DISCLOSURE STATUTES (INTERMEDIARY SYSTEM, REGISTRY AND WAIVER SYSTEM)
Section 453.120: Court order required to release information. Missouri Annotated Statute Section 453.121 (Supp. 1987) provides an Intermediary System. Ann. Stat. Section 453.121 (Vernon Supp. 1992) mandates disclosure of non-identifying info. In 1980, adult adoptee, James George petitioned the court to open his adoption file to locate biological relatives who might be willing to donate bone marrow transplant to treat his leukemia; the court, unable to get consent of the birthparents, denied the request. Networking search groups found his mother who eventually agreed to be tested, but no tissue match was obtained. (The mother refused to identify the father.) Section 453.121: Registry of birthparent and adult adoptee for identifying information. Non-identifying information may be requested and disbursed to adoptive parent, legal guardians, and adopted child at age of majority.

ADOPTION SEARCH/SUPPORT GROUPS (see "Key" on page 47)

Support Open Adoption Records
(SOAR) (SS)
4589 Hopewell Rd.
Wentzville, MO 63385

Sandy Hassler/Mary Ellen Hixon
Kansas City Adult Adoptees (S, SG)
PO Box 11576
Kansas City, MO 64138

Virginia Long (S)
Adoptee Searches, Inc.
PO Box 803
Chesterfield, MO 63006

Lindas Shipley Tremaine
MO Adoption Reform (S, SG)
708 Demaret Dr., B
Columbia, MO 65202
lshipley@socket.net

Carolyn Pooler
Adoption triad Support Network KKC
Liberty, MO
ganmother@aol.com
http://www.adoptiontriadsupportnetworkkkc.com

Judy Bock
Adoption Triad of the Ozarks
Columbia, MO
Atcofmidmo@socket.com
http://www.atcofmidmo.com

Sharon Fieker
Adoption Triad of the Ozarks
Springfield, MO
Bestyear95@yahoo.com
www.ichoosethisday.org/triad.htm

Janet Waer
STAC State Contact
2306 Meadowview Dr.
Jefferson, MO 65109

Carson Baxter (S, SG)
5061 Pernod St.
St. Louis, MO 63139
carsonbaxter@aol.com

Sandra Lombardo
705 Sandpiper St.
Raymore MO 64083

Woman's Day magazine, 11/02/93: True Story: "LOVE LOST AND FOUND ... When Linda finally told her parents she was pregnant, her distraught mother coerced into concealing her pregnancy and agreeing to give up the baby for adoption ... Finally, Bob grew discouraged and forced himself to try to forget her. On January 31, 1967, after 19 hours of hard and lonely labor, Linda gave birth to a baby boy ... Then in 1989, while visiting his mother for Thanksgiving, Bob suddenly felt an urge to find Linda right away ... At their second meeting, Linda confessed to Bob that the baby she had borne more than two decades before was really his child . . . Together they searched for the son Linda had given up for adoption ... Since Linda had falsified records when the baby was born, they kept having doors closed in their faces ... they enlisted the help of Virginia Long, a private investigator in St. Louis. Bob and Linda were the first guests on Long's new radio program that encouraged listeners to phone in clues that would help reunite adopted children with their natural parents . . . Nearly a year passed before any information surfaced ... Sitting in her son's living room, Linda thought about the many years she'd ached inside whenever someone asked, 'How many children do you have?' Now, at last, she could answer honestly, 'Three.'"

Lincoln County Journal, 06/04/91 . . . "THEY SAY GOOD THINGS COME TO THOSE WHO WAIT. Shirley Byington can attest to that first hand. She waited for 50 years for this moment; a chance to meet her sister, Pat Mauro. ... Byington was placed in a foster home in 1941, at the age of 4 by the order of th e court. She lived with her foster parents until she was 18. Pat was born in 1942. She, too, was placed in a foster home in Missouri. However, it wasn't until 1960 when Byington got in touch with her real father, who was living in St. Louis at the time, that she received some information on her background . . . her birth certificate, documents, even some family photos. Her real father died in 1963. Shirley and Pat have two other sisters (born in 1943 and 1945). They, too, were placed in foster homes. Maybe one day all four sisters will be reunited—Pat thinks so—but Byington is thankful for her reunion."

Dear AmFOR:... "I am seeking information on how to obtain adoption records. Often clients are adopted and have a desire to obtain information about their natural parents. Could you assist me or refer me to the appropriate source? Thank you for your assistance . . . Sincerely . . . ROBERT BONDURANT, ACSW, ST. ANTHONY'S MEDICAL & PSYCHIATRIC CENTER, St. Louis, MO."

Dear AmFOR: ... "I have been transracially adopted since I was two months old. I have wanted to find out more about my biological mother, but every time I try, people tell me I'm not old enough. I have talked to Social Workers, Counselors, and the Juvenile Court in St. Louis Missouri. I feel if I do research about adoption I will understand what my mother did; therefore, I am doing a paper on adoption. It would be helpful, personally and scholastically, if you could sent me any information on adoption and how I might go about finding out about my mother. Please send as soon as possible. Thank you ... Sincerely, KARA A., Holland, MI."

Dear AmFOR:... "Thank you for answering my letter so promptly. In the letter you said if I knew a name a searcher would be inexpensive. Well I do know my son's name. It is Jared. What I did not mention is I had a child in 1991, also placed for adoption. Her birth name is Rachel Quinn; adopted name is Abbey. They are being raised together . . . How can I find them using that information? I have no money for a paid search. I just recently started a job but it barely pays the rent. I don't know a lot about my children's parents . .. Anything will be of great help. Thank you .. . S.A., St. Louis, MO."

Dear AmFOR: . . . "Please send me a guide on how to find my sister who was given up for adoption in Missouri. The rest of us are known to each other except for this one sister. So long ago ... 1940 or 41, but still time to love another. I have her birth certificate but I don't know what to do as it all has to be done through mail. I would appreciate any suggestions . . . JUDITH D., Lenox, MO."

Dear AmFOR:... "I was adopted from Florence Crittenton Home for Unwed Mothers, Jackson County Juvenile Court, Kansas City, MO . . . Either my mother or my name before I was adopted was H.M.D. My adopter found this out by accident... I hope you can help me... JANA H., Morett, MD."

"Dear AmFOR: ... I was born in Clayton, MO February 3, 1969 and adopted February, 1970 . . . My adopter told me he thinks my birth surname was "Gray" or "Gay" ... Thank you for your help .. . Sincerely, JULIA T., Fort Riley, KS."

Montana

CENTRAL RECORDS OFFICES

	Accessible?	State (St), County (Co), Birth (B), Death (D), Marriage (M), Divorce (DV)
Vital Records To Verify Fees (rec = recorded message). Bureau of Records & Stats Dept of Health PO Box 4210 . Helena, MT 59604-4210 (406) 444-2685 www.vitalrec.com/mt.html	Restricted fee	Indices & Records St-B,D since 1907 St-M, Dv since 1943 inq. fwd; Co-B.D-Co. Clerk Co-B.Dv County Clerk

State Archives Address	Year Adoption Records Closed	Hospital Records Available?	Legal Notice Required?
State Archives 225 No. Roberts St. Helena, MT 59601	1973	Difficult	Unknown

Central Department of Motor Vehicles
Montana Highway Patrol
Drivers Licenses
303 Roberts
Helena, MT 59601

National Archives-Rocky Mountain Region
Denver Federal Center, Building 48
PO Box 25307
Denver, CO 80225-0307
(303) 236-0817; (303) 236-9354
    Hours: M-F:7:30AM-3:45PM, Tu: 7:30AM-4:45PM
    (Serves CO, MT, ND, SD, UT, WY)

Central Agency Holding Adoption Records	Non-Identifying Info Provided?	Adoption Decree From Court	State Registry
Family Services/Adoptions PO Box 8005 Helena, MT 59604 (406) 444-1675	Yes, by law; All Triad.	No; District Tribal Court	No

ADOPTEES BORN PRE-1967 CAN ACCESS ORIGINAL BIRTH CERTIFICATE ON REQUEST.

Section 40-8-126: closed hearings; court order required to release information. Conformed to Uniform Adoption Act (per Shephard's Acts) 1981. Section 40-8-122: medical and social history shall be provided to adoptive parent. Ann. Section 40-8-122 (1991) mandates disclosure of non-identifying information. SB-150 (1995) ends adoptees' right to petition court directly and makes it mandatory that the court appoint a confidential intermediary.

ADOPTION SEARCH/SUPPORT GROUPS (see "Key" on page 47)

Karen Virts (SS)
Missoula Adoption Reunion Registry
4104 Barbara Lane
Missoula, MT 59803

Rosemary Furnell (S SG)
Family Matters (SS)
214 - 12th Ave., S.
Shelby, MT 59474

Lynda Sowell
Child & Family Alliance
PO Box 2444
Great Falls, MT 59403

Jo Glass (SS)
20034 Pacific Coast Hwy., S.
Seattle, WA 98198

Post Adoption Center
(Referrals)
PO Box 634
Helena, MT 59624

Ella Gaffney
MT Adoption Resource
Box 634
Helena, MT 59624

Great Falls Tribune, 11/02/88: "LOCAL WOMAN LEADS BIRTH RECORDS BATTLE ... A Great Falls woman wants state legislators to loosen restrictions on original birth records of adopted children, complaining that state law allows district judges to block access to records. Jo Glass found both her biological mother and father within the last few years with the help of a court order from a district judge. But the judge could have denied her access to her birth certificate, under a 1975 state law allowing certain birth records to be confidential. The law states a person must have "good cause" to see the birth record . . . In her campaign, Glass said, she enlists the aid of two Miss Piggy puppets, which sport buttons bearing slogans such as "Don't treat adoptees like Cabbage Patch dolls." Glass ... is seeking petition signatures to make the effort most effective . . . She has already obtained 775 signatures including adoptive and natural parents."

Dear AmFOR:..." I recently started a search organization here in my hometown of Shelby, MT. At this time, unfortunately, due to new laws, we search groups are not allowed to do in-state searches. We can do out-of-state ones, until the next legislative session when we hope to have the laws changed ... I'm trying to get my hands on all the information I can in order to do my searches. I am a mother who relinquished my daughter in 1963. I have been hoping someday I can find her. I keep getting the old story that she died at childbirth. Well, she was okay when they "accidentally" brought her to see me in the hospital. Now they tell me she died a month later from a cold!! ... Sincerely, ROSEMARY FURNELL/DIRECTOR, FAMILY ANSWERS, 214 - 12th Ave., S., Shelby, MT."

Dear AmFOR:... "Since I last spoke with you, I made a few calls on my own to Montana and got hold of a woman with the Montana State Department of Family Services ... She was real anxious to help me in my venture to find my family. Within an hour, she had already called me back with the information I needed for a good start. She told me that I had 5 sisters and two brothers ... Last week I received my first letter from my oldest sister. She was so excited and happy to find out that I was looking for them. She also sent to me a lot of pictures of some of my family and of my mother. I have more family than I can memorize! I never expected so much. But, I am proud of every one of them. I have also talked with her and another one of my sisters. The whole family can't wait until I get to go to see them. Well, I just wanted to drop you a line and let you know how much luck I had. Thanks for all your help . . . Sincerely yours, MARGO F., Tupelo, MS."

Dear AmFOR:... "I spoke to you on the phone about 8 months ago. You sent me some information on possible contacts in Montana (where I was adopted). Thanks for your help. Keep me updated. I've finally decided it's time to get more involved and also actively search for my parents . . . Sincerely, GAYLE T. Palm Desert, CA."

Dear AmFOR: ... "I have always wanted to find my mom, but I don't know where to begin ... I have no idea where my papers are; my adopters have always kept them somewhere I haven't figured out yet. All I have is a certified copy of my birth certificate. I was born in Helena, MT on April 28, 1972. I have the doctor's name and the hospital. Yet all I know about my mother is she was 19 ... Thanks, T.J.T., Simi Valley, CA."

Nebraska

CENTRAL RECORDS OFFICES

	Accessible? Restricted: fee	State (St), County (Co), Birth (B), Death (D), Marriage (M), Divorce (DV) Indices & Records

Vital Records
To Verify Fees
(rec = recorded message).
Bureau Vital Stats.
Dept of Health
PO Box 95065
Lincoln, NE 68509
(402) 471 -2871 -rec
www.vitalrec.com/ne.html

Accessible?
Restricted:
fee

State (St), County (Co),
Birth (B), Death (D),
Marriage (M), Divorce (DV)
Indices & Records
St-B since 1904; D-pre'04
St-M Dv since 1909
Co-M County Court
Co-Dv District Court

State Archives
Address
State Historical Society Library
1500 and "R" Streets, NE
Lincoln, NE 68503

Year Adoption
Records Closed
1941

Hospital Records
Available?
Unknown

Legal Notice
Required?
No

Central Department of Motor Vehicles
Dept. of Motor Vehicles (Driver Records)
301 Centennial Mall, S.
Lincoln, NE 68508

National Archives - Central Plains Region
2312 E. Bannister Rd.
Kansas City, MO 64131: (816) 926-6272
Hours: M-F: 8AM-4:30PM, 3rd Sat: 9AM-4PM
(Serves IA, KS, MO, NE)

Central Agency
Holding Adoption Records
Dept. Social Services/Adoptions
PO Box 95044
Lincoln, NE 68509
(402 471-9333

Non-Identifying
Info Provided?
Yes, by law.
Adoptee,
Birthparents,
Siblings

Adoption Decree
From Court
No;
County Court

State
Registry
Yes

ADOPTEES (AGE 25) CAN ACCESS ORIGINAL BIRTH CERTIFICATE IF NO "BIRTH" PARENT VETO.

Section 45-113: court order required to release information. Nebraska Revised Statute Section 43-113 (Cum. Supplement 1984) provides an Intermediary System. Section 43-124: relative consent form provided by Bureau of Vital Statistics to match consents of natural relatives and adopted child over age 25 for release of identifying information. NE Rev. Stat. 43-107 (Supp. 1990) mandates disclosure of non-identifying info.

ADOPTION SEARCH/SUPPORT GROUPS (see "Key" on page 47)

Joyce Brown, Nancy Sullivan
Adoption Triad Midwest (SG)
PO Box 37273
Omaha, NE 68137

Adoption Triad Midwest
3711 North 108th Street
Omaha, NE 68164

Janet Fenton
CUB
4075 West Airport Road
Grand Island, NE 68803

Marge Brower
Adoption Triad-Midwest (SS
PO Box 489
Fullerton, NE 68638

Sandy Rolles (CUB) (SS)
9621 Parker St,
Omaha, NE 68114
Sandyrolls@cox.net

Linda Willson
La Vista, NE
cyrillawillson@aol.com

Omaha World Herald, 07/24/90: "ISSUES EXPLORED AT FORUM—PARENTS PROMOTE OPEN ADOPTION... Adoptive parents, birth parents and adopted children shared their experiences at a recent workshop titled, 'The Experts Speak Out.' The workshop was part of a weekend forum on adoption at Peony Park sponsored by the Child Saving Institute ... The new process of open adoption eliminates the curiosity of adopted children about their birthmothers. In open adoption, the birthmother and adoptive parents may exchange letters and pictures and may even visit each other... 'Over the years, adoption has been changing,' she said. 'There are different types of open adoption but you still need the agency behind you for counseling and support.'"

Dear AmFOR:... "This is the second agency to open their records. As far as I know, they are the first to combine open records with open adoption through an agency. These agencies are more important than they realize. Adoption reunions reduce stress. This benefits the individuals, the economy through increased productivity and the society through reduction of social pressure that has been a key influence in four successful revolutions. As true adoptions are peeled off, we will find kidnapped children 'laundered' through adoption with false papers, to conceal their true origins. The result will be a monumental international scandal, U.S. adoption courts and defects in our laws revealed as the central element. It's like cancer surgery. Painful, but necessary to protect the social body as a whole. I hope everybody supports Child Saving Institute . . . EUGENE AUSTIN, Tilden, NE."

Sunday World Herald, 02/02/92: "MOTHER, SON MEET AFTER 62 YEARS—GIVEN UP FOR ADOPTION IN ALLIANCE, MAN NEVER MOVED AWAY Yakima, Wash.-She was told he played In front of a Nebraska apartment with his red wagon. He was 4 years old. But when her search brought her to that street in Alliance, no one was there. She had a good cry and went back home to South Dakota. That was 58 years ago. It was the first time that Marjorie Melton tried to find her child, born June 2, 1930, in Alliance and adopted just 10 days after his birth. Tuesday evening at the Yakima airport, Ms. Melton, 82, and her son, William John Tragresser, were finally reunited . . . Not wanting to hurt the feelings of his 95-year-old adoptive mother, who was in a nursing home, Tragresser chose not to tell her he had found his birthmother. Mother and son first spoke on the telephone in May and again on Tragresser's birthday in June. The death of his adoptive mother around Thanksgiving paved the way for the reunion."

Dear AmFOR: . . . "In 1961 I relinquished my firstborn son to adoption through the coercion of my parents and Catholic Social Service. Apparently I was a slow learner, because I was back at CSS in 1964, and subsequently relinquished my second son to adoption. My first son and I have been reunited since June 6, 1986. I searched for my second son—without the blessings of CSS—and learned he was killed in an auto accident on June 6, 1984, more than two years before I located his adoptive family. The agency was aware of his death, but refused to give me the tiniest bit of information. Things got better. I married later in 1964. We have two sons born to us, three adopted daughters and a stepson—7 kids!... What a bunch!!... Sincerely, LINDA A-W, Omaha, NE."

Nevada

CENTRAL RECORDS OFFICES

Vital Records
To Verify Fees
(rec = recorded message).

Div. Health/Vital Stat	Accessible?
Dept of Human Resources	Immediate
4150 Technology Way - Suite 104	family;
Carson City, NV 89710	fee
(775) 684-4242	

www.vitalrec.com/nv.html

State (St), County (Co),
Birth (B), Death (D),
Marriage (M), Divorce (DV)
Indices & Records
St-B ,D since 7/1911
St-M.Dv since 1/68
Co-B,D,M County Recorder
Co-Dv County Clerk

State Archives	Year Adoption	Hospital Records	Legal Notice
Address	Records Closed	Available?	Required?
State Library	Unknown	Difficult	No
Archives Division			
100 Stewart St.			
Carson City, NV 89710			

Central Department of Motor Vehicles
Driver License Division
555 Wright Way
Carson City, NV 89701

National Archives - Pacific Sierra Region
1000 Commodore Dr.
San Bruno, CA 94066
(415) 876-9009
Hours: M-F: 8AM-4PM, W: 8AM-8PM
(Serves CA, except So. CA; HI, NV, except
dark Co.; Pacific Ocean area)

National Archives - Pacific Southwest
Region
24000 Avila Road, First Floor
Laguna Niguel, CA 92656; (714) 643-4241
Hours: Mon-Fri & 1st Sat: 8AM-4:30PM
(Serves AZ, So. CA and dark Co., NV)

Central Agency	Non-Identifying	Adoption Decree	State
Holding Adoption Records	Info Provided?	From Court	Registry
Dept. Child/Family Services/Adoptions	Yes, law gives	Sometimes;	Yes;
711 E. 5th St.	court discretion;	District Court.	Waiver System
Carson City, NV 89701	All Triad.		
(775) 684-4450			

(1986) ADOPTION DISCLOSURE STATUTES (REGISTRY AND WAIVER SYSTEM)
Section 127.140: closed hearing; court order required to release info. Nevada Revised Statute Section 127.007 (1986) provides a Registry System. No statement re fees. No separate provision for medical information. NM Ann. 40.7.52 (Michie 1980) gives courts discretion for disclosure of non-identifying info.

ADOPTION SEARCH/SUPPORT GROUPS (see "Key" on page 47)

Marsha L. Reinhart	Michael Sarkis	Dori Owen
4478 Casa Blanca	Adoptee Search Connection (SS)	165 Moore Lane
Las Vegas, NV 89121	9713 Quail Springs Ct.	Reno, NV 89509
	Las Vegas, NV 89117	

Las Vegas Review-Journal, 01/12/88: "SEARCH CONSULTANT'S JOB IS FINDING FAMILY TIES .
. . Michael Paris' clients know nothing of their past. But they're not suffering from amnesia. They're
suffering the phantom pains of adoption—either not knowing their own origins or not knowing the fate of
their birth child. Paris has a relatively obscure professional sideline. He is a family search consultant. As
Paris' phone message goes, 'We assist people searching for separated family members, whether by divorce, adoption or other disruption.' Certified by a private California-based organization called
Independent Search Consultants, Paris is one of approximately 75 ISC members nationwide. His Boulder
City service is Adoption & Family Search Consultants. Paris will only do a search on behalf of a minor with
the adoptive parent's permission. In general, he will only lead a search that culminates in a direct contact between
birthparent and birth child . . . Because each case has its idiosyncrasies, no two searches are alike. Paris declines
to elaborate on certain search methods. 'There are a lot of techniques and areas that are perfectly legal, but if
known would be shut off to adoptees. I will gladly share them with people searching.' He believes fervently in
the therapeutic value of a search, for both parties ... 98 percent of reunions are positive. For some males, that's
enough... 'Ninety-five percent of searchers are female, but we're seeing the male group go higher all the time.'
Some searches last years. Paris said his quickest search lasted two weeks, aided by an 'enlightened adoptive
mother' who had asked for and saved relevant information and by a loving birthmother who for 30
years had maintained an additional telephone listing under her maiden name in case her daughter came
looking. A search conducted by a consultant costs between $300 and $1,500, said Paris based on his own experience ... Search for immediate relatives, 'You can see results. You can see lives that are different... Once
you find that birthparent the ties to adoptive parents, in most cases, grow tremendously. I don't know
why. It just happens.'"

New Hampshire

CENTRAL RECORDS OFFICES

Vital Records
To Verify Fees
(rec = recorded message).
Bureau of Vital Records
71 South Fruit Street
Concord. NH 03301-2410
(603) 271-4650
www.vitalrec.com/nh.html

	Accessible?
	Immediate
	family;
	fee

State (St), County (Co),
Birth (B), Death (D),
Marriage (M), Divorce (DV)
Indices & Records
St-B,D,M since 1640
St-B.D since 1880
St-B,D,M Town Clerk
Co-Dv Superior Court

State Archives
Address
State Archives
71 So. Fruit St.
Concord, NH 03301

Year Adoption
Records Closed
1938

Hospital Records
Available?
Difficult

Legal Notice
Required?
No

Central Department of Motor Vehicles
Div. of Motor Vehicles (Driver Records)
10 Hazen Dr.
Concord, NH 03301

National Archives-New England Region
380 Trapelo Rd.
Waltham, MA 02154
(617)647-8100
Hours: M-F & 1st Sat: 8AM-4:30PM
(Serves CT, ME, MA, NH, RI, VT)

Central Agency
Holding Adoption Records
Dept. Child/Families/Adoptions
129 Pleasant Street.
Concord, NH 03301
(603) 271-4711

Non-Identifying
Info Provided?
Yes, by law;
Adoptee

Adoption Decree
From Court
Usually;
Probate Court

State
Registry
No;
Consent only

ADULT ADOPTEES (AGE 18) CAN ACCESS ORIGINAL BIRTH CERTIFICATE ON REQUEST.
Section 170-B: 19: closed hearings; court order to release information. NH Rev. Stat. Ann. Section 170-B: 19 II-C (Supp.
1985) allows access with consent only—no search or registry: identifying information may be obtained by adoptee over
age 21 with consent of birthparent. (Cum. Supp. 1975) Violating confidentiality of adoption proceedings—Misdemeanor.
Rev Stat Ann 170-B: 19 (1990, Supp. 1991) mandates disclosure of non-identifying info.

ADOPTION SEARCH/SUPPORT GROUPS (see "Key" on page 47)

Ginny Baynard
Morristown Post-Adoption Support
ginny_bay@yahoo.com

Randie Zimmerman
Adoptee Birthparent Support Central NJ
Hillsborough, NJ
Randie_Zimmerman@hotmail.com

Kelli A. Ross
Triad Support
6 Choate Road
Hanover, NH 03755

Pat Fox
PatFox1@aol.com

Paul Schibbelhute (AAC)
15 Seminole Drive
Nashua, NH 03063
pschibbe@aol.com

Tracy Pond
Birthmothers of New Hampshire
www.birthmothersofnh.cm

Dear AmFOR: ... "I found my son! Words cannot express my deepest gratitude. I'll never forget your
name and your help! ... DARLENE R., Bristol, NH."

New Jersey

CENTRAL RECORDS OFFICES

	Accessible?	State (St), County (Co), Birth (B), Death (D), Marriage (M), Divorce (DV)
Vital Records To Verify Fees (rec = recorded message). Bureau of Vital Stats PO Box 370 Trenton, NJ 08625-0370 (609) 292-4087 www.vitalrec.com/nj.html	Restricted; fee	Indices & Records St-B,D since 1/1878 St-M,Dv since 6/1878 Co-B,D,M,Dv

State Archives Address	Year Adoption Records Closed	Hospital Records Available?	Legal Notice Required?
State Library Archives & History 185 West State St. Trenton, NJ 08625	1941	Difficult	No

Central Department of Motor Vehicles
Division of Motor Vehicles
Bureau of Security Responsibility
25 So. Montgomery St Hours:
Trenton, NJ 08608

National Archives-Northeast Region
201 Varick St.
New York, NY 10014-4811; (212) 337-1300
M-F: 8AM-4:30PM, 3rd Sat: 8:30AM-4:OOPM
(Serves NJ, NY, Puerto Rico, Virgin Islands, federal census for all states. New York passenger arrivals on microfilm, also naturalization records for NY, NJ, Puerto Rico)

Central Agency Holding Adoption Records	Non-Identifying Info Provided?	Adoption Decree From Court	State Registry
Dept. Youth/Family Serv/Adoptions PO Box 717 Trenton, NJ 08625-0717 (609) 984-2380	Yes, by law; Adoptee	Seldom; Domestic, Superior	Yes; Intermediary

(1992) ADOPTION DISCLOSURE STATUTES (REGISTRY, INTERMEDIARY, WAIVER SYSTEM)
Section 9:3-31; records sealed; court order to release information. Section 9:3-41: prospective parents shall be provided with all available information relevant to child's development, personality, temperament and birthparent complete medical histories. Stat Ann Section 9:3-41.1 (West Supp. 1992) mandates disclosure of non-identifying info. Title 26 Rev Stat permits adoptee 21 or older access to orig. birth certificate; confidential intermediary system.

ADOPTION SEARCH/SUPPORT GROUPS (see "Key" on page 47)

Adoption Crossroads (SG)
85 Paramus Road
Paramus, NJ 07652
betglori@aol.com

Barbara Cohen (SG)
NJ Coalition For Openness
55 High Oaks Dr.
Wachtung, NJ 07060
BLCCohen@aol.com

Edna Cadillac
Angles & Extensions (SG)
PO Box 7247
Sussex, NJ 07461

Barbara Kelly
Adoption Reunion Coalition (SG)
15 Fir Pl.
Hazlet, NJ 07730

Joe Collins (L-PI)
H-6 Farmhouse Lane
Morristown, NJ 07960
joeadoptpi@aol.com

Diane LeMasson
Origins (SG)
289 E. Halsey Rd.
Parsippany, NJ 07054
DLeMasson@prodigy.net

Jane C. Nast (AAC)
Adoptive Parents for Open Records
(APFOR)
3 Harding Terrace/Fenwick
Mendham Township Cr. 32
Morristown, NJ 07960

Carol Gustavson (SG)
Adoptive Parents for Open Records
(APFOR)
9 Marjorie Dr.
Hackettstown, NJ 07480

Shea Campbell
Birthparent Support Group
Children's Aid & Family Services
scampbell@cafsnj.org

Nancy Heller
NJ Services for the Missing (SS)
PO Box 26
Gibbsboro, NJ 08026

Sandi Grimmie
Adoption Support Group of South NJ
(SC C)
32 Trotters Ln.
Smithville, NJ 98201

Cindi Addesso
Adoption Crossroads
15 North 15th St.
Hawthorne, NJ 07506
adesso@mindspring.com

Sue Wright
Origins
49 Richardson
New Brunswick, NJ 08901

West Central Search Support
of New Jersey
PO Box 3604
Trenton, NJ 08629

Janis Duncan, MSW
Adoption Support Network (SS)
505 W. Hamilton Avenue, #207
Linwood, NJ 08221

Birthdates
117 Nelson Ave.
Jersey City, NJ 07307

Maria Caliva
NJ Coalition for Openness
206 Laurel Place
Laurel Springs, NJ 08021

Pat Bennett
Concerned United Birthparents
Whippany, NJ
Paben48@comcast.net

Cindi Adesso
Full Circle Post Adoption Support
Paramus, NJ
cindilouwho@mindspring.com

Judy Foster
Jfoster7@optionline.net

Susan Durick
CHAT Triad Support Group
North Plainfield, NJ
chatssnj@comcast.net

Ruth Ann Morris (SS)
4 Michele Dr.
Middletown, NJ 07748

Pam Hasegawa
NJ Coalition for Openness
29 Hill Street
Morristown, NJ 07960
phasegawa@erols.com

Irene Gendron
Burlington County Birthmoms /
Adoptees Support Group
Pemberton, NJ
eastwestig@aol.com

John Peret/Mary Hunt
O.A.S.I.S.(S)
1733 Serpentine Dr.
Forked River, NJ 08731
mjshay@bellantic.net

Pamela Slaton (S)
45 Black Pine Lane
Mount Holly, NJ 08060
Pamelaobr@aol.com

NJ Adoption Resource
Clearinghouse
warmline@njarcb.org

Dear AmFOR:... "My brother and I were both born and adopted in Elizabeth, New Jersey, my birthdate is July 29, 1942 and I believe my brother was born in December 1944 ... and raised in Hillside, NJ. That is really all that I know ... I would greatly appreciate any help that you might be able to give me, as I really would like to find him soon . . . Most sincerely ... MS. BEATRICE L., LATOURETT, Tucson, AZ."

Dear AmFOR: ... "I would like to get information on how to conduct a search for my mother. I know I was adopted through a Catholic agency, that my records and my mother's maiden name are sealed in Trenton, NJ.... Thank you, LAURIE E., Lancaster, CA."

New Mexico

CENTRAL RECORDS OFFICES

Vital Records To Verify Fees (rec = recorded		State (St), County (Co), Birth (B). Death (D), Marriage (M), Divorce (DV)
Vital Stats Bureau	Accessible?	Indices & Records
PO Box 2610	Immediate	St-B ,D since 1880
Santa Fe, NM 87501	family; fee	St-M,Dv no state index
(505) 827-0121		Co-M County Clerk
www.vitalrec.com/nm.html		Co-Dv District Court

State Archives	Year Adoption	Hospital Records	Legal Notice
Address	Records Closed	Available?	Required?
State Records Center	1950	From doctor,	Yes
404 Montezuma St.		sometimes	
Santa Fe, NM 87501			

Central Department of Motor Vehicles
Transportation Dept.
Driver Services Bureau
PO Box 1028
Santa Fe, NM

National Archives-Southeast Region
501 W. Felix St./ PO Box 6216
Fort Worth, TX 76115; 87504 ; (817) 334-5525
Hours: M-F: 8AM-4PM, W: 8AM-9:PM
(Serves AK, LA, NM, OK, TX)

Central Agency	Non-Identifying	Adoption Decree	State
Holding Adoption Records	Info Provided?	From Court	Registry
Dept. of Social Services	Yes, by law	Always;	No;
Adoptions - Pera Bidg.	gives court	District Court	Intermediary;
PO Drawer 5160	discretion; Adoptee;		Waiver System.
Santa Fe, NM 87502	Birthparents		
(505) 827-8416			

(1986) ADOPTION DISCLOSURE STATUTES (CONSENT ONLY, INTERMEDIARY, WAIVER SYSTEM)
Section 40-7-53: court order required to release information. Identity of petitioner and birthparent shall not be released to each other without their consent; closed hearings; locked files. New Mexico Annotated Statute Section 40-7-53 (1986) provides access to records with consent only—no search or registry. Section 40-7-53: identifying information may be made available to adult adoptee about birthparent or to birthparent about adult adoptee with consent of parties. Non-identifying information available to adult adoptee without consent. Stat. Ann. 40-7-53 (Michie 1989) gives courts discretion regarding disclosure of non-identifying info.

ADOPTION SEARCH/SUPPORT GROUPS (see "Key" on page 47)

Elizabeth Avens
CUB
358 Joya Loop
Los Alamos, NM 87544

Leonie Boehmer (SS)
805 Alvarado Dr., NE
Albuquerque. NM 87108
BoehmerL@aol.com

Sally File
Operation Identity, Inc. (SG)
13101 Blackstone, NE
filefinder@aol.com

Cheryl Block
1411 Los Lentes, NE
Los Lunas, NM 87031

Rema/Adoption Search
PO Box 15206
Rio Rancho, NM 87174

Barbara Free
Operation Identity
1818 Somerville St. NE
Albuquerque, NM 87112

Karen J. Gregory
3600 Cerrillos Road
Santa Fe, NM 87505

Lee Morgan
Operation Identity
Albuquerque. NM
eaglesevephoto@comcast.net

Randa Phillips
Adoption Support Group
www.asgsf.org

Dear AmFOR: ... "I did give up the A.A.C. Hotline. It was taking 4-5 hours a day to man it correctly. Those were hours taken from my searching. Just decided I'd given to the A.A.C. all I could.

I'm glad to continue to act as a referral service from my phone (505) 293-3144. Please, if you know folks who need to be guided in the right direction, have them call me ... Always in search, SALLY FILE, OPERATION IDENTITY, 13101 Blackstone, NE, Albuquerque, NM."

Dear AmFOR: ..." I... am adopted ... I know few details of my heritage. I have always wanted to pursue looking for my mother, but wasn't sure how to go about it, without undergoing a lot of expense The facts that I do know are these: I was adopted approximately at the age of 4 months, and I was born in Santa Fe, NM (Bernalillo County). Please let me know if you can help with my search. Any and all information would be appreciated . .. Very truly yours, JEAN N., Aurora, MN."

Dear AmFOR: ... "I am 39 years old and adopted. I know my father's name and birth date, but I've always come up empty when it comes to obtaining any information that can lead to him. Could you please send me information on your organization? Thank you!... VALERIE A., Alamogordo, NM."

New York

CENTRAL RECORDS OFFICES

Vital Records		State (St), County (Co),	
To Verify Fees		Birth (B), Death (D),	
(rec = recorded		Marriage (M), Divorce (DV)	
NY STATE Dept. of Health	Accessible?	Indices & Records	
Vital Records Section	Immediate	St-B,D since 1880	
PO Box 2602	family: fee	St-M since 5/1915	
Albany, NY 12220-2602		St-Dv since 1/1963	
(212) 788-4521		Co-B,D,M,Dv Albany off.	

www.vitalrec.com/ny.html

Bureau of Records/Stats	Immediate	St-B,D since 1910	
NY CITY Dept. of Health	family; fee	St-M,Dv since 5/13/43	
125 Worth St., CM-4, Rm 13		City-B,D,M,Dv-City	
New York City, NY 12220-2603		Clerk each borough:	
(212) 788-4521		for pre-1910/1949	

State Archives	Year Adoption	Hospital Records	Legal Notice
Address	Records Closed	Available?	Required?
New York State Archives	1936	From doctor	No
Cultural Ed. Ctr., Rm. 11-0-40		or attorney	
Albany, NY 12230			

Central Department of Motor Vehicles	National Archives-Northeast Region
Department of Motor Vehicles	201 Varick St.
Public Service Bureau	New York, NY 10014-4811; (212) 337-1300
Empire State Plaza	Hours: M-F: 8AM-4:30PM, 3rd Sat: 8:30AM-4:OOPM
Albany, NY 12220	(Serves NJ, NY, Puerto Rico, the Virgin Islands, federal
	census records for all states, NY passenger, naturalization
	records for NY, NJ, Puerto Rico)

Central Agency	Non-Identifying	Adoption Decree	State
Holding Adoption Records	Info Provided?	From Court	Registry
Child/Family Serv/Adoptions	Yes, by law;	Never; Surrogate	NY Adoption Registry
40 N. Pearl St., Riverview Ctr. 6th fl.	Adoptee	Supreme, Family	PO Box 2602
Albany, NY 12243	Court		Albany, NY 12220-2602
(518) 474-9465			

PUBLIC ACCESS TU BIRTH INDEX **ONLY IN 5 BOROUGHS** of BRONX (Bronx Co), BROOKLYN (Kings County), MANHATTAN (New York County), QUEENS (Queens County), STATEN ISLAND (Richmond County) Section 114: records sealed; court order to release information. No mention of fact that child was born out of wedlock shall be included in files. New York Public Health Law Section 4138-B (Supp. 1984-85) provides a Registry System. Section 112: must include in petition all info. on child's medical history; Section 114: to be given to adoptive parent upon adoption. Section 114: may not disclose surname of child to adoptive parent except under court order. Unauthorized disclosure punishable as contempt of court - NY Domestic Rel. Law Section 114, McKinney 1976. In the 1970's Adoptees' Liberty Movement Assn. (ALMA) brought a class action suit by adoptees challenging Constitutionality of sealed records statutes in NY but the high courts refused to hear merits of the case. Effective July 27, 1992, NY State Registry no longer requires consent of adoptive parents in the registry to release identifying information between adoptees and birthparents; and the age requirement is lowered from age 21 to age 18. NY Soc. Ser. Law. Section 373-a (McKinney Supp. 1992) mandates disclosure of non-identifying info. Effective 4/01, $275 search fee repealed: check for any registration fees.

Joe Soll, President
Adoption Crossroads (SS)
National HQ
444 East 76th Street
New York, NY 10021
ccra@idt.net

Florence Fisher
ALMA HQ (SG)
Radio City Station, Box 727
New York, NY 10101
joesoll@adoptionhealing.com

Shelly Kosik
Reunions—The Next Step
305 E. 40th St., #12-V
New York, NY 10016

Ann Feldman (SG)
Adoption Alliance
17 Colton Ave.
Sayville, NY 11782

Iris Forschener
Adoption Crossroads (SG C)
7 Cheryl Pl.
North Massapequa, NY 11758

Rita Stapf
Adoption Crossroads (SS S)
PO Box 9025
Schenectedy, NY 12309

Richard Bliss - PI
39 Robisch Hill Road
Hortonville, NY 12745
sleuth@catskill.net

Adoptee Info. Service
19 Marion Ave.
Mt. Vernon, NY 10552

Holly Roth
Registry For Our Adoption Records
40 Springsteen Rd
Windsor, NY 13865

Toy Dupree
Manhattan Birthparent Group
New York City, NY
toyathome@msn.com

Sue Boyce (SS)
The Missing Connection
PO Box 712
Brownville, NY 13615

CUB
457 E. Maine Rd.
Johnson City, NY 13790
Connie Stang
4507 Windsor Terrace
Hamburg, NY 14075

Christine Losey
ANGELS (SG)
14 Baylor Circle
Rochester, NY 14624
ANGELSR5@aol.com

Marcia Cohen (SS)
B.V.S.S.
PO Box 299
Victor, NY 14564

Michele L. Tiedeman
PACES
6850 Akron Road
Lockport, NY 14094

Kathryn Blake
PACES
PO Box 1223
Amherst, NY 14226
kblake@adephia.net

Marjorie Moser
Origins (SG)
216 Carroll St.
Brooklyn, NY 11231

Carole Whitehead
Birthparent Supp Netwk (BSN)(SS)
37 Sylvia Lane
Old Bethpage, NY 11803
CAROLE401@aol.com

Mary Evans
ANSWERS
PO Box 67
Woodstock, NY 12498

Cathie Hanlon
Candid Adoption Talk
20 Fitzgerald Ct.
Monroe, NY 10950

Barbara Ilardo
Kinquest, Inc. (SS)
89 Massachusetts Ave.
Massapequa, NY 11758
mistical2@aol.com

Millie Fediw (SG)
Adoption Crossroads
20 No. Pine Dr.
North Massapequa, NY 11758

Ilene Mindlin
Adoptees/Birthparents-L.I.
134 Jerusalem Avenue
Massapequa, NY 11758

Richard Gauthier - PI
99 The Plaza
Atlantic Beach, NY 11509
priority101@aol.com

Anne Johnson
Family Finder
30 Grant Street
Potsdam, NY 13676
annehj@northnet.org

Denise McCarty
42 Morris St.
Auburn, NY 13021

Adoption Circle
401 E. 74th St., #17-D
New York, NY 10021

Diane Mees
Adoption Crossroads (SS)
PO Box 311
Shenrock, NY 10587

Kathy Lind
Bloodroots (SS C)
958 Comfort Rd.
Spencer, NY 14883

Phyllis Clearwater
B-KIDS (SS)
PO Box 43
Erin, NY 14838

Suffolk Adoption Search Support
10 Janice Ln.
Selden, NY 11784

Felicia Pin-one (SS S)
Birthparent Support Network (BSN)
93 Main St.
Queensbury, NY 12804

Beverly Thompson (S)
2350 Broadway
NYC, NY 10024

FINDEX/Far Horizons
PO Box 621
Cortland, NY 13045

Ronnie Richards
Triangle of Truths
4 Alder Lane
Liverpool, NY 13662

Wade G. Curry
74 Summit Ave.
Sea Cliff, NY 11579

Dominic/ Sarah Telesco
Center for Reuniting Families (SS)
51 Burke Dr.
Buffalo, NY 14215
dstelesco@aol.com

Susan Kelsey
ALMA
6101 Slocum Rd.
Ontario, NY 14519

Frank Piccareto
Adoptee Birthparent/FIND
104 Old Orchard Lane
Orchard Park, NY 14127

Jean Van Horn
Adoption Kin Ship (SS)
817 Taylor Dr.
Vestal, NY 13850

Eileen McCarthy (S) former ALARM
1355 Chelsea Rd.
Wantagh, NY 11793

BUSS (SS)
39 Tidd Ave.
Farmington, NY 14425

Cheryl Reidy
American Adoption Congress
38 Brookview Avenue
Delmar, NY 12054

Sandra Brown McDaniel
16 Gillett Lane
Cazenovia, NY 13035
SANDY21751@aol.com

Debra/John Tordoff (SG)
Jamestown Adoption Triad
644 Wade Hill Road
Gerry, NY 04740

Gail Davenport ACSW
Birthparent Support Network (BSN)(SS)
PO Box 120
North White Plains, NY 10603
GADS6@aol.com

Adoption Group of Orange County (SG)
PO Box 156
Chester, NY 10918

Leslie LaRocco
Bastard Nation
3356 Rt. 228
Alpine, NY 14805

Michael Colberg
Center for Family Connections
200 Park Avenue South #196
New York City, NY 10010

Hope A. Catricicala
Adoptees Political Action Coalition
PO Box 2807
Glenville, NY 12302

Dear AmFOR:..." In your October 16, 1987 letter to Governor Cuomo, you ask whether New York State would permit transmittal of medical information to an adoptee concerning a medical condition discovered in birthparents after an adoption. This office is responding because the Department of Health operates the Adoption Information Registry ... In the case you present in your letter, where you ask about information regarding a natural parent having AIDS, if the natural parent provides that information to the adoption agency, then the agency is apparently obligated to pass that information to the adoptive parents. In the other case you mention of a person trying to transmit the need for a bone marrow transplant, that situation would require a court to open adoption records to obtain the names of the natural parents. There is no guarantee that the courts in New York would actually open their records in such a case. The public policy in New York, as developed by both the courts and the Legislature, has favored strict confidentiality of all adoption records except for the non-identifying information available through the Registry. Earlier this year, this Department provided information about the New York Registry to Senator Levin of Michigan, who is proposing legislation for a national registry. I enclose a copy of the statute creating New York's Registry and a copy of Social Services Law Section 373-a, in hopes that the information will be helpful to you ... Sincerely, JAMES F. HORAN, ATTORNEY, STATE OF NEW YORK, DEPT. OF HEALTH, Albany, NY."

Quest: The Newsletter of Kinquest, Inc., Vol III, No. 4 (#12), 03/92: "VARIOUS NYS COURT RULINGS AFFECT ADOPTEES' AND BIRTH PARENTS' RIGHTS—Adoptee Seeking Medical Information Is Directed to the State Health Department's Registry ... Although it is agreed that genetic information was important, and that, indeed, some individuals might die for lack of it, the Court nonetheless declined to assist the adoptee, directing her, instead, to the Health Department and its Adoption Information Registry. Noting that one day natural parents might be required to leave tissue samples on file to permit genetic testing, the Court recognized that that day was not at hand. In the interim, the Court considered the registry sufficient protection for adoptees against genetic hazards."

Dear AmFOR:. . . "Thank you so much for the information you sent to me. I've requested information from numerous agencies and didn't receive anywhere near this amount of information or personal attention ... I've contacted Social Services in New York where I was adopted and got what information I could. And I also have the adoption decree from my mother. I contacted the hospital and they said that they destroy records after six years. I didn't know about the index card—could you possibly explain what that is? I've made a listing of all the Robinsons (birth name) across the country from the CD-ROM telephone directory that I have at my job. I have sent a letter to about 80 people in the area of my birth stating who I was and what I'm looking for (I've enclosed a copy of the letter). Now every time I go to the mailbox I get this weird feeling. I think I'm scared I'm going to get a letter saying—Stop Looking. I was surprised to have gotten two letters from people wishing me well in my search and they informed me that they were not related to me. I never thought people would respond in that manner. It really made me see things in a different perspective. I guess I just needed someone to help me realize that I'm not crazy to feel the way I do. My friends can't understand why I feel empty inside. Sometimes I can't understand it either. I have two loving adopters who would never be replaced in a million years, but I don't know how to explain how I feel. Well I've taken up enough of your time. Again, thank you for caring, not only about your own search, but for others you don't even know. You're one in a million ... Sincerely, KAREN B., New Fairfield, CT."

Dear AmFOR: ... "I have an adopted daughter who wishes to find her mother. It is very important to her; she is ... curious about her birth path. I love her very much and I have promised to stand by her and help in any way I can. She was born in Bronx, NY and the adoption took place in Manhattan, NY ... Sincerely, W.L., Westminster, CA."

Dear AmFOR: . . . "Thank you so much for all the information you sent me. It was very informative. I have just completed my husband's search., both mother and father. I am trying to become certified through ISC. My experience is in New York/New Jersey ... If you would add me to your very impressive list, I would appreciate it. Also, I would like any information on the laws of NY or Georgia. Thanks again for your help . . . Sincerely, GEORGI H.OLT, Marietta, GA."

Dear AmFOR: ... "I know very little about my parents, in fact, all I know is, I was born in Geneva, NY, to a young college student, on December 15, 1968. I would love to find my parents, to find out my history. Don't get me wrong, I'm not looking for a mother and father, I have one, I'm looking for myself. . . Thank you, M.M., Lakeland, FL."

Dear AmFOR:... "I would really like to know who my real parents are. I was adopted from Springville Hospital. I assume that I was born there; my name was changed when I was adopted. DOB: August 4, 1965. Thank you ... Sincerely, MARYJO L., Woodbourne, NY."

Dear AmFOR:.. ."I was born on May 29, 1968 in a Bronx hospital. The name of the hospital is unknown to me. At the age of two, I was adopted... I know I was named Nicholas by my parents, who I now wish to locate and meet with, or at least question as to my nationality, lineage and the circumstances surrounding my being given up ... There is not much information available to me by my adoptive parents regarding these matters. Perhaps this will make my search a futile endeavor, but I hope not. . . Any help your organization could offer to me would be greatly appreciated ... The work your organization is doing is fair, admirable and needed ... Sincerely, NICHOLAS T., Flushing, NY."

North Carolina

CENTRAL RECORDS OFFICES

		State (St), County (Co),
Address & Phone		Birth (B), Death (D),
To Verify Fees		Marriage (M), Divorce (DV)
(rec = recorded message).		Indices & Records
Div. Vital Records	Accessible?	St-B,D,M since 10/1913
1903 Mail Service Center	Public;	St-M,Dv no state index
Raleigh, NC 27699	fee	Co-M Deeds Registrar
(919) 733-3526		Co-Dv Superior Court
www.vitalrec.com/nc.html		

State Archives	Year Adoption	Hospital Records	Legal Notice
Address	Records Closed	Available?	Required?
State Library, Div. Archives	1938	Usually	No
109 E. Jones St.			
Raleigh, NC 27611			

Central Department of Motor Vehicles	National Archives-Southeast Region
Division of Motor Vehicles (Traffic Records)	1557 Saint Joseph Avenue
1100 New Bern Ave.	East Point, GA 30344; (404) 763-7477
Raleigh, NC 27601	Hours: M&W-F:7:30AM-4:30PM,
	(Serves AL, GA, FL, KY, MS, NC, SC, TN)

Central Agency	Non-Identifying	Adoption Decree	State
Holding Adoption Records	Info Provided?	From Court	Registry
Dept. Social Services/Adoptions	Yes, by law;	Always;	No
325 N. Salisbury/2401 Mail Serv. Ctr.	Adoptee.	Superior Court	
Raleigh, NC 27603			
(919) 773-4622			

(1987) ADOPTION DISCLOSURE STATUES

Section 48-13: No reference in records shall be made to birthparent marital status. Section 48-25: files not open to public. Section 48:26: court order required to release information. Section 48-9: Adoptive parent must be notified in cases where both birthparents have been adjudged insane or incompetent. Section 48-25: health history shall be given to adoptive parent and adopted child. Stat Section 48-25 (1991) mandates disclosure of non-identifying info. to adopted child over 21.

ADOPTION SEARCH/SUPPORT GROUPS (see "Key" on page 47)

Amy Bergman (AAC)
Adoption Issues & Ed. (AIE) (SG)
603 N. McNair Street
Washington, NC 27889

Jeffrey M. Lamb
53 Short Studer Rd.
Leicester NC 28748

Sandy Wilson
4101 Ivy Lane
Kitty Hawk, NC 27949

Robin Wilson (SS)
CUB
11 Sweetbriar Ln.
Chapel Hill, NC 27514

Julie Bailey (AAC)
PO Box 1582
Carraborg, NC 27510
Julesbai@aol.com

CUB
4916 Brentwood Dr.
Durham, NC 27713

Lynn Giddens (AAC)
PO Box 4153
Chapel Hill, NC 27515

Lynn Kopatich (SS)
CUB
2906 Plantation Rd.
Charlotte, NC 28226

Tammy Hall
Adoption Reunion Connection
PO Box 1447
Dunn, NC 28336

Christine Lee (L-PI, AAC)
Adoption Info Exchange (AIE)(SS);
Kinsolving Investigations (SS)
PO Box 1917
Matthews, NC 28106
mzchrisles@aol.com

Francie Portnoy, MALPC
Children's Home Society
PO Box 14608
Greensboro, NC 27415
fportnoy@bellsouth.net

Adoption Information
8539 Monroe Rd.
Charlotte, NC 28212
Kinston, NC 28501

Roberta MacDonald
Triangle Adoption Support Group
nccar@mindspring.com

Mari Cochran
WNC Adoption Network
Asheville, NC
info@wncadoptionnetwork.org
www.wncadoptionnetwork.org

Raleigh News & Observer, 05/21/89: "OPEN ADOPTION RECORDS ... As an adult adoptee, I am responding to a May 14 letter, 'Real' parents defined.' The writer says that 'parents who nurtured you, raised you ... are your REAL parents.' and that 'adoption records should remain sealed—never opened and permitted to wreak havoc on a family.' Actually, it is the deception of sealed records that wreaks havoc on adoptive families ... Our adoptive parents are our REAL parents. But our birth parents are also 'real,' in that they really do exist. For an adoptee to deny the existence of his birth parents is to deny the existence of a part of himself. . . SARAH B., Raleigh, NC"

The State in Charlotte, NC: "REAL CELEBRATION—25-YEAR-OLD AIKEN MAN REUNITES WITH BIRTHPARENTS ON NEW YEAR'S ... on New Year's Day, Aiken resident Jim Hopper got a new family. Hopper, a 25-year-old plumber, met his biological parents for the first time Friday. He and his parents, Linda Young and Robert Jaeckel, had been searching for each other for years without success .. . Long has computer access to all city directories in the United States and was able to get a list of all people named James Hopper. She then called each person on the list until she found the right one ... It cost Jaeckel and Young $1,050 to search for Hopper, Long said ... the trio said the cost and worry of the search was worth it."

Dear AmFOR:..." I hope you will be able to help me locate my brother. We were separated shortly after I was born. Social Services in Whiteville, North Carolina will not help me ... The papers they sent has that their records in 1962 indicated he had mild mental retardation . . . My brother's name is Tommy Jackson Bratcher. He was born November 3, 1959 at Columbus County Hospital, Whiteville, NC. I was told that my brother was dead, but I have found out he is still alive. Our mother died shortly after I was born. Our father gave us up for adoption. Our father is not in good health and would like to see his son before he dies. I would also like to meet my brother ... If you can help I sure would be glad .. . MRS. V.L.D.T., Society Hill, SC."

Dear AmFOR: . . . "Getting information on my natural parents is impossible here in North Carolina. I need your help . .. Sincerely, PHYLLIS A., Durham, NC."

Dear AmFOR:... "I do not know where I was born and I have no idea how the adoption system works. Although my parents are very loving, they have mixed feelings about my search ... I heard about your organization from an article in a magazine and thought writing you would be a good start. . . HOLLY P., Carrboro, NC."

Dear AmFOR:... "I surrendered my daughter to adoption in NC. Please forward me search info. NC is a TUFF STATE! With many restrictions . .. God bless, S.M."

North Dakota

CENTRAL RECORDS OFFICES

Vital Records
To Verify Fees
(rec = recorded message).
Div. of Vital Records
State Capital
600 E. Boulevard Ave.
Bismarck, ND 58505
(701) 328-2360
www.vitalrec.com/nd.html

Accessible?
Restricted;
fee

State (St), County (Co),
Birth (B), Death (D),
Marriage (M), Divorce (DV)
Indices & Record
St-B,D since 7/189
St-M since '25; M-7/49
Co-M County Judge
Co-Dv District Court

State Archives	Year Adoption	Hospital Records	Legal Notice
Address	Records Closed	Available?	Required?
State Archives	Unknown	Unknown	Unknown
North Dakota Heritage Center			
612 E. Boulevard Ave.			
Bismarck, ND 58505			

Central Department of Motor Vehicles
Driver License Division
600 E. Boulevard Ave.
Bismarck, ND 58505

National Archives-Rocky Mountain Region
PO Box 25307
Denver, CO 80225-0307; (303) 236-0817
Hours: M-F:7:30AM-3:45PM, Tu: 7:30AM-4:45PM
(Serves CO, MT, ND, SD, UT, WY)

Central Agency	Non-Identifying	Adoption Decree	State
Holding Adoption Records	Info Provided?	From Court	Registry
Children/Family Services/Adoptions	Yes, by law;	Unknown;	Yes;
600 E. Boulevard Ave	Adoptee:	District Probate	Intermediary
Bismarck, ND 58505	Birthparents	Court	

(1985) ADOPTION DISCLOSURE STATUTES (INTERMEDIARY SYSTEM. REGISTRY)
Section 14-15-16: closed hearings; confidential records. Conformed to Uniform Adoption Act (per She Shephard's Acts). ND Century Code Section 14-15-16 (Supp. 1985) provides an Intermediary System. Section 14-15 provides for medical information. Code Section 14-15-16 (1991) mandates disclosure of non-identifying info. Section 14-15-16: Non-identifying information about birthparent shall be provided to adoptive parent and adopted child age 21 or older. Adoption agency shall make reasonable efforts to contact birth parent of adult adoptee who desires contact or identifying information for adult siblings or adoptee.

ADOPTION SEARCH/SUPPORT GROUPS (see "Key" on page 47)
for referrals, contact:
The American Adoption Congress (AAC)
1000 Connecticut Avenue NW #9
Washington, DC 20036
(202) 483-3399; www.american-adoption-cong.org

Lutheran Social Services of North Dakota
Fargo, ND.org
(701) 235-7341

Dear AmFOR:... "In April of 19641 was adopted at the age of 6. In recent years I was told of an older brother who was also to have been adopted. But something happened and he was sent back to Child Protection. I can't get much more except his name and approximate age ... I have been requesting info from ND Department of Human Services ... PATRICIA H., San Bernardino, CA."

Ohio

CENTRAL RECORDS OFFICES

Vital Records
To Verify Fees
(rec = recorded message).
Div. of Vital Stats.
PO Box 15098
Columbus, OH 43215
(614) 466-2531-rec
www.vitalrec.com/oh.html

Accessible?
Public;
fee

State (St), County (Co),
Birth (B), Death (D),
Marriage (M), Divorce (DV)
Indices & Records
St-B,D since 12/20/08
St-M since 9/49; Dv-'48
Co-M, Dv Probate Judge

State Archives
Address
State Library Archives
Interstate Route 71 & 17th Ave.
1982VelmaAve.
Columbus, OH 43211

Year Adoption
Records Closed
1964

Hospital Records
Available?
Yes

Legal Notice
Required?
Unknown

Central Department of Motor Vehicles
Bureau of Motor Vehicles
Driver Licenses
PO Box 7167
Columbus, OH 43205

National Archives - Great Lakes Region
7358 South Pulaski Rd.
Chicago, IL 60629; (312)353-0162
Hours: M & W-F: 8AM-4:15PM
(Serves IL, IN, MI, MN.OH, WI)

Central Agency
Holding Adoption Records
Dept. Family Services/Adoptions
65 East State St., 5th fl.
Columbus, OH 43266

Non-Identifying
Info Provided?
Most agencies;
some for fee;
Adoptee, Adop. Parent

Adoption Decree
From Court
Usually;
Probate Court

State
Registry
Yes;

ADOPTEES BORN PRE-1964 CAN ACCESS ORIGINAL BIRTH CERTIFICATE ON REQUEST.
Section 3107.17: Closed Hearings; Court Order Required to Release Information. OH Rev. Code Ann. Section 3107.39-44 (Supp.1985) allows access to records with consent only. Section 3107.12/17: Non-identifying social history of birthparent may be inspected by adoptive parent and adoptee as Court so orders. Section 3107.38: identifying information about birthparent and siblings will be released to adult adoptee with their consent. Section 3107.42: unauthorized release of information is a Misdemeanor. Rev. Code Ann Section 3107-12 (Anderson 1989) mandates disclosure of non-identifying info. Adoptees' pre-1/64 birth records are public.

ADOPTION SEARCH/SUPPORT GROUPS (see "Key" on page 47)

ABORN
PO Box 27633
Cleveland, OH 44127
Jeep@aborn.org

Barbara Miller (SG)
Adoption Triad Support
980 Main St.
Wellsville, OH 43968

Joan Comett (SG)
Aftermath
2547 Loris Dr.
West Carrolton, OH 45449

Lucy Ruffher
Adoption Connection (SS)
PO Box 2482
Youngstown. OH 44509

Mary Howard
Birthmother's Support (SG)
27 S. Ludlow, #1126
Dayton, OH 45402

Carole Alard (SG)
Adoption Option, Inc.
PO Box 429327
Cincinnati, OH 45242

Christine Darr ISC
Adoption Triangle Unity (SS)
4144 Packard
Toledo, OH 43612

Linda Pellini
Adoption Network Ceveland
www.adoptionnetwork

Joanne Halbgewoks (SS)
(Formerly ALARM)
7523 Road 24, Rt. 2
Continental, OH 45831

Joanne Gall (SS)
Chosen Children
311 Springbook, #B-1
Dayton, OH 45405
ag802@mvcndayton.oh.us

Sue Langenhorst
12-Step Adoption Healing (SG)
2120PershingBlvd.
Dayton, OH 45420

Betsie Norris
Adoption Network-Cleveland
291 E. 222nd St., Rm. 229
Cleveland, OH 44123
Betsie@adoptionnetwork.org

Mary Fuller (SS C)
Insight to the Adoption Triad
2599 Riverside Drive 3-E
Columbus, OH 44903

Susan McGuire-ISC
5617 WintonRoad
Fairfield, OH 45014

Janet Huddleston ISC
3230 Nidover Dr.
Akron, OH 44312

Judy Braddock (SG)
Mum's the Word Support Group
381 BartleyAve.
Mansfield, OH 449903

Janet Anderson
Full Circle (SS)
4110 North Ave., #4
Cincinnati, OH 45236

Berta Yenney (SG)
Birthmothers Network
856 Pine Needles Dr.
Dayton, OH 45458
vnnybc@juno.com

Micki Glassbum (SS)(S)
SE Ohio Searchers (SOS)
109 North Plains Rd. #20
The Plains, OH 45780
Birthright
6779 Manchester Rd.
Clinton, OH 44216

Diana Creque
Full Circle (SG)
11690 Cymmes Valley
Loveland, OH 45410

Lisa Ginges
CUB (SS)
1446 Bensch Dr.
Toledo, OH 43614

Sue Gettings (SG)
Support for Birthparents
1983 Sitterly Rd.
Canal Winchester, OH 43110

Marjorie Drinnon
Support Adoption Trial
526 Hamilton St.
Bryan, OH 43506

Jean Batis (SS)
Sunshine Reunions (SS)
1175 Virginia Ave.
Akron, OH 44036

Adoption Network
302 Overlook Park Dr.
Cleveland, OH 44110

Deb Bryan, Jeanne Uram (SS)
Adoption Network
205 W. 30th St., Rm 14
Lorain, OH 44055
deb@adoptionnetwork.org
jeanne@adoptionnetwork.org

Burleigh G. Wall, L.P.I
Peace Maker Investigations
PO Box 902
Pataskala, OH 43062
P18856@aol.com

Dear AmFOR:... "I decided to try to locate some type of information concerning my parents.
But all I ran into was a lot of hassles and dead ends—because they claim my records are sealed and I need
$50 and a court order to open them. Well, I certainly don't have that kind of spare money so I put it on
hold for awhile. Last year, I landed myself in the hospital for 18 days not knowing what was wrong with
me; the doctors . . . kept questioning my heredity and I kept telling them I was adopted and had no
knowledge of my medical background. They told me to locate the hospital where I was born and maybe
they could help. Well, of course another dead end. I even contacted the adoption service I was adopted
through. They kept telling me they would get back with me and of course they never did . .. SCOTT B.,
Massillon, OH."

Oklahoma

CENTRAL RECORDS OFFICES

Vital Records		State (St), County (Co),
To Verify Fees		Birth (B), Death (D),
(rec = recorded message).		Marriage (M), Divorce (DV)
Vital Records Section	Accessible?	Indices & Records
1000 NE. Tenth, Rm. 117	Genealogy;	St-B,D since 10/1908
Oklahoma City, OK 73117	fee	St-M,D no state index
(405) 271-4040		Co-B.D Court Clerk
www.vitalrec.com/ok.html		Co-M,Dv Court Clerk

State Archives	Year Adoption	Hospital Records	Legal Notice
Address	Records Closed	Available?	Required?
State Archives/Records	1953	Difficult	Yes
200 NE 18th St.			
Oklahoma, OK 73105			

Central Department of Motor Vehicles	National Archives-Southeast Region
Dept. of Public Safety (Driver Records)	501 W. Felix St./PO Box 6216
PO Box 11415	Fort Worth, TX 76115; (817) 33 4-5525
Oklahoma City, OK 73136	Hours: M-F: 8AM-4PM, W: 8AM-9:PM
	(Serves AK, LA, NM, OK, TX)

Central Agency	Non-Identifying	Adoption Decree	State
Holding Adoption Records	Info Provided?	From Court	Registry
Dept. Child/Family Services/Adoptions	Yes, by law;	Usually;	Yes
907 South Detroit, Ste. 750	All Triad.	Children's	
Tulsa, OK 74120		District Court	
(918) 592-9149			

(1988) ADOPTION DISCLOSURE STATUTES (REGISTRY SYSTEM)

Section 60.17: closed hearings; court order required to release information. Conformed to Uniform Adoption Act (per Shephard's Act), 1981. No statement re fees. Section 60.5A: Persons required to consent to adoption must complete a medical history of child, birthparents to be filed with adoption petition. OK Stat Ann Tit. 10, Section 57 (West Supp. 1992) mandates disclosure of non-identifying info. Non-DHS disclosure requests will be sent to International Soundex Registry.

ADOPTION SEARCH/SUPPORT GROUPS (see "Key" on page 47)

Tracy Norsworthy/Cynlla Peters	Karen Slagle	Gary Strode
Oklahoma Adoption Triad (SS)	Shepherd's Heart (SG)	Adoption Triad of OK
PO Box 471008	158 Stevens Circle North	RR-3, Box 2110
Tulsa, OK 74147	Newalla, OK 74857	gstrode@webzone.net
	kcsl976@aol.com	
Jenny Kolp		Sue Scott
Adoption Connection	Carol Davis-Brake	Shared Heartbeats
Rt. 1, Box 613	Adoptive Families in Search	PO Box 12125
Roland, OK 74954	PO Box 2225	Oklahoma City, OK 73157
klop@ipa.net	Stillwater, OK 74076	

Deborah Oaks
401 South Ash Avenue
Altus AFB, OK 73521

Glenda Allen
Research Roots
PO Box 3311
Edmund, OK 73083
glendagri@aol.com

Samantha Franklin
OK Post-Adoption Support
Tulsa, OK
sfranklin568@yahoo.com

Dear AmFOR:... "I was born at St. Anthony's Hospital in Oklahoma City, OK on March 15, 1963 and adopted through Catholic Social Services. They informed me that I could have information when I was 18, only to be told at that time that I would have to be 21. At 21 I was told that the law had changed and that I could not get any information. Any assistance you can give me would be greatly appreciated . . . JOHN W., Norman, OK".

Dear AmFOR: ... "I am presently assisting a friend searching in Oklahoma for his natural parents. We have the court records and copies of his mother's birth certificate, but we are now at a stand-still... Any help in this matter would be appreciated ... Sincerely yours, MERRY ANN S., Phoenix, AZ".

Dear AmFOR: ... "I am a 37-year-old wife and mother of two teenagers. When I was three days old, I was adopted through a private agency in Oklahoma. My legal mother doesn't seem to know much about the circumstances or just doesn't want to tell me. Anyway I don't want to press the issue and hurt her feelings. But I can't stand not ever knowing the answers to all my questions. I love her and wouldn't change mothers for the world. I would like advice on how to go about locating my real mother without having to go to court if at all possible. I don't have much money. Any help in this endeavor will be appreciated ... A.S., Bedford, TX."

Dear AmFOR: . . . "My daughter is 21 years old and she and I would like to begin a search for her birthparents. We have limited information from the county social services adoption agency where she was placed with us. Can you please contact us with information on how we may start this procedure? .. . Sincerely, JO C., Broken Arrow, OK."

Dear AmFOR:... "I am an adoptee longing to find my roots. I was born on June 9, 1969, at St. Anthony's Hospital in Oklahoma City, OK. My legal adopters.... adopted me 10 months after my birth ... Sincerely, MICHELLE C., Goodwell, OK."

Dear AmFOR:... "Sixteen years ago on May 24, 1973, I gave birth to a boy and put him up for adoption through the Oklahoma State Adoption Agency. At that time I was at the Salvation Army Home for Unwed Mothers. During the past sixteen years I have tried to deny my own feelings and do as I was forced to do by my parents so long ago. But I can't anymore. If there is anyway I can find this child, or at least register with organizations should he decide to search one day, then I want to do so. I understand your organization helps people separated by adoption and you also support legislation that would open currently sealed adoption records . . . Can you do anything at all to help me in my search? Your response will be greatly appreciated . .. Sincerely, J.H., Stillwater, OK."

Dear AmFOR:.. . "Please allow me to go on file so that if and when my daughter (born 11/11/72) should want to find me she will know that I'm waiting . . . Thank you, CONSTANCE S., Bartlesville, OK."

Oregon

CENTRAL RECORDS OFFICES

Vital Records
To Verify Fees
(rec = recorded message).
DHS-Vital records
PO Box 14050
Portland, OR 97293
(971) 673-1190
www.vitalrec.com/or.html

Accessible?
Immediate
family;

State (St), County (Co),
Birth (B), Death (D),
Marriage (M), Divorce (DV)
Indices & Records
St-B,D since 7/1903
St-M since 1907
Co-B,D,M, Dv Co. Clerk

State Archives	Year Adoption	Hospital Records	Legal Notice
Address	Records Closed	Available?	Required?
State Library	1957	From doctor	Sometimes
Oregon Collections Room			
800 Summer St., NE			
Salem,OR97310			

Central Department of Motor Vehicles
Motor Vehicle Division
1905 Lana Ave., NE

National Archives-Pacific Northwest Region
6125 Sand Point Way, NE
Seattle, WA 98115; Salem, OR 97303
Hours: M-F: 7:45-4:00, Tu: 5:00-9:00
(Serves ID, OR, WA)

Central Agency	Non-Identifying	Adoption Decree	State
Holding Adoption Records	Info Provided?	From Court	Registry
Dept.Child/Family Services/Adoptions	Yes, by law;	Usually;	Yes;
500 Summer St., NE, 2nd fl	All Triad	District Court	Intermediary
Salem, OR 97310-1017			System

ADULT ADOPTEES (AGE 21) CAN ACCESS ORIGINAL BIRTH CERTIFICATE ON REQUEST.

Section 432.420: records sealed; court order required to release information. Section 7.211—separate records. Oregon Revised Statute Section 109.425 (1985) provides a Registry System. No fees statement. Section 19.342: Medical history of adopted child and birthparent required; must be available to adoptee at majority and give to adoptive parent when decree is granted. Section 109.430: non-identifying and identifying information shall be made available; Voluntary Adoption Registry for birthparents, adult adoptees, adult genetic sibling, adoptive parents of deceased adoptee, or adult siblings of deceased adoptee. No penalty statement available. Rev. Case Ann. Section 3107-12 (Anderson 1989) mandates disclosure of non-identifying info. Section 109.425 to .500 revised- Adoptee, age 18, may access original birth certificate on request, with ID.

ADOPTION SEARCH/SUPPORT GROUPS (see "Key" on page 47)

Sarah Atkins (SC)
11505 SW Dutchess
Beaverton, OR 97005

Carol Bridges (SG)
612 Cascade, #76
Woodburn, OR 97071

Pam Wilson/Donna Wells OARA (SS)
PO Box 882
Portland, OR 97207

Kathy Brown
So, OR Adoptee Rights Ass.(SOAR)
1076 Queens Branch Rd.
Rogue River, OR 97537

Heather Megyesi (SS C)
4633 SE 113th
Portland, OR 97266

Helen Gallagher ISC
Family Ties
4537 Souza
Eugene, OR 97402
helengal@efn.org

Dianne May
Adoptee Birthfamily Connection (SS)
PO Box 50122
DL_MAY@ prodigy.net

Ann Taylor
(SOAR)
PO Box 415
Ashland, OR 97520
actmwt@hotmail.com

Pat Florin
The Circle
635 Elkader Street
Ashland, OR 97520
pjflorin@jeffnet.com

Delores Teller
Portland, OR
teller@osure.edu

Kathlyn Krautscheld ISC
7778 SW. Salmon Ave
Redmond, OR 97756

Norma Benjamin
14394 Ehlen Road
Aurora, OR 97002

Katherine Pederson, Ed.M.
Triad Connection (SS)
550 SE 123rd St.
South Beach, OR 97366

Ruth Johnson
So. OR Adoptive Rights (SOAR)
1605 SW "K" St.
Grants Pass, OR 97526

Shannon Baker
The Circle-C-14
Medford, OR 97504

Nancy J. Finley
5236 SW Nebraska
Portland, OR 97219

Coco Brush
AAC, CUB
Portland, OR
cocobrush@yahoo.com

Nina Yates
Adoption Mosaic
Portland, OR

Dear AmFOR:... " All my life whenever I wanted join ... or... start school, go into the Service ... even when I applied for Social Security ... 'Where is your birth certificate?'... Never had one, no one seemed to see it as a problem ... it cause me a lot of anguish. I was just after my seventieth birthday a cousin sent a letter. In it was a genealogy of our family. I almost fell off the kitchen stool. My adopters adopted me when I was three weeks old ... Although the news was not something I wanted to hear, I am glad I got to know . . . something I suspected. A lot of things are clearer . . . My advice to adopters: PLEASE, PLEASE tell your child as soon as they start to walk. It's best YOU explain . . . I'm in search of my family. I understand I have two brothers . . Yours in search, DALE M., Grants Pass, OR."

Dear AmFOR:... "My adopted son Wayne Louis Falck would like to find his parents. We are not sure just how to go about it. I saw this story in a magazine with your address on it and decided to see you might help us. My husband was in the Air Force in Portland, OR in 1964. We answered an ad in the military paper wanting military personnel to adopt children through the Welfare Office in Portland. Wayne was eight months old when we adopted him. He had been in a foster home. They called him Sandy ... His mother's name was on the adoption papers but my husband had the lawyer cut it out. Could we request another copy? Or could they locate her for us? ... Sincerely, MARJORIE S., Houston, TX."

Dear AmFOR:... "I'm looking for my birthmother. I have a lot of the records ... My adopter is helping me search. Please send information .. . Thank you, ROBERT O., Florence, OR."

Dear AmFOR: ... "I have no idea who my real parents are and I can't talk about it with my adopters That's why I was really excited when one of my friends told me about you guys ... I really hope that you can help me! But this must remain a secret from my adopters ... L.S., Coos Bay, OR."

Dear AmFOR:... "I was born in the Good Samaritan Hospital (Wilcox). There was apparent family problems. The foster mother nicknamed me 'Pansy' in the hospital; it was my mother's favorite flower . . . Thank you, LORI M., Cathedral City, CA."

Pennsylvania

CENTRAL RECORDS OFFICES

Vital Records
To Verify Fees
(rec = recorded message).
Div. Vital Stats.
State Dept. of Health
PO Box 1528
New Castle, PA 16103
(724) 656-3100
www.vitalrec.com/pa.html

Accessible?
Public;
fee

State (St), County (Co),
Birth (B), Death (D),
Marriage (M), Divorce (DV)
Indices & Records
St-B,D since 1906
St-M, since 1941; Dv-'46
Co-M Marriage Lie. Clerk
Co-Dv Prothonotary at
County Seat

State Archives
Address
State Library Archives
Reference Section
PO Box 1026
Harrisburg,PA 17120

Year Adoption
Records Closed
Unknown

Hospital Records
Available?
Difficult

Legal Notice
Required?
Yes

Central Department of Motor Vehicles
Dept. of Transportation
Bureau of Accident Analysis
Operator Information Section
Driver Licenses
PO Box 8695
Harrisburg, PA 17105

National Archives - Mid-Atlantic Region
Ninth and Market Sts., Room 1350
Philadelphia, PA 19107
(215) 597-3000
Hours: M-F: 8AM-5PM, 2nd Sat. 8AM-4PM
(Serves DE, PA, MD, VA, WV)

Central Agency
Holding Adoption Records
Dept. Children/Youth/ Family/Adoption
PO Box 2675 Adoptee
Harrisburg, PA 17105
(717) 783-7376

Non-Identifying
Info Provided?
Yes, by law;

Adoption Decree
From Court
Never;
Common Pleas
Court

State
Registry
Yes;
Intermediary
Waiver System

ADULT ADOPTEES ACCESS ORIGINAL BIRTH CERTIFICATE IF "BIRTH" PARENT FILES WAIVER:
Section 2905; court order required to release information. Pennsylvania Stat. Ann. Tit. 23 Sec. 2905(b) (Supp. 1986) provides an Intermediary System. Section 2533: Medical history must be obtained for adoption petition. Section 2909: Medical history shall be delivered by attending physician or birthparent to intermediary for adoption records. Any identifying information shall be removed. Section 2405: non-identifying information shall be made available to adoptive parent, birthparent and adoptees at least 18 years old; court may contact birth parent and inform them of petition by adoptee over age 18, or adoptive parent, to gain access to identity of birthparent. If birthparent consents, information will be released. Section 2910: unauthorized release of information is punishable as 3rd degree Misdemeanor. Stat. Ann Tit. 23 Section 2909 (1991) mandates disclosure of non-identifying info.

ADOPTION SEARCH/SUPPORT GROUPS (see "Key" on page 47)

Mary Alice Mull
Adoption Forum of Harrisburg (SS)
100 No. Front St.
Wormleysburg, PA 17043

Kathy Lowenberg
Origins (SG)
1032 Hemlock Farms
Hawley, PA 18428

Barbara Hakel
PA Adoptee Search Team (PAST) (S)
8130 Hawthorne Dr.
Erie, PA 16509

135

Barbara Hakel
PA Adoptee Search Team (PAST)(S)
3130 Hawthorne Dr.
Erie, PA 16509

Chris Blank
Pittsburgh Adoption Connection-
Butler (SS)
815 Saxonbure Rd.
Butler, PA 16001

Sherel Kissell
PA Adoption Connection of Western PA
Canonsburg, PA
sherel@verizon.net

Janet Kelly
Landsdale Adoption Connection (SS)
1167 Hi 11 Dr
Lansdale, PA 19446

Glenda Shay
PA Adoption Connection of Western PA
Fort Hill, PA
gshay@aol.com

Linda Szybowski
Adoption Forum-Delaware Co. (SS)
2175 Franklin Ave.
Morton, PA 19070

Judy Cotton
Adoption Forum
Reading, PA
Judycotten21@gmail.com

Nancy M Newman
PA Adoption Legislation Coalition
24 North Marion Avenue #127
Bryn Mawr, PA 19010

Jewell McCliment
PA Adoption Exchange
Department of Welfare
PO Box 2675
Harrisburg, PA 17105

Kinsearch
424 Bryant Drive
Pittsburgh, PA 15214

Bob Aafetz
Adoption Forum
Bucks County, PA
roberthafetz@comcast.net

LisaFrey
NW PA Adoption Connection (SS)
632 North Michael St.
Edensburg, PA 15857

Abigail Lovett
Adoption Forum
PO Box 582
New Hope, PA 18938

Holly Watson
Open Line Adoption Connection
817 East Third Street
Oil City, PA 16301

Jane Hoover
Harrisburg Adoption Connection (SS)
7728 Manor Dr.
Hamsburg, PA 15201

Broken Trails (SG)
PO Box 71
Keedsville, PA 17084

Jean Vincent
Pittsburgh Adoption Lifeline (SS)
PO Box 52
Gibsonia, PA 15044

Chris Frank
CUB
2800 W Chestnut Ave.
Altoona, PA 16603

Carol Chandler
Adoption Healing (SG)
532 Landsdale Place
Pittsburgh, PA 15528
tocarol@earthlink.net

Karen Deluca
Adoption Forum
PO Box 12502
Philadelphia, PA 19151
Karen_Deluca@msn.com
heimstra@sas.upean.edu

Carol Bravin
Adoption Lifeline of Altoona (SG)
414 28th Ave.
Altoona, PA 16601

Ellen Berman
ENCORE
683 Hidden Hill Farm Lane
York, PA 17403

Kristi Blazi (SS)
Adoption Forum
1060-5 Cold Stream Circle
Emmaus, PA 18049
blax2001@hotmail.com

Dear AmFOR:. .. "Thank you for answering so quickly . . . Both my doctor and I have tried to obtain a copy of my hospital records without success. They claim to need my mother's name to locate them even though it's a very small hospital and we can provide birth statistics and even footprints. I suspect that "adoption" is stamped all over the file. I am considering legal action but I'm not sure the law is on my side. In the meantime, my doctor has agreed to make one more attempt by going over the head of the medical records people directly to the chief of staff... In my case, the agency is the state Social Services and they are paranoid. They will not even release non-identifying information and have pulled an Assistant Attorney General into the picture to justify them ... I believe that the identifying information is clearly severable but they simply would rather a judge make the decision to open the records ... A genealogist who is sympathetic to our plight sneaked into the Washington County file and found a period during which every child social services obtained guardianship for was listed a "Baby _____" with no last names. As I am in this time frame, we got no useful information. I am without any leads to help me play detective . . . I look forward to hearing from you . . .
Sincerely, ANN W., Salisbury, MD."

Dear AmFOR:... "I am a mother who surrendered my son born August 31, 1966. About 4 months ago I requested from the agency, Jewish Family and Children's Services in Pittsburgh, PA, copies of the Original Certificate of Birth, Surrender Agreement, non-identifying information and whether they would make contact with either my son or his adopters to determine whether there was any interest or desire for a reunion. After several months of telling me that they had to have a legal committee meet to determine what their policy should be with respect to my request and others, they have determined that their policy is to not give any information, including non-identifying to parents or adoptees, based on current PA Law, unless directed to do so by court order. I am currently petitioning the court which is the Orphan's Court of Allegheny County, PA ... the secretary told me that they got it, but that the best that she felt the judge could or would be able to do, was put it all in the file! I have still not heard from Judge Zavarella, himself. In the meantime, please add me to your Petition for Open Records . . . Sincerely, CAROL C.F., Rowayton, CT." Author's Note: Carol was later reunited with her son.

Dear AmFOR: ... "I am a mother who searched and successfully found the daughter who was surrendered to adoption. I am in the process of trying to organize a support group for relinquishing mothers in Pittsburgh, PA... Looking forward to receiving information from you ... Sincerely, GLENDA S., Carnegie, PA."

Rhode Island

CENTRAL RECORDS OFFICES

Vital Records
To Verify Fees
(rec = recorded message).
Div. of Vital Records
3 Capitol Hill, #101
Providence, RI 02908
(401) 222-2811
www.vitalrec.com/ri.html

Accessible?
Genealogy;
immediate
family; fee

State (St), County (Co),
Birth (B), Death (D),
Marriage (M), Divorce (DV)
Indices & Records
St-B,D,M since 1853
St-Dv since 1/1962
Co-B,D,M Town Clerk
Co-Dv Family Court

State Archives Address	Year Adoption Records Closed	Hospital Records Available?	Legal Notice Required?
State Library Archives 337 Westminster St. Providence, RI 02903	Before 1930	Difficult	No

Central Department of Motor Vehicles
Registry of Motor Vehicles
State Office Building
Providence, RI 02903

National Archives-New England Region
380 Trapelo Rd.
Waltham, MA 02154; (617) 647-8100
Hours: M-F & 1st Sat: 8AM-4:30PM
(Serves CT, ME, MA, NH, RI, VT)

Central Agency Holding Adoption Records	Non-Identifying Info Provided?	Adoption Decree From Court	State Registry
Dept. Children/Families/Adoptions 101 Friendship Street Providence, RI 02908 (401) 528-3605	Yes, but law gives court discretion. All Triad.	Seldom; Probate Family Court	Yes

(1987) ADOPTION DISCLOSURE STATUTES (REGISTRY SYSTEM)
Section 20-7-1780: non-identifying information shall be released at the discretion of the adoption agency. Section 15-7-22: violation of adoption provisions or false statements is punishable by 1 year in prison and/or $500 fine for first offense. RI Gen. Laws Section 8-10-3 (Supp. 1991) gives courts discretion regarding disclosure of non-identifying info. State registry operated by Family Court, Providence, RI.

ADOPTION SEARCH/SUPPORT GROUPS (see "Key" on page 47)

Dorene L. Morin
American Adoption Congress
8 Oyster Place
Warren, RI 02885
Dorene.Morin@brown.edu

Linda Brown
96 Everett Ave.
Providence, RI 02906

B. Jane Cacciatore (S)
30 Glen Drive
East Greenwich, RI 02818
BJC1080@aol.com

Dear AmFOR: ..." I recently obtained your name from a magazine article ... I have spoken to the agency in RI through which my parents got me and they were not able to help me very much at all. I asked if they would contact my biological mother and ask if she wanted to see me, but they would not even do that. It seemed that they were very concerned about possible lawsuits against them. I would greatly appreciate information on how to find or contact my biological parents; also ... on Rhode Island laws. Thanks, LIANNE S., New York, NY."

South Carolina

CENTRAL RECORDS OFFICES

Vital Records
To Verify Fees
(rec = recorded message).
2600 Bull Street
Columbia, SC 29201-1797
(803) 898-3630
www.vitalrec.com/sc.html

Accessible?
Immediate
family;
fee

State (St), County (Co),
Birth (B), Death (D),
Marriage (M), Divorce (DV)
Indices & Records
St-B ,D since 1/1915
St-M since 7/50; Dv-'62
Co-M Probate Judge
Co-B,D,M,Dv County Clerk

State Archives
Address
State Library,
Dept. Archives & History
1430 Senate Street
Columbia, SC 29201

Year Adoption
Records Closed
1963
open to age 18+

Hospital Records
Available?
No, if finalized
pre-1961

Legal Notice
Required?
No

Central Department of Motor Vehicles
Driver License Division
PO Box 1498
Columbia, SC 29202

National Archives-Southeast Region
1567 Saint Joseph Avenue
East Point, GA 30344; (404) 763-7477
Hours: M & W-F: 7:30AM-4:30 PM.
   (Serves AL, GA, FL, KY, MS, NC, SC, TN)

Central Agency
Holding Adoption Records
Dept. Youth Services/Adoptions
PO Box 1520
Columbia, SC 29202-1520
(803) 898-7524

Non-Identifying
Info Provided?
Yes, but law gives
court discretion

Adoption Decree
From Court
Usually;
Family Court

State
Registry
Yes

(1985) ADOPTION DISCLOSURE STATUTES (REGISTRY SYSTEM)

Section 20-7-1780: closed hearings; records sealed; court order required to release information. Section 20-7-1740: birthparent shall provide medical history of birth family of adopted child. Sec. 20-7-1780: Registry System; non-identifying information shall be made available to adoptive parent, birthparent and adopted child, about each other, at discretion of the agency; identifying information shall be made available to adoptee over 21 and to birthparents and siblings through the filing of corresponding affidavits. SC Code Ann. Section 20-7-1780 (Law. Co-op. Supp. 1991) gives agencies discretion regarding disclosure of non-identifying info.

ADOPTION SEARCH/SUPPORT GROUPS (see "Key" on page 47)

Pollie Robinson
Tammy Hall
Adoption Reunion Connection
263 Lemonade Road
Pacolet SC 29372
Jrobin474@aol.com

Marci-Jo Mishoe (SS)
Adoptees Birthparents in Search (ABIS)
4327 Helene Dr-
Charleston, SC 29418

BrendaCraig
Craig Locating Service (SS)
PO Box 849
Roebuck, SC 29376
Craiglocatmgsen@aol.com

Karen Conner (SS)
Adoptees Birthparents in Search (ABIS)
PO Box 13
Lexington.SC 29071

Patti Courtney
Adoption & Reunion Center (SS)
126 Brown Log Road
Pacolet, SC 29302

Mary Bishop
Adoptees & Birthparents
258 North Suber Rd-
Greer, SC 29651

Karen Conn / Missing Piece
PO Box 507
Campobello, SC 29376

Janet Davis
Bits & Pieces (SG)
PO Box 85
Liberty, SC 29657

Alta McNatt
Adoption Support of CSRA (SS)
PO Box 7966
North Augusta, SC 29861

Mildred Szakacsi
Adoptees Adult Liberation & Triad (SS)
1725 Atascadero Dr.
Columbia, SC 29206

Cyndi Walters (AAC)
Adoption Search for Life (SS)
PO Box 66
Anderson, SC 29622
cpwalters@aol.com

Liz White
Adoption Reunion Connection
PO Box 239
Moore, SC 29369

Margit Benton (ISC)
2238 Bailey Drive
Charleston, SC 29405
margritB@aol.com

Carol Harrington Courdin ISC
1350 Roddington St.
Mt. Pleasant, SC 29464
gourdin@home.com

Heather Lowe (SG)
Birthmother Support
10839 Dorchester Rd.
Summerville, SC 29485
hslowe@earthlin.net

Dear AmFOR:... "I certainly appreciate your letter... I told you in my first letter that I had not met my child due to the hostility and fears of her adopters. I currently have an attorney in South Carolina looking into filing for Shannon's original birth certificate. I plan to go forward with court action. I feel that having her original records sealed and ... being sent away and having a child in secret and alone has greatly damaged my sense of self-worth and self respect. To still face rejection and denial twenty-six years later is indeed hard to swallow ... My daughter surprised me when she expressed doubts that I was her real mother. Since Catholic Charities called her adopter and told her that I had located Shannon, surely the adopters knew . . . My sister Erica did make an appointment under a false name at the beauty parlor where she works. But how else were we to see her? This, believe it or not, was the social worker at Catholic Charities' idea ... It really helps to talk about this subject that for so long was taboo. I would be glad to share my story, if I could help even one person find that missing part of themselves and have a positive reunion experience ... Thanks again for your help and kind, sympathetic ear ... JANET J., Harrisonburg, VA."

Dear AmFOR:... "I would like to locate my biological parents. I have contacted the adoption agency. I was sent a few bits of information ... I am at a stand-still since they cannot give me access to my files unless it is of an emergency nature ... Being a mother myself, I feel very strongly about finding my own parents, if for no other reason than to tell them that I turned out just fine... Sincerely, RENEE OPPENHEIM PEACOCK, N. Charleston, SC."

Dear AmFOR:... "My adopter has told me the name of my mother on the adoption papers ... I can't afford lawyer fees and I am hoping your organization can help. Maybe my mother is looking for me ... ANN R., Belvedere, SC."

South Dakota

CENTRAL RECORDS OFFICES

Vital Records
To Verify Fees
(rec = recorded message).
Center for Vital Records — Accessible?
209 East Missouri. Suite 1-6 — Restricted
Pierre, SD 57501-2536 — fee
(605) 773-4961
www.vitalrec.com/sd.html

State (St), County (Co),
Birth (B), Death (D),
Marriage (M), Divorce (DV)
Indices & Records
St-B,D since 7/1905
St-M,. Dv since 7/1905
Co-B.D.M Co Treasurer
Co-Dv Court Clerk

State Archives — Year Adoption — Hospital Records — Legal Notice
Address — Records Closed — Available? — Required?
South Dakota Archives — Never — No — No
Cultural Heritage Center
900 Governors Dr.
Pierre, SD 57501

Central Department of Motor Vehicles
Department of Public Safety
Driver Improvement Program
118 West Capitol
Pierre, SD 57501

National Archives-Rocky Mountain Region
Denver Federal Center, Building 48
PO Box 25307
Denver, CO 80225-0307; (303) 236-0817
Hours: M-F:7:30-3:45PM, Tu 'til 4:45 PM
   (Serves CO, MT, ND, SD, UT, WY)

Central Agency — Non-Identifying — Adoption Decree — State
Holding Adoption Records — Info Provided? — From Court — Registry
Dept. Social Services/Adoptions — Yes, by law; — Adoptee access — Yes
700 Governor Dr. –Kneip Bldg. — Adoptee; — to court records
Pierre, SD 57501-2291 — Adoptive Parents
(601) 773-3227 — Circuit Court

(1986) ADOPTION DISCLOSURE STATUTES (REGISTRY SYSTEM)
Section 20-7-1780: closed hearings; records sealed; court order required to release information. Section 20-7-1780(e)
Supp. (1985) provides a Registry System. SD Codified Laws Ann. Section 25-6-15.2 (Supp. 1992) mandates disclosure
of non-identifying info. to adoptive parent or adoptee at age 18.

ADOPTION SEARCH/SUPPORT GROUPS (see "Key" on page 47)

Andrea Sindt (CUB) — Shirley Shinneman (ALMA) — Carolyn S. Rosemore
41004 259th Street — 1325 So. Bahnson — 217 West 3rd Street
Mitchell, SD 57301 — Sioux Falls, SD 57103 — Miller, SD 57362

Dear AmFOR: . . . "Little is being done towards "adoption reform" in S.D. We would like to be more
informed on what we can do in our state of South Dakota ... Thank you, ANDREA HARMES-BINDT,
CABSG (Closed Adoption Support Group), Mitchell, SD."

Tennessee

CENTRAL RECORDS OFFICES

	Accessible?	State (St), County (Co), Birth (B), Death (D), Marriage (M), Divorce (DV) Indices & Records
Vital Records To Verify Fees (rec = recorded message). TN Vital Records Dept of Health 421 5th Avenue North Nashville, TN 37243 (615) 714-1763 www. vitalrec. com/m. html	Immediate family; fee	St-B ,D since 1/1914 St-M,Dv since 1945 St-B,D,M Co Court Clerk Co-Dv Court Clerk

	Year Adoption Records Closed	Hospital Records Available?	Legal Notice Required?
State Archives Address State Library & Archives 403 7th Ave. No. Nashville, TN 37219	1950	Difficult	No

Central Department of Motor Vehicles
Department of Safety
Driver Licenses
PO Box 945
Nashville, TN 37202

National Archives-Southeast Region
1557 Saint Joseph Avenue
East Point, GA 30344; (404) 763-7477
Hours: M&W-F 7:30AM-4:30PM, Tues: 7:30AM-9:30PM
(Serves AL, GA, FL, KY, MS, NC, SC, TN)

Central Agency Holding Adoption Records	Non-Identifying Info Provided?	Adoption Decree From Court	State Registry
Dept. Children's Services/Adoptions 436 Sixth Avenue North Nashville, TN 37243-1290 (615) 741-9206	Yes, but law gives gives court discretion	Usually; Probate Court pre-1950 adoptions; Chancery Court post-1950	Yes; Intermediary Waiver System

ADULT ADOPTEES ACCESS ORIGINAL BIRTH CERTIFICATE IF NO "BIRTH" PARENT VETO:

Section 36-1-129/131: records sealed; court order required to release information. Tennessee Code Annotated Section 36-1-141 (Supp. 1986) and Tennessee Code Annotated Section 36-1-140 (pertains to siblings) provide to Intermediary System. No separate medical information provision. Section 36-1-139; procedures exist for reuniting pre-adoptive siblings when they reach age 18 or over. Section 36-1-149; adopted child over 18 may request non-identifying information about birthparent. Section 36-1-132; birthparent illegal repossession of adopted child is guilty of abduction. (Note: Tennessee home Society Director Georgia Tann mass kidnapped over 5,000 children sold to adopters nationwide, primarily in Hollywood/Southern California, New York, Kentucky and Tennessee, 1940's, 50's, 60's). Disclosure from confidential records-Misdemeanor: $250-S 1,000 fine and/or up to one year in prison-TN. (Supp. 1999) Section 36-1-125 to 141; Adult Adoptee access to original birth certificate. CHS records are now wide open for S130 plus copy fee.

ADOPTION SEARCH/SUPPORT GROUPS (see "Key" on page 47)

Denny Glad ISC
Tennessee Right To Know
5182 Oak Meadow Ave.
Memphis, TN 38164
dglade@bellsouth.net

TN Searchers for Truth (SG)
7721 White Creek Pike
Joelton, TN 37080

Anne Byrn
Birthparent Support Group
c/o Miriam's Promise
Nashville, TN
annebyrnf@miriamspromise.org

[Note: Find your adopted Tennessee ancestors, listed by county in "Nineteeth Century Tennessee Adoptions, Legitimations and Name Changes" by Alan N. Miller, Genealogy Publishing Company.]

Sheila Hunt (SC)
PO Box 3826
Kingsport, TN 37664

Norma Mott Tillman (L-PI)
UFO.REUNET
PO Box 290333
Nashville, TN 37229

Debbie Norton
Tennessee Right To Know (SS)
PO Box 34334
Memphis, TN 38134

Sandra Freeman (SS)
Group for Openess in Adoption
518 General George Paton Rd.
Nashville, TN 37221

Sue Campbell ISC
ROOTS (SS)
PO Box 9662
Knoxville, TN 37940
sis21@msn.com

Sheri Kalt - PI
1424 Randall Park Dr.
Knoxville, TN 37922
PVTeyeTN@aol.com

Nadeen Hart, ISC
FAITH (SS)
181 -1 /2 W. Sevier Ave.
Kingsport, TN 37660

Sue Abernathy
(formerly ALARM)
408 Valeria Ct.
Nashville, TN 37210

Kathy Albaum
Birthparents Search
for Answers (SS)
2750 Ward Rd.
Millington, TX 38053

Jamie Johnson
ALMA
PO Box 15064
Chattanooga, TN 37415

Susan Thompson
Rights of Origin (SG)
7110Westway Cir.
Knoxville, TN 37919

Robert Filipcazak (S)
Family Reconnections
701 Shannon Lane
Atoka, TN 38004
HM2Flip@yahoo.com

Norma Samsel CUB (SS)
2601 Holston Dr.
Morristown, TN 37814

Jalena Bowling
Tennessee Right To Know (SS)
6100 Chester St.
Arlington, TN 38002
FFMJ26B@bellsouth.net

Sharon Mauk
1504 East Sevier Avenue
Kingsport, TN 37664

Holly Spann
CUB
21 Vaughn's Gap Unit J 163
Nashville, TN 37205

Ann Tarkington
Openness In Adoption
6107 Hillsboro Road
Nashville, TN 37215

Dear AmFOR: . . . "Thank you for yours of the 6th. The cutoff deadline for new bills has passed for this year in Tennessee, but we do have some bills pending which will make access to records somewhat easier . . . Very truly yours, DOUGLAS HENRY, JR., SENATOR, Nashville, TN."

Dear AmFOR: ..." Keep up the good work. I know gradual progress is being made. Did you see Unsolved Mysteries recently? There was a story concerning the Tennessee Children's Home and the "black market" babies that were sold to anyone who could pay the price. I have worked for two years on one of those and have not yet located her. If you could mention this in an article it might help. Her name at birth was Charlotte Temple Cook, born in Baptist Hospital, Nashville, TN on January 31,1951. Her mother has been searching unsuccessfully for many years. These records are separate and apart from all other adoption records in Tennessee. It is impossible to locate any information because of the scandal... Sincerely, NORMA TILLMAN, PI, (UFO), P.O. Box 290333, Nashville, TN 37229"

Dear AmFOR:... "You have been, by far, the most helpful in my search... AmFOR's packet of materials was a God-send. I have also requested information from other organizations. Every response, with AmFOR as the exception, wanted astronomical fees for conducting searches and/or materials on how to search. You can imagine my utter disbelief of actually having helpful information! I felt such hope and support as I eagerly read your materials. Making the decision to search was one of the hardest things I've ever done. Thanks to you and AmFOR, it looks as if the actual search will be much easier. I am in the process of filing a "search request" with the Department of Human Services. Due to the age requirement in Tennessee (21), I had to wait until after my birthday this month. I have been searching for a support group for searching adoptees in the Nashville area... AmFOR is providing a much-needed service and a wonderful support system!!! I'll let you know my results!... Sincerely yours, CHRISTIE S., Nashville, TN."

143

Dear AmFOR:... "I was adopted and want to find out who my family is ... I am so tired of doors being closed on me. It seems like for every step forward, I take 10 backwards. Please help me ... Sincerely, JACKIE W., Cookeville, TN."

Dear AmFOR:... "I was born on November 5, 1965 in Knoxville, TN. I have known all my life that I was adopted ... I guess one could say that I have all the same questions that any adopted child would have. My adopters that I have today have been the greatest and I have no doubt that they love me ... but I still wonder. And that is a natural feeling to have, so I'm told . . . Sincerely, DONNA S., Lenoir City, TN."

Dear AmFOR: . . . "DHS located my mother and she refused to give them permission to release identifying info to me. They do not know who my father was, so they could not search for him ... I waited a year and asked them to contact my birthmother again, and they told me once they contacted someone, they would not do it again. Where can I go from here? ... EILEEN Y., Charleston, SC."

Dear AmFOR:... "I am the mother of a girl born October 1970 in Tennessee. I allowed her to be adopted in order to give her the home that, at that time, I could not provide. Hardly a day has gone by without me thinking of her ... I hope to meet my daughter and be a part of her life. I thank her adopters for being there and I love them for loving her. I don't wish to ever take her away from them, but I do feel there is room in her life for all of us ... Thank you, V.S., Upland, CA."

Texas

CENTRAL RECORDS OFFICES

Vital Records To Verify Fees (rec = recorded message). Bureau Vital Statistics 1100 West 49th Street Austin, TX 78711-2040 (888) 963-7111 www.vitalrec.com/tx.html	Accessible? Immediate family; fee	State (St), County (Co), Birth (B), Death (D), Marriage (M), Divorce (DV) Indices & Records St-B ,D since 1903 ;M-'66 St-Dv since 1/1968 Co-B,D,M Co Clerk Co-Dv District Court

State Archives Address State Library, Archives 1201 Brazos Austin, TX 78711	Year Adoption Records Closed 1935	Hospital Records Available? Difficult	Legal Notice Required? Yes

Central Department of Motor Vehicles
Dept. of Public Safety
License Issuance & Driver Records
PO Box 4087
Austin, TX 78765

National Archives-Southeast Region
501 W Felix St.
PO Box 6216
Fort Worth, TX 76115; (817) 334-5525
Hours: M-F:8AM-4PM, W:8AM-9PM
(Serves AK, LA, NM, OK, TX).

Central Agency Holding Adoption Records Dept. Protective Services/Adoptions PO Box 149030 (E-558) Austin, TX 78714 -9030 (512) 438-3412	Non-Identifying Info Provided? Yes, by law; Adoptee, Adop. Parents	Adoption Decree From Court Usually; Chancery, District, Circuit Court	State Registry Yes

(1986) ADOPTION DISCLOSURE STATUTES (REGISTRY SYSTEM)

Texas Human Resources Code Section 49.001 (Supp 1986) provides a Registry System. No fees statement. Section 16.032: parents and/or child placing agency will complete health, social, education, genetic history of adopted child and provide summary to adoptive parent at/before placement and to adopted child at majority and to surviving spouse or progeny of adoptee. Section 49.001: Voluntary Adoption Registry—adoptee over age 21, birthparent over age 21. Putative father who acknowledges paternity and siblings may, with proper consents of party(ies) gain access to identifying information. (Note: Thacker case, 1992, exposed 'legal baby selling' under private adoption law even by unlicensed baby brokers exists in Texas.) TX Fam. Code Ann. Section 16.032 (West Supp. 1992) mandates disclosure of non-identifying info.

ADOPTION SEARCH/SUPPORT GROUPS (see "Key" on page 47)

Mary C. Rizzo, ISC, Cindy Segal Marywood Search Support PO Box 91271 Austin, TX 78709 robertr650@aol.com	Linda Crenweldge Orphan Voyage (S C) 1305 Augustine Ct. College Station, TX 77840	Peggy Dom Orphan Voyage (SS) 5811 S. Minster Houston, TX 77035
Pat Rutherford (L-PI) Worldwide Tracers PO Box 173006 Arlington, TX 76003	Pat Palmer, ISC Searchline of Texas (SS) 1516 Old Orchard Irving, TX 75061 searchlinepat@aol.com	Joanne Slate Post-Adoption Center Support (SG) 7475 Callashaw Rd. San Antonio, TX 78229 Joann@TexasCradle.com

Patricia Martinez Domer
Adoption Counseling & Search
206 Lochaven
San Antonio, TX 78213
PDonner@email.msn.com

The National Locator (Military Locator)
PO Box 39903
San Antonio, TX 78218

McRoy Grotevant
The Adoption Institute
PO Box 27261
Austin, TX 78755

Child and Family Resources (SG)
2775 Villa Creek, #240
Dallas, TX 75234

David Duffey
Marywood Post Adoption Services
510 West 26th Street
Austin, TX 78705

Bill Betzen (ACSW)
Catholic Charities
304 Harwood Rd.
Bedford, TX 76021
txcare@txcare.org

Carolyn Shaw (SG C)
Adoption Knowledge Affiliate, Inc. (AKA)
2121 S. Lamar, #112
Austin, TX 78704

Triad Support Group
510 W. 26th St.
Austin, TX 78705

Gina Shelton (S)
Adoption Search & Reunions
10103 Appleridge Dr.
Houston, TX 77070

Nancy Kvapil (S)
HC02 Box 431
Dripping Springs, TX 78620

Adoptees Adoptive/Birthparents in
Search (SS)
4208 Roxbury
El Paso, TX 79922

ALMA
PO Box 5735
Austin, TX 78763

Bonnie P. Solecki
Texas Adoption Search Services
PO Box 14142 & 3408 Wendell Dr.
Fort Worth, TX 76117
txsearch@nash.com

Alicia Lanier
Adoption Triad Forum (SG)
PO Box 832161
Richardson, TX 75083
AliciaKLa@aol.com

Beckie Scott
Triangle Search
5738 Crest Grove
Corpus Christi, TX 78415

Mikko
Adoption Healing
5324 West Northwest Hwy
Dallas, TX 75220

Mona McDonald (SS)
Mehtodist Family Services
6487 Whitbug Rd
San Antonio, TX 78290

Bonnie Solecki
PO Box 14142
Fort Worth, TX 76117

Glenda Allen (S)
RESEARCH Roots
PO Box 2424
Coppell.TX 75019
glendalpi@aol.com

Adoption Knowledge Affiliates
Westover H lls Church
8332 Mesa
Austin, TX
aka@adoptionknowledge.org

Linda Strength
Adoptee Reunions
PO Box 8445
Bacliff, TX 77518
Srchgrl@wt.net

Marilyn Morris-Rose (S)
Peace of Mind
PO Box 371
Pasadena, TX 77504
mrose@wt.net

Carol Demuth (SG)
PO Box 460024
Garland, TX 75046
Cldemuth@aol.com

DFW Triad Support Group
Dallas, TX
dfwtriad@yahoo.com
tapestry@irvingbible.org

Dear AmFOR:... "I recently received a pamphlet from your organization. There are some very interesting statistics given. As a person who is actively involved in providing post-adoption services—including
search, etc. I would appreciate your providing me the source of these statistics so that I can do some additional
reading on my own. This information will be helpful to me as I advocate for adoptees, adopters and parents
... Sincerely, BOB PARKHILL, LPC, CSW-ACP, DIRECTOR OF SOCIAL SERVICES, Abilene, TX."

Dear AmFOR: ... "I was adopted through West Texas Children's Aid and Welfare Home in Abilene,
Texas (Tayler County). I am unable to secure any records from the Vital Statistics through the County and
District Clerks, to the Public Library ... My mother was supposed to be from Seymour, Baylor
County, Texas. She was born between 1917 and 1922. She was supposed to have placed a male child
either 2 years before or after my placement with this same agency. I would appreciate any help you can give
me. Thank you for your time, effort and consideration... Sincerely, ANN C., Abilene, TX."

Dear AmFOR:. . . "[Regarding] Betty Pearl Stauffer (her birth name) was born January 3, 1944 in San Antonio, TX and adopted a t 19 mo. by a Lutheran Minister in San Antonio ... I am helping my friend, Pat (Stauffer) Armstrong to try to locate Betty Pearl, her sister ... Anything you can tell me to assist us is greatly appreciated. I would love to play some tiny part in reuniting my friend with her sister. Sincerely, DARLENE D., Houston, TX."

Dear AmFOR:..." I was successful finally five years ago, I found a brother. And as luck would have it, he was the youngest. On his original birth certificate, it stated he was the sixth live birth. My father had denied there were any children. There were six all together, four adopted out at birth ... I knew about them. I loved my Dad and didn't want to distress him so couldn't pursue the search with his blessing ... The youngest was born when I was ten, my parents were in the process of a divorce. They married others ... each had children, they had children ... Mom begged me to find the kids, she said the law was that I could find them. But she wasn't allowed to ... I told her about the search and how hard it was to get a scrap of information. The 'Secret Files' are hard to penetrate than Fort Knox. My poor Dear Mother paid the price of being a young girl in love with her husband. They tried to make a living, working for themselves. In the years of the Depression. It wasn't good news for her to tell her hubby she was pregnant just fourteen months after the last baby . . .So four babies were adopted out... with a kiss and a lifetime of regret... She would tell me it's a sister's birthday ... or a brother's. There are two sisters for me to find... yet I want them all to know Mom didn't adopt them out because she didn't love them ... it was because she was thinking of them and their welfare before herself. God Bless you and your cause. I hope I'm able to bring my search to a successful conclusion and I hope it's because you are a success in your quest to open the Files . . . Sincerely yours in Search, B.J. M., Livingston, TX."

Dear AmFOR:... "My son is over legal age ... I don't know how to go about finding him or making it known to him that I am looking. I have read all the books in the library in my town, and I am sorry to say that they mostly pertain to adopting . . . JUANITA T., McKinney, TX."

Dear AmFOR:... "The Edna Gladney Center, through which I was placed, thinks I should be content to know my mother was 5'6" had hazel eyes and blond hair and weighed 113 pounds. I have signed their registry and in October 1991 my mother contacted them to ask about the registry. They wouldn't release the forms to her "because she has to request in writing" . . . TRISH P., Columbus, IN."

Dear AmFOR:... "My husband and I divorced and not too long after that was forced to put my boys up for adoption. My husband and I divorced .. . and my oldest son and I were on welfare and food stamps. The welfare office lost track of our case and for 2 months I had no money. My oldest was 16 months old and 3 months before my youngest my born. For those 2 months I still had to feed and care for my children. So I wrote checks to feed and care for my boys. They arrested me for " misdemeanor theft by worthless check." Ten days before my court date I went with our minister from church and my welfare worker (to tell them their computer messed up) to see the judge trying my case. The judge decided the circumstances didn't matter (never been in trouble before) and he was going to "make an example" of me for the whole country. He advised me to do something with my boys because he was going to send me to jail. It was called "shock probation" and I would spend 30-190 days in the county jail. The minister, welfare worker and I left and I singed the papers that day to place my boys up for adoption through the Methodist Mission home in our state. I placed one condition on the adoption for the boys—that they never be separated. They are only 13-1/2 months apart in age and were very close. About 8 months after they left a very loving couple adopted both my boys. The couple and I feel comfortable writing back and forth and, once a year, I get pictures of my sons. My sons still ask about me and when they're old enough will be told how to reach me. The parents are very loving and I admire them for what they have done. They write me and tell me they love and admire me for my courage . .R.L.B., Longview, TX"

147

Utah

CENTRAL RECORDS OFFICES

Vital Records
To Verify Fees
(rec = recorded message).
Bureau of Vital Stats
PO Box 141012
Salt Lake City, UT 84114
(801) 538-6105
www.vitalrec.com/ut.html

Accessible?
Immediate
family; fee

State (St), County (Co),
Birth (B), Death (D),
Marriage (M), Divorce (DV)
Indices & Records
St-D since 1905
St-M, Dv no state index
Co-B,D Co Clerk
Co-M,Dv County Clerk

State Archives Address	Year Adoption Records Closed	Hospital Records Available?	Legal Notice Required?
LDS Genealogical Society of 35 North West Temple Salt Lake City, UT 84102	Utah Unknown	From doctor	No

Central Department of Motor Vehicles
Driver License Division
1095 Motor Ave,
Salt Lake City, UT 84116

National Archives- Rocky Mountains Region
Denver Federal Center, Building 48
PO Box 25307
Denver, CO 80225-0307; (303) 236-0817
Hours: M-F: 7:30AM-3:45PM,
TU:7:30AM-4:45PM
(Serves CO, MT, ND, SD, UT, WY)

Central Agency Holding Adoption Records	Non-Identifying Info Provided?	Adoption Decree From Court	State Registry
Dept. Social Services /Adoptions 120 N. 200th West/PO Box 45500 Salt Lake City, UT 84103 (801) 538-4398	Yes, by law; Adoptee	Never	Yes

(1992) ADOPTION DISCLOSURE STATUTES (REGISTRY SYSTEM)

Section 78-30-15: records sealed; court order required to release. Utah Code, Section 78-30-17: child placement agency shall provide detailed health, genetic, social history of birth family to adoptive parent and adopted child over 18. Section 78-30-17: non-identifying health, genetic and social history of adoptee shall be available to adoptive parent, adoptee's guardian, children or spouse of adoptee and adoptee's adult siblings. Sect 78-30-18: Mutual Consent Voluntary Adoption Registry for identifying information. No fee statement. Code Ann. Section 16.032 (West Supp. 1992) mandates disclosure of non-identifying info.

ADOPTION SEARCH/SUPPORT GROUPS (see "Key" on page 47)

Sharlene Lightfoot
Adoption Connection of Utah (SS)
1349 Mariposa Ave.
Salt Lake City, UT 84106

Donnie Davis
Birthmother / Adopte Suport Group
Salt Lake City, UT
Pdj27@aol.com

David L. Barss
Salt Lake City Legs
PO BOX 174
North Salt Lake, UT 84054

Bonnie Cox Schulte ISC
PO Box 41
Hopper, UT 84315

Leslie Carpenter
Adoption Lifeline-Ogden Group
175 No. Iowa Ave.
Ogden, UT 84404

Louise Brown /Adoption Forum (SG)
98 Garden Park #24
Orem, UT 84057

Charlotte Staten
Searchfinders/LAMB (SS)
672 E 2025 South
Bountiful, UT 84010
cstaten@networld.com

THE FAMILY HISTORY CENTER
35 North West Temple Street
Salt Lake City, UT 84140

Salt Lake City is the headquarters for The Church of Latter-day Saints (Mormon) Family History Center with branches nationwide and worldwide. All branches have computer and/or microfilm versions of ANCESTRAL NAME identifiers, SOCIAL SECURITY DEATH INDEX (you don't need to know the Social Security Number to access), and BIRTH RECORDS by location—the largest genealogical resource in the world. Staff will not research for you but are helpful guides. Their new Internet Website is as www.familysearch.org that will eventually be a repository for 600 million names, extracted from vital records, worldwide.

Adoption search resources may be outdated and limited to referrals to search groups and registries, unless you know the name, or similar spelling. The main library at Salt Lake City houses more documents and books than its branches—including The Ultimate Search Book, now being reviewed for possible distribution to the branch libraries.

Dear AmFOR:... "I was born on September 9, 1967 at LDS hospital in Salt Lake City, UT and adopted through LDS Social Services ... My grandfather was the attorney who handled the adoption, but he says the records are sealed and that I would have to petition the court to have them unsealed and it would be very expensive to do so. I have placed my name with Utah Adoption Registry, but no match has yet been made ... Any assistance you can give me will be greatly appreciated ... Sincerely, ALLISON F., Bountiful, UT."

Vermont

CENTRAL RECORDS OFFICES

Vital Records
To Verify Fees
(rec = recorded message).
Vital Records Section
PO Box 70
Burlington, VT 05402
(802) 863-7275
www.vitalrec.com/vt.html

Accessible?
Public;
fee

State (St), County (Co),
Birth (B), Death (D),
Marriage (M), Divorce (DV)

Indices & Records
St-B,D,M since 1857
St-Dv since 1860
Co-B,D,M City Clerk

State Archives
Address
Public Records/Gen. Serv.
U.S. Route 2 - Middlesex
PO Drawer 33
Montpelier, VT 05602

Year Adoption
Records Closed
1946

Hospital Records
Available?
Difficult

Legal Notice
Required?
No

Central Department of Motor Vehicles
Driver Licenses
Department of Motor Vehicles

National Archives-New England Region
380 Trapelo Rd.
Waltham, MA 02154; (617) 647-8100
Montpelier, VT 05602   Hours: M-F & 1st Sat: 8AM-4:30PM
(Serves CT, ME, MA, NH, RI, VT)

Central Agency
Holding Adoption Records
Dept. Social & Rehab/Adoptions
103 South Main Street.
Waterbury, VT 05671
(802) 241-2259

Non-Identifying
Info Provided?
Yes, by law;
Adoptee;
Adoptive Parents

Adoption Decree
From Court
Rarely;
Probate Court

State
Registry
No;
Consent only

(1986) ADOPTION DISCLOSURE STATUTES (CONSENT ONLY)
Section 451/452: records sealed; court order to release information. Vermont Statute Annotated Title 10 Section 462 (Supp. 1986) allows access to records with consent only—no search or registry. No fees statement. No separate medical information provision. Section 462: consent to disclosure of identifying information may be filed with the court by an adoptee at age 21 or by a birthparent of adoptee. Section 461: court shall release non-identifying information after notice and hearing by all interested parties and after determination that disclosure is warranted after considering relative effects of disclosure. No penalty statement. Stat. Ann. Section 78-30-17 mandates disclosure of non-identifying info.

ADOPTION SEARCH/SUPPORT GROUPS (see "Key" on page 47)

Marge Garfield
Adoption Search and Support (SS)
771 Bayne Road
East Calais, VT 05650
beleaf4u@aol.com

Carolyn Flood ISC
B&C Search Assistance of VT (SS)
50 N. Mail St.
St. Albans, VT 05478
cbflood@sover.net

Kim Butterfield
(Referrals)
PO Box 267
Williston, VT 05495

Mary Lighthall
Adoption Alliance
613 Hill's Pt. Road
Charlotte, VT 05445
mlight@accessvt.com

Enoch Tompkins
Adoption Alliance of VT (SS)
Falls Road
Shelburne, VT 05482

Maureen Vincent
Adoption Alliance of VT (SS)
17 Hopkins St.
Rutland, VT 05701

Susan Wadia-Ellis
The Adoption Connection
PO Box 401
Putney, VT 05346

Wendi Whitmaker (ISC)
30 Martindale Road
Shelburne, VT 05482

Adoption Alliance of VT (SS)
91 Court St.
Middlebury, VT 05753

The Saginaw News, 03/04/92, "HOMELESS MAN REUNITED WITH UNKNOWN TWIN SISTER: Charlottesville, VA. (AP) Thirty-five years after they were adopted as infants by two different families, a homeless Massachusetts man and the twin sister he didn't know existed have been reunited. "I feel like a void has been filled," Peter LaLonde said after he stepped off a bus Monday in Charlottesville to meet Claudia Lam. 'I had always felt that something was missing in my life,' Ms. Lam said. 'I didn't know what it was but I knew something wasn't right.'... Ms. Lam's search started four years ago when she contacted an adoption agency in Burlington, VT. and learned she had been separated from a twin brother in infancy. Ms. Lam spent the next four years calling agencies and police departments. She said her search was given greater urgency by a need to relay medical information about her congenital heart disease. A year-and-a-half after a stroke prompted her to request that adoption records be opened, Ms. Lam - received a letter two weeks ago revealing her brother's name."

Dear AmFOR: ... "I found out two years ago that I was adopted. I am having a hard time getting matching information . .. My amended birth certificate states I was born January 7, 1956 in Burlington, VT but my (amended) baptism certificate states I was born January 2, 1956 in Bristol, CT. I was adopted through Catholic Charities, Burlington, VT, who recently provided scant background info. from my file. What now? .. . Respectfully yours, CATHERINE C., VT."

Virginia

CENTRAL RECORDS OFFICES

Vital Records		State (St), County (Co),
To Verify Fees		Birth (B), Death (D),
(rec = recorded message).		Marriage (M), Divorce (DV)
Bureau of Vital Records	Accessible?	Indices & Records
PO Box 1000	Immediate	St-B ,D since 6/14/12
Richmond, VA 23201	family; fee	St-M since 1853; Dv-1918
(804) 662-6200		Co-B,D, Health Dept.
www.vitalrec.com/va.html		Co-M.Dv County Clerk

State Archives	Year Adoption	Hospital Records	Legal Notice
Address	Records Closed	Available?	Required?
State Library Archives	Unknown	Usually	Usually
11th Street at Capitol Square			
Richmond, VA 23219			

Central Department of Motor Vehicles
Division of Motor Vehicles
Driver Learning & Information Dept.
2300 West Broad St.
Richmond, VA 23220

National Archives-Mid-Atlantic Region
Ninth & Market Street, Room 1350
Philadelphia, PA 19107; (215) 597-3000
Hours:M-F:8AM-5PM, 2nd Sat: 8AM-4PM
(Serves DL, PA, MD, VA, WV)

Central Agency	Non-Identifying	Adoption Decree	State
Holding Adoption Records	Info Provided?	From Court	Registry
Div. Social Services/Adoptions	Yes, by law;	Usually;	No
730 E. Broad St.	Adoptee	Circuit Court	
Richmond, VA 23219			
(804) 692-1872			

ADULT ADOPTEES (AGE 18) CAN ACCESS ORIGINAL BIRTH CERTIFICATE ON REQUEST.

Section 63.1-235: separate files, etc., security negative microfilm copies. Section 63.1-236: identifying information will be released after notice and hearing by all interested parties and after determination that disclosure is warranted after considering relative effects of disclosure. No penalties statement available. Code Ann. Section 63.1-223 (Michie 1992) mandates disclosure of non-identifying info.

ADOPTION SEARCH/SUPPORT GROUPS (see "Key" on page 47)

Adoptees/Birthparents Self-Help Group
603 14th St.
Virginia Beach, VA 23451

Billie Quigley
Adoptees and Natural Parents (SS)
949 Lacon Dr.
Newport News, VA 23608

Kaye Adams
Adult Adoptees in Search (SS)
PO Box 203
Ferrum, VA 24088

Cathy C. Holland
Parents & Adoptees Together (SS)
2500 Lauderdale Dr.
Richmond, VA 23233

Pat Lubarsky (AAC)
9706 Rhapsody Dr.
Vienna, VA 22181
PL9706@aol.com

Mary Zoller (AAC)
3225 Kensington Avenue
Richmond, VA 23221

Adoptees & Natural Parents
15 Caribbean Ave.
Virginia Beach, VA 23451

Anita L. Steagall
PO Box 192
Abingdon, VA 24212

Sandra Shaw, Dixie Wilson
Adoptee & Natural Parents (SS)
202 Old Landing Rd.
Yorktown, VA 23692

Adoptee/ Birth Parents Support
Alexandria, VA
ABSNmail@verizon.net
Alexandria, VA 22312

Tracy Mayo
Adoptee-Birthparent Support
PO Box 8273
McLean, VA 22106
tlmayol@aol.com

Tim Morgan
Adoptees & Natural Parents
7622 Windy Hill Road
Gloucester, VA 23061

Joann Jewell-ISC
2047 Retreat Dr.
Mechanicsville, VA 23111
searchline@aol.com

Metro International Reunion Registry
Alexandria, VA
Metro.reunionregistry@verizon.net
http://metroreunionregistry.org

Rebecca Ricardo
Coordinators Inc.
Richmond, VA
rcardo@c2adopt.org

Los Angeles Times, 03/06/91: "WOMAN LOOKING FOR MOTHER FINDS SHE IS HER CO-WORKER . . . Roanoke, VA-Tammy Harris had spent nearly a year looking for her [biological] mother. Joyce Schultz had been trying to find her daughter for nearly 20 years. They had lived two blocks from each other and had worked together at a convenience store for six months before Schultz's eavesdropping led to the startling discovery that they were mother and daughter.

Dear AmFOR: . . . "We are currently involved with a statewide study on adoption and any statistic indicating the need for more openness in adoption is of great interest! I look forward to hearing from you ... We appreciate the work you are doing . . . Sincerely, LAURIE LIPPOLD, ACSW, ADOPTION RESOURCE CTR., CHILDREN'S HOME SOCIETY-WA."

Dear AmFOR: . .. "My husband is adopted by his foster parents. His mother is touchy about telling him about his past. We have a daughter and we feel it is important to know his health history. He also wants to know who his mother is. We don't know where to begin . .. P.D., Norfolk, VA."

Dear AmFOR: ... "I spoke to one of the social workers at DSS and she informed me that I could only obtain non-identifying information. Since receiving that information, I would like to know more about my parents and my biological history . . . [Eight months ago] I wrote to the Commonwealth of Virginia asking how to go about taking this a step further and if I would be required to petition the courts. I have received no reply. I also contacted several agencies, but received no reply . . . MICHELLE P., Baldwinsvile, NY."

Dear AmFOR: ... "I was raised by my mother and a series of stepfathers ... When I was 16-3/4 I gave my consent for that stepfather to "legally" adopt me. I had to sign permission due to my age. However, I consented without knowledge that he was not my father. Do you think I can get records opened based on this legal technicality? . . . The adoption occurred in Alexandria, VA. .. My mother is non-supportive!! Thank you for your prompt reply. God Bless!! . . . D.C., Puyallup, WA."

Dear AmFOR: ... "This letter is to inquire about a son that I gave up for adoption, at Mary Washington Hospital, Fredericksburg, VA. in August, 1971... I am very interested in finding out where he is and if he is okay . . . Sincerely. P.I.G.H., King George. VA."

Dear AmFOR: ... "I have been searching for my parents . . . most of my efforts have yielded minimal results at best. . . CHRISTINA C., Dumfries, VA."

Dear AmFOR: ... "I am very interested in finding my parents . . . The State of Virginia has sealed records which can only be opened to a third party and then only to answer specific questions—not to find addresses and names! ... MARY B., Fairbanks, AK."

Washington

CENTRAL RECORDS OFFICES

Vital Records To Verify Fees (rec = recorded message). Center for Health Statistics PO Box 9709 Olympia, WA 98507 (306) 236-4300 www.vitalrec.com/wa.html	Accessible? Public; some restricted: fee	State (St), County (Co), Birth (B), Death (D), Marriage (M), Divorce (DV) Indices & Records St-B,D since 7/1907 St-M, Dv since 1/1968 Co-B,D,M, Co. Auditor

State Archives Address State Library 1120 Washington St., SE (EA-11) PO Box 9000 Olympia, WA 98504	Year Adoption Records Closed 1953	Hospital Records Available? Sometimes	Legal Notice Required? Yes

Central Department of Motor Vehicles
Division of Licensing
Department of Motor Vehicles
211 12th Ave SE
Olympia, WA 98501

National Archives- Pacific Northwest Region
6125 Sand Point Way, NE
Seattle, WA 98115: (206) 526-6507
Hours: M-F: 7:45-4:00, Tu 5:00-9:00
(Serves ID, OR, WA)

Central Agency Holding Adoption Records Dept. Children's Services/Adoptions PO Box 45710 Olympia, WA 98504 (360) 902-7986	Non-Identifying Info Provided? Yes, by law; Adoptee Family Court	Adoption Decree From Court Always; Superior, System	State Registry No; Intermediary

(1992) ADOPTION DISCLOSURE STATUTES (INTERMEDIARY, WAIVER SYSTEM)
Section 26.33.060: closed hearings. Section 26.33.350: records sealed; court order required to release information. No fees statement available. Section 26.33.340: disclosure of non-identifying information for medical purposes. Sectn 26.33.350: medical information to adoptive parent prior to placement, mental. physical, sensory handicapped, etc. Section 26/33/340; non-identifying information necessary for medical purposes. Rev. Code Ann. Section 26.33.350 (West Supp. 1992) mandates disclosure of non-identifying info.

ADOPTION SEARCH/SUPPORT GROUPS (see "Key" on page 47)

Jodie McBride
Scattered Roots
Olympia, WA
www.scatteredroots.org

Pat Owen, Joan DeGroot (SS)
Washington Adoptees Rights
Movement (WARM)
5950 6th Ave, So. #107
Seattle, WA 98108

Debby Lewis (SG)
Washington Adoptees Rights
Movement (WARM)
20 Hall Ave.
Yakima, WA 98902

Washington Adoptees Rights
Movement (WARM)
PO Box 2667
Olympia, WA 99507

Ronald Johnson
Touched by Adoption (SS)
1105 Colonial Dr.
College Place, WA 99324

Darlene Wilson
SW WA Adoption Suport
6608 NE 14th Avenue
Vancouver, WA 98684
wasearcher@msn.com

Shea Grimm
Bastard Nation
12865 N.E. 85th St., Ste. 179
Kirkland, WA 98033

Martha Faulkner (S)
2030 Dexter Ave., N., #A207
Seattle, WA 98109

Irene Dilley
CUB
10014 NE 35th
Vancouver, WA 98660

Rita Zastrow
63 Bear Gulch Road
Aberdeen, WA 98520
zastrow@olynet.com

Patricia D. Rudd
2513 Cedar Street
Everett, WA 98201
scarpat@w-link.net

Donna Grubbs (S)
2838 Kelly Rd.
Bellingham, WA 98226

Michele Heiderer (S)
16315 Jim Creek
Arlington, WA 98223

Carole Slaybaugh
Rt. 1, Box 17
Pomeroy, WA 99347

Nancy Carton ISC (S)
12740 Bel-Red Rd.
Bellevue, WA 98005

Susan R. Fair ISC
3705 S. Ridgeview Dr.
Spokane, WA 99206

MaryLou Netzer
PO Box 742
Sumner, WA 98390

Joan M. DeGroot
2409 Baker Avenue
Everett, WA 98201

William Elgenberger
Safe Passage
4022 39th Avenue South
Seattle, WA 98201
willverine@aol.com

Marilyn Dean ISC
Washington Adoptees Rights
Movement (WARM)
9901 SE Shoreland Dr.
Bellevue, WA 98004

Betty Rogers
Adoption Search & Reunion (SS)
5301 Tieton Dr.
Yakima, WA 98908

Ann Koch Pelto ISC
Adoption Search & Reconciliation (SS)
14320 SE 170th
Renton, WA 98058

Donna Portuesi ISC
Adoption Search & Counseling (SS)
6201 15th Ave. NW, #P-210
Seattle, WA 98107
asccare@aol.com

Richard Hastings (SG)
Washington Adoptees Rights
Movement (WARM)
1119 Peacock Ln.
Burlington, WA 98233

Racnel Stomme
Three Roots Triad Group
Seattle, WA
www.three-roots.com/groups

Carol Vandenbos ISC (AAC)
14435 22nd Ave., SW
Seattle, WA 98166
CaroleVandenbos@aol.com

Diane Sams ISC
303 East Paradise Rd.
Spangle, WA 99031
SamsSearch@aol.com

Celeste Maier (SS)
377 Draper Valley Rd.
Port Angeles, WA 98632

Tracey Williams
Bellingham Birthmothers
5236 Nielsen Road
Femdale, WA 98248

Deb Underwood (S)
13624 SE 20th Circle
Vancouver, WA 98660

WA Adoption Reunion Movement
(WARM) - Seattle, WA
warm@warmsearch.org

Marcia S. Long
725 Suzanne Court
Langley, WA 98260
jerryl@Whidbey.com

Janet Nixon Baccus
Baccus Genealogical Research
5817 144th Street East
Puyallup, WA 98373

Carole Atkinson/WARM
7835 Forest Ridge Lane NE
Bremerton, WA 98311

Treina Stauffer
A Loving Journey
Federal Way, WA
alovingjourney@aol.com

Trish Parnell
Research World
PO Box 5666
Vancouver, WA 98668

Jennifer Robinson
Given Right
Federal Way, WA
givenright@msn.com

Zoe Waggoner
Adoption Resource Center (SG)
3300 NE 65th St.
Seattle, WA 98115

Mary Lively (SS)
Adoptee Birthparent Reunion Searches
1509 Queen Anne Ave., N #331
Seattle, WA 98109

Donna Dorian-Nichols
The Healing Circle (SS)
4124 Olympic Blvd. W.
Tacoma, WA 98466

Deesa M. Haas (S)
2506 10th W.
Seattle, WA 98119

Janet Mackey (SS)
N. 1114 Locust Rd.
Spokane, WA 99206

Julie Dennis
Reunions Online
21904 Marine View Dr. PMB-138
Des Moines, WA 98198
bn@bastards.org

155

Marlene Smith
Madrona Research
PO Box 29001 PO Box 2144
Bellingham, WA 98228
marlenesmi@juno.com

Eunice Zeilstra, L-PI
EZ Investigations
PO Box 2144
Mt. Vemon, WA 98273

Phyllis Nevill
Birthparent Support
1024 NE 180th Street
Seattle, WA 98155
pmeville@aol.com

Jeann Macomber - ISC
1230-101st Place NE
Belleview, WA 98004

Jolene Johnson (S)
7919 NW 11th Court
Vancouver, WA 98665
jolene@pacifier.com

Jonell Kalamar (S)
SEEK
PO Box 1569
Port Orchard, WA 98366
jkalama@aol.com

Dear AmFOR:... "I was adopted through an agency in Seattle, WA in 1963. My adopters are the best. They will always be Mom and Dad. I am now happily married. I'm interested in my medial history; my husband and I would like to have a child of our own. I have tried calling the Ballard Hospital where I was born. They said that all medical records are confidential of course... Please send anything that you think would be of help... Thank you!... KATHLEEN L., Prosser, WA."

Dear AmFOR: ... "I was adopted towards the end of 1968, or perhaps early in 1969. I am considering starting a search for my mother. I would very much appreciate any information you have on the legislation in Washington regarding the rights of adoptees at the time I was adopted and at present. I am also open to any suggestions as to how to go about starting my search . . . Thank you for your time and attention, LEE K."

West Virginia

CENTRAL RECORDS OFFICES

Vital Records
To Verify Fees
(rec = recorded message).

Vital Registration
350 Capitol Street, Room 165
Charleston, WV 25305
(304) 558-2931

Accessible?
Immediate
family; fee

State (St), County (Co),
Birth (B), Death (D),
  Marriage (M), Divorce (DV)
Indices & Records
St-B ,D since 6/14/12
St-M since 1853; Dv-1918
Co-B,D,M Health Dept.
Co-Dv Circuit County Clerk

State Archives
Address
WV Historical Society
1900 Kanawhe Blvd., E.
Charleston, WV 25305

Year Adoption
Records Closed
Unknown

Hospital Records
Available?
From Doctor

Legal Notice
Required?
Sometimes

Central Department of Motor Vehicles
Driver Improvement Division
Department of Motor Vehicles
1800 Washington St., E.
Charleston, WV 25311

National Archives- Mid-Atlantic Region
Ninth & Market Streets, Room 1350
Philadelphia, PA 19107; (215) 597-3000
Hours: M-F 8AM-5PM; 2nd Sat: 8AM-4PM
(Serves SL, PA, MD, VA, WV)

Central Agency
Holding Adoption Records
Dept. Social Services/Adoptions
350 Capitol Street, Room 691
Charleston, WV 25330
(304) 558-6444

Non-Identifying
Info Provided?
Yes, by law;
All Triad

Adoption Decree
From Court
Usually;
Juvenile;
Circuit Court

State
Registry
Yes

(1985) ADOPTION DISCLOSURE STATUTES (REGISTRY SYSTEM)
West Virginia Code Section 48-4-10 (Supp. 1985) allows access to records with consent. WV Code Section 48-4-10 (Supp. 1992) mandates disclosure of non-identifying info.

ADOPTION SEARCH/SUPPORT GROUPS (see "Key" on page 47)

Judi Padlow
37 21st St.
McMechen, WV 26040

Society's Triangle
411 Cabell Court
Huntington, WV 25703

Loretta Hopson/ Legacies (SS)
826 Honaker Ln.
Charleston, WV 25312
legacies92@aol.com

Dear AmFOR: ... "I am trying to locate my son, who was born "out of wedlock." He was born in Wheeling, West Virginia at the "Ohio Valley General Hospital" on September 2, 1944. My mother put me in the "Florence Crittenton Home" for unwed mothers; he was adopted out from there. In those days we had no rights. They weren't even going to let me see him, but I kicked up such a fuss they had to—to get me calmed down. "He" was beautiful.. In 1987, he was here in Mackinaw City, MI inquiring some information from someone I know ... From what these people told me, he has a "tour bus service" or "travel agency" in his name of "Vieau." He left his business card with them. But somehow the card was lost. It would have been so simple if they hadn't lost the card, as I could have called him and got in contact with him that way. So, that's my predicament. Do you think you could help me locate my son? Thank you ... Sincerely, MRS. A.D., Cheboygan, MI."

Dear AmFOR: ... "I gave up 2 children—one in '84—daughter born at Appalachia Hospital—I never saw her—son at General Hospital... All I want is to see a photo of my kids ... Please help me if you can ... M.A.Q, Hickory, WV."

Dear AmFOR: ... "I was so excited when I read your letter. Especially when I got to the part, there is a mother looking for her daughter in Hickory. I said to myself could that be me she is looking for? It is close to Kentucky. Which on the border line of West Virginia. It could be a possibility it might be her! Do I have to be legal age for you to locate my parents? With the information I have, how long will it take for the search? . . . There is something that I found out! This adoption took place in Feb. of 1976. I was born July 19, 1972. My caseworker was a lady named Mrs. Church. I have an enclosed letter of information that might be useful to you ... Sincerely, LISA L., Efland, NC."

Dear AmFOR:... "I obtained your address from a national directory on adoptee search listings from my local library. I am very interested in your organization and its cause, and believe your services and knowledge can be of benefit... I was born on May 2, 1974 and the adoption was finalized approximately six months thereafter ... I am asking for help and I am not sure where to go from here. I have tried a search myself and have been unsuccessful. I plan to continue my search regardless of the obstacles I have already encountered, being optimistic that so many other adoptees and their parents have been successfully reunited. I sincerely wish to have the opportunity to meet my parents if they too have a mutual desire Sincerely, JACOB G., Terre Haute, IN."

Wisconsin

Vital Records		State (St). County (Co).
To Verify Fees		Birth (B). Death (D),
(rec = recorded message).		Marriage (M). Divorce (DV)
Vital Records	Accessible?	Indices & Records
PO Box 309	Fee	St-B.D since 1814
Madison. WI 53701		St-M since 4/1835
(608) 266-1371		St-D since 10/1907
www.vitalrec.com/wi.html		Co-B.D,M. Dv-no Co index

State Archives	Year Adoption	Hospital Records	Legal Notice
Address	Records Closed	Available?	Required?
State Historical Society	1929	From doctor	Sometimes
University of Wisconsin			
816 State St.			
Madison. WI 53706			

Central Department of Motor Vehicles	National Archives - Great Lakes Region
Department of Transportation	7358 South Pulaski Rd.
Driver Record File	Chicago, IL 60629; (312) 353-0162
PO Box 7918	Hours: M & W-F: 8AM-4:15PM,
Madison WI 53707	Tu: 8AM-8:30PM
	(Serves IL. IN, MI. MN. OH, WI)

Central Agency	Non-Identifying	Adoption Decree	State
Holding Adoption Records	Info Provided?	From Court	Registry
Dept. Child/Family Services/Adoptions	Yes. by law.	Never;	Yes;
PO Box 8916	Adoptee	Probate Court	Intermediary
Madison. WI 53708-8916			
(608) 266-2860			

ADOPTEE ACCESS TO ORIGINAL BIRTH CERTIFICATE w/ "BIRTH" PARENT CONSENT

Section 48.93; locked files; court order required to release information; records sealed. Wisconsin Statute Annotated Section 49.933 (Supp. 1986) provides an Intermediary System. Section 48.93: copy of child's medical record shall be to adoptive parent at time the decree is granted, shall also make information available to adoptive parent at age 18. 48.93: non-identifying information shall be given to adoptive parent at time of adoption; shall also make info to adopted child at age 18. WI Stat Sec Ann. 48.432 (West Supp. 1991) mandates disclosure of non-identifying info.

ADOPTION SEARCH/SUPPORT GROUPS (see "Key" on page 47)

Mary Niebuhr, ISC	Elton Smith	UP Connection (SG)
4221 Tomscott Trail	6706 Revere Ave.	725 American Ave.
Madison. WI 53074	Milwaukee. WI 53213	Waukesha. WI 53188

Linda Day (SG)
530 N. 109th St.
Milwaukee, WI 53226

Carolyn F. Seierstad (ISC)
Milestone Search & Support
3214 Berkshire Rd.
Janesville, WI 53546
bluejay@jvinet.com

Mary Emery Weidling
I CARE Registry
N. 5080, 17th Ave.
Mauston, WI 53948
mary@icareregistry.com

Pat Helgerson ISC
Adoption Resource Network (SS)
PO Box 174
Coon Valley, WI 54623

Doug Henderson PhD (AAC)
4308 Heffron Street
Stevens Point, WI 54481

Maureen Vande Hogen (SS)
Adoption Roots Traced (SS)
855 E. Lake St. #77
Green Bay, WI 54305
mswedl@intaccess.com

Kelly
AID
PO Box 2043
Oshkosh, WI 54903

Sharon Kay Halverson ISC (S)
RFD 1, Box 197-A
New Lisbon, WI 53950

Adoption Triad Outreach (Registry)
PO Box 370691
Milwaukee, WI 53237

Virginia
AID (SS)
PO Box 5045
Madison, WI 53705

Shelley Borreson (SS)
Adoption Information & Direction (AID)
PO Box 8221
Eau Claire, WI 54702

"Dear AmFOR: . . . Thank you for contacting my office with your viewpoints on open records and the misunderstandings associated with the provision. The information was extremely informative. It is my understanding that much of this information was provided in testimony at a recent public hearing. Committee members, therefore, are aware of the realities of adoptees and birthparents.

A charge associated with an adoption search was place in the budget by the Govrenor and was not removed thereafter. The provision is likely to stay in the budget as it was the Governor's initial proposal, but I would recommend writing a letter to him to voice your concerns.

Original birth certificate fees are attached to my bill, as well, as the Assembly version, in order to pay for the costs associated with the influx of requests as project by the State Fiscal Bureau. I have enclosed a copy of my bill, SB 174, for your information. If you should have any questions, comments or suggestions, please feel free to contact my office ... Sincerely, RUSS FEINGOLD, STATE SENATOR, Madison, WI."

Wyoming

CENTRAL RECORDS OFFICES

Vital Records		State (St), County (Co),
To Verify Fees		Birth (B), Death (D),
(rec = recorded message).		Marriage (M), Divorce (DV)
Vital Records Service	Accessible?	Indices & Records
Hathaway Building, 1ˢᵗ floor	Restricted;	St-B, D since 7/1909
2300 Capitol Avenue	fee	St-M, Dv no state index
Cheyenne, WY 82002.		Co-B,D,M County Clerk
(307) 777-7591		Co-District Court Clerk
www.vitalrec.com/wy.html		

State Archives	Year Adoption	Hospital Records	Legal Notice
Address	Records Closed	Available?	Required?
State Archives	Unknown	Unknown	Sometimes
Barren State Office Bldg.			
2301 Central Ave.			
Cheyenne, WY 82002			

Central Department of Motor Vehicles
Department of Revenue
Driver Licenses
122 West 25th St.
Cheyenne, WY 82001

National Archives-Rocky Mountain Region
Denver Federal Center, Building 48
PO Box 25307
Denver, CO 80225-0307; (305) 236-0817
Hours: M-F:7:30AM-3:45PM, Tu: 7:30AM-4:45PM
(Serves CO, MT, ND, SD, UT, WY)

Central Agency	Non-Identifying	Adoption Decree	State
Holding Adoption Records	Info Provided?	From Court	Registry
Dept. Family Services/Adoptions	Yes, by law;	Unknown	No
Hathaway Building	Adoptee;		
2300 Capitol Avenue, Rm. 317	Adoptive Parents		
Cheyenne, WY 82002			
(307) 777-6203			

(1987) ADOPTION DISCLOSURE STATUTES (INTERMEDIARY SYSTEM)
Section 1-22-104; records sealed; court order required to release information. No fees statement. Sec. 1-22-104: if child has not lived with petitioner for more than 6 months, child must have medical examination. Section 1-22-106: medical history of birthparents and adopted child given to adoptive parent after adoption and to adopted child at age of majority. Section 1-22-116 (1988) mandates disclosure of non-identifying info.

ADOPTION SEARCH/SUPPORT GROUPS (see "Key" on page 47)
Debbie Fomento
100 S. 30th, #13
Laramie, WY 82070

> *Dear AmFOR:...*" I found your organization in a magazine article I read. I've been trying to find my parents for two years. If there is any chance of you helping me, please inform me as soon as possible ... Thank you, HOLLY D., Rawlings, WY".

GENEALOGY RESOURCES FOR U.S. POSSESSIONS & TRUST TERRITORIES

AMERICAN SAMOA

American Samoa Freedmen Mailing List and Archivest
For anyone with a genealogical interest in Freedmen in
American Samoa Historic Preservation Office
Ancestry.com - U.S. Federal Censuses
Census images available by subscription: 1920, 1930
Family History Centers; FamilySearch web site
Geographic Names Information System (GNIS)
National Archives and Records Administration
Genealogical Research at the National Archives
Guide to Archival Holdings at NARA's Pacific Region
Search Microfilm Publications; SamoaGenWeb
WorldGenWeb Project; SAMOA Mailing List/Archives

GUAM

Ancestry.com - U.S. Federal Censuses
Census images available by subscription: 1920, 1930
Court Web Sites - Guam
Links to the web sites of various levels of judicial courts.
Family History Centers in Guam; FamilySearch web site
Geographic Names Information System (GNIS)
Guam Freedmen Mailing List and Archives
GuamGenWeb; The WorldGenWeb Project.
Guam Vital Records Information
LibDex - The Library Index - Guam
Genealogical Research at the National Archives
Guide to Archival Holdings at NARA's Pacific Region
Search Microfilm Publications
United States Funeral Homes Directory - Guam
The Vietnam Veterans Memorial - Guam
Midway Island General: MidwayIsland.com
Past Residents of Midway Island
Ancestry.com - U.S. Federal Censuses 1920
Libraries, Archives & Museums:
Family History Library Catalog

PANAMA CANAL ZONE

Ancestry.com - U.S. Federal Censuses
Census images available by subscription: 1920, 1930
El Canal de Panamá - The Panama Canal
Canal History; Canal Zone Vital Records Information
Family History Centers in Panama; FamilySearch web site
LibDex - The Library Index - Panama
Library of Congress / Federal Research Division / Country
Panama Canal Museum; Panama Canal Society Foundation
The Panama Canal Society of Florida; starting in 1932.
Panama Canal Zone Birth and Death Records
Commission now issued by the U.S. Department of State
The Panama Canal: The African American Experience
National Archives and Records Summer 1997,vol. 9, no. 2.
Records of Panama Canal- (Record Group 185) 1848-1984
National Archives Records; Roosevelt Medal Descendants

PUERTO RICO

La Genealogia de Puerto Rico /Genealogy of Puerto Rico
G'S Adoption Registry - Born 1900-1999 Puerto Rico
Hispanic Genealogy Address Book: Puerto Rico
The Jatibonicù Taino Tribal Nation of Borikén
PRRoots.com - Puerto Rican Roots; Court Web Sites
Latin American Network Information Center - LANIC
Libraries, Archives & Museums ;WorldGenWeb Project
Family History Centers Puerto Rico; FamilySearch web site
LibDex - The Library Index - Puerto Rico
Search Microfilm Publications Services for the Public
RootsWeb: Genealogy Mailing Lists: USA/PR
Puerto Rican Genealogist Mailing List
Puerto Rico Freedman MailingList
Geographic Names Information System (GNIS)
1898 La Guerra Hispano Americana en Puerto Rico
Historia de la Guerra Hispano Americana en Puerto Rico
History of the 65th Infantry Regiment,3rd div, Korean War.
The Vietnam Veterans Memorial - Puerto Rico

VIRGIN ISLANDS

Ancestry.com - U.S. Federal Censuses, 1920, 1930
Ancestry.com searchable indexes; maps, 1513-1990
Danish West Indies (U.S. Virgin Islands)
Maps, resource guide, index of wills 1671-1848, 1722
Geographic Names Information System (GNIS)
LibDex - The Library Index - Virgin Islands
Genealogical Research at the National Archives
FamilySearch web site; Search Microfilm Publications;
NewspaperArchive.com - Historical Newspapers Online
Daily News of Virgin Islands, The
Catholic Dioceses/ Parishes within US- Virgin Islands
United States Funeral Homes Directory - Virgin Islands
US Virgin Islands - formerly the Danish West Indies.
USVI Mailing List Archives; WorldGenWeb Project
U.S. Virgin Islands - St. Thomas, St. Croix, St. John
The Vietnam Veterans Memorial - Virgin Islands
Virgin Islands Freedman Mailing List
Virgin Islands Vital Records Information

TRUST TERRITORIES NORTHERN MARIANAS

Family History Library Catalog; FamilySearch web site
Genealogy Helplist - Northern Mariana Islands
Geographic Names Information System (GNIS)
MicronesiaGenWeb; The WorldGenWeb Project.
National Archives Pacific Region
Guide to Archival Holdings at NARA's Pacific Region
Search Microfilm Publications Services for the Public
Northern Mariana Islands Vital Records Information
North Mariana Islands Council for the Humanities
Northern Mariana Freedmen Mailing List and Archives
Pacific Islands Association of Libraries and Archives

U.S. Possessions and Trust Territories

American Samoa

Vital Records Address To		State (St), County (Co), Birth (B), Death (D),
Verify Fees	Accessible?	Marriage (M), Divorce (DV) Indices & Records
Registrar Vital Stats	Public;	St-B, D since 1900
Vital Stats Section	fee	St-M, Dv since 1900
Government of American Samoa		
Pago Pago AS 96799		

(011) (684) 633-1405; 633-1406

ARCHIVES AND LIBRARIES WITH HOLDINGS IN GENEALOGY

Territorial Archives
Office of Archives & Records Management
Dept. of Administrative Services
American Samoa Government
Pago Pago AS 96799
(684) 633-1609; (684) 633-1290

Guam

Vital Records Address To		State (St), County (Co), Birth (B), Death (D),
Verify Fees	Accessible?	Marriage (M), Divorce (DV) Indices & Records
Office Vital Stats	Fee	St-B, D, M since 10/26/01
Health/Social Services		St-Dv Clerk Superior Court

PO Box 2816
Agana. GU 96910
(011) (671) 735-7292

ARCHIVES AND LIBRARIES WITH HOLDINGS IN GENEALOGY

Territorial Archives
University of Guam
Micronesian Area Research Center
University of Guam Station/Mangilao
Mangilao, GU 96923
(011) (671) 734-4473

ADOPTION RECORDS:

Superior Court
Guam Judicial Center
120 West O'Brien Drive
Agana. Guam 96910

Panama Canal Zone

CENTRAL RECORDS OFFICES

Vital Records Address To Verify Fees	Accessible?	State (St), County (Co), Birth (B), Death (D), Marriage (M), Divorce (DV) Indices & Records
Panama Canal Commission Vital Statistics Clerk 1111 – 19th Street NW-Suite 510 Washington, DC 20522-1705 (202) 955-0307	Public; fee	St-B, D, M, Dv since 5/04 through 9/1979

Puerto Rico

CENTRAL RECORDS OFFICES

Vital Records Address To Verify Fees	Accessible?	State (St), County (Co), Birth (B), Death (D), Marriage (M), Divorce (DV) Indices & Records
Dept. of Health Demographics PO Box 11854 - Fernandez Junco Sta San Juan, Puerto Rico 00910 (787) 767-9120	Public; fee	St-B, D, M since 1900

ARCHIVES AND LIBRARIES WITH HOLDINGS IN GENEALOGY

City, County and Regional Archives and Libraries
Conservation Trust of Puerto Rico
PO Box 4747
San Juan, PR 00905
(809) 722-5834

ADOPTION RECORDS:

Administration for Children & Families
Adoption Unit/Post Adoption Services
PO Box 15091
Santurce, Puerto Rico 00910
(787) 724-7474

National Archives - Northeast Region
201 Varick St.
New York, NY 10014-4811
(212) 337-1300
Hours: Mon-Fri 8AM-4:30PM
3rd Sat 8:30AM-4:00 (microfilm only, not naturalization records)
(Serves Puerto Rico, New York, New Jersey and the Virgin Islands; federal census records for all states and New York passenger arrivals on microfilm; also naturalization records for Puerto Rico, New York, New Jersey.)

Virgin Islands

CENTRAL RECORDS OFFICES

U.S. Possession	Vital Records Address To Verify Fees	Accessible?	State (St), County (Co), Birth (B), Death (D), Marriage (M), Divorce (DV) Indices & Records
Virgin Islands (St. Croix)	Registrar Vital Stats Chas. Harwood Memorial Hospital-Christiansted St. Croix, VI 00820	Public; fee	St-B, D since 1840 St-M, Dv Certified copy not avail; inq. fwded if sent c/o Chief Deputy Clerk, Territorial Court of VI, POBox 929 Christiansted, St. Croix VI 00820
Virgin Islands (St. John; Thomas)	Registrar Vital Stats Old Municipal Hospital St. Thomas, VI 00801	Public; fee	St-B since 7/06; D-1/C6 St-M Certified copy not avail; inq. fwded if sent c/o Bureau Vital Records/Stats, Dept. of Health, Charlotte Amalie, St. Thomas, VI 00801; Dv-Certified not avail; inq. fwded-send c/o Clerk, Territorial Court of VI, PO 70, Charlotte Amalie, St. Thomas, VI 00801

Central Agency Holding Adoption Records
Dept. Children/Youth/Families (Adoptions)
1303 Hospital Building A-Knudstansen Complex
Charlotte Amalie
St. Thomas, VI 00802

ARCHIVES AND LIBRARIES WITH HOLDINGS IN GENEALOGY

Virgin Islands/St. Croix
Independent Publications & Miscellany
St. Croix Landmarks Society
Centerlien Road
Frederiksted, VI 00840
(809) 772-0593

Virgin Islands/St. Thomas
Territorial Archives and Library
Virgin Islands Dept. of Conservation & Cultural
 Affairs - Division of Libraries, Museums &
Archeological Services
Location: 20 Dronningens Gade St. Thomas VI 08802
Mailing Address: PO Box 390 (mailing address)
St. Thomas, VI 00801
(809) 774-0630

National Archives-Northeast Region
201 Varick St.
New York, NY 10014-4811
(212) 337-1300
Hours: Mon-Fri 8AM-4:30PM
3rd Sat 8:30AM-4:00
(microfilm only, not naturalization records)
(Serves the Virgin Is. Puerto Rico, NY, NJ;
federal census records for all states & NY
passenger arrivals on microfilm; also naturalization
records for Puerto Rico, NY, NJ

Trust Territory of Marianas

CENTRAL RECORDS OFFICES

State (St), County (Co),
Birth (B), Death (D),
Marriage (M), Divorce (DV)

Vital Records
Address To
Verify Fees · Accessible? · Indices & Records
Director, Health Services · fee plus · St-B, D, M,D,V since 1900
Trust Territory of Pacific Islands · addl. fee per 100 words
PO Box 307
Saipan, MP 96950
Northern Marianas
(670) 234-6401, ext. 15

ARCHIVES AND LIBRARIES WITH HOLDINGS IN GENEALOGY

Independent Publications and Miscellany
Commonwealth Council for Arts and Culture
PO Box 553 CHRB
Saipan CM 96950

INTERNATIONAL SOUNDEX REUNION REGISTRY (ISRR.net) - Oldest, Largest & Free

---

FOR OFFICE USE ONLY

RN	$	DOB		COUNTRY	STATE	I
STAFF						II

Official Registration Form
-- Confidential --

MAIL TO: ISRR, P.O. BOX 371179, LAS VEGAS, NV 89137

COMPLETE BOTH PAGES of this form, use BLACK ink, THEN PRINT, SIGN & MAIL

Please read the guidelines on page 4. This will help you fill out the form correctly.

This registration is my FIRST ENTRY ☐   an UPDATE ☐

I AM THE: ADOPTEE/CHILD ☐   BIRTH PARENT ☐   BIRTH SIBLING ☐   OTHER: (explain) _____

PRESENT NAME: _____   REFERRED BY: _____

ADDRESS: _____   CITY: _____   STATE: _____   ZIP: _____

TELEPHONE
NUMBER(S)   HOME: (___) _____   SOCIAL SECURITY #: _____

WORK: (___) _____   E-MAIL: _____

Information About the CHILD

BIRTH DATE (Month/Day/Year) _____   TIME _____ AM ☐ PM ☐   BIRTH WEIGHT _____ lb ____ oz

HOSPITAL (Birth Place) _____   ATTENDING PHYSICIAN (Or Other) _____

CITY OF BIRTH _____   COUNTY _____   STATE _____   COUNTRY _____

MALE ☐   FEMALE ☐

NAME GIVEN AT BIRTH _____

NAME GIVEN AT ADOPTION _____

ADOPTIVE PARENT'S NAMES _____

BIRTH CERTIFICATE #'s -- File # _____   Registrar # _____

IF THIS WAS A PLURAL BIRTH (Twins/Triplets, etc.), How many MALES? ____ How many FEMALES? ____

Were they separated by adoption?   YES ☐   NO ☐   Their Name(s) _____

COURT OF JURISDICTION _____   CITY _____   STATE _____

ATTORNEY OF RECORD _____   DATE OF FINAL DECREE _____

This adoption was -- PRIVATE ☐   BY AN AGENCY ☐   SOCIAL WORKER/INTERMEDIARY _____

NAME OF PLACEMENT AGENCY _____   CITY _____   STATE _____

INTERNATIONAL SOUNDEX REUNION REGISTRY, Inc.

Information About the BIRTH PARENTS (at time of separation):

Including all info you know is very important. It helps ISRR determine relationship. Please enter everything you know here. Update ISRR when you acquire additional data. Get your non-identifying info from an agency. Click on "Get More Info" at www.isrr.net for guidelines.

	Birth Mother	Birth Father
NAME(S)		
Maiden Name		
Used At time of Birth		
Signed on Relinquishment/Consent		
BIRTH DATE	Age At Birth	Age At Birth
BIRTH PLACE		
MARITAL STATUS		
RELIGION		
EDUCATION		
OCCUPATION		
MILITARY BRANCH		
ANCESTRY		

	HEIGHT	WEIGHT	HAIR	EYES	HEIGHT	WEIGHT	HAIR	EYES
DESCRIPTION								
OTHER CHILDREN								
PARENT'S NAMES								

REMARKS: (use a separate sheet if needed)

-- To help ISRR use contributions wisely, please keep your address, phone number & email current and notify ISRR if you are married --

I, the undersigned, hereby give my permission to the International Soundex Reunion Registry to release this vital information to the person(s) for whom this search is conducted. I understand that permission is necessary to activate registration, facilitate contact and for verification of identity, and my relationship to that person or persons.

X _____   Date _____
Signature Required

ALTERNATE ADDRESS AND/OR PHONE _____

THIS IS YOUR REGISTRY - YOUR CONTRIBUTION IS TAX DEDUCTIBLE

Registration remains free because of the generosity of those we serve -- ISRR is a non-profit 501(c)3 tax exempt corporation

© 1993-2009 International Soundex Reunion Registry

PLEASE PRINT, SIGN AND MAIL THIS FORM TO:
ISRR, P.O. Box 371179, Las Vegas, NV 89137

WE LOOK FORWARD TO SERVING YOU!

ISRR will notify you only when a match is made. If you wish confirmation that your form has been received, include a self-addressed stamped envelope with this registration or update. Please do not send anything that requires signature, or to volunteers to wait in line at the post office. Thank You.

168

"The only thing that lives on is truth; It passes in secret from one heart to another;
It passes in mother's milk to her child."
—The Egyptians.

International Searching

Search Basics and Directory of Resources
by Country, Alphabetically

International Search Resources

1. INTERNATIONAL VITAL RECORDS.

CONSULAR SERVICES.

Consular Services Abroad. A document is issued by an American embassy or consulate reflecting the facts of a birth abroad of a child acquiring US citizenship at birth through one or both parents (an FS-240 record), along with the Certification of Birth (DS-1350), and are acceptable as proof of birth and US citizenship for all legal purposes. For a Report of the Death of an American Citizen, a document is issued by an American embassy or consulate reflecting the facts of a death of an American citizen, based on the local death certificate. For a Certificate of Witness to Marriage. A document is issued by an American embassy or consulate reflecting the facts of a marriage abroad in which at least one party is an American citizen. A consular officer must have attended the ceremony. This accommodation was discontinued in 1987.

How To Apply for a Copy of These Records. Submit a signed, written request including all pertinent facts of the occasion along with the requester's return address and telephone number. Only the subject, parent, or legal guardian may request a birth record. If the request is for an SF-240, the original FS-240, or a notarized affidavit attesting to its disposition, must be included with the request. If a birth record is to be amended or corrected, appropriate certified documents supporting the request must be included. Where to Write and Obtain Forms: US Department of State, Passport Services, Vital Records Section, 1111 – 19th Street NW, Suite 510, Washington, DC 20524; (202) 955-0307..

OBTAINING VITAL RECORDS DIRECTLY FROM A COUNTRY.

It should be kept in mind that copies of the original certificate might be on file in several jurisdictions depending on the country. Similar records are also kept by various religious denominations, and some copies and originals are held by archives and libraries the world over., including the largest collection held by the Mormon Genealogical Library-- accessible via any of 3,000 Family History Centers in the United States and abroad. The main address is: THE FAMILY HISTORY LIBRARY, 35 North West Temple Street, Salt Lake City, Utah 84150 USA. Online, go to http://www.ancestry.com

In pre-revolutionary Russia all civil status documents were registered by the church. Such registrations were first introduced in 1722, when Peter I decreed the mandatory registration of births of the Orthodox population. For the non-Orthodox, birth registration was introduced later—for Lutherans in 1832, for Catholics in 1826, for Muslims in 1828, for Jews in 1835, and for Old Believers in 1874. In the other socialist countries civil status documents are registered by agencies of civil registry—called bureaus in the Polish People's Republic, services in the People's Republic of Bulgaria, and so on—which are under the jurisdiction of local agencies of authority. In the capitalist countries documents of civil status are usually registered, depending upon the type of document; at the city hall (for births) or with the police (for deaths). Marriages are registered either at church registries (Spain, Greece, Portugal) or at the city hall (France, Federal Republic of Germany) or else by a judge (in some states of the USA).

2. INTERNATIONAL RED CROSS SERVICES –Tracing and Messaging.

To search for a family member in any country, contact the local chapter of the RED CROSS near you. They have a person experienced in (1) international traces, (2) international messaging. Your request will be sent through Red Cross channels to the appropriate overseas office for processing.

The American Red Cross (HQ)
431 18th NW
Washington, DC 20006 USA
(202) 737-8300
http://www.redcross.org/
email-info@redcross.org

International Red Cross
Tracing and Messaging
(410) 764-5311
http://www.redcross.org/services/intl/tracing.html

3. EUROPEAN CENSUS.

First censuses for the following countries were: Austria 1815, Russia 1897, France 1801, Saxony 1825, Prussia 1810 Spain 1789, Bavaria 1818, Norway 1815, Sweden 1749, Greece 1836, Switzerland 1860, Great Britain 1851.

170

4. PRIVATE INTERNATIONAL SEARCH-SUPPORT ORGANIZATIONS AND REGISTRIES
(Always enclose SASE with sufficient postage or International Postage Reply Coupons.)

Americans for Open Records (AmFOR)
PO Box 401
Palm Desert, CA 92261 USA
http://AmFOR.net/UltimateSearch

American Adoption Congress (AAC)
PO Box 42730
Washington, DC 20015 USA
(202) 483-3399
http://american-adoption-cong.org

International Message Bank
22 Willesden Road
Toronto Ontario M2H 1 V5
CANADA

International Soundex Registry (ISRR)
(oldest/largest registry with MedicAlert;
(see Chapter 1)
PO Box 2312
Carson City, NV 897.. USA
http://www.isrr.net

Concerned United Birthparents (CUB)
2000 Walker St. (National HQ)
Des Moines, IA 50317 USA
http://CUBirthparents.org

Adoptees' Foreign Searches
PO Box 360074
Strongville, OH 44136 USA
(216)238-1004

NORCAP (UK./USA Searches)
Ann Caffari
112 Church Rd.
Wheatley, Oxfordshire OX33 1LU
United Kingdom
enquiries@norcap.org

Overseas Brats
PO Box 29805
San Antonio, TX 78229 USA
(210)349-1394

Pam Martin
25433 Via Estudio
Launa Niguel, CA 92677
USA

5. INTERNATIONAL SOCIAL SERVICES (ISS). International Social Services (ISS), founded in 1924 in Germany, is headquartered in Switzerland, and has branches in Argentina, Australia, Canada, Finland, France, Great Britain, Greece, Hong Kong, Italy, Japan, the Netherlands, Spain, the United States of America, and Venezuela. ISS also has correspondent offices in approximately 100 other countries. ISS is concerned with a variety of social services, primarily concerning family matters that involve foreigners and which result in crossing international borders such as parental kidnap and custody matters. The ISD also contacts relatives and others from whom people have become unexpectedly or involuntarily separated, "political" and other types of refugees.

ISD helps couples adopt children from other countries and has also been instrumental in helping adoptees and birthparents locate and contact each other, especially when they are in different countries. On November 12,1987, ISD held a conference titled "Adoptees Seek Their Original Family." A report on this conference was printed in the News Service of German Associations for Public and Private Welfare, Issue #5, 1988, p. 148 et seq.

Headquarters
International Social Services
32, quai du Seujet
CH-1201 Geneva
Switzerland
Phone: 22 317454
FAX: 22-73-80-949

Canada
International Social Services-Canada
Box 3503 Station C
Ottawa K 1 Y 4G 1 Ontario
Canada

France
Service Social d'Aide aux Emigrants
72 Rue Regnault
F-75013 Paris
France

Germany
Internationaler Sozialdienst
Deutscher Zweig e.V.
Am Stockbom 5-7
6000 Frankfort-am-Main 50, FRG
Germany

Great Britain
Internal'l Social Services-Great Britain
39 Cramer House, 39 Brixton Rd.
London SW9 6DD
Great Britain

The Netherlands
Stichting.International Social Services
Stationweg 147
NL-2515 BM's-Gravenhage
The Netherlands

Spain
Service Social International
Consejo Superior de Protection
de Menores
Cea Bermudez 46, E
28003 Madrid
Spain

United States of America
International Social Services
American Branch, Inc.
95 Madison Ave.
New York, New York 10016
(212) 532-6350, ext. 351

6. INTERNATIONAL ADOPTIONS

Citizenship. Effective in 2001, United States citizenship is now acquired by adoption. Prior to 2001, an alien child who was adopted by a U.S. citizen was eligible for citizenship immediately after adoption, if applied for. State law as to access to adoption records applies.

Adoption Laws and Records. North American adoption records are not typical of the rest of the world. With the exception of the Soviet Union, where all citizens' birth, marriage, and death records were made uniformly confidential (not available to public access), most countries do not impose a seal of secrecy upon its vital records. Countries where a shift away from parental views of "children as possessions", where histories and biologies are "owned", find no need of the term "adoption" in free societies. New Zealand's Adoption Information Act of 1985 requires a "show cause" to seal, rather than to open, an adoption record. In England, Scotland, and other countries, the institution of adoption appears to be working to the satisfaction of society where those countries have truly open, accessible vital records. Ethnic groups peripheral to American society—African-Americans, Eskimos, Polynesians, Native Americans, and early Hawaiians—have practiced kinship fostering to a greater extent than has the white, anglo-saxon population. Former Yugoslavia (now Bosnia-Herzegovina) offered 3 types of adoption—closed, open, and "incomplete" adoption.

Islamic Law prohibits adoption but recognizes other systems of caring for the Muslim child—if the system provides psychological, health, social, educational, and financial assistance, and being eligible for a testament while preserving the child's original origin.

> *Politics of Adoption* by Mary K. Benet, Free Press, MacMillan Publishing, NY, 1976: "Punishment for unauthorized disclosure from a 'sealed' (confidential) record in California and Connecticut is exceeded only by punishment for the same offense in the former Soviet Union."

> According to Anne Merrill, International Concerns for Children (911 Cypress Dr., Boulder, CO 80303; 303/494-8333): "Foreign adoptions more often involve children 'abandoned with no records.' Searching out birth family for information is the most reliable way for adoptees worldwide."

> *USA Today*, 5/26/93, page 13A: "Treaty Helps Foreign Adoptions —Adoption Advocates Are Working on International Treaty to Curb Corruption . . . Each country has its own widely varying adoption laws and administrative procedures. This lack of uniformity breeds corruption, bribery, and baby-selling.

> The sad truth is, international adoption can be cruelly exploitative; citizens of wealthy nations 'buying up' future human resources of poorer ones ..."

Missing & Abducted Children

1. MISSING CHILDREN & INTERPOL. Interpol is a source of assistance when children are thought to have been taken out of a country. If taken out of the United States, contact the office of Interpol in the US: U.S. Central Bureau, U.S. Dept. of Justice, Shoreham Bldg, Rm. 800, Washington, DC 20530; (202) 272-838

IN CANADA, missing child search: National Clearinghouse Royal Canadian Mounted Police, (613) 993-7425.

BLOCK CHILD'S PASSPORT: To block passport of a missing child, for a "welfare and whereabouts" search to locate a child and determine physical condition; or to obtain Consular Report of Birth (Form FS- 240) or Certification of Birth (Form DS-1350 or FS-545), for foreign-born children adopted in the U.S., contact: Office of Citizens' Consular Services; U.S. Dept. of State - Rm 4811; Washington, DC 20520 USA. (202) 647-3444

2. INTERNATIONAL RECIPROCAL AGENCIES. The countries listed below were signatories to the Hague Convention on Civil Aspects of International Child Abduction as of June 1, 1992. Some signatory countries do not have reciprocal agreements with all other members (for return of abducted children). In case of abduction, or for info on a country's current status with regard to the Hague, contact your central authority, or Mr. Adair Dyer, First Secretary (in English, French, or Spanish), The Hague Conference on Private International Law, Permanent Bureau, 6, Scheveningseweg, 2517 KT-The Hague, Netherlands; telephone 31/70-363.33.03; telex 33383; telefax 31/ 70-360.48.67 ... Or: One World: For Children, PO Box 124, Corunna, MI (517) 725-2392.

U.S. Central Authority: Offices of Citizens Consular Services, Child Custody Division, Rom 4817, Dept. of State, Washington, DC 20520; (202) 647-3666 (Sally Light, Jack Markey, Jim Schuler). Signatories by Country: Argentina, Australia, Austria, Belize, Canada, Denmark, Ecuador, France, Germany, Hungary, Ireland, Israel, Luxembourg, Mexico, Norway, Portugal, Spain, Sweden, Switzerland, United Kingdom, United States, and Yugoslavia.

3. PRIVATE CHILD RESCUE GROUPS FOR HIRE. Another resource for international missing children situations is CHILD QUEST INTERNATIONAL, 1190 Coleman Ave., San Jose, CA 95110; (408) 287-4673. This non-profit organization claims 1,544 child rescues from countries outside the U.S., on funds raised from royalties from 'missing child photo-labels,' on candy machines, and a few corporate donors. In *Rescue My Child*, author Neil Livingston reveals how parents retrieved their children from other countries when the American government would not intervene for diplomatic reasons. A private group of ex Delta Force Commandos rescues children from other countries on behalf of their custodial parents—their usual 6-digit fees are commensurate with the risks, and they maintain a low profile. Since 1993 their last known point of contact is: Don Feeney, Security Training Seminars, Corporate Training Unlimited, PO Box 41627, Fayetteville, NC 28309; phone (919) 864-9806; FAX (919) 864-3106.

Open Records Worldwide

Anglo-Celtic Countries: Common law countries, such as England and Australia, tend to have biases favoring "blood ties," families and privacy. With the exception of Canada, from the 1970's on, these biases have resulted in open records (subject to occasional vetos).

Other First World Traditions: In Continental Europe, Quebec, Japan and Korea which have divergent adoption customs, mostly using Civil law traditions, birth certificates (and sometimes other adoption records) are available to adoptee (except in Quebec, Luxembourg, a few others). Scandinavians have most progressive open records systems.

Developing World: Practices vary widely. Records were never expressly sealed, except in China, India and Poland. Focus has been on care of unwanted children. In Argentina, past regimes facilitated kidnapping of infants and coerced adoptions with aid of sealed records; Argentinian activist groups now promote open records as a "universal right."

International Policy: The United Nations Rights of the Child Project which the United States refused to ratify, and Hague Intercountry Adoption Treaty Conferences both recognize the child's right to identity and heritage, freedom from discrimination due to circumstances of birth and freedom of association with one's biological family. These agreements have given rise to the International Council on Social Welfare Adoption Guidelines found at: http://www.adoptionscentrum.se/guidelines/english.htm

Afghanistan

Department of Population
Registration and Vital Statistics
Ministry of the Interior
Sharlnow, Kabul, Afghanistan

Afghanistan has required all males to register for identification cards since 1952. Efforts to strengthen the registration of vital records in Afghanistan have been of limited success. Documents are provided for free.

During the Wars in Iraq and Afghanistan, from 2003 through 2009 an estimated 1.6-million Afghani civilians were displaced to neighboring countries, along with nearly 100,000 Iraqis fleeing to Syria and Jordan *each month*. As of 2010, the number of civilian casualties in Afghanistan is estimated to be over 100,000 while the number of civilian casualties in Iraq is still highly disputed. The number of actual war orphans in these countries is unknown. There is no adoption law in these Muslim countries, only guardianship; an unknown number of Iraqi and Afghani children have been smuggled to unknown destinations (Wikipedia.com).

Albania

Drejtoria Qendore e Statisikave
Keshili i Ministrave (Kryemistrial)
Bulevardi Deshmoret e Kombit
Tirane, Albania

Registration is required of all residents. Documents are provided for free.

Algeria

Service d'Etat Civl des Communes
Ministere de l'Interieur
Alger, Algeria

Vital registration began in Algeria in 1882 and included principally Muslims in the North. By 1905 coverage also included Muslims in the South. Today the registration of vital records is considered to be incomplete.

Angola

Direccao Nacional dos Registos
Notariado e Identificacao
Ministerio de Justicia
Luando, Angola

Vital registration began for Europeans earlier in this century and efforts have been made to expand registration throughout the country. The civil strife there has made this an impractical goal for the nation.

Antigua and Barbuda

Registrar General's Office
High Court
High Street
St. John's, Antigua
(809) 462-0609

Antigua was discovered by Columbus in 1493 and became independent in 1967. The Registrar General has records from August 1, 1856.

Argentina

Director of Civil Registration
Office of Civil Registration
(Capitol, Province) Argentina

Additional information is available from the National Registry of Persons in Buenos Aires. Each state maintains its own vital records and issues the national identification card for the National Registry of Persons. Vital registration began on August 1, 1886 in Argentina. The current registration is considered to be 90 percent complete. The fee for documents varies from state to state.

SEARCH RESOURCE

Abuelas de Plaza de Mayo
Corrientes 3284 - Piso 4 - Dto. "H"
1193 -Cap. Fed. - Republica Argentina
T.E.: 89-3475

ABDUCTED CHILDREN IN ARGENTINA

When in 1976, the Armed Forces seized control of the government of Argentina, they began to implement a systematic plan of destruction and of violation of the most fundamental human rights.

In this manner they caused 30,000 persons to disappear, persons of all ages, from the most diverse social backgrounds. Among the disappeared there are hundreds of children who were kidnapped along with their parents or who were born in the clandestine detention centers where their pregnant mothers had been taken. Many of the children were registered as children of members of the repressive forces; others were abandoned while others were left in institutions as children whose identity was unknown. In this way they made children disappear and destroyed their identity, depriving them of their rights, freedom, and natural families.

In order to locate the disappeared children, the Grandmothers of May Square work on four different levels; denunciations before national and foreign governments, before the judiciary, advertisements in the press directed to the general public, and personal investigations. After dramatic years of searching without stop, they were able to locate 48 disappeared children, of whom 5 had been murdered. Of the remaining 43, 27 are already with their legitimate families and others are in close contact with their grandparents, with their true identity and history restored to them by court orders.

In order to help this work, the Association has created a technical team made up of 18 professionals including lawyers, doctors, and psychologists. Each one of the disappeared children has a case pending before the judiciary; and when new information is received, it is added to their files so that, as time passes, it will be able to determinate the real identity of all of the children and of those responsible for their kidnapping or illegal adoption.

In order to preserve for the future the data obtained from the blood tests* used in identifying the children, a genetic data bank has been created by National Law No. 23.511, where the genetic histories of all the families whose children have been abducted will be stored.

> *Omaha World Herald*, 9/3/93, page 4: "Argentina Takes Custody of Cult Children" . . . Buenos Aires,
> Argentina (AP) - About 30 adult members of a cult have been arrested and 300 children living with
> them—including some Americans—were placed in protective custody in government-run orphan homes,
> a court official said Wednesday. The adults of the Children of God sect were charged with 'conspiracy to
> kidnap and conceal children,' court secretary Jorge Sica said. 'From 60 to 70 percent of the children are
> foreigners from Britain, France, the United States, Canada, Brazil, Venezuela and other countries,' Sica said
> . . . Initial testimony showed that some of the children 'were subjected to sexual acts or suffered physical abuse
> and injuries from leaders of the groups,' prosecutor Carlos Villafane told station Radio Mitre."

*The Blood Center of New York, and the Association for the Advancement of Science (also in the U.S.) have developed a way to use blood and tissue samples to establish family relationship to a 99.95 certainty.

Armenia

Russian-American Genealogical Archival Services (RAGAS)
PO Box 236
Glen Echo, MD 20812
(202)501-5206

Cost for a Birth, Marriage, or Death Certificate $20.00

By an agreement between the United States National Archives Volunteer Association and the Archives of Russia Society, RAGAS receives and processes requests for vital records in some of the former Soviet republics. Although at this time RAGAS is able to deal mainly with Russia, Belarus, and Ukraine they might be able to help you with your inquiries regarding Armenia. There is a $2.00 shipping fee. The service also is available at an hourly rate. (See "Russia" for application forms.) The National Library of Armenia also has records. Contact them at Terian 72, Yerevan 375009, Armenia; Tel: (011) (7) (8852) 56-45-74. Also, the Armenian Library and Museum of America, 65 Main St., Watertown, MA 02172; (617) 926-2562.

SEARCH RESOURCES

Armenian Genealogical Records Search
410 East Sumac Ave.
Provo, UT 84601
U.S.A

Armenian Historical Society of Australia
59 Fourth Ave.
Willoughby, New South Wales 2068
Australia

Los Angeles Times, 4/25/93, page B3: "Armenians Rally at Consulate to Mark Genocide Anniversary . . . Wednesday was a day of worldwide mourning for Armenians, who consider the date to be the anniversary of the start of a campaign by the Ottoman Turks in 1915 to massacre the Armenian minority in Turkey . . . Turkish officials reject the accusation that 1.5 million Armenians were slaughtered, saying that perhaps 300,000 died as a result of famine and mass deportation ... .

... President Bush issued a proclamation to the nation's one million Armenians ... that avoided using the word 'genocide,' but called April 24 a 'day of remembrance.' But for Armenian-Americans who lost family members to persecution in Turkey, Wednesday was clearly more than that... 'I do this for my children and my grandchildren, that they never forget, and they never lose their hope that justice will be done to us,' Ajamian said."

Los Angeles Times, 6/14/93, page B5: "There's Always the Danger of Culture Being Lost... The philosophy here is to give a quality education in the American sense as well as to make sure that the Armenian heritage is preserved. Because it is a very rich culture and heritage. It's centuries old. For example, Armenians were the first to accept Christianity as their national religion."

Ararat, Winter 1988, by Mary Louise Foess: "Return Trip: The Incredible Story of How a Young Woman Fought for Her 'Lost' Armenian Identity ... I want ancestral ties. I learned from Uncle that most of the family was killed in the genocide. I also wanted contact with blood relatives, the physical contact of hugging and kissing these dear people, full knowledge of all the circumstances surrounding my birth and subsequent surrender, and most of all, the opportunity for my relatives to know the 'lost' baby. The truth of my origins or existence shall not be hidden anymore ... Like my sealed adoption record, the splendor and beauty of these people and their tragedy (actually mine, too, because my ancestors were killed, too) seemed to be some deep, dark secret... My heritage is beautiful yet rare. It is my time now to come back ... To deny or ignore your ethnic heritage and ancestors, to me, is to deny God... I don't want you or any of my descendants to ever have a sense of rootlessness as I had, or even worse, the feeling of never being able to know what others take for granted: the truth of one's origins and the love of one's birth family."

Australia - Australian Capital Territory

Office of the Registrar General of Births, Deaths and Marriages

Office of Registrar General
(255 Canberra Ave., Fyschwick, ACT 2609)
PO Box 225
Canberra City, ACT 2608, Australia
(011)(61)(6) 207-0460
www.ovs.acr.gov.au

The Registrar General holds records from January 1, 1930.

Records of interest are also available at the National Library of Australia, Parkes Place, Canberra, A.C.T. 2600

SEARCH RESOURCES

Federation of Australian
Historical Societies
Box 40
Civic Square
Canberra ACT 2600
Australia

Heraldy & Genealogical Society
of Canberra
Box 585
Canberra ACT 2600
Australia

Military History Society of Australia
Box 30
Garran ACT 2605
Australia

Australian National University
Historical Society
Box 1112
Canberra ACT 2600
Australia

The long-awaited A.C.T. Adoption Act 1992 was finally passed March 30, 1993, and implemented in July. Under the Act adopted people over the age of 18 years, their birthparents, and adoptive parents all have rights to identifying information about each other. Children and other descendants have similar rights. A contact veto is available to a wide range of persons in both the adoptive and birth family. No penalty is attached to breaking the veto.

Australia - New South Wales

Registry of Births, Deaths, and Marriages
191 Thomas St.
PO Box 30 G.P.O.
Sidney, New South Wales 2001, Australia
(01)(61)(2) 228-8511
www.bdin.nsw.gov.au

The Registry has records from March 1, 1856. Payment must be made in Australian dollars using an international money order or bank draft made payable to the Registry of Births, Deaths, and Marriages. If your request is urgent, you may call them at (011)(61)(2) 228-7777. There is an additional charge of Au $20.00.

The Family History Library of The Church of Jesus Christ of Latter-day Saints in Salt Lake City, Utah has microfilmed original and published vital records and church registers of New South Wales. Consult your nearest Family History Center. Records of interest are also available at the National Library of Australia, Parkes Place, Canberra, A.C.T. 2600; Tel. (011)(61)(62)621-111.

Quest: The Newsletter of KinQuest, Inc., Vol. III, No. 4 (#12), 03/92: "Parent Finders, National Capital Region, Inc. of Canada reports that the states of Queensland and New South Wales in Australia have each passed legislation giving access to identifying information to both adoptees over the age of 18 years and their birthparents. Unlike similar legislation passed in nearby New Zealand in 1985, there is no compulsory counselling, no mediation, and no veto option on information being released. Support services are available but optional for a nominal fee, which may be waived. At the time that the legislation was passed, it was vigorously noted that State Contact Registries are not effective. Of 154 politicians eligible to vote in the House, only 1% voted against the legislation."

SEARCH RESOURCES
Adoption Search-Support

Post-Adoption Resource Center
PO Box 239
bondi, New South Wales 2026
Australia
parc@bensoc.asn.au

Royal Australian Historical Society
History House
133 MacQuarie St.
Sydney New South Wales 2000
Australia

Nepean Family History Society
125 Maxwell St.
South Penrith
New South Wales 2750
Australia

Australian Jewish Historical Society
166 Castlereagh St.
Sydney New South Wales 2000
Australia

Presbyterian Historical Society
Box 100
Sydney, New South Wales 2000
Australia

New South Wales Military
History Society
12 Irvine Crescent
Ryde, New South Wales 2112
Australia

Church of England Historical Society
GPO Box 2902
Sydney New South Wales 2001
Australia

Australian Catholic Historical Society
154 Elizabeth St. - 2nd Fl. Suite !
Sydney, New South Wales 2000
Australia

Society of Australian Genealogists
Richmond Villa
120 Kent St.
Sydney, New South Wales 2000
Australia

Australia - Northern Territory

Office of the Registrar of Births, Deaths and Marriages
Department of Law
Nichols Place
G.P.O. Box 3021

Darwin, Northern Territory 0801. Australia
(01)(61)(8) 8999-6119
www.nt.gov.au/justice/bdm

The Office of the Registrar has birth records from August 24,1870, marriage records from 1871, and death records from 1872. If your request is urgent, there is an additional fee of Au $10.00.

The Family History Library of The Church of Jesus Christ of Latter-day Saints in Salt Lake City, Utah has microfilmed original and published vital records and church registers of the Northern Territory. For further details on their holdings, please consult your nearest Family History Center.

Records of interest are also available at the National Library of Australia, Parkes Place, Canberra, A.C.T. 2600; Tel.: (011)(61)(62)621-111

Adoption legislation changes have been accepted in the N.T, effective May 3, 1994, with parents and adoptees having equal rights. There are to be veto options against both information and contact. Adopters are to be notified when parents apply for the birth certificate. There have been approximately 400 adoptions in the N.T.

Australia - Queensland

Office of the Registrar of Births, Deaths and Marriages

(110 George St., Brsibane. Australia)
PO Box 15188
City East, Queensland
Queensland 4002, Australia
(01)(61)(7) 3035-1000
www.justice.qld.gov.au

The Office of the Registrar General has records from March 1, 1856. When writing please make the international bank draft in Australian dollars and make payable to the Registrar General. If your request is urgent, there is an additional charge of Au $10.50.

The Family History Library of The Church of Jesus Christ of Latter-day Saints in Salt Lake City, Utah has microfilmed many of the original and published vital records and church registers of Queensland. For further details on their holdings, please consult your nearest Family History Center.

Records of interest are also available at the National Library of Australia, Parkes Place, Canberra, A.C.T. 2600; Tel.: (011)(61)(62) 621-111.

SEARCH RESOURCES

Australia - South Australia

Principal Registrar of Births, Deaths and Marriages
Department of Public and Consumer Affairs
Edmund Wright House
59 King William St.
G.P.O. Box 1351
Adelaide, South Australia 5001, Australia
(01)(61)(8) 8204-9599
www.ocha.sa.gov.au/bdm

ADOPTION RECORDS:
(Records and original birth certificates
 are open on request)
GPO Box 292
Adelaide, South Australia 5001, Australia
www.adoptions.sa.gov.au

The Registrar has records from July 1, 1842. Enclose an additional Au $1.00 per certificate for airmail postage. If your request is urgent, there is an additional charge of Au $15.00. Please make your international bank draft in Australian dollars payable to the Principal Registrar.

The Family History Library of The Church of Jesus Christ of Latter-day Saints in Salt Lake City, Utah has microfilmed original and published vital records and church registers of the Northern Territory. For further details on their holdings, please consult your nearest Family History Center.

Records of interest are also available at the National Library of Australia, Parkes Place, Canberra, A.C.T. 2600; Tel.: (011)(61)(62) 621-111.

SEARCH RESOURCES

Mrs. Diane Roundhill
War Babes Down Under
47 Phillip Highway
Elizabeth 5112
South Australia

Paulina Allman
Austr Relinquishing Mothers Society
51 North Terrace
Hackney, South Australia 5069
Australia

Adoption Jigsaw
20 McKenzie Road
Elizabeth Downs 5113
South Australia

55 King William Rd.
Adoption Jigsaw
PO Box 252
Hillarys Perth 6025
Western Australia

Australian Maritime Historical Society
Box 33
Magill, South Australia
Australia

South Australia Genealogy & Heraldry
Box 13
Marden 5070
South Australia

Historical Society of South Australia
Institute Building
122 Kintore Ave.
Adelaide
South Australia

State Records-Norwich Centre
55 King William Road
North Adelaide 5006
(Records held include State Children's
Dept., Destitute Person's Dept. and
Social Welfare Dept.)

Government
Family Information Service
Dept. for Family & Community
Services
4 Rowells Rd.
Lockleys 5032
South Australia

Non-Government
Ivy Marks
Jigsaw SA, Inc.
PO Box 567
Prospect East 5083

ARMS (Assn. Of
 Relinquishing Mothers)
c/o Jigsaw SA Inc.
220 Victoria Square
Adelaide, S. Australia 5006
This organization exists
to provide support specifically for
relinquishing mothers.

The Sunday Mail, 12/26/93, pages 5-6: "The Two Sides of an Adoption . . . Special report by John Church—Despite new adoption laws introduced in 1989, South Australians on all sides of the dilemma are still hurting. The laws mean future generations of adopted kids and their birthparents will have open access to all information they want or require . . . adopted kids who have grown up, are finding the information now available has come too late—their parents are either untraceable or dead... There are an estimated 26,500 adoptees in South Australia and many more people related or affected by that figure.

Yet despite its wide impact there is no centre where people can go to get specific information on adoption. Jigsaw president, Valma Gay, would like to set up a national centre in South Australia.

She works diligently from a poky office at the back of her flat, where Jigsaw, an agency helping people find out about their origins, makes contact (after consent) with birth relatives, operates.

Valma has her own story. At 19 she was raped and became pregnant. In a small country town such scandal was just not acceptable ... Forty years later she says the now four-year-old laws giving greater access to adoptees and parents searching for their lost relations are a step in the right direction... In Queensland, for example, applicants make vetoes for life unless they decide to change it.

Since the new South Australian laws were introduced (in 1989), 3544 adoptees or parents have applied to the Department of Family and Community Services (FACS) for information about their lost blood relatives. Conversely, 1345 people have vetoed the access of any information to relatives searching for them.

Case One: An identity he may never find—David Perron, big and hefty, with tattoos splashed across his arms and hands, is a bloke who looks unlikely to have deep-seated emotional problems about his mother. He was adopted by a small-town couple, and says he 'can't stand' his female adopter, but regards his Male adopter as the 'sweetest man I ever met' ... He has been haunted by a desire, perhaps an obses- sion, to meet his birthmother ... For most of his life he has searched for a clue to his origins. Three years ago he tried again under new laws, learning the name of his mother and father, some loose details about them and receiving authority to have his real birth certificate opened. Since then he's drawn blanks ... The less cynical might feel more pity for a man who feels so strongly about an identity, an origin ...

Case Two: In a Rundle Mall toilet, the woman, shielded perhaps with dark glasses, handed a veto application to a government officer. So frightened was she that her secret would be discovered, the anonymous toilet meeting was the only way she could feel safe.

The Adoption Privacy Protection Group lobbies for people like her and their right to privacy and a life which is not chased by a past they wish to forget... Women like this are so scared their spouses will find out that things like meeting in a toilet to lodge a veto suddenly become acceptable... Both incoming and outgoing Ministers admitted the solutions to the adoption dilemma will never be the right answer for everyone."

The Sunday Mail, 12/27/92: "6 Brothers, Sisters Unite ... Emotion-packed months of searching and shock discoveries have all but ended with the reunion in Adelaide yesterday of six brothers and a sister for the first time in 35 years ... With respective clans of each of the seven present, the look-a-like brothers, sisters, aunts, uncles and cousins tallied 35—many had never met before ... 'It's like walking into a whole new world.'"

Dear AmFOR: ... "Thanks so much for writing back to me ... The records department had sent me a letter saying that they had found the G.I. that I was looking for. But when I saw the date that he had died on it just didn't add up.

So I had to confront my mother with the info. that I got back from the records dept. When she looked at the letter she said that she thought they had made a mistake in the U.S. ... Well, that wasn't the case. Three days later my mother phoned me up and said that what she had told me was a lie, all these years and that Theodore Shultz wasn't my natural father. She said that she did know him in 1944 and all about him.

So then of course I had to ask who was my father. Oh Lori, I can't tell you what a blow it was to me to hear this information. I believed everything she told me. I have wasted 16 years looking for the poor man ... MRS. DIANE R., Elizabeth, South Australia."

Australia - Tasmania

Registrar General of Births, Deaths and Marriages
15 Murray St.
Nichols Place
G.P.O. Box 198

Hobart, Tasmania 7001. Australia
(011)(61)(3) 6233-3793
www.justice.tas.gov.au/bdm

ADOPTION RECORDS:

Adoption Information Service
Department of Health and Human Services
GPO Box 539, Hobart, Tasmania 7001, Australia
www.dhhs.tas.gov.au/health_and_wellbeing/
children_and_families/related_topics/adoption_and_information

The Registrar General has records from 1803 now that church registers from 1803 to 1838 have been added to the Registrar's records. If your request is urgent, there is an Au $20.00 fee per document.

The Family History Library of The Church of Jesus Christ of Latter-day Saints in Salt Lake City, Utah has microfilmed original and published vital records and church registers of the Northern Territory. For further details on their holdings, please consult your nearest Family History Center.

Records of interest are also available at the National Library of Australia, Parkes Place, Canberra, A.C.T. 2600; Tel.: (011)(61)(62) 621-111

SEARCH RESOURCES

Genealogical Society of Tasmania
Box 640-G
Hobart Tasmania 7001
Australia

Margaret Humphreys/Child Migrant Trust
28-A Musters Rd.
West Bridgeford, Nottingham NG2 7PL
United Kingdom

ADOPTION INFORMATION INQUIRY - TASMANIA

The Tasmanian Adoption Act, 1988 was passed in September, 1988, and the access to information provisions were proclaimed to commence on 1 July, 1989. The Tasmanian Act is similar in most respects to the Victorian Adoption Act (upon which it was largely modeled). Adoptees are able to apply for identifying information (including the original birth certificate) from the Department once they reach 18 years of age. While the original birth certificate will be released to an adult adoptee as a right, identifying information will only be released if agreed to by the parents.

Birthparents are entitled to identifying information only with the adoptee's consent.

Adopters may have non-identifying information about the adoptee's parents without restriction but can only obtain identifying information with the parents' consent. However, adult adoptees must be informed the information is being given.

Close relatives have access to non-identifying information about the adoptee, if the Director of Community Welfare is convinced there are circumstances which make it desirable. The adoptee (if over 18) or the adopters (if the adoptee is a minor) must give consent.

The Act provides discretionary power for the Director of Community Welfare regarding the release of distressing information. The Director may release medical or psychiatric information to a medical practitioner instead of directly to the applicant. There is mandatory counseling for all persons seeking access to identifying or non-identifying information, unless applicants are resident outside Tasmania. Clients can choose to have it either on an individual or group basis. Extended counseling is also available on request. It is of an information-giving rather than therapeutic nature.

An Adoption Information Register has been established by the Adoption Information Service of the Department of Community Welfare. The intention with the Register is to provide people with a full spectrum, from refusal to authorize the release of any identifying information (except the birth certificate, access to which is an absolute right) through to full contact. The system is self-regulatory and depends on the cooperation of those concerned.

Of the almost 1,000 names placed on the Register prior to the commencement of the legislation, only six had expressed a desire for no contact with the other party.

The cost of the publicity campaign associated with the legislation was estimated to be $15,000. The Department charges fees of up to $160 for registration, search, and the provision of information and outreach. Private counseling is conducted on a fee-for-service basis.

Australia - Victoria

Registry of Births, Deaths and Marriages
595 Collins Street
PO Box 4332
Melbourne, Victoria 3001, Australia
(01)(61) 1300 369 387
www.online.justice.vic.gov.au/bdm/home

ADOPTION RECORDS:
Adoption and Family Information/DHS
Level 20, 570 Bourke Street
Melbourne, VIC 3000, Australia
(01)(61)(3) 8608-5700

With the incorporation of early church records, the Registry now has records from 1837. Vital registration began on July 1, 1853. If your request is urgent, there is a charge of Au $26.00.

The Family History Library of The Church of Jesus Christ of Latter-day Saints in Salt Lake City, Utah has microfilmed many of the original and published vital records and church registers of the Northern Territory. For further details on their holdings, please consult your nearest Family History Center.

Records of interest are also available at the National Library of Australia, Parkes Place, Canberra, A.C.T, 2600; Tel.: (011)(61)(62) 621-111.

SEARCH RESOURCES: Adoption Search-Support

Geelong Adoption Program
37 Retreat Rd.
Newtown Victoria 3220
Australia

Adoption Jigsaw
G.P.O. 5260-BB
Melbourne 3001
Australia

Royal Historical Society of Victoria
459 Collins St.
Melbourne Victoria 3000
Australia

Australian Institute of Genealogical
Studies
Box 60
Oakleigh Victoria 3166
Australia

Genealogical Society of Victoria
98 Elizabeth St., Rm 1, 1st Fl.
Melbourne Victoria
Australia

Adoption Information Service
488 St Kilda Road
Melbourne, Victoria 3004
Australia

ADOPTION INFORMATION INQUIRY-VICTORIA

The adoption information provisions of the Victorian Adoption Act, 1984 were proclaimed to commence in April, 1985. It was the first Act by any Australian State allowing increased access to adoption information and as such served as a model for similar legislation in Western Australia, South Australia, Tasmania, and New Zealand.

In Victoria adult adoptees have the legal right to apply for a copy of their original birth certificate and any other information held in the adoption records of the Community Services Department or the private adoption agency involved in the placement. This includes information that may identify parents.

Parents and relatives are also entitled to apply for information about the adopted person. No information identifying the adopted person is released until the Department or agency has contacted the other party(s).

Only 22 people and one organization, opposed to increased access, provided submissions; eight were anonymous. The majority of those opposed were adopters. From their physical appearance, a number of the submissions in this category, both signed and unsigned, seemed to be from the same author.

A number of those opposed to increased access assured the Committee that they were speaking on behalf of a 'silent majority' who were not willing to come forward. However, the Committee found no evidence to support this assertion. The percentage of people opposed to increased access was very small.

The only fee imposed by the Department is a $20.00 registration charge.

> *Newsletter of Adoption Jigsaw* ... "Rhonda, her husband and youngest son, came from Victoria during the recent school holidays, to spend some time with Lisa, and her family (and adoptive mum) getting to know each other after meeting earlier this year ... They sure are alike! I wish them much happiness now and in the future. It was a great pleasure. Thanks, LISA, VALMA."

Australia - Western Territory

Registrar General of Births, Deaths and Marriages
Level 10, 141 Georges Terrace
Perth, Western Australia 6000. Australia
(01)(61)(8) 9264 1555
www.justice.wa.gov.au/

ADOPTION RECORDS:

Past Adoption Services
Department of Child Protection
PO Box 6334
East Perth 6882, Western Australia
www.childprotection.wa.gov.nu

The Registrar General has records from September 9, 1841. Genealogists may obtain birth records more than 80 years old, marriage records more than 40 years old, and death records before 1980. If your request is urgent, there is an additional charge of Au $12.00.

The Family History Library of The Church of Jesus Christ of Latter-day Saints in Salt Lake City, Utah has microfilmed original and published vital records and church registers of the Northern Territory. For further details on their holdings, please consult your nearest Family History Center.

Records of interest are also available at the National Library of Australia, Parkes Place, Canberra, A.C.T. 2600; Tel.: (011)(61)(62) 621-111.

SEARCH RESOURCES

Western Australia Genealogical Society
Box 7
West Perth 6005
Western Australia

Glennis Dees - President
Adoption Jigsaw WA
PO Box 252-Hillarys
Western Australia 6025

Royal Western Australia
Historical Society
Sterling House
49 Broadway
Nedlands 6009
Western Australia

ARMS (Assn. Of Relinquishing
Mothers)
PO Box 521
Perth, 6162
Western Australia

The Western Australian, 4/3/91: "Adoption Blackout Popular... More than 1,000 people have lodged applications demanding their identities be kept secret from family members trying to contact them under new adoption laws.

Since the veto register was set up in December (1990), 1,114 people have paid to have their names included because they do not want contact with either the children they gave up or, in the case of adopted children, their natural parents. People who break the veto face a $2,500 fine or six months' jail... Family and Community Services Minister Robert Webster said the authorities expected more than 12,000 applications for birth certificates during the next year... Vetoes can still be lodged by making an appointment at any Family and Community Services Center. Applications for birth certificates cost $117 while those who use the veto register are charged $50.

The Advertiser, 10/93: "'Only Child' Finds She Has Dozen Half-Brothers and Half-Sisters ... Perth-Dorothy Pitman was brought up as an only child by adopters. Mrs. Pitman always wished for an older brother, but when she began the frustrating search for her origins in 1984, the idea of discovering siblings had not entered her mind. In fact, she found 12 half-brothers and sisters. When adoption agency Jigsaw phoned Mrs. Pitman with the news, they asked first whether she was sitting down. 'They told me I was one of 13 children,' she said ... Robert was the last and most difficult to find because his records had been destroyed, official practice until the 1930s."

Jigsaw Pieces, Western Australia, September, 1994: "Update on Legislative Changes:... No more applications for information of Original Birth Certificates will be taken by the Department for Community Development until the new law (which is expected to be proclaimed in December 1994) takes effect early in 1995. The Department is presently dealing with the backlog of applications. Any applications lodged before 1st June will be dealt with."

The West Australian, 1/29/93: "Friends United as Father/Son ... In 1989, Ray joined the same company as Peter and they worked together for four years not knowing that they were father and son . . . Tracey simply said, 'Peter, Ray is your father.' And Peter replied in time-honored Australian tradition: 'Bullshit.' But she convinced Peter and he went to Ray, his work mate, his friend, his step-father in-law. And the first words he said: 'So you're the old bastard, eh?' And Ray's reply, 'Yes I am.' The jigsaw was complete."

WESTERN AUSTRALIA: THE ADOPTION OF CHILDREN (AMENDMENT) ACT, 1985
The Adoption of Children (Amendment) Act, 1985 was passed by the Western Australian Parliament on December 13, 1985. Those sections dealing with accessing adoption information were proclaimed to commence on April 24, 1986.

This Act allows adult adoptees to apply to the Director-General for access to their original birth certificate. The provision of such information by the Director-General is subject to the applicant attending a mandatory counseling session offered by either the Department or "other approved counseling services"; a further condition is that there be no objection to the release of the information registered by the birth parents on an Adoption Contact Register held by the Department of Community Services.

There was no provision in the 1989 Western Australian Act for granting access to identifying information to parents or relatives (except in special circumstances).*

The Adoption Contact Register is administered by the Department. The Western Australia version also operates as a "veto register" solely for birthparents who do not wish identifying information about themselves to be released to adoptees. The veto is of indefinite duration and may be removed or amended at any time. As of September 20,1989, 257 vetoes had been received by the Department.

During the mandatory counseling session, the counselor is obliged to release to the applicant potentially distressing information held on Department of Community Service's adoption records. Available non-identifying information is also passed on to the applicant. The counselor is required to explain the effect of any veto placed in the Adoption Contact Register by the parents.

Breaches of any section of this Act carry penalties of $2,500 or six months imprisonment.

*At time of writing a review of the legislation is under way in Western Australia. Its main aim is to examine the operation of the entire Act, including the possibility of access to information by parents and relatives.

Austria

Sandesamt

(Town), Austria

Additional help is available from the Department for Personal Registration (Federal Ministry of the Interior, Herrengasse 7, A-1014 Vienna, Austria). There is no central office for vital records in Austria. To obtain copies of birth, marriage, and death certificates, write to the Civil Registration District Office in the town where the event occurred. Vital records are on file from 1784. Current vital registration is complete.

SEARCH RESOURCES
Genealogisch Heraldisch
Gellschaft "Adier"
1 Haarof 4A
A-1014 Vienna/PO Box 25
Austria

Orange County Register, (CA) 12/25/94: "After Four Decades, CA Woman Is Reunited With [Parents] in Austria . . . Catherine Watkins celebrates her 42nd birthday today. But the biggest present she's ever gotten—Christmas or birthday—came a little earlier. Her husband, an employee of Continental Airlines, sent Watkins from Garden Grove to Austria a month ago so she could be reunited with her [mother] .

Watkins was adopted in 1953 by a U.S. Army lieutenant and his wife who were stationed in Salzburg, Austria. She hadn't seen her [mother] since she was a toddler and learned of her whereabouts only in October . . . She tried a half-dozen agencies that help locate Birthparents, but none could help with an overseas adoption. Then she was referred to Leonie Boehmer in New Mexico who specializes in finding [parents] in Austria, Germany and Switzerland. Boehmer secured Watkins' original birth certificate and arranged for the police to contact her mother, now Rosa Podrascanin.

It turned out that Podrascanin had been hoping all those years to hear from Sonja: Rosa's stepparents had taken the baby against her will when she was 17 and poor, unwed and struggling to survive... From other family members, Watkins figures she was handed more than 100 bouquets: 'I didn't have enough arms for all the flowers.'

The trip also brought Watkins to an unexpected bonus: She met her [father] as well, a wealthy horse trainer who was 16 when she was born."

Azerbaijan

Russian-American Genealogical Archival Service (RAGAS)
P.O. Box 236
Glen Echo, Maryland 20812
(202) 501-5206

By an agreement between the United States National Archives Volunteer Association and the Archives of Russia Society, RAGAS receives and processes requests for vital records in some of the former Soviet republics. Although at this time RAGAS is able to deal mainly with Russia, Belarus, and Ukraine, they might be able to help you with your inquiries regarding Azerbaijan. There is a $2.00 shipping fee. The service also is available at an hourly rate. (See "Russia" for application forms.)

Bahamas

Registrar General's Department
Office of the Attorney General
P.O. Box N 532
Nassau, NP, Bahamas
(242) 322-3316

The Registrar General has birth and death records from January 1, 1850, and marriage records from January 1, 1799.

The Family History Library of The Church of Jesus Christ of Latter-day Saints in Salt Lake City, Utah has microfilmed original and published vital records and church registers of the Bahamas and the Caribbean. For further details on their holdings, please consult your nearest Family History Center.

Bahrain

Registrar of Births and Deaths
Ministry of Health
PO Box 12
Manama, State of Bahrain

Birth registrations are nearly comprehensive; however, overall registration is incomplete.

Bangladesh

Bangladesh Demographic Survey and Vital Registration System
Bangladesh Bureau of Statistics
Gana Bhavan Extension Block-1
Sher-A-Bangla Nagar
Dhaka 7, Bangladesh

While some records exist from 1873, modern vital registration began in 1960. Marriages and divorces are filed with Ministry of Law and Parliamentary Affairs. The Directorate of Archives and Libraries, National Library of Bangladesh also has records; contact them at Sher-e-Banglanagar, Agargaon, Dhaka 7, Bangladesh.

Barbados

Registration Office
Supreme Court of Barbados
Law Courts
Coleridge Street
Bridgetown, Barbados WI
(809) 426-3461

The Registration Office has birth records from January 1, 1890, marriage records from 1637, and death records from January 1, 1925. There are also baptismal records before 1890 and burial records before 1925. These can be requested using the birth and death application forms, respectively.

For persons over 60 years of age, the cost is BD $1.00. Make international bank draft payable in Barbados currency.

The Family History Library of The Church of Jesus Christ of Latter-day Saints in Salt Lake City, Utah has microfilmed original and published vital records and church registers of Barbados and the Caribbean. For further details on their holdings, please consult your nearest Family History Center.

SEARCH RESOURCES
Barbados Historical Society
Bridgetown Barbados
British West Indies

Belarus

Russian-American Genealogical Archival Service (RAGAS)
P.O. Box 236
Glen Echo, Maryland 20812
(202)501-5206

By an agreement between the United States National Archives Volunteer Association and the Archives of Russia Society, this agency will receive and process requests for vital records in Belarus. There is a S2.00 shipping fee per document. The service also is available at an hourly rate. (See "Russia" for application forms.)

Belgium

Registres de l'Etat Civil
(Town), Belgium

Three is no central office for vital records in Belgium. To obtain copies of birth, marriage, and death certificates, write to the town where the event occurred. Vital records are on file from 1796 and the current registration is considered to be complete.

There are also records at the General State Archives; contact them at Archives Generales du Royaume (AGR), Algemeen Rijksarchief, rue de Ruysbroeck 2, B-1000 Brussels, Belgium; Tel. (011)(32)(2)513-76-8880; FAX (011)(32)(2) 513-76-81.

SEARCH RESOURCES

Flemish Society for Femilienkunde	Ofice Genealogical de Belgique	Vlaamge Vereining
c/o Von Haverbeke	Musees Royaux d'Autre d' Historique	Voor Familiengeschiedenis
Hyacintensioon 33	Parc du Cine	Van Heybeeckstraat 3
Oostende	Brussels B-1040	Antwerpen-Merksen B-2-6
Belgium	Belgium	Belgium

ADOPTION SEARCHES

Suzanna Byme
The Old Vicarage
Stationssraat 66, 3580 Neer Pelt
Brussels
Belgium

Dear AmFOR:... I would like to say that my remark to use violence was not understood correctly. What I mean to say is that we probably could use the GREEN PEACE way of acting. I am not the aggressive sort of person, but I feel that we should do some more now in some countries on behalf of the adoption triangle. You also asked me about the legal situation on Adoption in Belgium. This has not changed much last years. But if you would like to know more please write to: B. Steenkiste, Vereniging voor Adoptiegezinnen, Hamerstraat 19, 1040 Brussels. Tel. 2/2180626 (Belgium is 32) ... With regards, RENE HOKSBERGEN, Adoptie Centrum, University Utrecht, Faculteit Der Sociale Wetenschappen, Heidelberglaan 1, 3584 CS CS Utrecht.

Belize

Registrar General
The General Registry
Judiciary Department
Court House Plaza
PO Box 87
Belize City, Belize
(011)(501)(2)72-053

The Registry has birth and death records from 1885 and marriage records from 1881 to the present.

The Family History Library of The Church of Jesus Christ of the Latter-day Saints in Salt Lake City, Utah has micro-filmed original and published records of Belize and South America. For further details on their holdings, please consult your nearest Family History Center.

Benin

Maire

(Town), Benin

Vital registration began in Benin, formerly known as Dahomey, in 1933 and included mostly French citizens and foreigners. By 1950 registration included most residents within 15 miles of a registration center.

Bermuda

Registry General
Ministry of Labour and Home Affairs
Government Administration Building
30 Parliament St.
Hamilton 12, Bermuda
(809)295-5151

The Registry General has birth and marriage records from 1866 and death records from 1865 to the present.

SEARCH RESOURCE

Bermuda Historical Society
c/o Bermuda Library
Par-la-Villa Park
Hamilton
Bermuda

St. George Historical Society
St. George
Bermuda

Dear AmFOR:..." I am an... adoptee who is searching for mother and sister. Please could you send me information about your organization and any helpful hints on searching . . . Thanks, Christina R. Pembroke, Bermuda."

Bhutan

Registration, Census and Immigration Division
Department of Registration
Ministry of Home Affairs
Thimphu, Bhutan

Vital registration is considered to be 70 percent complete.

Bolivia

Direccion Nacional de Registro Civil
Ministerio del Interior, Migracion, y Justicia
Av. Arce No. 2409
La Paz, Bolivia

The first laws authorizing vital registration were passed in 1898; modern vital registration in Bolivia began July 1,1940.
Current vital registration is considered to be incomplete.

Bosnia and Herzegovina

Civil Registration Office
(Town), Bosnia and Herzegovina

Vital records are on file from 1946. Records before that were kept by the local churches.

For pre-1991 searches, see "Yugoslavia."

> *Los Angeles Times,* 7/24/93: "Bosnia's Orphans of Rape: Innocent Legacy of Hatred ... By Sarajevo
> government order, these youngest citizens of Bosnia-Herzegoina are growing up in institutions gener-
> ously supplied by foreign charities with everything the babies need, with the exception of parents.
>
> The Bosnian government has prohibited adoption of the children of rape in hopes that their natural moth-
> ers will someday learn to accept them or that the war will end soon and the rejected babies can be placed
> in other Bosnian homes . . . Civic and officials of the Egyptian Agency for Humanitarian Aid, which
> opened the children's home three months ago, believe that some of the natural mothers may later realize
> their babies are innocent victims and choose to take them back.
>
> 'That is what would be best for the babies,' said the 30-year-old doctor who has two sons of her own. 'In
> my opinion, adoption* would be a good solution but only after time, maybe two years, and only to
> Bosnian couples.'
>
> None of the mothers has yet decided to reclaim her child. But Cici said two have paid visits to the safe
> house to see their offspring under encouragement of aid agency counselors . . . 'My view is that for the
> children, it is better if they stay here in Bosnia-Herzegovina or at least in temporary shelter in Zagreb,'
> said Selimovic Harun. 'I believe these women will eventually give the children up for adoption, but
> conditions in Bosnia-Herzegovina are not suitable for that now.'
>
> 'Not one of the woman I spoke with, and I spoke with them for hours, had even a minimal wish to take
> their babies. We had to put blindfolds on them for the deliveries,' said Asim Kurjak, head of obstetrics and
> gynecology at Zagreb's Holy Spirit Hospital. 'The babies are innocent third parties'... Kurjak told of on
> 17-year-old so consumed with shame and fear that she threatened to kill herself if the hospital staff made

any record of her having given birth. For the benefit of her tradition-bound family, the teenager's delivery after a rape-induced pregnancy was noted in her medical charts as surgery to remove a kidney stone.'

He estimates that 500 to 600 children of rape have been born in the last few months; he speculates that many more are probably trapped with their mothers in the 70 of Bosnia's now under Serbian control.. . Kurjak said he had already received numerous letters from desperate childless couples seeking to adopt, including one from a wealthy Cairo family who offered to build a new wing for his hospital in reward for being favored with a Bosnian newborn.

'The government is concerned it could be accused of selling its children, as happened in Romania,' Kurjak said."

*Author's Note: If Bosnia's orphans become adopted with falsified birth records, they are 'child of no one' whether they remain in Bosnia or are adopted abroad.

Omaha World-Herald, 8/5/92, page 12: "Orphans Reach Safety of Rural Germany ... Zerbst, Germany— Nina stretched out her arms for a hug and smiled in the sunshine. For the first time in a long time, the tiny 2-year-old with soft brown curls was in no danger of dying.

She and 37 other children from a Bosnian orphanage made it to safety Tuesday, surviving a wrenching, 60-hour odyssey that took them from the blood-stained streets of Sarajevo to the peace and relative plenty of rural Germany.

Nine of the 48 survivors of the sniper attack were separated from the others and prevented from traveling on after their names were identified as being Serbian, according to Vera Zoric, the director of the Ljubica Ivezic orphanage ... The Flying Tigers sent members to intercept the children's bus after it stopped in the town ofFoinica outside Sarajevo ... Saxony-Anhalt state officials said the children will stay in Germany as long as the hostilities persist in Bosnia-Herzegovina. They will not be available for but will be returned to Sarajevo when the fighting stops."

Dea rAmFOR: ... "'Flying Tigers' is a CLA-owned charter airline. They have moved stolen children to the U.S. for sale into adoption, under a Congressional and Presidential mandate to 'save foreign children from the hazards of war.'... Serbia kidnapped 10,000 children from Croatia and Bosnia just after WWII. They know about such activity by USSR and U.S. That's why they stopped the bus and removed Serbian children. They believe the children are gone forever . . .

If the hostility ends and the children are returned with the same kind of publicity, INCLUDING RE-TURN PHOTOS, it is safe to assume that we now have the support of a powerful segment of the federal government. Probably to conform to the new International Adoption Convention and counter hostile UN reports. If the hostilities end and there is no publicized return, nothing has changed and this is just another Orwellian propaganda ploy ... EUGENE AUSTIN, P.O. Box 115, Tilden, NE 68781."

Botswana

Registry of Births, Deaths, Marriages
Ministry of Home Affairs
Private Bag 002
Gaborone, Botswana
(011)(267) 360-1000

The Registrar has birth records from 1915, marriage records from 1895, and death records from 1904. In 1966 Botswana became independent, and vital registration became compulsory in 1969. The registration is not considered to be complete. Send your request for divorce records to The High Court of Botswana, Private Bag 1, Lobatse, Botswana; Fax (011)(267)332-317.

Brazil

State Archives

(Town. State). Brazil

Vital registration began on September 9, 1870. Records are kept by the Civil Registration Office in each town and are sent regularly to the State Archives of each of Brazil's states. Divorces are on file at the State Archives and at the court where the decree was issued.

SEARCH RESOURCE

Institute Genealogie Brasilia

Rua Conselheirocrispano 53

Sao Paulo SP

Brazil

Los Angeles Times, 4/1/90, page M-3: "To Be a Child, Fair-Haired, Fair-Skinned and Poor in Brazil... Baby Trade: Americans and Europeans eager to adopt need only U.S. dollars and the assistance of Casa Alegre to realize their dreams.

When Maria Lourdes, mother of five malnourished children, was asked by her wealthy patroa if she could 'borrow' Maria's 4-year-old, she readily agreed. The woman, for whom Maria washes clothes, said she wanted the galega (fair-haired, fair-skinned child) strictly for amusement. Maria sent her daughter just as she was: untidy, barefoot, without a change of clothes or her little pink comb with its missing teeth. The patroa promised to return the child the following morning . . . The little girl had been given to a wealthy American missionary who directed a 'children's home' in Recife that specialized in overseas adoptions . . . Each year, nearly 1,500 children legally leave Brazil to live with adoptive parents in Europe, the United States and Israel. But if one adds the clandestine traffic that relies on false documents and bureaucratic corruption in Brazil and abroad, exploiting the emotions and ignorance of poor women like Maria, the estimated number of children leaving rises to 3,000 a year, or roughly 50 a week ... The adoption had cost nearly $3,000, excluding the air fare and per-diem expenses in Brazil. One-third went directly to the 'orphanage' (as they called it); another $800 to the legal intermediary, a local 'adoption' lawyer who was a son-in-law of the orphanage director ... It also claimed that all the children made available for international adoption were either orphans or abandoned by their mothers ... When I asked about traffic in babies, the director had a ready answer: it was true... Sometimes she, herself, fought with parents over the release of their children so that they could be free for adoption. Some [mothers], she added, resist signing the legal adoption papers even though they are in no position to care for another child . . . 'When I am very angry,' she once said, 'I think to myself, 'Why doesn't that rich American woman who stole my little blonde come back and get the rest of us as well.'""

Weekly World News, 6/11/91: "Meet the World's Youngest Parents ... (Porto Velho, Brazil) Emilia Filho is only 7 years old—but she's already a mom! The pint-sized parent gave birth to a bouncing baby girl six months ago, making her the world's youngest mother. And Emilia says she is so delighted with motherhood that she wants another child as soon as possible.

Her parents are even allowing the baby's father, 11-year-old Manuel Ferraz, to live with them until he and Emilia are old enough to marry. 'Doctors told us last year that our daughter has a hormone disorder which has caused her reproductive organs to mature much earlier than normal,' said Hermes Filho. 'We knew she and Manuel were sweet on each other and we tried to warn them about pregnancy. 'But boys will be boys, I guess ...'"

Dear AmFOR . . . "International Adoption Assistance, Inc., IAA, is a Pennsylvania corporation with special expertise in the assistance of adopting children from Brazil and provides services which are in accordance with both United States and Brazilian law ... Our corporation offers a dignified and expedient approach for those people who are exploring the viability of international adoption ... The Brazilian law permits adoption by foreigners. The adoption for foreigners is a complete and full adoption and is available to both single persons and married couples. The adoptive parent(s) must be over twenty-one

(21) years of age and at least sixteen (16) years older than the adopted child. Brazilian authorities have initiated the practice of issuing birth certificates showing the [adopter(s)], as the parent(s), leaving out the names of the parent(s). This procedure is followed in order to safeguard the confidentiality of the adoption . . . Additionally (subject to conditions) our past [adopters] have agreed to speak with prospective adopters on a CONFIDENTIAL basis ... Sincerely, CLAUDIA F. RICHARDS, President, INTERNATIONAL ADOPTION ASSISTANCE, INC., Norristown, PA, USA."

DearAmFOR:.. . "Update on International Adoption Assistance:

1. Corporate file number 91281721; 2) For-profit Pennsylvania business corporation;

3. Corporate officers: Anthony Richards; Claudia Furtado Richards;

4. Corporate address: 194 Eaton Square, Morristown, PA 19401;

5. Filing date: 05/16/91; Effective 04/15/91;

6. No notary or attorney listed;

7. Numerous arrests in Brazil of Brazilian citizens who participate in such activity;

8. Information sent to PA Attorney General; Reply, dated 07/30/92, from Joseph A. Curcillo, III; They want to act, but they have no authority under PA law; They forwarded the file to their rep, Tom Gallagher, Interpol, Lyon, France;

9. I sent file to Brazilian Embassy, emphasizing that U.S. will extradite U.S. citizens who commit crimes against other jurisdictions without leaving U.S.;

10. PA computer lacks the capability of linking officers' names to other corporations.

Hopefully, there may be action later . .. Sincerely, EUGENE AUSTIN, Tilden, NE."

Brunei

Registrar of Births and Deaths
Medical and Health Department
Ministry of Health
Bandar Seri Begawan 2062, Brunei

Vital registration began in 1923 for births and deaths and 1948 for marriages. Current registration is considered to be complete.

Bulgaria

Executive Committee
Town Council
(Town), Bulgaria

Registration began in 1881 and is more than 90 percent complete.

TRANSINFORMA was the first private Bulgarian Translation and information agency with seven departments, 500 free-lance specialists, and 24 representatives in all the regional towns. TransAdopt Department dealt with legal adoption of Bulgarian children by foreign adopters. Check for current address or alternate entity via your public library Internet access to worldwide telephone directories.

Burkina Faso

Center for the Civil Status
(Town), Burkina Faso

Registration began in 1933 for French citizens and expanded in 1950 to include all residents living within 15 miles of the registration centers.

Burundi

Department de la Population
Ministere de l'Interieur
BP 160, Gitega
Bujumbura, Burundi

Vital registration began in 1922. Even though efforts have been made to include all areas, the registration is not considered to be complete.

Cambodia

Director, National Institute of Statistics
Ministry of Planning
Phnom Penh, Cambodia

Records are not generally available for any event before 1980; all archives were destroyed during the 1975-1079 regime and it has been difficult to reestablish civil institutions.

Los Angeles Times, 03/31/91: "A Land of Widows and Orphans Remains U.S. Enemy . . . Cambodia: In the ultimate victim nation, still a target of economic sanctions and menaced by Pol Pot, a traffic jam is reason to hope ... The mortality rate is about 133 per thousand live births, and one of five children dies before age 5. This country of mostly women and children, of widows and orphans, is our enemy—officially . . . World aid, particularly American, is channeled to the 300,000 refugees in camps along the border of Thailand, where amenities are better than in Phnom Penh. There are mostly women and children in the camps, too. The men are usually old. Younger men are in the jungles on the other side of the border."

Cameroon

Ministere de l'Administration Territoriale
B.P. 7854
Yaounde, Cameroon

Registration began in 1917 for western Cameroon and in 1935 for the entire country. Divorces are recorded on the marriage and birth certificates of both parties.

Canada - Alberta

Government Services. Alberta Registrations
Box 2023
Edmonton. Alberta T5J 4W7
Canada
(780) 427-7010
www.servicealberta.gov.ab.ca/vitalstatistics.cfm

Vital Statistics has birth records from 1853, marriage records from 1898, and death records from 1893. Make payment payable to "Provincial Treasurer."

Other sources are the Alberta Culture Center (Provincial Library, 16214 114th Avenue, Edmonton, Alberta T5M 2Z6), the Provincial Archives of Alberta (12845 102nd Ave., Edmonton, Alberta T5N OM6), the National Archives of Canada (395 Wellington, St., Ottawa, K1A ON3; Tel. 613-995-5138); and the National Library of Canada (same address; Tel. 613-995-9481; Fax 613-996-4424).

The Family History Library of The Church of Jesus Christ of the Latter-day Saints in Salt Lake City, Utah has microfilmed original and published records of Alberta and Canada. Consult your nearest Family History Center.

Alberta's Post Adoption Reunion Registry has been operating since 1985 for adult adoptees, parents, birth siblings of adult adoptees. Parties may consent or veto contact. Search services have been offered to adoptees since 1995 and to birth families since 1996.

SEARCH RESOURCES

Passive Registry
Alberta Social Services
D. Keith Owen
10030 107th St. - 12th Fl.
Edmonton Alberta T5J 3E4
Canada
postadoption.registry@gov.ab.ca

Ray Ensminger
PO Box 52053
Edmonton, Alberta T6G 2T5
Canada
Search/Support Groups

Triad
PO Box 5114
Station A
Calgary Alberta T2H 1X1
Canada

Birthparent & Relative Group
5317-145 Ave.
Edmonton Alberta T5A 4E9
Canada

Parent Finders
PO Box 12031
Edmonton Alberta T5J 3L2
Canada

Adoptive Parent Support
NCAC
12133-41 St.
Edmonton Alberta T5W 2M5
Canada

Alberta Family History Society
Box 30270 Station B
Calgary Alberta T2M 4PI
Canada

Genealogy
Alberta Genealogical Society
Box 12015
Edmonton Alberta T5J 3L2
Canada

Brooks Branch
Alberta Genealogical Society
Box 1028
Brooks Alberta T0J 0J0
Canada

Edmonton Branch
Alberta Genealogical Society
Box 754
Edmonton Alberta T5J 2L4
Canada

Grande Prairie Branch
Alberta Genealogical Society
Box 1257
Grand Prairie Alberta T8V 4Z 1
Canada

Historical Society of Alberta
Box 4025 Station C
Calgary Alberta T2T 5M9
Canada
Lethbridge Branch
Alberta Genealogical Society
1032 Lakeway Blvd.
Lethbridge Alberta T1 K 3E5
Canada

Medicine Hat Branch
Alberta Genealogical Society
Box 112
Medicine Hat Alberta T 1 A 7E8
Canada

North American Genealogical Society
507 - 30th Ave.
SW Calgary Alberta
Canada

Red Deer Branch	Wetaskian Branch	Ukranian Hist. & Gen. Soc. of Canada
Alberta Genealogical Society	Alberta Genealogical Society	Box 30270 Station B
Box 922	5320 - 47th Ave.	Calgary Alberta T2M 1V1
Red Deer Alberta	Wetaskian Alberta T9A OK8	Canada
Canada	Canada	

Dear AmFOR: ... "In my mind, Illumination on Adoption was a very fitting theme for this conference. As an adoptive parent, I feel it is important to open lines of communication with organizations such as the American Adoption Congress (A.C.C.), which has traditionally held a low opinion of adopters.

Throughout the conference I encountered a fair amount of negative feedback towards adopters, both from adoptees and from parents. At one of the sessions (Myths and Lies We Have Been Told), I was horrified to hear some of the stories told by adoptees ... Those of us in organizations like the A.P.A. are more aware of some of the problems we and our children might encounter. However, there are far too many parents who do not receive adequate information in this regard. One of the results of this can be lies that are told to adoptees by their adopters. More openness and honesty in adoption is not something to fear.

Another insight I got at this conference was an understanding for a sometimes forgotten person in the adoption process, the father. I happened to meet a father from North Carolina who is seeking custody of his son, who is now in Alberta ... By attending conferences like this, we as adoptive parents can learn a great deal more about the adoption process and how it affects us and our children ... submitted by LANA BULGER, Bassano, Alberta in ADOPTIVE PARENTS NEWSLETTER, 6325 60 Ave., Red Deer, Alberta T4N 5T9."

Dear AmFOR:... "We wanted to thank you and your organization for your support per your letter to Ms. Julia Turnbull, Calgary, Alberta, Canada. According to our Calgary sources your letter along with others the Mikulaks' have received has caused quite a stir. We, nor our attorney have had any contact with the Mikulaks or their attorney, Ms. Julia Turnbull. Dennis and our children have sent cards for birthdays, Christmas, Easter and etc. to Dennis' son. The ones with return addresses have been opened, resealed with tape and returned. We are working very diligently in trying to make the public aware of the injustice being done to Dennis' son, Dennis and our family. Your help is appreciated.

Recently Jon Ryan and ourselves appeared on Donahue and although the format was not exclusively on Birthfathers' trying to stop the adoption of their children, we felt we were successful in getting our story told to the audience. Again thank you for your time and consideration ... Sincerely yours, DENNIS AND AMY BERGMAN, Ernul, NC."

Canada - British Columbia

British Columbia Vital Statistics Agency
PO Box 9657-DTN Prov. Govt.
Victoria, British Columbia V8W 9P3
Canada
(250) 952-2681
www.vs.gov.bc.ca/

Ministry of Health has vital records from 1872 and some baptismal registers from 1849. Birth certificates are issued only to the individual, parents of the child, or an authorized agent. Death certificates are issued to anyone who has a valid reason. The charge for 24-hour service is Can $50.00. Genealogists should request a genealogy verification extract. Extended genealogical search costs Can $50.00.

Other repositories to contact are: The National Archives of Canada (395 Wellington. St., Ottawa, K1A ON3; Tel. 613-995-5138), the National Library of Canada (same address; Tel. 613-995-9481; Fax 613-996-4424), and the British Columbia Archives (655 Belleville St., Victoria, British Columbia V8V 1X4; Tel. 613-687-5885).

The Family History Library of The Church of Jesus Christ of the Latter-day Saints in Salt Lake City, Utah has microfilmed original and published records of British Columbia. For further details, please consult your nearest Family History Center.

British Columbia's adult adoptees and parents must file a "no contact declaration," if contact is not desired, through Ministries of Health, Seniors and Vital Statistics.

SEARCH RESOURCES

Adoption - Search / Support
Nancy Kato
Forget Me Not Family Society
1146 Kent Street
White Rock, BC
Canada V4B 5TA

Jim Kelly, Joan Vanstone
Parent Finders of Canada
3998 Baybridge Avenue
West Vancouver, B C V6K 3E4
Canada
jkelly@portal.ca/cansoftauniserve.com
parentfinders@parentfinders.org
jvanstone@parentfinders.org

Adoption Research Project
3231 Williams Rd.
Richmond
British Columbia V7E 1 H8
Canada

Alice Metzger
TRIAD of Canada
432 - Obed Ave.
Victoria, BC V9A 1K5

Parent Finders
3960 Westridge Ave.
W. Vancouver B.C. V7V 3H7
Canada

Canadian Adoptees Reform
202-4381 Fraser St.
Vancouver, BC V5V 4G4
Canada

Forget Me Not Family Society
www.adoptioncircles.net

Origins BC
www.originscanada.org

M. Elaine Turner
Parent Finders
4152 Chestnut Dr.
Prince George, BC V2K 2T5
Canada
dtumer@telvs.net

Genealogy Groups
Abbotsford Genealogical Club
1913 Westbury Crescent
Abbotsford B C V25 1B9
Canada

B C Genealogical Society
Box 94371
Richmond B C V6Y 2A8
Canada

B C Historical Assoc.
3450 W. 20th Ave.
Vancouver British Columbia
Canada

Chase Dist Family History Assn.
Box 64
Anglemon, B C V0E 1AO
Canada

Cowichan Valley Genealogical Soc
7631 Bell-McKinnon Rd., RR4
Duncan British Columbia
Canada

Kamloops Family History Society
Box 1162
Kamloops B C
Canada

Adoptive Families Association
www.bcadoption.com

Kelowna and Dist. Gen. Society
Box 501, Station A
Kelowna, B C VI Y 7A1
Canada

Langley Genealogical Society
21107-88th Ave.
Langley, B C V2A 6X5
Canada

Nanaimo Genealogical Club
Box 1027
Nanaimo B C V9R 5Z2
Canada

Powell River Genealogy Group
Box 446
Powell River, B C V8A 5C2
Canada

Prince George Family History Society
Box 1056
Prince George BC V2L 4V2
Canada

Quesnel Branch BCGS
Box 4454
Quesnel B C V2J 3J4
Canada

Revelstoke Genealogy Group
Box 309
Revelstoke B C V0E 2SO
Canada

Vernon District Family History Soc
Box 1447
Vernon British Columbia
Canada

Victoria Genealogical Society
Box 4171, Station A
Victoria B C V8X 3X8
Canada

The Vancouver Sun, 06/29/91: "Adoption Reunion Registry to Ease Search for Family ... Adoptees who want to find their [parents] will find it easier this fall when the new provincial active adoptive reunion registry opens in Victoria. That's the good news ... but the bad news, say search and support groups, is the possibility a fee of $275 will be charged, effectively barring low-income people from using the service."

Dear AmFOR: ... "I returned a year ago from my Native people in the Prince George, British Columbia area. While I was there it was mentioned that it would be nice to set up a year's project to research and seek out the Native children who were adopted out into the United States. Many of these children may not even know where they are from in Canada or what Band they belong to. They may not want to know their real families but they may want to know exactly where they are from.

Usually the original last name may lead us to the Band (Tribe). Bands are set up in Clans and each Clan has several family names. For instance, the Band I am from has the names Monk, Prince, Alexes, Joseph, etc. The children may just want information. What ever the needs, we would like to hear from them.

Many of my people and the Native people across Canada have wondered what became of the many apprehended children. So many of these children were adopted out into the United States.

If anyone has information about any adopted Canadian Indian kids or you yourself are an adopted Canadian Indian child and don't know where you are from but you have your original last name, or you just need to tell someone your story please write. Even if you are listed as Metis, mixed Native or Indian descent, original band unknown, please don't hesitate. If anyone has information about kids in jails or prisons, please let us know.

Please keep in mind a lot of these children we seek may be in their late 30's. Please help us, and help our concerned families. We would just like to know what happened to our children . . . B.M. MONK, RE-SEARCH SPECIALIST, BROKEN TRAILS ADOPTED CANADIAN INDIAN RESEARCH CENTER, RD 2 - Box 196, Belleville, PA 17004.

Author's Note: Disclosure terms for underage adoptees, aboriginal and other, rely on a best interests determination. For aboriginal children under age 19, the superintendent or adoption agency may disclose information about the child's community or band to the [adopters]. The superintendent may also disclose identifying information so that the child can be contacted by a designated representative of his/her Indian band or aboriginal community.

Canada - Manitoba

Vital Statistics
Department of Family Services
254 Portage Ave.
Winnipeg, Manitoba
Canada R3C OB6
(204) 945-3701

The Manitoba Office of Vital Statistics has records from 1882. If your request is urgent, there is a Can $50.00 fee for a 24-hour rush service.

The Manitoba Provincial Archives (200 Vaughan St., Winnipeg, Manitoba R3C 1T5; Tel. 204-945-3971; Fax 204-948-2008) also has records.

The National Archives of Canada (395 Wellington. St., Ottawa, K1A0N3; Tel. 613-995-5138) and the National Library of Canada (same address; Tel. 613-995-9481; Fax 613-996-4424) have extensive holdings.

The Family History Library of The Church of Jesus Christ of the Latter-day Saints in Salt Lake City, Utah has microfilmed original and published records of Manitoba and Canada. For further details on their holdings, please consult your nearest Family History Center.

SEARCH RESOURCES

(Active Registry for Adult Adoptees and Passive Registry for Birthparents):

Adoption Registry Coordinator
Manitoba Community Services
114 Garry St., 2nd Fl.
Winnipeg Manitoba R3C 1G1
Canada

Post Adoption Registry,
Child & Family Support
270 Osbome St., N
Winnipeg Manitoba R3C 1 V7
Canada

Genealogy

Brandon Branch
Manitoba Genealogical Society
Box 1332
Brandon Manitoba R7A 1A8
Canada

Dauphin Branch
Manitoba Genealogical Society
Box 2066
Winnipeg Manitoba R3C 3R4
Canada

Historical & Scientific Society of
Manitoba
Provincial Library
Legislative Building
Winnipeg Manitoba
Canada

Jewish Historical Societ- W Canada
403-322 Donald St.
Winnipeg Manitoba R3B 2H3
Canada

La Societe de Historic de St. Boniface
CP 135
Winnipeg Manitoba R2Il 3R4
Canada

Manitoba Historical Society
147 James Ave.
Winnipeg Manitoba
Canada

Mennonite Genealogical Society
Box 1086
Steinbach Manitoba
Canada

Dear AmFOR:... "I was adopted, and was wondering if you—or do you know of any organizations that could help me find some information on my mother or father, or both. I live in Lancaster, but was born in Canada - Manitoba, I was told, in '65. My birth name is Kimberly Rose Marie Van Venka; here is a photocopy of a birth certificate that I have, if it could be some help. I'd appreciate any kind of help you could offer me, anything at all... Thank you, DONNA MARIE WERONOWSKI, East Aurora, NY."

Canada - New Brunswick

Department of Health and Community Services
Service New Brunswick Vital Statistics
Box 1998
Fredericton, New Brunswick E38 5G4 Canada
(506) 453-2385
www.snb.xa/e/0001e.asp

The Division of Vital Statistics has records from January, 1888. If your request is for genealogical purposes, you may obtain a non-certified extract of the birth, marriage, or death record. Records are also available at The Provincial Archives of New Brunswick, Bonar Law-Bennett Building, Dineen Dr., University of New Brunswick, Fredericton (P.O. Box 6000, Fredericton, New Brunswick E3B 5H1; Tel. 506-453-3288; FAX 506-453-3288). The National Archives of Canada (395 Wellington, St., Ottawa, K1AON3; Tel. 613-995-5138) and the National Library of Canada (same address; Tel. 613-995-9481; Fax 613-996-4424) have extensive holdings.

The Family History Library of The Church of Jesus Christ of the Latter-day Saints in Salt Lake City, Utah has microfilmed original and published records of New Brunswick and Canada. For further details, please consult your nearest Family History Center.

Passive Registry

Genealogy

Postadoption Services
DepL of Health & Community Services
PO Box 5100
Fredericton New Brunswick E3B 5G8
Canada

Centre d'Etudis Acadiennes
Universitie de Moncton
Moncton New Brunswick E1 A3E9
Canada

New Brunswick Historical Society
Box 575
St. John's New Brunswick
Canada

New Brunswick Genealogical Society
Box 3235, Station B
Fredericton New Bnmswick E3A 2WO
Canada

Irene Praeg
Parent Finders-New Brunswick
16 Grove Avenue
Rothesay, New Brunswick E2E 5K3
Canada

Canada - Newfoundland

Vital Statistics Division
Department of Health
PO Box 8700
St. John's, Newfoundland
Canada A 1B4J6
(709) 729-3308

The Newfoundland Department of Health has records from 1892. There is a Can $4.00 charge for each three-year period searched. The Provincial Public Libraries Services (Provincial Reference and Resource Library, Arts and Culture Centre, St. John's, Newfoundland A 1B 3A3; Tel. 709-737-3954; FAX 709-737-3009) and the Provincial Archives of Newfoundland (Colonial Building, Military Road, St. John's A 1C 2C9; Tel. 709-733-9380) also have materials of interest. The National Archives of Canada (395 Wellington St., Ottawa, K1AON3; Tel. 613-995-5138), and the National Library of Canada (same address; Tel. 613-995-9481; FAX 613-996-4424) have extensive holdings.

The Family History Library of The Church of Jesus Christ of Latter-day Saints in Salt Lake City, Utah has microfilmed original records of Nova Scoria. For further details, please consult your nearest Family History Center.

SEARCH RESOURCES

Passive Registry

Geneaology

Postadoption Services
PO Box 4750
St. John's Newfoundland A 1 C 5T7
Canada

Newfoundland Historical Society
Colonial Building
Military Road
St. John's Newfoundland A 1C 5E2
Canada

Newfoundland and Labrador
Genealogical Society
Memorial University of Newfoundland
St. John's Newfoundland A 1C 3C7
Canada

Adoption Services
Department of Social Services
PO Box 8700
St. John's Newfoundland A1B 4J6
Canada

Canada - Northwest Territories

Registrar General

Dept. of Health / Vital Statistics
Bag 9 / 107 MacKenzie Road
Inuwik, NT V0E 0T0 Canada
(867) 777-7420
www.hlthss.gov.nt.ca/

The Northwest Territories Registrar General has records from 1925. The Public Libraries Services of the Northwest Territories (PO Box 1100, Hay River, Northwest Territories XOE OROI) also has materials of interest.

The National Archives of Canada (395 Wellington St., Ottawa, K1AON3; Tel. 613-995-5138), and the National Library of Canada (same address: Tel. 613-995-9481; FAX 613-996-4424) have extensive holdings.

The Family History Library of The Church of Jesus Christ of Latter-day Saints in Salt Lake City, Utah has microfilmed original records of Nova Scotia. For further details, please consult your nearest Family History Center.

SEARCH RESOURCES
(No Registry in Legislation; send letter indicating desire for reunion)

Family & Children's Services
Department of Social Services
Government of the N.W.T.
PO Box 1320
Yellowknife, N.W.T. XI A 2L9
Canada

Canada - Nova Scotia

(for records after October 1, 1908

Deputy Registrar General
Nova Scotia Dept. of Health
1723 Hollis St./PO Box 157
Halifax, Nova Scotia B3J 2T7
Canada
(902) 424-8381

(for earlier records:)

Public Archives of Nova Scotia
6016 University Avenue
Halifax, Nova Scotia
Canada B3H 1W4
(902) 424-6060,
Fax (902) 424-0516

The Department of Health has birth and death records from October 1, 1908, and marriage records from 1907 to 1918, depending where the marriage occurred.

Other sources are the Nova Scotia Provincial Library (3770 Kempt Road, Halifax B3K 4X8; Tel. 902-424-2460; FAX 902-424-0633), the National Archives of Canada (395 Wellington St., Ottawa, K1AON3; Tel. 613-995-5138), and the National Library of Canada (same address; Tel. 613-995-9481; FAX 613-996-4424).

The Family History Library of The Church of Jesus Christ of the Latter-day Saints in Salt Lake City, Utah has microfilmed original records of Nova Scotia. For further details on their holdings, please consult your nearest Family History Center.

Since 1996, Nova Scoria's adoption registry permits adult adoptees and parents contact. Others, such as adopters and siblings, may register only with consent of adoptee or parent. For further information, contact Parent Finders: 902-435-0287. (See below for address.)

SEARCH RESOURCES

Passive Registry

Director of Family & Children's
   Services
Dept. of Social Services
PO Box 696
Halifax Nova Scotia B3J 2T7
Canada

Adoption Search-Support

Parent Finders - Nova Scotia
PO Box 23148
Dartmouth, Nova Scotia B3A4S9
canada
Genealogy

Amherst Township Historical Society
37 Clifford St.
Amherst Nova Scotia B4H 2G3
Canada

Annapolis Valley Historical Society
Town Hall - Box 299
Middleton Nova Scotia BOS 1PO
Canada

Bridgetown & Area Historical Society
RR3
Bridgetown Nova Scotia BOS 2GO
Canada

Canso Historical Society
RR1
Canso Nova Scotia BOH 1HO
Canada

Cape Breton Genealogical Society
Box 42
Shelbourne Nova Scotia BOW ISO
Canada

Chestico Museum &
Historical Society
Box 37
Port Hood Nova Scotia BOE 2WO
Canada

Chezzetocook Historical Society
Grand Desert
Truro Novia Scotia
Canada

Colchester Historical Society
29 Young St. - Box 412
Truro Nova Scotia B2N 5C5
Canada

Cole Harbor Rural Heritage Society
Bisset Rd., RRl
Dartmouth Nova Scotia B2W 3X7
Canada

Eastern Marine Arts, Tech & Crafts
Heritage Society
Box 606
Halifax Nova Scotia B3J 2T1
Canada

Federation of Museums
Heritage & Historical Societies
5516 Spring Garden St., Ste. 305
Halifax Nova Scotia B3J 1 G6
Canada

Genealogical Committee-Nova Scotia
Historical Society
Box 895
Armdale Nova Scotia
Canada

Guysborough Historical Society
Box 140
Guysborough Nova Scotia BOH 1NO
Canada

Hantsport & Area Historical Society
Box 31
Hantsport Nova Scotia BOP 1PO
Canada

Historical Association-Anapolis Royal
Box 358
Anapolis Royal Nova Scotia
Canada
 Canada

Box 46
Ingonish Nova Scotia BOC IKkO
Canada

Inverness Historical Society
Box 161
Inverness Nova Scotia BOE 1NO
Canada

Kings Historical Society
Box 11
Kentville Nova Scotia
Canada

La Societe Historique
Acadienne de la Baie Sainte Marie
St. Anne's College
Church Point Nova Scotia BOW 1MO
Canada

Lunenberg Heritage Society
Box 674
Lunenberg Nova Scotia
Canada

Lunenburge Co. Historical Society
Lehave Nova Scotia
Canada

Lunen Co.
Nova Scotia BOR 1 CO
Canada

Mabou Gaelic & Historic Society
Box 175
Mabou Nova Scotia BOE 1X0
Canada

North Cumberland Historical Society
 Box 52
Pugwash Nova Scotia BOK 1LO
Canada

Nova Scotia Genealogical Society
37 Primrose St.
Dartmouth Nova Scotia B3A 406

Ingonish Historical Society
Nova Scotia Historical Society
Box 1102
Hallifax Nova Scotia B3J 2X1
Canada

Parrsboro Shore Historical Society
Parrsboro Nova Scotia BOM ISO
Canada

Port Hastings Historical Society
Box 131
Port Hastings Nova Scotia BOE 2TO
Canada

Queen's Co. Historical Society
270 Church St.
Liverpool Nova Scotia B3H 1Z9
Canada

Royal Nova Scotia Historical Society
Halifax Nova Scotia B3H 1T9
Canada

Sackville Heritage Society
83 Tamarack Circle
Lower Sackville Nova Scotia B4C 1E4
Canada

Scotian Railroad Society
Box 798
Armdale Station Halifax, N.S. B31. 4K5
Canada

Shelbourne Historical Society
Box 39
Shelbourne Nova Scotia BOT 1 WO
Canada

South Shore Genealogical Society
Box 471
Bridgewater Nova Scotia B4V 2X6
Canada

Tatagamouche Historical Society
Box 29
Tatagamouche Nova Scotia BOK 1 VO
Canada

West Hants Historical Society
Box 17, Courthouse
Windsor Nova Scotia BON 2TO
Canada

Weymouth Historical Society
Box 158
Weymouth Nova Scotia BOW 3TO
Canada

Yarmouth Historical Society
22 Collins St.
Yarmouth Nova Scotia B5A 3C8
Canada

Canada - Ontario

Registrar of Vital Statistics
189 Red River Rd / PO Box 4800
Thunder Bay, Ontario P7B 6L8
Canada
(807) 343-7459
www.serviceontario.ca

Archives on Ontario
77 Greenville Street
Toronto, Ontario M7A 2R9
(416) 327-1600

On November 1, 2005, The Adoption Information Disclosure Act (bill 183 authored by Sandra Pupatello) was passed by the Legislative Assembly, permitting disclosure to an adult adoptee of that adoptee's original full name, birth certificate, and the names of "birth" parent – and, to "birth" parents, the disclosure of an adoptee's legal (adoptive) name. The "birth" parent is permitted to file a "contact veto," similar to a restraining order, to prevent contact but it does not prevent release of the person's name unless they file a "restricted disclosure veto" demonstrating that their "safety is at stake."

The Office of the Registrar General has birth records from 1896, marriage records from 1911, and death records from 1921 to the present. They will issue certificates to the individual, the individual's parents or children, and to an attorney. These certificates cost Can $22.00. Any other requests are considered genealogical searches, and the charge is Can $22.00 per certificate.

Other sources include the Provincial Library (Ministry of Culture and Communications, 77 Bloor St., W, Toronto M7A 2R(; Tel. 416-314-7627; FAX 416-314-7635), the National Archives of Canada (395 Wellington St., Ottawa, K1AON3; Tel. 613-995-5138), and the National Library of Canada (same address; Tel. 613-995-9481; FAX 613-996-4424).

The Family History Library of The Church of Jesus Christ of the Latter-day Saints in Salt Lake City, Utah has microfilmed original records of Ontario and Canada. For further details on their holdings, please consult your nearest Family History Center.

ADOPTION SEARCH & SUPPORT GROUPS

Adoption Council of Ontario
http://www.adoption.on.ca

Adoption Support Kinship (ASK)
http://askaboutreunion.org

Birthmothers of Canada
Http://www.birthmothersofcanada.org

Parent Finders - National Capital Region
http://www.parentfindersofottawa.ca

SEARCH RESOURCES

Active Registry for Adult
Adoptees & Passive Registry for
Birthparents

Adoption Information Unit
Ministry of Community and Social Serv.
24th FL, 2 Bloor St., W.
Toronto, Ontario M7A 3E9

Fay Rath
Adoption Roots & Rights
187 Patricia Avenue
Donteter, Ontario NOL1GI
Canada
fayrath@execu.link.net

Adoption Roots & Rights
3 John Davies Drive
Woodstock, Ontario N4T1M9
Canada

Pat Fenton
Adoption Council
3216 Yonge St
Toronto, Ont. M4N 2L2
Canada
aco@adoption.ca

Joan Marshall (ISC)
Adoption Reunion Searehline
POBox65043-Merivale
Nepean, Ontario K2G5Y3
Canada

Searchline of Canada
63 Holbron Ave.
Nepean Ontario K2C 3H1
Canada

Sharon Chianelli, P.I.
47 Abbey Dawn Dr.
Bath, Ont. KOH 1GO
Canada
shasam@adan.kingston.net

Irene Garcia
Parent Finders One
47 Trieste Place
Hamilton, Ontario M4Y 2T7
Canada

Judy Grove
Adoption Council of Canada
180 Argyle Ave. # 329
Ottawa, Ontario K2P 1B7
Canada
aac@adoption.ca

Mr. Terry Romanchuk
Parent Finders-Windsor
PO Box 85
Cottham, Ontario NOR 1 BO
Canada

Irene Praeg
Parent Finders-Rothesay
1401 Gulf Blvd #109
Cleanvater, FL 34630
USA

Arlene
Parent Finden.-Brockville
PO Box 2002
Brockville, Ontario K6V 6N4
Canada

Monica Byme
Parent Finders-Nat'l. Capital
PO Box 5211 - Station F
Ottawa Ontario K2C 2H5
djl28@freenet.carleton.ca

Parent Finders - KW
49 Selkirk Street
Cambridge, Ontario N1S 1Z2
Canada

Parent Finders - National Capital
PO Box 21025 - Ottawa South
Ottawa, Ontano K 1 S 5N 1
Canada

Parent Finders
146 Richmond St.
Thorold Ontano L2V 2H4
Canada

Parent Finders
36 Woodbridge Rd.
Hamilton Ontario L8K 3C9
Canada

Parent Finders
PO Box 272
Willowdale Sta. A
North York Ontario M2N 5S9
Canada

David Latta
Parent Finders
384 Femdale Ave
London Ontario N6C 2YB
Canada
David Latta@hotmail.com

Parent Finders
1543 Duffenn Ave.
Wallaceburg Ontario N8A 2M7
Canada

Parent Finders - Windsor
PO Box 16
Ruthven Ontario NOP 2GO
Canada

Family Connection
25 Irwin Ave.
Toronto Ontario M4Y 1 L4
Canada

Ottawa Children s Aid
1370 Bank St.
Ottawa Ontario K1H 7Y3
Canada

Adoptive Parent Support
NCAC
RR-2 Brampton
Ontario L6V 1A1
Canada

Genealogy

Brant Co. Branch OGS
PO Box 2181
Brantford Ontario N3T 5Y6
Canada

Brantford Historical Society
Public Library Bldg.
Brantford Ontario
Canada

Brantford Historical Society
Public Library Bldg.
Brantford Ontario
Canada

Bruce and Grey Branch OGS
Box 1606
Port Elgin Ontario NOH 2CO
Canada

Canada Historical Assoc.
395 Wellington St.
Ottawa Ontario K1A ON3
Canada

Centre D'Exchanges Genealogiques
56 First Ave.
Ottawa Ontario K1A ON3
Canada

Elgin Co. Branch OGS
Box 416
St. Thomas Ontario N5P 3V2
Canada

Essex Co. Branch OGS
Box 2, Stat. A
Windsor Ontario N9A 6J5
Canada

Glengarry Genealogical Society
RR 1
Lancaster Ontario KOC 1NO
 Canada

Greenville Historical Society
Box 365
Prescott Ontario KOE 1TO
Canada

Halton-Pelel Branch OGS
Box 373
Oakville Ontario L6J 2J6
Canada

Hamilton Branch OGs
Box 904
Hamilton Ontario L8N 3P6
Canada

Heraldy Society of Canada
125 Lakewav Dr
Ottawa Ontario K115A9
Canada

Historical Society of Mecklenburg-
42 Noranda Street
Toronto Ontario
Canada

Huron Co Branch OGs
Box 469
Goderich Ontario N7A 5C7
Canada

Kawartha Branch OGS
PO Box 162
Peterborough Ontario K9J 6Y8
Canada

Kent Co. Branch OGS
Box 964
Catham Ontario N7M 5L3
Canada

Kingston Branch OGS
Box 1394
Kingston Ontano K7L 5C6
Canada

Lambton Co. Branch OGS
Box 2857
Samia Ontario N7T 7W1
Canada

Leeds and Greenville Branch OGS
Box 536
Brockville Ontario K6V 5V7
Canada

London Branch OGs
Box 871 Station B
London Ontario N6A 4Z3
Canada

Niagra Peninsula Branch OGs
Box 2224 Station B
St. Catherine's Ontario L3M 6P6
Canada

Nipissmg Branch OGS
Box 93
North Bay Ontario P1B 8G8
Canada

Ontario Genealogical Society OGS
40 Orchard view Blvd. - Ste. 253
Toronto Ontario M4R 1B9
Canada
Ontario P7C 4V9, Canada

1466 Bathhurst St.
Toronto Ontario M5R 3J3
Canada

Ottawa Branch OGS
Box 83446
Ottawa   Ontario K1 G 3H8
Canada

Oxford Co. Branch OGS
Box 1092
Woodstock Ontario N4S 8A5
Canada

Perth Co. Branch OGs
Box 9
Stratford Ontario N5A 6S8
Canada

Quinte Branch OGS
Box 301
Bloomfield Ontario KOK 1 GO
Canada

Sault and Disrict Branch OGS
Box 1203
Sault Ste. Mane Ontario P6A 6N1
Canada

Simcoe Co Branch OGS
Box 892
Barrie Ontario L4M 4Y6
Canada

Societe Canadienne de Genealogie
19 Rue Charlotte (Hull-Ottawa)
Ottawa Ontario
Canada

Sons of Scotland
19 Richmond St., W.
Toronto Ontario,
Canada

Storemount-Dundee-Glengany Hist Soc.
Box 73
Cornwall Ontario K1H 5T5
Canada

Sudbury District Branch OGS
c/o Sudbury Public Library
200 Brady St.
Sudbury Ontario P3E 5K3
Canada

Thunder Bay District Branch OGS
Box 373 Station F
Thunder Bay

Ontario Historical Society
 Toronto Branch OGS
 Box 147 Station Z
 Toronto Ontario M5N 2Z3
Canada

United Empire Loyalists Assoc.
23 Prince Arthur Ave
Toronto Ontario M5R 1B2
Canada

Waterloo-Wellington Branch OGS
Box 603
Kitchner Ontario N2G 4A2
Canada

Whitby-Oshawa Branch OGS
Box 174
Whitby Ontario L IN 5S1
Canada

Canadian Living, 12/1/91: "Retying the Cord: Adult Adoptees and Their [Birth]parents Discover the Joys of Each Other's Company ... At age 19, Dominique Laundry started looking for her mother. Her childhood with her adopters in Sudbury, Ontario was happy, but occasionally, particularly on birthdays and holidays, she would wonder about the woman who had given her up for adoption. 'In the back of my mind, there was always this thought of a person without a name or a face. My parents and I talked about it often,' she says.

In 1986, she registered with the Adoption Disclosure Register (ADR), a service of the Adoption Information Unit of the Ontario Ministry of Community and Social Services, which keeps records of the more than 200,000 adoptions that have taken place in Ontario since the 1920s. But, until recently, the ADR would not release the identify of a parent or adoptee unless both of them had placed their names on the ADR list. When Dominique applied, her birthmother hadn't registered. Dominique was shocked. 'Both my mother and I bawled our heads off for a little while,' she says.

However, unknown to Dominique, about 500 kilometers away in Ottawa, her mother was thinking about the baby she'd put up for adoption. Gail Masterson never expected to see her daughter again, but when she heard about the ADR, Gail put her name in.

A few months later after the ADR had matched their names, Gail and Dominique met. Dominique recalls the moment: 'It was scary. My heart was racing so fast.' After their first awkward 20 minutes, Gail and Dominique were talking a mile a minute—one of the many traits they share ... Until 1987, Dominique's adoptive parents could have blocked her reunion with her birthmother ... This loosening of regulations finally united one Toronto woman with her family.

Patricia (a pseudonym) was adopted in 1931, a fact she didn't uncover until she was 45 years old. Her parents had sworn their family and friends to secrecy. Wanting to know her medical background—her own children were marrying and having children—she registered with the ADR in 1979, but she never heard a word. Nearly 10 years later, after the new amendments came into effect and the ADR conducted a search, Patricia discovered the reason for the long silence: her mother had died in 1953 ... Judith Kizell, president of the National Capital Region branch of Parent Finders, searched, along with the father, for their daughter for three years. 'I wanted to know if she was alive and well,' says Judith, pointing out that others feel the same. 'Nearly every mother I've ever met has never forgotten her child.' Finally, last year, she found her ... Of the 17,000 adoptees registered with the ADR in Toronto, only 9,377 have asked the province to conduct a search. Adopters have dimmed the natural curiosity of many ...
A few reunions are disappointing—reality doesn't always measure up to fantasy. Some are exceptionally happy. But, no matter what the outcome, most people don't regret the search. As Gail Masterson says, "You never know until you do it. Now I think my life wouldn't be as full." Patricia says, 'It's given me the satisfaction of knowing my roots. I think that's the main thing, to know where I came from."

Dear AmFOR: ... "Must have something to do with the fact that I am adopted that makes me run from cameras. I never look in pictures like I think I should yet I don't what I look like. If that makes sense. Probably because I was the odd one out in a family of dark brown hair, hazel eyes, curly hair and high foreheads ... I just found out that the man I thought was my father isn't!!!! Keep up the work but remember it is not worth ruining your health over it... then who is going to be around to stimulate some of these articles written to and about you!!! Take care of yourself. .JUDITH KIZZELL BRANS, Nepean, Ontario, Canada."

Canada - Prince Edward Island

Dept. of Health Services / Div. of Vital Statistics
12 Douses Road
PO Box 3000
Montague, Prince Edward Island C0A 1R0
(902) 838-0880
www.gov.ca/vitalstatistics/

The Division of Vital Statistics has records from 1906. Make your fee payable to "The Minister of Finance." Records are also available at The Public Archives and Records Office located at the George Coles Building, Richmond St., Charlottetown (PO Box 1000, Charlottetown, C1A 7M4; Tel. 902-368-4290). The National Archives of Canada (395 Wellington St., Ottawa, K1A ON3; Tel. 613-995-5138), and the National Library of Canada (same address; Tel. 613-995-9481; FAX 613-996-4424) also have extensive holdings.

The Family History Library of The Church of Jesus Christ of the Latter-day Saints in Salt Lake City, Utah has micro-filmed original and published vital records and church registers of Prince Edward Island. For further details, please consult your nearest Family History Center.

SEARCH RESOURCES:

(No Registry in Legislation: Send Letter Indicating Desire for Reunion):
Dept. of Health & Social Services
PO Box 200
Charlottetown PEI C1A 7N8

Adoption Search Support

Parent Finders
RR #2
N. Wiltshire PEI C0A 1Y0
Canada

Genealogy

PEI Genealogical Society
2 Kent St. - Box 902
Charlottetown PEI C1A 7M4
Canada

Canada - Quebec

La Director de l'etat Civil
2535 Boulevard Laurier
Quebec, Quebec, G1V 5C6 Canada
(418) 643-3900
www.etatcivil.gouv.qc.ca

Archives Nationales du Quebec
1210 Ave de Seminaire
St. Foy, Quebec
Canada G1V 4N1
(418) 643-1322

Genealogy Department
Bibliotheque de la Ville de Montreal
1210 Sherbrooke East
Montreal Quebec
Canada H2L 1L9
(514) 872-5923

Vital records are not kept in a central repository in Quebec. The Archives Nationales due Quebec and the Bibliotheque de las Ville de Montreal have extensive collections of vital records. Contact them, or write to the parish where the event took place. The National Archives of Canada (395 Wellington St., Ottawa, K1A ON3; Tel. 613-995-5138), and the National Library of Canada (same address; Tel. 613-995-9481; FAX 613-996-4424) also have extensive holdings.

The Family History Library of The Church of Jesus Christ of the Latter-day Saints in Salt Lake City, Utah has micro-filmed original records of Quebec. For further details, please consult your nearest Family History Center.

SEARCH RESOURCES

(Active Registry for Adult Adoptees & for Parents of Adult Adoptee)
The Adoption Secretariat
3700 Bern St.
Montreal Quebec H2L 4G9
Canada

Adoption Search-Support

Pat Danielson
Parent Finders - Montreal
190Davignon
Dollard des Ormeaux, Quebec H9B 1Y5
Canada

Association de parents
    pour l'adoption qubecoise
www.quebecadoption.net

Service des Programmes a la
Communatue - Ministers de la Sante
et des Services Sociaux
1075 Chemin Ste-Foy
6e etage
Quebec G1S2M1
Canada

Mouvement Retrouvailles
www.mouvement-retrouvailles.qc.ca

Genealogy

Brome Co. Historical Society
Box 690
Knowlton Quebec J0E 140

Compton Co. Historical Society
RR 2
Sawyerville Quebec J0B 3A0
Canada

Institut Genealogique Drouin
4184 St. Denis
Montreal Quebec
Canada

Centre Genealogiques
C P 845
Hauteville
Montreal Quebec
Canada

Jewish Genealogical Society-Montreal
4605 St. Kevin Apt. 5
Montreal P Quebec H3W 1N8
Canada

English-Speaking
Quebec Family History Society
Box 1026
Pointe Claire P Quebec H9S 4H9
Canada

Societie Genealogiques des Cantons
1041 Rue Kingston
Sherbrooke P Quebec
Canada

Societe de Genealogie de Quebec
C P 2234 Vellie de Quebec
P Quebec G 1 K 7N8
Canada

Societie Genealogique - Francaise
C P 335 Place de Armes
Montreal P Quebec H2X 3H1
Canada

Societe de Historic et de Genealogiques
55 Rue de Roacher
Revieire du Loop P Quebec
Canada

Parent Finders Montreal
www.home.primus.cal~pfmt1

Societe Genealogique Trivluvienne
893 Rue Richard
Trois Rivieres P Quebec G8Y 4A5
Canada

Registry in the U.S.
Deanna Rogers
Quebec Quest Registry
1-810-686-3988
11:00 a.m. - 1:00 p.m. EST

Information on Duplessis' Children
Duplessis' Children Association
Attn: Stan Van Duyse, M.D.
Medi-Lex
333 Henri Bourassa
Montreal Nord (Quebec) H1H 1H6
Canada

Societe de Bernier D'Ameriquw
5569 Bernlanger
Montreal P Quebec
Canada

Sunday World Herald, 5/23/93, page 18-A: "Orphans Falsely Labeled Retarded: Thousands Sue Canadian Nuns, Alleging Abuse in the 1950s and '60s ...Montreal—On March 17,1955, Herve Bertrandwas an ordinary 11-year-old boy attending classes at the Mount Providence orphanage in Montreal. On March 18, he became an 'idiot.' The reason: The provincial government paid mount Providence, operated by Roman Catholic Nuns, 75 cents a day each for the care of orphans. For mentally retarded children, it paid $2.75.

The orphanage decided on what it called a 'change of vocation,' transforming itself into a mental institution and declaring its charges to be retarded. Thousands of children in similar Quebec facilities were falsely labeled mentally retarded in the 1950s. Many of them were sent to psychiatric hospitals and put in overcrowded wards with real mental patients and only a few overworked nuns to supervise them. The orphans say they were beaten with straps, paddles and fists, sexually and psychologically abused, restrained in straitjackets for weeks at a time, plunged into ice water, lashed to beds.

A group of about 4,000 former residents of the institutions in the 1950s and '60s has filed a class-action lawsuit against seven religious orders that operated a dozen orphanages or mental hospitals. It accuses them of physical, sexual and psychological abuse and seeks damages of $1.2 billion. The complainants say 90 percent of those selected for the 'change of vocation' were born illegitimate and were considered more shameful . . . One of the former "idiots," as they were called at the time, has earned a doctoral degree. Others have not fared as well. They suffer from a lack of self-esteem, chronic depression, paranoia and anxiety, said Dr. Stan van Duyse, who has examined many of the 'Duplessis children.'"

Dear AmFOR: . . . "Our five-hours long television program broadcasted throughout Quebec has been a full success. During this TV program, we made a public inquiry. The question was, "Are you against or for the right to origins?' People from everywhere in Quebec could ask this question in calling-up a toll-free number (2 __. 1,000).

There were so many people who tried to call up this phone number at the same time that the (switchboard) blew out... The reason is that about 10,000 people tried to call at the same time. Until this unexpected event, the initial result of the inquiry is: 2,672 for the right to origins and 2 against!

Do you know a group or someone who could help a mother from Quebec who is searching for her birthson who has been adopted in Kansas. The baby boy was born in Quebec City, on March the 30th, 1962 at the Creche Saint-Vincent de Paul. parents lived in a city somewhere in Kansas in 1964. The baby boy was 2 years old and a half when he was adopted. His male adopter was a German-American, 34 years old. The female adopter was a French-American, 29 years old. The fictitious name of the baby boy was Joscelin Paris. If you have an idea, send me the answer please... CECILE COMEAU, MOUVEMENT RETROVAILLES, Charlesbourg, Quebec."

Canada - Saskatchewan

Vital Statistics - Saskatchewan Department of Health
100-1942 Hamilton Street
Regina. Saskatchewan S4P 4W2, Canada
(306) 787-3251
www.health.gov.sk.ca/ ·

The Saskatchewan Department of Health has records from 1878. Genealogical photocopies may be requested for birth, marriage, and death certificates. The Provincial Library (1352 Winnipeg St., Regina S4P 3V7; Tel. 306-787-2985; FAX 306-787-8866) also has materials of interest. The National Archives of Canada (395 Wellington St., Ottawa, K1A ON3; Tel. 613-995-5138), and the National Library of Canada (same address; Tel. 613-995-9481; FAX 613-996-4424) also have extensive holdings.

The Family History Library of The Church of Jesus Christ of the Latter-Day Saints in Salt Lake City, Utah has microfilmed original records of Saskatchewan. For further details on their holdings, please consult your nearest Family History Center.

SEARCH RESOURCES
(Active Registry for Adult Adoptees & Passive Registry for Birthparents):

Post-Adoption Services
2240 Albert St.
Regina Saskatchewan S4S 3V7
Canada

Search/Support Groups

Parent Finders
PO Box 123
Mervin Saskatchewan S0M 1Y0
Canada

Adoptive Parent Support

NCAC
154 Batouche Crescent
Saskatoon Saskatchewan S7M 5B3
Canada

Genealogy

Saskatchewan Genealogical Society
Box 1894
Regina Saskatchewan S4P 0A0
Canada

Saskatoon Genealogical Society
323 Hilliard St E
Saskatoon Saskatchewan S70 0E5
Canada

Canada - Yukon

Yukon Health and Human Resources
Division of Vital Statistics
PO Box 2703
Whitehorse, Yukon
(867) 667-5207
www.hss.gov.yk.ca/

The Division of Vital Statistics has some birth records from 18988 and complete records from 1925. Birth and marriage certificates are issued in a wallet-size and framing size. The framing size is a more complex document. A photocopy of the original birth or marriage certificate is also available but it is a restricted document. If your request is urgent, please enclose an additional fee of Can $2.00.

The Yukon Archives (PO Box 2703, Whitehorse Y1A 2C6; Tel. 403-667-5321; FAX 403-667-4253) also has materials of interest.

The National Archives of Canada (395 Wellington St., Ottawa, K1A ON3; Tel. 613-995-5138) and the National Library of Canada (same address; Tel. 613-995-9481; FAX 613-996-4424) have extensive holdings.

The Family History Library of The Church of Jesus Christ of the Latter-day Saints in Salt Lake City, Utah has microfilmed original records of Ontario and Canada. For further details on their holdings, please consult your nearest Family History Center.

SEARCH RESOURCES

Passive Adoption Registry

Director of Family & Children's Services
PO Box 2703
Whitehorse Yukon Y1A 2C6
Canada

Genealogy

Yukon Historical Society
White Horse
Yukon Territory
Canada

Cape Verde

Direccao Geral dos Registos e Notariado
Ministerio de Justica
C.P. 204
Praia, Cape Verde

Birth and marriage records through 1910 for family members.

Cayman Islands

Registrar General
Tower Building
George Town
Grand Cayman, Cayman Islands, BWI
(345) 244-3404

Central Africa Republic

Center for the Civil Status
(Town), Central African Republic

Registration began 1940 for French citizens, foreigners; by 1966, entire population.

Chad

Civil Registrar
Direction de la Statistique
B.P. 453
N'Dajamena, Chad

Vital records are generally unavailable, presumed destroyed in the February-December 1980 civil strife.

Chile

Director General del Servicio de Registro Civil e Identificacion
Ministerio de Justicia
Hurfanso 1570
Santiago, Chile
(011)(562) 698-2546
www.resistro.civil.cl/

Registration began January 1, 1885. There is no divorce in Chile.

China

Population Registration
Ministry of Public Security
(City), China

Administrative Division for Population Registration
Third Bureau, Ministry of Public Security
14 Dong Chang An Jie, Beijing, China

China uses a household registration system to record and identify each person in China. The registration is handled by the local police office. Current vital registration is considered to be 90 percent complete. When writing include two International Postal Reply Coupons, available at your local post office, with your request.

The Family History Library of the Church of Jesus Christ of Latter-day Saints in Salt Lake City, Utah has microfilmed original and published records of China. For further details on their holdings, please consult your nearest Family History Center.

Genealogical Research Center
www.libtarv.sh.cn/english/

China - Hong Kong

General Register Office
3/F, Low Block
Queensway Government Offices
66 Queensway   Hong Kong (HKSAR), China
(011) (852) 2867-2785
www.info.gov.hk/immd/

While church registers date from the colonial period, vital registration in Hong Kong began in 1872. Current registration is considered to be complete. Divorces are registered by the Registrar of the Supreme Court. There is a HK $12.40 fee to send each certificate by registered airmail and an additional charge of HK $20.00 to search for a record.

The Family History Library of the Church of Jesus Christ of Latter-day Saints in Salt Lake City, Utah has microfilmed original and published records of Hong Kong and China. For further details on their holdings, please consult your nearest Family History Center.

China - Macau

Conservatoria do Registro Civil de Macau
Secretario-Adjunto para Administration,
Rue do Campo, No. 162
Edificio Adminstracao Publica, 15
Andar, Macau, China

While church registers date from the colonial period, the vital registration office n Macau has birth records from 1890 and marriage and death records from 1900. The codes have been changed over the years with a new code going into effect in May, 1987. The office is adding photocopies of church registers from January 1, 1900.

China - Mongolia

Population Registration
Ministry of Public Security
(City), Mongolia

Mongolia uses a household registration system to record and identify each person in the country. The registration is handled by the local police office. Current vital registration is considered to be 85 percent complete.

China - Taiwan

Civil Registration Service
Department of Civil Affairs
9F. No. 1 Shifu Rd., Xinyi District
Taipei City 110, Taiwan
Republic of China

(011)(886)(2) 383-2741

China uses a household registration system to record and identify each person in China. The registration is handled by the local police office. Current vital registration is considered to be complete. Materials of interest are also found at The National Central Library at 20 Chungsham South Road, Taipei, Taiwan, Republic of China; Tel. (011)(866)(02)361-9132

The Family History Library of the Church of Jesus Christ of Latter-day Saints in Salt Lake City, Utah has microfilmed original and published records of China. For further details on their holdings, please consult your nearest Family History Center.

From "A Mother's Ordeal: One Woman's Fight Against China's One-Child Policy"...Chi An, a serious student and dedicated party activist from Shenyang, Manchuria, was trained as a nurse during the Cultural Revolution. When the Chinese government launched its sweeping family planning campaign during the early 1980s, Chi An—then a young mother—was recruited as a population-control worker. She was trained to enforce the "one-couple, one-child" policy through coercive peer counseling pressuring uncooperative women to "think clear" about their pregnancies. She hunted down runaway women who were illegally pregnant and helped administer forced sterilizations, late-term abortions and in cases where women carried illegal fetuses to term, lethal injections.

Disturbed by a series of harrowing "birth-control" experiences, Chi An applied for a visa to join her husband who was studying at a university in the U.S. Not long after she arrived in America. The tables were turned. Chi An found herself pregnant. Since Chi An and her family planned to return to China she was forced to seek permission from Chinese officials to have a second child. The Chinese authorities responded with a resounding "no." After much anguished debate, Chi An and her husband decided to cut their ties to their homeland and applied to the U.S. government for asylum. America was not responsive and instead initiated deportation procedures. China expert Steven Mosher stepped in, helping Chi An win her case and ultimately effecting a policy change that protects families in similar situations....by STEVEN W. MOSHER, Harcourt, Brace & Company..

Los Angeles Times, 9/22/90: "Hong Kong Mothers-to-be Dash to U.S. to Give Birth: They Want American Passports for Their Children When the Colony Reverts to China in 1997"... Seven years before China is scheduled to assume control of Hong Kong, hundreds of mothers-to-be are journeying to the United States in an ingenious jet-age dash to have their children born on American soil for what has become a pried possession-a U.S. passport. The United States automatically bestows citizenship on anyone born here and an increasing number of Hong Kong parents are taking advantage of the law to give their children a new home before the People's Republic of China takes control of the Colony from Britain in 1997....the rich could buy their freedom in Canada, New Zealand, Australia or even the tiny Pacific nation of Tonga. But for the middle-class, the routes are limited.

In the wake of China's brutal crackdown on pro-democracy demonstrators last year in Tien An Men Square, hundreds-and perhaps thousands-have come to the United States to give birth. The parents cannot automatically become U.S. citizens and get no immediate benefit from having their children born here ... The rush to leave Hong Kong before China assumes control has reached a jittery level for many of the colony's 5.7 million residents. An estimated 1,000 people a week are now emigrating to new homes

Colombia

Registro de la Nacional del Estado Civile
AC 26 #51-60 - CAN
Bogota, Colombia
(011)(57)(1)284-8976
www.registraduria.gov.co

Records began June 3, 1852, and were kept by parish priests. Government registries were set up in 1934. Death records have been kept since 1969.

> *Los Angeles Times:* "Young Stowaway Orphan's Tale Takes Turn for Worse: ... INS doesn't believe Colombian's story; major parts of it don't stand up. He may be sent back tonight despite celebrity status.
>
> He was orphaned, he said, when his parents were killed in a bus accident. He lived on the streets of Cali and slept in an abandoned airplane. He stowed away to the United States on June 3 because he wanted to go to college ... The Miami Herald ran a color picture on the Sunday front page. NBC's 'Dateline' did a feature, and after the wire services picked up his story, the boy received adoption offers from as far away as Port Townsend, WA... Gillermo Resales turned out to be Juan Carlos Guzman, not 13 but turning 17. His mother and stepfather were alive. And as for his account of enduring sub-zero temperatures and a lack of oxygen while clinging to the landing gear of a plan traveling at 30,000 feet—immigration officials don't believe it. Today, Guzman is scheduled to be deported to Colombia."
>
> Examiner, 7/11/89: "9-Year-Old Mom Has Made Her Family Rich and Happy ... A nine-year-old mother has made her family rich and happy, but a dark cloud still looms over her baby ... On Christmas Day last year, Marta Artunduaga became the world's youngest registered mom when she gave birth to a baby girl, Olga, at the age of nine ... Doctors who delivered Marta's baby in Pitalito, Colombia, gifted her with a live cow—no small present for a poor family ... Now, thanks to the generosity of readers around the world who were saddened to learn of Marta's misery, the family shares a charming villa, equipped with electricity and a telephone ... Now, Marta's mom has succeeded in opening a small grocery store, and there's enough food for everyone—even the flocks of cousins who have moved in. The only shadow that mars this otherwise ideal picture is the priest's refusal to baptize Olga. The baby is cruelly referred to as 'the child of sin' by many in the small town."

Comoros

Registrar General
Moroni, Comoros

Comoros became independent from France in 1975.

Congo

Direction Nationale de l'Etat Civil
Ministere de l'Interieur
B.P. 880
Brazzaville, Congo

Vital registration began in 1922.

Costa Rica

Direccion de Registro Civil y Notariado
Tribunal Supremo de Elecciones
AP 10218-1000
San Jose, Costa Rica
www.tse.go.cr/

Registration began in 1881 and is considered complete.

Croatia

Civil Registration Office
(Town), Croatia

Vital records are on file from 1946.

Cuba

Directora de Registros y Notarias
Registro Civil
Ministerio do Justicia
13 Calle O No. 216
3/23 y 25 Vedado
Havana, Cuba 10400 (053) 32-4536

Registration began June 17, 1870, with key changes in 1885 and January 1, 1986.

Cyprus

c/o Registrar
District Office
(Town), Cypress

For further information, in the USA, contact Cyprian Consulate, 4219 Coolidge Ave., Los Angeles, CA 90066 USA; Tel. (310)397-0771.

Czech Republic

Ministry of the Interior
Archivni Sprava
Tridadr, Milady Horakove
133, 166 21 Prague, Czech Republic

The Archives charges an hourly fee for a search. Registration began in 1919, and church records are available from 1785. Records are also available at the Nardni Knihovna v Praz (National Library), located at Klementinum 190, 110 01 Prague, Czech Republic; Tel. (Oil) (42) (2) 266-541; FAX (011)(42)(2) 261-775. The Czechs do not practice adoption.

Denmark

Lutheran Pastor
(Town), Denmark

The Central Office can also advise you:

Central Office of Civil Registration
Ministry of the Interior
Datavej 20, PO Box 269
3460 Birkerod, Denmark
(Oil) (45) 82-7200, FAX (011)(45) 82-5110

For further assistance contact:

Ministry of Ecclesiastical Affairs
Frederiksholms Kanal 21
DK 1220 Copenhagen, Denmark
(011)(45) 3392-3390, FAX (011)(45) 3392-3913

Civil registration is administered by the Lutheran Church. Church registers are on file from the 1600s. The Central Office does not make their records public but can advise you where to write.

The Family History Library of the Church of Jesus Christ of Latter-day Saints in Salt Lake City, Utah has microfilmed original and published records of Denmark For further details on their holdings, please consult your nearest Family History Center.

Djibouti

Police Nationale
Service de la Population es Postes et Telecommunications
Section Etat Civile
BP 37
Djibouti, Djibouti
Formerly known as French Somaili and later as the French Territory of the Affairs and the Isaas, Djibouti became independent in 1977. The registration is considered to be incomplete.

Dominica

Registrar General's Office
Supreme Court
Bay Front
PO Box 304
Rouseau, Commonwealth of Dominica
West Indies
(809) 448-2401

Dominica became independent in 1978. The Registrar General's Office has records from April 2, 1861; but the office was burned in June, 1979, with the loss of many records. Current registration is considered to be complete.

Dominican Republic

Direcion General Estado Civil
Calle Paul Harris Esq. Horacio Vicioso
Santo Domingo. Dominican Republic

For records before 1930 write to:

Archive General de la Nacion
 Cesar Nicolas Penson 91
Plaza de la Cultura
Santo Domingo, Dominican Republic

Registration began January 1, 1828 and is considered incomplete.

Ecuador

Director General de Registro Civil, Identificacion y Cedulacin
Ministerio de Gobiemo
Av. Amazonas 743 v Veintimilla
Ed. Espinosa
Quito, Ecuador

Older records are available at the Archive Municipal (National Museum Building, Quito, Ecuador). Modem vital registration began January 1,1901. The National Library also has records. Contact them at Universidad Central del Ecuador, P.O. Box 166, Quito.

Egypt

Department of Civil Registration
Ministry of Interior
Abassia, Cairo, Egypt

While Egypt had the world's first vital records registration program, dating from Ramses n in 1250 B.C., current registration began in 1839. Only births and deaths are registered. Marriages are kept by the religious denomination, and divorces are kept by the court issuing the decree. The National Library and Archives also has records. Contact them at Comiche El-Nil Street, Boulac, Cairo.

El Salvador

Legal Office

Registro Civil
Alcaldia Municipal
(City),·El Salvador

Central Office:

Direccion General de Estadistica y Censos
Ministerio de Economia 43a. Avenida Norte y la. Calle
Ponient
AP 2670
San Salvador, El Salvador
(011)(503) 23-1520

Records began in 1860 and are recorded in each town. Divorces are recorded on the original marriage certificate.

Times: "Leukemia Patient Dies Hours Before Mother Arrives From El Salvador . . . Newport Beach-A leukemia patient whose mother in El Salvador finally won permission from federal authorities to visit him one last time, died Thursday afternoon just hours before her plane landed. Fernando Pedrosa, 25, died about 5 p.m. at Flagship Health Care while his mother was on her way to see him . . . Local INS officials said they were not aware of the situation until last week. On Tuesday, an emergency permit was granted by the INS to allow the mother to enter the United States for 60 days on humanitarian grounds."

Equatorial Guinea

District Judge
Ministerio de Justica, Culto y Registro
Malabo, Equatorial Guinea

Equatorial Guinea, the only Spanish-speaking nation in Africa, became independent in 1968.

Eritrea

Registrar
Ministry of the Interior
Asmara, Eritrea

Vital registration is not considered to be comprehensive.

Estonia

Russian-American Genealogical Archival Service (RAGAS)
PO Box 236
Glen Echo, Maryland 20812
(202) 501-5206

Director General, State Vital Records
Lossi Plats - Rnu Mat 67
EE0100 Tallinn, Estonia

By an agreement between the United States National Archives Volunteer Association and the Archives of Russia Society, RAGAS receives and processes requests for vital records in some of the former Soviet republics. Although at this time RAGAS is able to deal mainly with Russia, Belarus, and Ukraine they might be able to help you with your inquiries regarding Estonia. There is a charge per document with a shipping fee per document. The service also is available at an hourly rate. (See "Russia" for application forms.)

Records are also available at the National Library (Eesti Rahvusraamatukogu), located at Tonismagi 2, Tallinnn, Estonia EE0106; Tel. (011)(7)(142) 442-094.

Ethiopia

Urban Areas:

Regin 14 Administration - Vital Statistics
PO Box 356
Addis Ababa, Ethiopia

Rural Areas:

Registrar
Ministry of the Interior
Addis Ababa, Ethiopia

Vital registration is not considered to be complete.

Fiji

Registrar General
Crown Law Office
Box 2213
Suva, Fiji
(011)(679)211-598

Registration began in 18744. Records are also available at the National Archives, P.O. Box 2125, Suva, Fiji; Tel. (011) (679) 304-144; FAX (011)(679) 302-379.

Finland

Pastor	or:	Registrar
Lutheran Church		District Registrar
(Town), Finland		(Town), Finland

Records from the local parishes and the registrars are forwarded to:

Population Registration Center
Ministry of the Interior
PL 7
SF-00521 Helsinki, Finland
(011)(358)(0) 189-3909Cost for a certified Birth Certificate..... Price Varies

Over 90 percent of Finland's vital records are registered by the Lutheran Church. Non-Lutherans have been allowed to register with their respective churches or the government since 1917. These records are forwarded to the Population Register and are not open to public inspection. A file is kept on every resident of Finland, immigrant or citizen, as well as those who have emigrated from Finland. Current registration is considered to be complete. Church registers date back to 1686.

When writing, include two International Postal Reply Coupons, available at your local post office.

The Family History Library of The Church of Jesus Christ of Latter-day Saints in Salt Lake City, Utah has microfilmed many of the original and published vital records and church registers of Finland. For further details on their holdings, please consult your nearest Family History Center.

SEARCH RESOURCES

Adoption Search Support

Ann Koch Pelto, ISC
14320 S.E. 170th
Renton, WA 98058
USA

Genealogy
Finnish Genealogical Society
Soumen Sukutukumusseura R Y
Sukutukimusosasto
Snellmaninkatu 9-11
Helsinki 17
Finland

France

Le Marie
(Town). France
Vital records are on file from the late 1700s. Current registration is considered to be complete.

SEARCH RESOURCES

Genealogy

Centre d'Entr'Aide
Genealogique Les Fresnes
52/55 Bd de Charrones
75000 Pans 150
France

Centre Genealogique de Paris
64 Ru de Richilieu
75002 Pans 150
France

Centre Genealogique due Centre
81 Rue de Foix

41 Blois
France

Centre Genealogique de l'ouest
2 Impasse Copernic
44 Nantes

France

Groupment Genealogique de Lorraine
duNord
172 Grand Rue

59 Roubalx
France

Cercle Genealogique de Lorame et
Barrois
Archives Department Sales
Rue de la Monnaie
54 Nancy
France

Eguipe Genealogique Sedanzise
3 Place Crussy
08 Sedan
France

Centre Genealogique de Picardie
124 Chausse Marcae
80 Abbeville
France

Centre Genealogique du Sud-Ouest
2 rue Ducau
33 Bordeaux
France

Centre de Researchs Genealogique et
Heraldiques du Languedoc
12 Place Roger Salengro
34 Montpeleier
France

Cercle Genealogique de l'Albigeois
Maitre Congard
81 Viane
France

Cercle Genealogique d' Alsace
Archives du Bas Rhin
5 Rue Fischart
67000 Strasbourg
France

Cercle Genealogique de Tourraine
23 rue de la Chevalerie
37 Tours
France

Groupe des Genealogistes du Cambresis
8 Rue Watteau
59 Cambrai
France

Societe Dugrand Armorial de France
179 Bd Hussman
7500 Paris
France

International Genealogical Friendship
Society
141 Bd Malesherbes
17 Paris 17E
France

Les Vieux Noms de France
17 RueCaumartin
75009 Paris
France

Paris World News Service, 8/71: "France Has No Bastards ... In the eyes of a new French law, 'natural' children will soon be as legitimate as children born in wedlock. They will have the same rights to support and inheritance. And the illegitimate child may also have several fathers contributing to his support. The law provides that children born out of wedlock, in adultery or as a result of other irregularities have the right to use their father's name and shall no longer be obliged to bear their mother's. The court shall decide who is the father, or fathers ...

Los Angeles Times: "France May Limit Artificial Pregnancies" ... Medicine: controls sought by government would be among world's strictest. 'We want to stay very close to nature,' one official says ... Paris—France's conservative government said Wednesday that it will seek to impose strict controls on artificial impregnation, including a requirement that infertile couples have the consent of the sperm donor and a judge's permission before receiving an embryo implant.

The government was spurred by a growing national debate this week following the birth of twins to a 59-year-old, post-menopausal British woman, who received an embryo implant at an Italian clinic. The doctors who did that implant say a 62-year-old Italian woman, Rosana Della Corte, now is three months pregnant after a similar treatment."

Dear AmFOR: . . . "I was wondering if your organization could assist me as I begin my search for my parents. I have heard of your organization on several occasions. . . . I was born on February 1, 1964, in Columbia, Missouri to a woman named Jeanine Marquis who was attending the University of Missouri in Columbia at that time. It is unclear if she was in graduate or undergraduate school. She was 21 years old, Catholic, unmarried and originally from Poitiers, France. It is my understanding that she was in the States specifically to attend school so it is possible that she returned to Europe eventually. My name was Louise Marquis prior to the adoption. I have no information about my father.

There are many reasons for my interested in pursuing my heritage. It is important to me and my future family to have some knowledge of the health history of my ancestors, and I must admit that there is a natural curiosity to know some information about my background. I realize that these quests don't end as expected, however, I am ready to unveil whatever information I can find in relations to these circumstances. Again, any assistance you could offer to point me in the right direction would be very helpful . . . Sincerely, SUSAN KONOP, Webster Grove, MO."

Gabon

Registrar of Births, Marriages and Deaths
Ministeres de l'Linterieur et de la Justice
Libreville, Gabon

Registration begun in 1940 for French citizens and in 1972 for the entire population. Currently the registration is considered to be incomplete. (Gabon was formerly French Equitorial Africa)

Gambia

Ministry of Health - The Quadrangle
Banjal, Gambia
(011)(220) 227-872

Gambia became independent in 1970. Vital registration is 50 percent complete for births and 10 percent complete for deaths. The National Library also has records; write PO Box 552, Banjul, Gambia.

Georgia

Civil Registry Agency/ Ministry of Justice
4 Vani Street
0154 Tblisi, Georgia
www.cra.gov.ge/index.php?m=2

By an agreement between the United States National Archives Volunteer Association and the Archives of Russia Society, RAGAS receives and processes requests for vital records in some of the former Soviet republics. Although at this time RAGAS is able to deal mainly with Russia, Belarus, and Ukraine they might be able to help you with your inquiries regarding Estonia. There is a $20 charge per document with a $2.00 shipping fee per document. The service also is available at an hourly rate. (See "Russia" for application forms.)

Records are also available at the National Library (Gruzinskaia Gosudarstvennaia Respublikanskaia Biblioteka), located at ul. Ketskhoveli 5, 38007 Tbilisi, Georgia; Tel (011)(7)(883) 22.

Germany

Standesamt
(Town), Germany

Write to the Civil Registration District Office or the parish church in the town where the event occurred. Vital records are on file as early as 1809 but usually from 1875. Current registration is considered to be complete. When writing, include two International Postal Reply Coupons, available at your local post office.

The Family History Library of The Church of Jesus Christ of Latter-day Saints in Salt Lake City, Utah has microfilmed many of the original and published vital records and church registers of Germany. Consult your nearest Family History Center.

The Red Cross operates the Holocaust and War Victims Tracing and Information Center, Baltimore, MD. Your local chapter has inquiry forms.

German adoption records have been open since the late 1970s. The office in Germany that handles adoptions is the Adoptions vermittlung (Adoption Placement Office), a subdivision of the Jugendamt (Youth Office). Each municipality has its own branch of the Jugendamt. Inquiries about German adoptions should be directed to:

Jugendamt
Adoptions vermittlung
[5-Digit Postal Code] [Name of City or Town]
Germany

SEARCH RESOURCES

Adoption Search-Support

Leonie Boehmer (Searcher)
William Gage
GeborenerDeutscher (newsletter)
805 Alvarado, NE
Albuquerque, NM 87108 USA
BoehmerL@aol.com
wmlgage@aol.com

Margit Benton
2238 Bailey Dnve
North Charleston, SC 29405 USA
margitb@aol.com

Missing in Adoption
Joan E. Kelly
13109 Ring Road
St. Charles MI 48655
USA

International/Tracing Services:

Internationaler Sozialdienst
(Deutscher Zweig) e.V
Am Stockbom 5-7
60439 Frankfurt/Main
Germany

Deutsches Rotes Kreuz
Suchdienst München
InfanteriestraBe 7 A
80797 Munchen
Germany

Earnest Thodes
Address Book for Genealogy
Genealogical Publishing Company, Inc.
1001 North Calvert Street
Baltimore, MD 21202
USA

Genealogical Societies

FEDERAL REPUBLIC OF
GERMANY - GENERAL

Deutsche Arbeitsgemeinschaft
Genealogischer Verbande
70193 Stuttgart 1
Germany

Der Herald Verein fuer Heraldik
Genealogie und Verwandte
Wissenschaften
Archivstrasse 12-14
14195 Berlin 33 (Dahlem)
Germany

ANHALT
Arbeitsgememschaft fuer Mitteldeutsche
Familienforschung Amalienstrasse 1
34117 Kassel
Germany

Verein fuer Familien-und
Wappenkunde in Wuerttemberg
un Baden
70047 Postfasch / 105441 Stuttgart
Germany

Landsverein Badische Heimat
Auschuss fuer Familienforschung
Heilbronstrasse 3

BAVARIA-UPPER
Bayensche landverem
fuer Familienkunde e.V
WinzererstrastraBe 68
80797 Munchen/Munich
Germany

BAVARIA-FRANCONIA
Gessellschaft fuer
Familienforschung in Franken e.V.
Archivstrasse 17 (Stratsarchiv)
90408 Nurmberg
Germany

BREMEN
Gesellschaft fuer Familienforschung
"Die Maus"
Prasident Kennedy Platz 2
Stadtarchiv
28203 Bremen
Germany

COLOGNE-KOELN
Westdeutsche Gellschaft fuer
Familienkunde
Postfach 101471
51063 WullstraBe 96
Germany

HAMBURG
Genealogische Gesellschaft
Sitz Hamburg e.V
Postfach
302042 Hamburg
Germany

HESSEN-DARMSTADT
Hessiche Familiengeschichtliche
Vereinigung e.V.
Schloss
64283 Darmstadt
Germany

HESSEN-NASSAU
UND FRANFORT-MAIN
Familienkundliche Gesellschaft
fuer Nassau und Frankfurt e.V.
NiederwaldstrastraBe 5
65187 Weissbaden
Germany

HESSEN-KURHESSEN
UND WALDECK
Gesellschaft fuer Familienkunde
In Kurhessen und Wieck e.V.
Postfach 410328
34065 Kassel
Germany

HESSEN-FULDA
Vereinigung fuer
Familien-und-Wappenkunde Fulda e.V.
Taunusstrasse 4
36043 Fulda
Germany

LOWER SAXONY
Sidersachische Landverein
fuer Familienkinde e.V.
Kobelingerstrasse 59
30159 Hanover
Germany

Genealogisch-Heraldische
Gesellschaft
Sitz Gottigen
Theaterplatz 5 (Streadtsarchiv)
37073 Gottigen
Germany

LOWER SAXONY-
EAST FRIESLAND
Arbeitsgruppe Familienkunde und
Heraldik
Der Ostfriesishen Landschaft
Burgermeister Mueller Platz 2
26603 Aurich
Germany

LOWER SAXONY-EASTPHALIA
Familienkundliche Kommission
fuer Niedersaschsen und Bremen
Appelstrasse 9
30167 Hannover
Germany

LUEBECK
Arbeitskreis fuer
Familienforschung
Wakenitzstrasse 19
23564 Luebeck
Germany

NORDREHEIIN-WESTPHALEN-
RHINELAND
Westdeutsche Gesellschaft fuer
Familienkunde e.V.
Rheinalle 34
53173 Bonn I
Germany

NORDHEIM-
WESTFALEN/WESTFALIA
Westfalische Gesellschaft fuer
Genealogie
und Familienforschung
Warendorferstrasse 25
48145 Muenster (Westfalen)
Germany

OLDENBURG
Oldenburgische Gesellschaft
fuer Familienkunde
Lerigauweg 14
26131 Oldenburg
Germany

RHEINLAND PFALZ-
THE PALITINATE
Arbeitsgemeinschaft fuer
Pfalisch-Rheinische
Familienkunde e.V.
Rottstrasse 17 (Stradtsarchiv)
67061 Ludwigshafen/Rhein
Germany

RHEINLAND PFALZ-
THE RHINELAND
West Deutsche Gesellschaft Fuer
Familienkunde e.V.
Rheinalle 34 5300 Bonn-Buell
Germany

Roland Zu Dortmund e.V.
Dutelstrasse 1
44319 Dortmund
Germany

RHINELAND PFALZ -
UPPER RHINE
Hessesche Familienschlichte
Vereinigung e.V.
Stadtsarchi Schlosse
64283 Darmstadt
Germany

SAARLAND
ArbeitsgemeinschaftfuerSaarlandische
Familienkunde zum Rauenhuebel 120
66333 Voelklingen
Germany

Vereinigung fuer die Heimatkunde
in Ladkreis Saarlouis e.V.
Landratsamt
Postfach 360
66740 Saarlouis
Germany

SCHLESWEG HOLSTEIN
Schlesweg Holsteinische Gedellschaft
fuer Familienforschung
Gartenstrasse 12
24103 Kiel
Germany

MIDDLE GERMANY- BRANDENBURG, MECKLENBURG AND SAXONY	ASTERN GERMANY-SILESIA, AST AND WEST PRUSSIA, POMERANIA	GERMANS FROM CZECHOSLOVAKIA DETENDEUTSCHE)
ArbeitsgemeinschaftfuerMitteldeutsche	Arbeitsgemeinschaft Ostdeutscher	Vinigung Sudentendeutscher
Familienforschung e.V.	Familiforschung e.V.	Familienforschung
Sitz Marburg	Ernesst-Moritz-Arndt Strasse 25	Juttastrasse 30
Emilienstrasse 1	53225 Bonn	90480 Nurmberg
34121 Kassel	Germany	Germany
Germany		

Excerpted from *Deutsche Presse Agentur/ap Allgemeine Presse* (Karlsruhe)—2/1/89: "Illegitimate Offspring Have Right to Information—The Way to Name of True Father Opened for Children . . . The Federal Constitutional Court in Karlsruhe has broadened the right of children born out of wedlock to get information about their birthfathers. The Court, in a decision rendered on Tuesday (01/31/89), announced that the current ruling, by which even those of age could only contest their legitimacy and demand information about their true father in limited exceptional cases, violates a basic right.

According to the opinion of the Constitutional Court, children at the age of majority also have the right to clarification of their heritage if their mother is legally married (to someone other than the child's biological father). In their decision, the judges in Karsruhe obligated the legislature to change the constitutional ruling accordingly ... the decision does not contain what the proceedings seemed to promise. It was expected that the Federal Constitutional Court would, with its investigation as to when illegitimate children could ascertain their father, turn to a much more significant question: the heavily discussed problem of whether or not children produced by artificial insemination with the sperm of an unknown donor have a right to the determination of the biological father remains unresolved."

Wall Street Journal, 7/15/93: "What's in a Name Greatly Interests German Officialdom . . . You Can't Just Call Your Son Sascha, a Couple Learned, Without Suing the State ... Bremerhaven—Olafand Silke Witte had a simple desire: To name their son Sascha. German officials had a simple reply: No. They demanded that he also have a middle name . . . Names that officials find odd can be rejected out of hand. Second names can be required—as in the case of little Sascha—to nail down a child's sex. (Though Sascha is a common boy's name in Germany.) Changing a name is a complicated procedure that can cost $1,500. And the surname married people take is a perennial subject of controversy and even legislation. The state plays were rough, too. For the first 13 months of his life, Sascha barely existed in the eyes of Germany. He did, however have a passport, a pink sheet of paper that gave his names as 'WITTE, WITHOUT.' A friendly official has supplied the document so the Wittes could take the baby with them to Denmark on vacation. The name game, which became a minor cause celebre, finally ended for them in March, when a newspaper headline declared: 'Sascha Can be Sascha.' Acting as his own lawyer, Mr. Witte had fought decisions at a local bureau of vital statistics (which Germans call the registry), by the state of Bremen's interior department and by a court. He finally won on appeal... Mr. Ahnert says names like Gott (God) , Zufall (coincidence), and Bierstuebl (little beer bar) are recent rejected examples of parental willfulness. Curiously, one name that many Germans believe is verboten—Adolf—isn't. Guenter Bahrtdt, who is in charge of another Berlin registry, says the name can't be done away with: 'Otherwise, we'd have to forbid names like Khomeini and those of other bad statesmen. That couldn't be'... At the moment, one of the five most popular names for newborn babies is Kevin—a name completely alien to Germany but now all the rage because of Kevin Costner and because of a movie called 'Kevin Allein zu Haus.' The title in the States was 'Home Alone.'"

Excerpted from *La Habra Star*, 2/18/93: "39-Year Wait Is Over... Daughter Given Up for Adoption by German Woman Is Reunited With [Birth]mother in CA ... On Friday, after 39 years. La Habra resident Christine Galvin was reunited with the baby girl she gave up in Germany.

Years of searching and months of preparation went into the reunion ... Barbara Britton's knees trembled as she left the plane and descended the stairs.

"I saw her right away," she said. "I said, 'There she is, there she is.' I tried to get to her just as fast as I could" ... Galvan reached down, grabbed Britton's hands, and kissed them. 'That's the last thing I kissed when I gave her up,' Galvan said ... Once while Britton was in the care of her adopters, Galvan thought about avoiding the adoption deal. But the wife of the American serviceman who adopted Britton invited Galvan to see her baby's new home. It was then that Galvan was convinced. 'I just couldn't take her away and bring her back to poverty,' she said.

That was the last time Galvan saw Britton. Until Friday. Since then, they both searched for each other. Britton off and on; Galvan more recently after seeing a *Geraldo* show which discussed finding children given up for adoption ... Finally, after document requests and international computer probes, the search paid off. Last September, Galvan sent a letter to Britton, who lives in Georgia. Eight days later, contact was made."

Geborener Deutscher, Summer 1994: "The USA Meets Germany: Too Many Years Apart ... There was a little girl whose life began in June 1957 in Stuttgart, Germany, when she was adopted by a loving U.S. military couple, although she was actually born on June 29,1955 and known as Lieselotte Inge Bemhardt for her first two years.

'For as long as I can remember, I have struggled with the question of 'Who am I?' For most of my life, I searched for the sense of belonging ... On August 5, 1992, I received the news I was looking for, although not exactly as I had dreamed or hoped. I learned that my mother had died in Germany 7 years prior (8/9/85), but that I had a brother remaining in Stuttgart, Germany named Wolfgang Bemhardt.'"

Los Angeles Times, 7/14/92: "A Need to Know: Better Access to Holocaust Data May Help Ed Haven Learn His Mother's Fate ... Palm Desert—Bronislava Rechtszafen had a plan. After bribing a guard so she and her son could escape the Warsaw Ghetto in 1942, she moved into an apartment in the city. There, she made an agreement with a neighbor.

Whenever she and her son left the apartment, she would walk on one side of the street and the neighbor would accompany the boy on the other. Rechtszafen hoped that it the Nazis captured her, the ruse would protect her blond, Aryan-looking son. The strategy worked. On one of their walks, Nazis seized the dark-haired Jewish woman but ignored 9-year-old Edward.

Today, Ed Haven can't remember much about his mother's disappearance. 'I just know that all of a sudden she was gone,' he says. But for 50 years, Haven has wondered what happened to the woman he remembers only as being tall and gentle . . . Now, Haven may find out. The National Archives has begun microfilming and cataloguing names of 300,000 to 500,000 Holocaust victims from records of transport, medical experiments, death camps and forced labor camps.

The records were opened to the public in 1973, but cataloguing makes them 'more accessible,' says U.S. Archivist Don W. Wilson. News of the project has increased requests from relatives who have never known the fate of their loved ones, the American Red Cross says.

The Los Angeles Chapter of the Red Cross has received about 140 calls since the project was announced two months ago. About 106 people made requests all of last year, a spokesman said. Nationwide, the Red Cross has received about 2,000 requests, double the normal rate . . . The Red Cross will send Haven's request to the War Victims Tracing and Information Center in Baltimore, MD., which will forward it to the Central Tracing Agency in Arolsen, Germany. The process will probably take one to three years. Usually, about 50 of such searches are successful, a Red Cross spokesman says.

Los Angeles Times, 6/19/93: "Holocaust Survivors Reunited at Last... Friendship: 'He saved my life and I saved his, says one pair separated since 1945 . . . Nearly fifty years ago, suffering from typhoid fever and walking miles between Nazi concentration camps, George Donnenberg got some help from a friend named Walter Berger.

We were walking from one camp to another and Walter was holding me up under my arm, otherwise they would have shot me,' Donnenberg said. 'If you couldn't walk, they shot you.'

Donnenberg and Berger locked arms again Friday for the first time since 1945 in an equally emotional moment... About six months ago, he said, he met a man in Brooklyn who knew that Donnenberg was living in the Los Angeles area and was in the camera business. Three months later, Donnenberg received a phone call in his Thousand Oaks photo shop ... The two hope to take a trip to Europe together, tracing the remnants of all the camps where they were imprisoned."

The Ottawa Citizen, 5/24/91: "Former E. German Rulers Made Foes Give Up Children . .. Berlin—The Communist rulers of the former East Germany forced some of their political foes to give up their children, Berlin officials said Thursday.

Authorities said they had documented eight cases so far but expected to find evidence of more ... 'It is now known that the state was acting as a kidnapper,' said Thomas Krueger, chief of the city's youth and family department... She speculates that the forced separations were stopped in the early 1980s after word of the program was leaked to western news media ... The Communists ruled East Germany for 40 years before their downfall in 1989."

Los Angeles Times, 2/16/92, page A7: "East German Hospital Reportedly Used to Drown Tiniest Newborns ... Hamburg, Germany—Some premature babies born at a hospital in former East Germany were drowned and officially listed as 'abortions,' a news magazine reported Saturday ... A midwife who had worked at Erfurt's Women's Hospital in the 1960s and returned to work there in 1982 was quoted as saying she had often witnessed the drowning of weak, underweight babies in buckets of water. When she found the practices still in use in 1982, he complained to the hospital director."

Los Angeles Times, 11/20/92, page A5: "Legal Wrangling Continues Over Secretive German Colony ... Santiago, Chile—In January, 1991, the Chilean government tried to solve an embarrassing problem, one with international implications, through a legal maneuver: It decreed that Colonia Dignidad, a controversial colony of Germans in Chile, no longer existed as a legal entity ... The Supreme Court ruled recently that the government decree against the colony was unconstitutional. The government, however, insists that Dignidad has never been dedicated to the purpose for which it was founded—to help Chilean orphans—and says it will continue its legal battle against the community.

Legal complications are not new to Paul Schafer, Dignidad's founder and leader. When he came to Chile in 1961 and founded the community on a farm near the southern town of Parral, Schafer was wanted in Germany on charges of sexually abusing minors.

Schaefer, who had led a breakaway Baptist sect in West Germany, brought with him dozens of adults and children when he set up the new community in Chile. The population of Colonia Dignidad (Dignity Colony) eventually grew to 250 Germans.

Ghana

Registrar of Births and Deaths
Central Registry Office
Ministry of Local Government
PO Box M270
Accra, Ghana

Registrar of Marriages
Registrar General's Department
POBox 118
Accra, Ghana

A system for registration began in 1888 in Accra and Christianborg and was expanded to other principal towns in 1912; however, registration for the entire nation did not begin until 1965. Births are on file from 1912 and deaths from 1888.

When writing, include two International Postal Reply Coupons, available at your local post office.

The Family History Library of The Church of Jesus Christ of Latter-day Saints in Salt Lake City, Utah has microfilmed many of the original and published vital records and church registers of Ghana. For further details on their holdings, please consult your nearest Family History Center.

Gibraltar

Registrar General
Registry of Births, Deaths and Marriages
277 Main Street
Gibraltar
(011)(350)7-2289

For Divorce Records:

Registrar
Supreme Court of Gibraltar
277 Main Street
Gibraltar

The Registrar has birth records from October 3, 1848, stillbirth records from November 24, 1951, marriage records from April 10, 1862, and death records from September 1, 1859. Registration was not compulsory for births until January 20, 1887, for marriages until July 17, 1902, and for deaths until January 1, 1869.

Current vital registration is considered to be more than 90 percent complete. The Supreme Court has divorce records on file from November 6, 1890.

Payment must be made by certified check payable to "Gibraltar Government Account."

Greece

Department of Civil Registry
Stadiou 27 / Dragatsamiou 2. Klasthmonos Sq.
101 83 Athens, Greece

Vital registration started in 1924. Current registration is considered to be complete. The Division of Citizenship of the Ministry of the Interior (14 Euripidou St., Athens 150 59, Greece) directs the work of the local registrars.

Grenada

Registrar General's Office
Ministry of Health
Church Street
St. George's, Grenada
West Indies
(809) 440-2030

The Registrar General has records from January 1, 1866. Current vital registration is considered to be complete. The local churches also have their own records.

When writing, include two International Postal Reply Coupons, available at your local post office.

The Family History Library of The Church of Jesus Christ of Latter-day Saints in Salt Lake City, Utah has microfilmed many of the original and published vital records and church registers of Grenada. For further details on their holdings, please consult your nearest Family History Center.

Guatemala

Director, Registro Civil - Municipalidad de Guatemala
21 Calle 7-77 Zona 1
Guatemala City, Guatemala

Vital registration began January 1, 1877, and is recorded in the Office of Civil Registration in each town. Current vital registration is considered to be complete.

On July 20, 2008 *NBC Dateline* ("To Catch A Baby Broker") exposed the kidnappings and fraudulent, black market adoptions of Guatemalan children by unknowing American families via Guatemalan Baby Brokers, "facilitators" and the "jaloras" (baby finders who work for facilitators). Before 2008, adoptions were handled privately for profit, not by the Guatemalan government. Since 2008, Guatemala's government took over, eliminating private adoption in an effort to clean up corruption. Americans For Open Records (AmFOR.net) takes the position that adoption in the U.S. is a multi-billion dollar industry that, like any other business, relies on "supply and demand." Were it not for would-be adopters creating the "demand" for adoptable children worldwide (instead of Legal Guardianships that require more accountability than adoption) there would not be such corruption in the process of creating the "supply" of children with a price on their heads.

Guinea

Chef de Statistisques de la Population
BP 3495
Cankry, Guinea

Guinea-Bissau

Direction Generale de l'Identificacion et du Registre Civile
Ministerio de Justice - Caxa Postal
Bissau, Guinea-Bissau

Vital Registration began in 1976 and is not complete

Guyana

Registrar, General Register Office
Ministry of Home Affairs
GPO Building - Robb Station
Georgetown, Guyana

Registration in Guyana began in 1880 and is not complete. The National Library also has records.; contact them at PO Box 10240, Georgetown, Guyana.

Haiti

Service National de ;'Inspecion et de Control de le'etat Civil
Ministre de le Justice
Port au Prince, Haiti
www.anhhaiti.org

Registration began in 1880 and is not complete. Haiti-born adoptees currently being trafficked by baby brokers for adoptions in the United States, Canada and France will have a difficult time when they begin searching for answers to *"Who am I?"* and *"Are my parents looking for me?"* On January 7, 2010, a 7.0 earthquake destroyed Port au Prince, killing an estimated 200,000 inhabitants and leaving [at least] tens of thousands of children assumed orphaned, in addition to 380,000 pre-earthquake orphans (estimated by UNICEF). In the midst of the chaos, while survivors searched the rubble for missing parents and children, American would-be adopters, the Catholic Church, international adoption agencies, and independent adoption facilitators applied pressure on the Haiti government to airlift alleged orphans before confirming whether the parents and relatives are still alive. The first 500 or so alleged orphans were airlifted to the U.S. [according to the U.S. State Department] and 900 children were in process of being adopted from Haiti and placed in U.S. homes. According to the *Toronto Star* (in "First Haitian Children Arrive Today" by Allen Woods, 1-24-10), "In all, 154 Haitian children were approved for fast track adoption process, agreed to by Canadian and Haitian governments. Officials suspect Officials suspect many alleged orphans are being illegally spirited out of their homeland by childless couples and organized traffickers [including sexual predators]. It is known that 53 children were airlifted to Pittsburgh (*ABC World News*, 1-19-10): Catholic leaders pushed both Haiti and U.S. governments to airlift an *unknown number* of children to South Miami. Others were taken by Baptists groups to Idaho and to Austrian-based SOS Villages

Honduras

Archive Nacional de Honduras

6a Avenida 408

Tegucigalpa, Honduras

Registration began January 1,1881. The National Library also has records. Contact them at 6a Avenida Salvador Menieta, Tegucigalpa.

Los Angeles Times Magazine, 12/16/90: "The Baby Trade . . . Every 40 hours last year, an American arrived in Honduras to adopt a child. Sometimes the babies came from women who decided they couldn't afford to take care of another child. Sometimes the babies were stolen or purchased cheaply for what amounts to resale. In every case, the adopting parents face the question whether theirs is an act of charity or exploitation ...'It was like we were going baby shopping. She couldn't speak English. and I couldn't speak Spanish. I tried to tell her I would always love the child'... Last year, Americans unable or unwilling to adopt at home brought back to the United States about 8,000 children from 25 nations. Overwhelmingly it is developing countries like Honduras that supply the children. In 1989, Asian countries, led by South Korea, supplied about 5,000; a few hundred came from Africa and the poorer European nations, and the rest—about 2,600 children—from Latin America. Every 40 hours an American adopted a child in Honduras We're like one family formed at the root by necessity.

'... Adoption Department doesn't have the personnel, funds or mandate to thoroughly investigate where the children come from. 'That responsibility rests with the lawyers. Ours begins only when the child enters the adoption process' ... Of dozens of white adopters I have interviewed in three years. almost all said they would consider adopting a Latino child abroad before a black child at home John, an adoptive parent, wants to meet the mother. to see what she looks like, to ask her what there may be in the family. He is an orphan himself, and he has faced unanswered questions all his life.

Hungary

Civil Registration Office

(Town). Hungary

Vital records are on file from 1895. The National Archives also has records; contact Magyar Orszagos Leveltar, Becsi kapu ter 4, Budapest 1 H-1250; Tel. (011)(36)(1) 156-5811.

SEARCH RESOURCES

Mrs. K Benedek	Mme. K. Nemeth-Bokor
Senior Legal Counsellor	Director Adjoint, Ministere de la Justice
Dept. of International Law	Counsellor Superieur
Ministry of Justice	Budaapest
Budapest	Hungary
Hungary	

Dear AmFOR:... "Thank you very much for the wide variety of the articles on the issue of adoption in the USA and your organization. I inquired about the women you have mentioned in your letter who participated in Abduction/Adoption Conference three years ago. It's not surprising that there is no input from the Hungarian counterpart at these meetings because the system is unregulated in some questions As a matter of fact, my dissertation is about this issue to which I'm trying to collect written materials from different sources. If it is suitable and possible for you to have my dissertation translated into English I would be glad to send on e copy when it is completed in 1996.

I'd like to mention some of the problems that are typical in the Hungarian system:

- there's no act of child protection or any kind of standards according to adoption
- the system of adoption by foreigners is not regulated, there is no state guarantee
- rights of biological parents are ignored absolutely
- professional social work is completely missing in this field, because the training of social workers started only five years ago
- the network of foster parents is not organized adequately
- decision-making depends on individual preferences, monitoring doesn't function
- the black market exists, etc. ...

Sincerely, FISZTER E., Budapest, Hungary."

[Copied to AmFOR] "Dear Michelle . . . The information I'm going to share with you is all the non-identifying material that's in our record. Some of it may raise more questions than it answers. I hope that it will have meaning for you. I know that you'll find it interesting and perhaps important . . . Your birthparents were born in Hungary and emigrated to the United States and probably owing to the political unrest in Hungary. They were married in the United States when your mother was 18 years old and your birthfather was 25 and their family already on the way. Your mother, who professed the Catholic faith, completed 8th grade. Your father seemed undecided whether to be Protestant or Catholic. He was employed as an electronics technician, and by the time you were born, was in his third year of college, working toward a degree in business administration . . . When you were born your birthmother was 29 years old and had had nine pregnancies. There were three boys, 11, 8 and 4 years of age, and two girls, 10 and 6 years old. There had also been one stillborn child and two miscarriages. Your father to school so that one day their life would be easier. They were first known to this agency when their fifth child was expected. The many pressures of sustaining an adequate family life within their limited resources had begun to weigh heavily upon them. They planned to place this child for adoption, but decided not to. With a sixth child on the way, their desperation was overwhelming. They saw no alternative at that point but to plan adoption, thereby rescuing all of the children from a severely limited future. The decision was deeply painful for your parents, but they felt that this time they must not falter, that they must remain steadfast. Immediately after you were born your mother had a tubal ligation. She and your father signed relinquishments on February 14, 1968, their last contact with this agency. They asked for a letter telling them about the placement and some non-identifying background information about your new family. You were taken from the hospital to your foster home on January 25, 1968. You were placed with the Fields on March 1, 1968, and the adoption was final on April 11, 1969. And that's the beginning of your story.

If you wish to talk about this material again, or if you have any questions in the future, please feel free to call or write to me ... Best wishes, Very sincerely ... SYLVIA KAHN, Adoption Worker, County of Los Angeles, Dept. of Children's Services."

Iceland

The National Registry of Iceland
Norgartunia 24
150 Reykjavik, Iceland
(011) (354) 569-2950
www.thejodskra.is/en

The National Registry has records on all residents of Iceland from 1953. They maintain these records as part of a national identity system. Prior to this time, records were kept by the local, usually Lutheran, church. These church registers go back to 1785. The current vital registration is considered to be complete.

The Family History Library of The Church of Jesus Christ of Latter-day Saints in Salt Lake City, Utah has microfilmed many of the original and published vital records and church registers of Iceland. For further details on their holdings, please consult your nearest Family History Center.

India

Chief Registrar of Births, Deaths and Marriages
(Capital City; State, Union or Territory), India

Records began in the mid-1800s for Europeans. The Christian Marriage Act took effect in 1872, the Parsee in 1936, and the Hindu in 1955. The Bengal births and Deaths Registration Act took effect in 1873 and the Births, Deaths, and Marriages Registration Act in 1886.

> *Los Angeles Times*, 2/9/92, page A 12: "Researchers Find Widespread Infanticide of Girls in India . . . Chicago—In what is purported to be the first documentary evidence of the extent of infanticide in India, U.S. researchers reported Saturday that 72 of all deaths of infant girls in a rural southern India region were the result of such murders.
>
> Speaking at an American Assn. for the Advancement of Science meeting; the researchers said one in every 10 female births in rural areas of Tamil Nadu state ended in infanticide; and they suspect that a much higher percentage of infanticides actually occurred. The slaying of female babies occurred because males are considered to have higher value to families, in part because they are better able to support parents in their old age.
>
> The study sheds new light on previous reports that the Indian subcontinent and China have as many as 60 million fewer women than would normally be expected.
>
> *Dear AmFOR:*... "I am currently a senior at Allegheny College and am interested in a summer internship with your organization. I learned of Americans for Open Records while researching public interest jobs regarding human rights.
>
> Recently in India, my concern with human rights violations was fueled by daily exposure to the shocking abuses that many were forced to endure. As a volunteer at both Mother Theresa's Home for the Very Sick and Dying and at two orphanages, I became acutely aware of the transitory nature of my assistance ... It is my desire now to advocate human rights through an educational medium, such as those promoted by Americans for Open Records . . . Sincerely, AUDREY B-S., Meadville, PA."

Indonesia

Burgerlijke Stand
(Town), Indonesia

Records began in 1815. All Indonesians in Jakarta were registered in 1929. Births and deaths are with the Minister of Internal Affairs and in each town on individual forms called triplikats. Marriages and divorces are filed with the denomination and the vital registration office, and in the Indonesian Department of Religious Affairs.

Iran

Civil Registration Organization
Ministry of the Interior
Eman Khomaini Street
Central Building No. 184
Teheran, Iran 11374

ID cards have been required for Iranian men since 1918; and now, every Iranian is issued an ID card. Marriage and divorce records are kept by the Notarial Office and Court of Justice.

Iraq

Director of Vital and Health Statistics
Ministry of Health
Alwiyah, Baghdad, Iraq

Records began in 1947. Marriages are recorded by the religious denomination, and divorces are kept by the court that issued the decree.

During the Wars in Iraq and Afghanistan, from 2003 through 2009 an estimated 1.6-million Afghani civilians were displaced to neighboring countries, along with nearly 100,000 Iraqis fleeing to Syria and Jordan *each month*. As of 2010, the number of civilian casualties in Afghanistan is estimated to be over 100,000 while the number of civilian casualties in Iraq is still highly disputed. The number of actual war orphans in these countries is unknown. There is no adoption law in these Muslim countries, only guardianship; an unknown number of Iraqi and Afghani children have been smuggled to unknown destinations (Wikipedia.com).

Ireland, (Republic of)

General Register Office (GRO) sland)
Convent Road
Roscommon
Co. Roscommon, Ireland
(011) (353) (0) 90 6632900
www.groireland.ie/

AOPTION RECORDS:
Adoption Board (An Bord Uchtala)
Shelbourne House
Shebourne Road
Dublin, Ireland
www.adoptionboard.ie

The Registror General has records from January 1, 1864. Vital registration is considered to be complete. (For Northern Ireland see "United Kingdom—Ireland.")

The Family History Library of The Church of Jesus Christ of Latter-day Saints in Salt Lake City, Utah has microfilmed many of the original and published vital records and church registers of Ireland. For further details on their holdings, consult your nearest Family History Center.

SEARCH RESOURCES:

Adoption Search-Support
Anne O'Connor
An Bord Uchtala-Adoption Board
Shelbourne House, Shelbourne Rd.
Ballsbridge, Dublin 4 - Ireland.

The Irish Genealogical Research
Society (So. Ireland)
Glenholme, High Oakum Rd.
Mansfield Notts England
United Kingdom

O'Mahoney Records Society
Ardnalee
Putland Rd.
Bray County Wicklow
Republic of Ireland

The Butler Society
Kilkenny Castle
Kilkenny County Kilkenny
Republic of Ireland

Dear AmFOR:... "I seek lineage information about my great-grandmother . . . Mary Costello, born in 1841 in County Mayo, Ireland... married John Corbett in 1865... departed Ireland about 1869 for New Jersey to join John. They moved to Newburgh, New York where they lived out their lives with more children than I know. Any source of information concerning family she left behind would be most gratefully received. Thank you ... Sincerely, MARY M., Westbrook, CT, USA"

Los Angeles Times, 11/28/96, Front Page: "Ireland's 'Orphans' Search for Their Past... 2,000... infants were quietly shipped to the United States between 1949 and 1972 . . . Irish adoptees are demanding answers... paternity involving priests..." Contact the Barnardos Adoption Advice Center, Christchurch Square, Dublin 8, Republic of Ireland. (Phone: 011-353-1-454-6388).

Israel

Registrar
Immigration Service and Population Registration
Ministry of the Interior
PO Box 2420
Jerusalem, Israel

For marriage records, write to the Rabbinate in the town where the event took place.

SEARCH RESOURCES
Central Archives, Jewish History
Box 1149
Jerusalem
Israel

> *Omaha World-Herald*, 2/23/94: "Russia Suspects Children Illegally Smuggled to Israel... Jerusalem—Russia is investigating whether children from the former Soviet Union are being smuggled to Israel for illegal adoptions, a children's rights group said. Yitzhak Kadman, chairman of the National Council for the Child, said a Russian diplomat asked him last week for help regarding the disappearances of hundreds of children from orphanages and hospitals since the collapse of the Soviet Union ... Israel is a rife target for illegal child trafficking because there are no laws regulating overseas adoptions, officials said ... so many couples don't know they are often being handed forged documents ... in Kfar Saba, near Tel Aviv, a Russian immigrant doctor was fined the equivalent of $6,000 for selling three Russian babies to Israeli couples for $20,000 apiece ... An increasing number of foreigners, particularly those from the United States and Western Europe, have traveled to Russia in search of orphans since the breakup of the Soviet union at the end of 1991 ... Abuses such as bribery, child-selling and falsifying medical certificates have emerged in the past two years.

Italy

Stato Civile
(Town), Italy

Vital records are on file for most areas from the early 1800s, but more are available from 1870. For birth records, contact the State Archives or parish priest.

SEARCH RESOURCES

Adoption - Genealogy Searches

Alberta Sorenson
Family Search Services
PO Box 3315
Walnut Creek, CA 94598
DickandErnie57@aol.com

Genealogy, Italy

Carolyn B. Ugolini
1011 E. 11780 South
Sandy, UT 84094, USA

Institute Araldiico Genealogico
Conte Guelfi Camjani
Via Torta - 14
Firenze, Italy

Genealogy, Rome, N. Italy

Giovanni Tata
510 East 3950 North
Provo, UT 84604, USA

Geborner Deutscher, Spring 1991: "Search Help Offered for Italian-Born, American Adoptees ... Between 1950 and 1970. over 3,700 Italian-born 'orphans' were admitted to the United States and adopted by American parents. These children are all now adults, ranging in age from 20 to 40, and many may already have felt the basic, human desire to know more about their heritage, but were deterred from pursing that desire for want of knowing where to turn for help with a foreign search.

John Campitelli of Los Angeles, California, and Diana Smithson of Albuquerque, New Mexico, are two such adoptees who have decided to undertake the arduous task of searching for their parents ... If you are seeking a reunion with your parents or a child surrendered to adoption, or merely wish to obtain information about searching in Italy, then we would like to invite you to write (see "Search Resources" above).

Los Angeles Times, 2/14/92: "Honoring His Father ... In writing 'Unto the Sons,' Gay Talese Finds Keys to Understanding His Heritage ... New York—At 600, Gay Talese has finally decided to understand—but not forgive—his immigrant father. Like so many stories of fathers and sons, this one is about guilt and a grudge.

Developing a sense of history, of where you came from, can explain so many things'. .. 'The Kingdom and the Power' digs into his Italian ancestry to answer a nagging question: How did his father, a 16-year-old tailor's apprentice from Calabria, come to ply his trade in a New Jersey resort town?

Talese's exhaustive look at the roots of Italian-American immigration reaches back into antiquity and European history before focusing on the drama of his father's 1920 arrival at Ellis Island in New York, the port of entry for millions of would-be Americans. After 10 years of patient digging, he has filled 633 pages with military history, sociology and ruminations on the meaning of leaving one's native land.

It's a hugely relevant theme, 500 years after Columbus, and Talese suggests that the stories of Italian-Americans mirror other cultures as well. Most Americans are from somewhere else, he says, and even the most long-buried loyalties can erupt when a nerve is struck. To complete 'Unto the Sons,' he spent years in Italy compiling the biographies of obscure family members. He rummaged through diaries, dusted off archival records and interviewed hundreds to find the truth that, he says, 'has most deeply affected my life.'

Driven by his own demons and the belief that Mafia stereotypes still cloud Italian-Americans, Talese has endeavored to retell a familiar story—this time free from melodrama and Hollywood endings. As in previous works, he focuses on ordinary people and how they affected history.

What better place to start than his father? ... Talese suggests that a 'village' mentality' explains all. Although immigrants from Sicily and other regions may travel thousands of miles from their homes, they retain a strong sense of place and ethnic pride ... Like many first-generation Italian-Americans, Talese carries the inner village with him at all times. If skeptics need more proof, he adds, they should look no farther than New York Gov. Mario Cuomo, whose ancestors also hail from southern Italy.

'He [Cuomo] chooses to remain close to his area of familiarity, which in this case happens to be Albany,' says Talese. 'He doesn't stay away from home very much, and his closest adviser is his son, talking about family connections. His wife is Sicilian. This man, I suggest no less than me, has a village mentality'... There's an old Southern Italian saying: 'Never educate your children beyond yourself.' But Joseph Tales, for all his stubborn, conservative ways, insisted that his son get a college education and venture out into the world."

Dear AmFOR:... I am looking into my Italian family heritage, background history. names, family tree, genealogy. Anything at all that you can help me with or any information on how to go about finding out about my family name, genealogy with origins in Calabria, Italy.".

Myself: Maria Morelli	Father:	Louis P. Morelli
Born: Pittsburgh, PA	Born: :	Calabria, Italy
DOB: 7/24/59	Grandfather:	Clementine Morelh

Thank you very much, MARIA ESTES (MORELLI), Brookings, OR."

Ivory Coast

Registrar
Ministries of Interior and Justice
Abidjan 01. Ivory Coast

Registration began in 1933 for French citizens, expanded in 1950 to include some residents, and in 1964 opened to the entire nation. Current registration is not complete.

Jamaica

Registrar General's Office
Twickenham Park
Spanish Town   (876) 579-7845
St. Catherine, Jamaica   www.rgl.gov.jm/

Vital registration began January 1, 1878.

Japan

Director General
Civil Affairs Bureau, Second Division
Ministry of Justice
1-1-1 Kasumigaseki, Chiyoda-ku
Tokyo 100, Japan
(011)(81)(3) 3580-4111

Japan instituted the system of KOSEKI or family registers on February 1, 1872. Current registration is considered to be complete. Japan also requires each resident to have a national identification card. Both of these systems are administered by the Ministry of Justice.

The Family History Library of The Church of Jesus Christ of Latter-day Saints in Salt Lake City, Utah has microfilmed many of the original and published vital records and church registers of Japan. For further details on their holdings, please consult your nearest Family History Center.

> *Los Angeles Times*, 2/15/92, page D-l: "Views From the Camps ... Contrasting Images of WWII Internment ... Internees lost their houses and farms, their livelihoods and their freedom, and were transported from their homes to inhospitable, often primitive camps in the middle of nowhere. Nobody was formally charged with any crime, and two-thirds of the people interned were native-born Americans. At the same time that thousands of Japanese-Americans were serving in the war, their parents and families were being shunted into the internment camps."

> *Los Angeles Times*, 7/21/92, page A17: "Japanese Seek U.S. Surrogate Mothers ... Infertile Japanese couples are hiring Asian-American women to bear their children, paying as much as $45,000, a lawyer who arranges the surrogate mother deals said. 'We're dealing with a substantial number of Japanese couples that are coming to this country to have children,' said Noel Keane, a lawyer who heads the Infertility Center of New York. Keane, whose center also have offices in Indianapolis and Larkspur, California, said most of the Japanese seeking surrogates prefer Asian-Americans because in Japan, children of mixed blood may be looked upon with disdain."

Jordan

Registrar
Department of Civil Status
Ministry of the Interior
PO Box 2740
Amman, Jordan

Vital registration began in 1926 and is considered to be complete for births and about 60 percent for deaths.

Kazakhstan

Russian-American Genealogical Archival Service (RAGAS)
PO Box 236
Glen Echo, Maryland 20812
USA
(202) 501-5206

Office of Registration of Civil Events (ZAGS)
287 Bwizakov Street
Almaty, Republic of Kazakhstan

By an agreement between the United States National Archives Volunteer Association and the Archives of Russia Society, RAGAS receives and processes requests for vital records in some of the former Soviet republics. Although at this time RAGAS is able to deal mainly with Russia, Belarus, and Ukraine they might be able to help you with your inquiries regarding for Kazakhstan. There is a charge per document with a shipping fee per document. The service also is available at an hourly rate. (See "Russia" for application forms.)

The National Library also has records; contact Kazakhskaia Biblioteka, ul. Abaia 14,480013 Alma-Ata, Kazakhstan; Tel.(011)(7)(327)696-586.

Kenya

Department of Civil Registration
Office of the President
PO Box 49179
Nairobi, Kenya

Although church registers were kept from colonial times, modem vital registration for Europeans did not begin until 1904. Registration was expanded to include Asians in 1906 and the entire population by 1971. Currently, registration is not considered to be complete. When writing, please include two International Postal Reply Coupons, available at your local post office. The Registrar will accept an international bank draft payable in U.S. dollars.

Kenya is divided into districts; the original birth and death certificates are kept at the District Registry. Duplicates are sent to the Central Registry.

The Family History Library of The Church of Jesus Christ of Latter-day Saints in Salt Lake City, Utah has microfilmed many of the original and published vital records and church registers of Kenya and Africa. For further details on their holdings, please consult your nearest Family History Center.

Kiribati

Registrar General of Births, Deaths and Marriages
Civil Registration Office
PO Box 75
Bairiki, Tarawa, Kiribati

Civil registration began in the late 19th century. Records are also available at The National Archives and Library. Write to the following address for information: PO Box 6, Bairiki, Tarawa, Kiribati; Tel. (011)(686)21-337; FAX (011)(686)28-222.

Korea - North

Police Department
(Town), North Korea

Korea has maintained national population registers from the time of the United Silla Kingdom (668-935 A.D.). In 1896, a law on population registration was issued that required the registers to be updated annually. Currently, individuals register and update their family listings with the local police department.

Korea - South

Director General
Bureau of Registry
Ministry of Court Admission
37, Sosomoon-dong, Chung-ku
Seoul, 110-310, Korea

or to:
Registrar
Ministry of Home Affairs
(Town of current residence), Korea

Korea has maintained national population registers from the time of the United Silla Kingdom (668-935 A.D.). In 1896, a law on population registration was issued that required the registers to be updated annually.

Currently, individuals may register and update their family listings at either the Ministry of Home Affairs' office in the town where they now live or at the Ministry of Court Administration's offices in the family's recognized "hometown" or "ancestral home.'" This dual registration system means that both registers need to be searched.

There are about 250,000 Korean Americans and Koreans living in Los Angeles and Orange Counties. The first wave of Korean immigration occurred from 1895 to the 1930's, bringing about 9,000 laborers, "picture brides", students, and political exiles to this country. The second and larger wave began about 1970. Immigration peaked in 1987, when 36,000 Koreans entered the U.S., but has declined to about 15,000 a year, due in large part to the booming South Korean economy.

SEARCH RESOURCES:

Jo Rankin
Association of Korean Adoptees (A.K.A.)
San Diego, CA 92138, USA
jorankin@juno.com

Korean Adoptee Network
874 Philip Court
El Dorado, CA 95762, USA
CAANet@aol.ocm

Mihee-Natalie Lemoine
Korean Overseas Adoptees (KOA)
K. PO Box 1964
Seoul, Korea 110-619
chonihee@hotmail.com

Dear AmFOR:... "'Korea, The Unknown War,' by Halliday & Cummings. Penguin Books, 1988, page 38, children stolen from Korean Communist villagers by a joint U.S./ROK force, waiting transport to the special POW camp for children shown on page 175. Page 168, children killed by the U.S. Army rather than allow North Korean forces to recover them. Survivors were brought to the U.S. for adoption ... These activities exist because the U.S. State Department and Immigration/Naturalization Service, with knowledge and approval of every President since WWII, encourage U.S. citizens to adopt foreign children stolen for that express purpose. Note Congressional proposals to subsidize such adoptions ... Sincerely, EUGENE AUSTIN, Tilden, NE."

TIME magazine, 10/9/89, page 89: Living ... "One couple I know adopted twins through a lawyer,'says Pierce. "After several weeks, the couple found that the twins were deaf. They had paid the lawyer $25,000. Did they sue? No. By the time they had found out, they had become too fond of the twins to jeopardize their future ... Experts insist the secrecy that once surrounded adoption was a cure for which there was no disease ... With fewer kids coming from South Korea, parents are looking elsewhere, (says) Los Angeles author and adoption consultant Reuben Pannor. Too many adoptive couples leave the mother high and dry. They change phone numbers, move away or otherwise discourage further contact. Until an adoption is finalized, the birthmother is treated royally and seductively,' he says. 'Then the contact is brutally broken off."

Saginaw News (Michigan), 2/24/91: "Foreign Adoption Sours; Risk Is Not Uncommon . . . Grand Rapids—When Noreen and Tim Bosma met the 3-1/2 year-old Korean boy at the airport five years ago, they immediately fell in love with him. They knew he had rickets—a nutritional disease, and knew he had been found wandering along on the streets of Taegue, a note with his name and birth date pinned to his shirt. But what the Grand Rapids couple didn't know was that adopting the child would disrupt their marriage, expose their children to physical and possible sexual abuse, and drain them emotionally and financially . . . After much soul-searching, they did what they had once thought was unthinkable: They gave up the child, legally terminating their parental rights.

Dear AmFOR: ... "I was adopted at the age of 2 in Seoul, Korea. I would like you to send me some information about how to go about searching for my 'real' parents . . . Thank you, BECKY Y-S R., Herndon, VA".

Kuwait

Department of Central Civil Registration
Ministry of Public Health
PO Box 5286
13053 Safat, Kuwait

Birth, marriage, divorce, and death records are available from 1964. A new system of national identity cards was established in 1988.

The Wall Street Journal, 6/5/92: "Man Eyes Woman, She Smiles Back; This Is a Good Date? ... Kuwait Is Bribing Its Youth To Marry and Have Babies; But Singles Don't Buy In ... Kuwait—Kuwait has kicked out most of the half-million Palestinians who lived here before the invasion, and made it tougher for some foreign workers to obtain residency permits or to bring in their wives. But the stickier side of the population equation remains unsolved: How to get Kuwaitis to reproduce with one another in a country with its feet in the West and its soul in the Koran ... At a pizza parlor on the Salmiya strip, 23-year-old Tareq Amin, the professor's brother, sulks into his Pepsi cup. He can't go home, he says, because a cousin is there—fresh bait in his mother's relentless scheme to snare him a Kuwaiti wife.

"I want to meet a girl alone. I want to get to know her. I want to talk to her face to face," Mr. Amin sighs ... Still, eugenics, or "Kuwaiti-ization," as Kuwaitis call it, is hot. The emirate recently doubled the bribe it pays Kuwaiti men to choose Kuwaiti brides, to $14,000, and raised the monthly allowance it gives Kuwaiti couples to have more children, to $167 per child... The Marriage Committee, an Islamic charity, also wants to chip in. It plans to pay Kuwaiti men $3,500 for each additional Kuwaiti wife they marry after their first. (Islamic law lets men have as many as four wives. Polygamy accounts for about 10 of Kuwaiti marriages.)... In Islam, as in Kuwait, children are the sole property and nationality of their father."

Kyrgyzstan

Russian-American Genealogical Archival Service (RAGAS)
PO Box 236
Glen Echo, Maryland 20812
USA
(202) 501-5206

Chief, Registry Office
Ministry of Justice
140 Kalima Street
Bishkek, Kyrgyzstan

By an agreement between the United States National Archives Volunteer Association and the Archives of Russia Society, RAGAS receives and processes requests for vital records in some of the former Soviet republics. Although at this time RAGAS is able to deal mainly with Russia, Belarus, and Ukraine they might be able to help you with your inquiries regarding Kyrgyzstan. There is either the flat fee or hourly rate plus $2.00 shipping fee per document. (See "Russia" for application forms.)

The National Library also has records. Contact them at Gosudarstvennaia Respublikanskaia Biblioteka, ul. Ogonbaeva 242, 720873 Bishkek, Kyrgyzstan.

Laos (Lao People's Democratic Republic)

Laos does not have an organized system of vital registration.

Latvia

Russian-American Genealogical Archival Service (RAGAS)
PO Box 236
Glen Echo, Maryland 20812
USA
(202) 501-5206

Latvian Archives of the Registry Department
Latvian Ministry of Justice
24 Kalku Street
Riga 1623, Latvia

By an agreement between the United States National Archives Volunteer Association and the Archives of Russia Society, RAGAS receives and processes requests for vital records in some of the former Soviet republics, Russia, Belarus, and Ukraine and they might be able to help you with your inquiries regarding Latvia. There is either the flat fee or hourly rate plus $2.00 shipping fee per document. (See "Russia" for application forms.)

The National Library also has records. Contact them at Kr. barona iela 14, Riga, Latvia, 226011; Tel. (011) (7) 280-951.

Lebanon

Vital Statistics Bureau
(District), Lebanon

does not have an organized system of vital registration.

Los Angeles Times, 4/15/91: "In Lebanon, Ramadan Brings New Hope For Orphans . .. Mideast: Social Welfare Institutions in Lebanon (SWI) is the largest organization of its kind in the Arab world. Established in 1971, it has 13 branches but is best known for the Islamic Orphanage in Beirut... Of the 4,000 children at the orphanage, the majority are from broken homes or have only one parent.... Children who have lost both parents are, according to Muslim law, legally under the care of the next of kin and therefore not orphans in the Western sense of the word. Orphanage Director Nahida Thahabi said Lebanon's 15-year civil war 'greatly increased the number of social cases we see.'

The 5 who have no acknowledged families whatsoever are foundlings, abandoned by their unwed mothers or rejected by parents because they are physically or mentally handicapped . .. Although Islam forbids adoption, the orphanage's concern for these foundlings and their future won them a fatwa, or religious ruling. A practice, called takefful, or guardianship, allows a childless Muslim couple to 'adopt' an abandoned child by claiming in front of a Muslim court that the child is in fact theirs.

Thousands of children have grown up in the Islamic Orphanage through the years. And every year, a reunion is held at the end of Ramadan."

240

Lesotho

Senior District Administrator
PO Box MS 174
Masera, Lesotho
(201) 797-5533

Vital registration began in 1880.

Liberia

Bureau of Health and Vital Statistics
Ministry of Health and Social Welfare
PO Bag 3762
Monrovia, Liberia

Liberia gained its independence in 1847. While the system of vital registration has been worked on for years, including a United Nations project to improve the process, the registration is not complete. Limited records are available for the past 20 years.

Los Angeles Times, "The Orphaned Children of Liberia". .. "Unresolved civil war leaves troubled African

nation with haunting problem . . . Many children in Liberia have no parents. They are orphans of war. At least

10,000 'unaccompanied' youngsters survive in Liberia, according to the International Red Cross ... The intense fighting drove as many as 1 million people—nearly half the population—into miserable refugee camps in Sierra Leone, the Ivory Coast and Guinea. The Liberians who stayed faced shortages in water, food, health care and other essentials. But the most heart-wrenching domestic problem is orphaned children... The United States is providing food, but many in Liberia—founded by freed American slaves—expect greater generosity."

Libya

Registrar
Civil Registration Section
Secretariat of Utilities
Tripoli, Libya

During the period of Italian control, vital registration was begun in urban areas. Modern vital registration began in 1968. Currently births and deaths are computerized but not complete. Marriage and divorce records are kept by the religious law courts.

Each household in Libya is required to keep a family registration booklet, which gives the vital information on each person in the family. These booklets have serial numbers and are copied and registered at the local Civil Records Office. All changes must be recorded with the government.

Liechtenstein

Amtsvorstand/Zivilstandsamt des Fürstentums Liechtenstein
St. Floringasse 3
   9490 Vaduz, Liechtenstein

The National Archives also has copies of vital records. Contact them at Liechtensteinisches Landesarchiv, 9490 Vaduz, Liechtenstein; Tel. (011)(41)(75)66111. Vital records are available from 1878.

Lithuania

Russian-American Genealogical Archival Service (RAGAS)
PO Box 236
Glen Echo, Maryland 20812
USA
(202)501-5206

Civil Registry Department
K. Kailinasko 21
Lt 2600
Vilnius, Litthuania
(011) (370) 2634720

The Lithuanian National Archives has early vital records:
Centrinis Valstybinis Istorijos Archyvas
Gerosios Vilties Gatve 10
232015 Vilnius, Lithuania

By an agreement between the United States National Archives Volunteer Association and the Archives of Russia Society, RAGAS receives and processes requests for vital records in some of the former Soviet republics. Although at this time RAGAS is able to deal mainly with Russia, Belarus, and Ukraine they might be able to help you with your inquiries regarding Lithuania. There is a shipping fee per document. The service also is available at an hourly rate. (See "Russia" for application forms.)

The National Library also has records. Contact them at Lietuvos nacionaline Martyno Mazvydo Bibliotek, Gedimino pr. 51, 2635 Vilnius, Lithuania; Tel. (011)(7)629-023; FAX (011)(7) 627-129.

Luxembourg

Registrars of the Civil Status
(Town), Luxembourg

Send your requests for events before 1979 to:
Luxembourg State Archives
BP6
L-2010 Luxembourg, Luxembourg
(011) (352) 478-6661

Vital records are generally on file from 1795.

SEARCH RESOURCES
Association Luxembourgeoise de
Genealogie et Heraldique
c/o Mr. George Kiessel
Santegaas
L-5401 Bech-Kleinmacher
Grand Duchy of Luxembourg

Macedonia

Civil Registration Office
(Town), Macedonia

Vital records are on file from 1946. Records before that were kept by the local churches.

Madagascar

Direction du Controle de la Tutelle des Collectivites
Ministere de l'Interieur
Antanarivo, Madagascar

Vital Registration began July, 1878. Currently, registration is estimated 80 of births, 50 of deaths.

Malawi

Registrar General
Ministry of Justice
PO Box 100
Blantyre, Malawi

The Registrar General has birth and death records from 1886, marriage records from 1903, and divorce records from 1905. These early records are mostly from Europeans living in Malawi.

Malaysia

Registrar-General of Births and deaths
National Registration Department
No. 20, Persiaran Perdana
Presint 2
62551 W.P.
Putrajaya, Malaysia
www.jpn.gov.my/jpn_english.html

Records begin in the 1800s. The National Registration Department, established in 1948 and computerized in 1990, requires everyone 12 and older to carry a national ID. Marriage and divorce records depend on religion and where event occurred.

Maldives

For Birth and Death Records write to:

Ministry of Health, Ameenee Magu
Male 20379, Republic of Maldives
www.health.gov.nv

For Marriage and Divorce Records write to:

Registrar
Ministry of Justice
Male, Maldives

Registration began in the 1500s, but the modern system did not begin until the 1950s.

Mali

Direction Nationale de l/Administration Territoriale
Ministere d'Etat Chanrge de l'Administration
Territoriale et de la Securite Interieur
Bamako, Mali

Vital registration began in 1938 but is not considered to be complete.

Malta

Send your requests to:

Director
Public Registry
Ministry of Justice and Parliamentary Affairs
197 Merchants Street
Valletta, Malta
(011)(356)225-291

The Public Registry has records from 1863. No separate divorce records are kept. Divorce information is annotated onto the marriage record. Current vital registration is considered to be complete.

The Family History Library of The Church of Jesus Christ of Latter-day Saints in Salt Lake City, Utah has microfilmed original and published records of Malta. For further details on their holdings, please consult your nearest Family History Center.

Marshall Islands

Registrar's Office
PO Box 546
Majuro, Marshall Islands 96960

Records begin November 12, 1952, with some earlier records at the Hawaii State Bureau of Vital Statistics

(see "Hawaii"). Personal checks are not accepted.

Information is also available from the Alele Museum of the Marshall Islands, PO Box 629, Majuro, Marshall Islands 98960; Tel. (011)(692) 625-3550; FAX (011)(692) 625-3226.

Mauritania

Secretariat l'Etat Civil Postes et Telecommunications
BP 195
Nouakchott, Maritania

Vital registration began in 1933 for French citizens as well as all residents within 15 miles of the registration centers.

Mauritius

Registrar General
Civil Status Office
Prime Minister's Office
Emmanuel Anquetil Building, 7th Level
Port Louis, Mauritius   www.gov.mu/portal/site/civilstatussite

The Registrar General has birth and death records from 1539, marriage records from 1579, and divorce records from 1793. The law of April, 1667, formally established registration there. Mauritius is one of the few countries in Sub-Saharan Africa where the modern registration of births and deaths is considered to be complete.

Mexico

Oficina del Registro Civil
(Town, State), Mexico

or:

Director General
Direccion General del Registro Nacional
de Poblacion e Identificacion Personal
AlbanilesNo. 18
Col. Ampliacion Penitenciaria
C.P. 15350
Mexico D.F., Mexico
(011)(52)(5) 789-5331 or 789-4543; FAX (011)(52)(5) 789-5250

Records begin in 1859. Mexico currently requires each resident to have a national identity card. This office also registers all births, marriages, divorces, and deaths. The registration is considered 90 percent complete for births, 72 percent for deaths.

The National Archives of Mexico has many of the early records. Contact them at Archive General de la Nacion, Eduardo Molina y Albaniles 15350, Mexico D.F., Mexico. For further information, see their published services. Archives Estatales Y Municiplaes de Mexico.

The Family History Library of The Church of Jesus Christ of Latter-day Saints in Salt Lake City, Utah has microfilmed original and published records of Mexico. For further details on their holdings, please consult your nearest Family History Center.

Los Angeles Times, 1/28/91: "Missing Children: A Mexico Connection . . . Borders: Couple say son is among those abducted to Mexico. Officials there say youngsters are (then) taken to U.S. in illegal adoptions . . . Most of the more than 9,400 children classified as missing or abducted in the United States are believed to be somewhere in (Mexico). The Abeytas, however, think their child is one of a small but growing number who end up in Mexico, where the children are harder to trace—and to return if found.

Likewise, Mexican officials say, an unknown number of abducted Mexican children are taken, legally and illegally, across the border into the United States. Of particular concern, they say, is the trafficking, or illegal adoption, of Mexican children by American couples through shady lawyers and adoption rings.

... The problem is the lack of a central information network, [which] makes it difficult to locate a child in Mexico,' says an official at the U.S. Embassy. A non-custodial parent removing a child from the custodial parent is a crime in many [U.S.] states, but in Mexico it is not a crime anywhere. That makes recovery difficult. Sometimes the U.S. Embassy may locate a child and make visits to check on his or her welfare, but it has no power to send the child back to the United States . .. Washington is urging Mexico to sign the Hague Convention of mutual support in kidnap cases, requiring signatories to return found children to their country of origin . . . California and Mexico share information on 'missing persons' cases . . . Sometimes they are the offspring of poor, uneducated teenagers who are paid : or coerced into giving up their children. U.S. officials acknowledge that some Americans will pay a lot of money to adopt a Mexican baby or to obtain a birth certificate that says they are the natural parents. 'It is easy to get a baby in Mexico to get 'legitimate' documents that reflect non-facts,' the U.S. Embassy official says. 'It is very difficult to work a legal adoption and to get a U.S. visa when the legal adoption is done. You put all of this together and you get what the Mexicans call 'child trafficking.'"

Los Angeles Times, 8/6/92, page E-l: "Still Together—As Father Wished ... in 1986, Chris and Sharon Bisgaard read a Times story about Constance Towers Gavin, wife of the then-ambassador to Mexico. She was seeking homes for children orphaned by the Mexico city quake. The Bisgaards contacted Gavin, who matched them with the Torres Mendoza girls. Gavin had made a promise to the girls' father, who was terminally ill and had lost his wife in the quake. He had two wishes: that his daughters stay together and that an American family adopt them ... They don't want the girls to forget their father's love and concern for their future. Says Sharon: 'It was never our intention to absorb the girls and have them forget where they came from.'"

Dear AmFOR: ... "I am now 19 years old and I feel like my life can't go on. I feel as though I have a missing link in my life ... My real mom is Mexican and my dad is Black ... I have been searching in my heart for years but I have been searching in the natural for a couple of months ... Sincerely. LA MANTA S. B., West Covina, CA."

Dear AmFOR:. . . "I'm working with Acapulco and Mexico City TV programs about child psychology, sociology, false child abuse laws, and have been teaching anthropology and child psychology at the State University ... With the students of the University, I have put together a large exposition of murals saying: 'Adoption and foster care are not the solution, they are just the 'escape-valve' of a capitalist-absolutist-repressive system ... we worked day and night, over a lot of AmFOR news clips, photographic and graphic material; we also wrote about Sealed Records! The public was shocked . . . Many professionals, who came to the Exposition, congratulated me and told me that before they didn't know the problem at all ... Write me soon . . . Love, DR. M. JOHNSON LOMBARDI, Acapulco, Mexico."

Micronesia-Federated States of Micronesia

Clerk of Courts
State of Losrae
Leiu, Losrae, ECI 96944

State of Courts
State of Truk, FSM
Moen, Truk, ECI 96942

Clerk of Courts
State of Yap, FSM
Colonia, Yap WCI 96943

Clerk of Courts
State of Pohnpei, FSM
PO Box 1449
Kolonia, Pohnpei, ECI 96491

Records begin November 12, 1952, with some earlier records at the Hawaii State Bureau of Vital Statistics (see "Hawaii"). Personal checks are not accepted, and there is a typing charge of 100 every 100 words.

The Family History Library of the Church of Jesus Christ of the Latter-Day Saints in Salt Lake City, Utah, has microfilmed original and published records of Micronesia and the Pacific. For further details, consult your nearest Family History Center.

Moldava

Archiva Nationala a Republicii Moldovei rvice (RAGAS)
(Moldovan National Archives)
Str. Gheorgihe Asaci. Nr. 67-B
Republica Moldova
(011) 373-22-73-56-27

By an agreement between the United States National Archives Volunteer Association and the Archives of Russia Society, RAGAS receives and processes requests for vital records in some of the former Soviet republics. Although at this time RAGAS is able to deal mainly with Russia, Belarus, and Ukraine they might be able to help you with your inquiries regarding Moldava. There is a $2.00 shipping fee per document. The service also is available at an hourly rate.

The National Library of Moldova also has records. Contact them at Biblioteca Nationala al Republic Moldova, ul 31 August 78a. 2776112 Chisinau, Moldova; Tel. (011)(7)(042) 22-1475.

Monaco

Mairie de Monaco
Bureau of the Civil Status
Monte Carlo, Monaco

Monaco began vital registration in 1793. Current vital registration is considered to be complete.

Montenegro

Civil Registration Office
(Town), Montenegro

Records begin in 1946. The National Library (Nardona Biblioteka, P.O. Box 57, 81250 Cetinje, Montenegro) also has records.

Montserrat

Register General's Office
High Court Registry
Government Headquarters
Brades, Montserrat
(011) (604) 4491-2129

Records begin February 12, 1862. Your request should state in which of the three districts the event occurred. Registration is complete.

Morocco

Chef, Division d'Etat Civil
Ministere de l'Interieur
Rabat, Morocco

Records begin in 1915 for the French and foreign population. In 1931 registration was extended to all Moroccans. With independence in 1956, registration became formalized for the entire country. Morocco began a major effort in 1987 to computerize all of its records. Marriages and divorces are kept by the denomination of court of record.

Mozambique

Direccao National dos Registros e Notoriados
Av. Vladimir Lenine n. 565, 2 Andar
C.P. 2157
Maputo, Mozambique

Vital registration is not considered to be complete.

Myanmar (Burma)

Office of Divisional Health Director
Yangon Health Division
No 520. West Race Course Road
Yongon (Rangoon). Myanmar   Registration is complete.

Namibia

Subdivsion of Birth. Deaths and Marriages
Ministry of Home Affairs - Cohen Building
Kasino Street / Private Mail Bag 13200
Windhoek. Namibia

Nauru

Registrar General
Republic of Nauru
Nauru Island

Nauru's current vital registration is considered to be complete. Nauru uses the Australian dollar as currency.

Nepal

Registrar, Civil Registration. Vital Statistics Office
Ministry of Home Affairs
Singha Durba, Katmandu. Nepal

Although there are records from the colonial period, vital registration has been nearly comprehensive in the past ten years; marriages since 1983, divorces since 1985.

The Netherlands

Burgerlijke Stand
(Town), The Netherlands

Current records are kept by the town Burgerlijke Stand. Older records are usually deposited in the Provincial or Municipal Archives. Vital records are on file from 1811. Current vital registration is considered to be complete.

The Royal Library, Netherlands National Library, also has records. Contact them at Koninklijke Bibliotheek, Postbus 90497, 2509 LK, The Hague; Tel. (011)(31)(70)314-0911; FAX (011)(31)(70)314-0450.

The Family History Library of The Church of Jesus Christ of Latter-day Saints in Salt Lake City, Utah has microfilmed original and published records of The Netherlands. For further details on their holdings, please consult your nearest Family History Center.

SEARCH RESOURCES

Central Bureau Voor Genealogie
Box 1755
2502 He Hague
The Netherlands

Roots
Postbus 125, 2000 AC
Haarlem Holland
The Netherlands

To Locate Fathers:

Association of Liberation Children
Secretariat Postbus 3207
5203 De S Hertogenbosch
The Netherlands

Dear AmFOR:... "I need any help you can give me. I'm 20 years old and was adopted at birth, but I want
to find my real mother. She placed me up for adoption in California, but it is quite possible
she is back in her homeland, The Netherlands. What can be done to find my mother? . . . Sincerely,
MELANIEA. RUARK, Springfield, MO."

New Zealand

Births, Deaths and Marriages
Level 3. Boulcott House   PO Box 16-526
47 Boulcott Street
Wellington, New Zealand
(011) (64) (4) 474-8150
www.bdm.govt.nz

The Registrar General has birth and death records from January 1, 1848, and marriage records from 1854. Current vital
registration is considered to be complete. The fee plus postage costs may be paid in your local currency to the New
Zealand Consulate, which will then forward your application to the Registrar General. Application forms sent directly to
the Registrar General must be accompanied by an international bank draft payable in New Zealand dollars.

The National Archives of New Zealand also has records. Contact them at PO Box 6148, Te Aro, Wellington; Tel. (011)(64)
485-6109; FAX (011)(64) 482-8789.

The Family History Library of The Church of Jesus Christ of Latter-day Saints in Salt Lake City, Utah has microfilmed
original and published records of New Zealand. For further details on their holdings, please consult your nearest Family
History Center.

Original birth certificate is available to adult adoptees. Other adoption issues have been raised in Parliament in 2003, while
the head of Adoptions, an advocate for children, is accused of being "anti-adoption" in the *Sunday Star-Times*, 5/03.

SEARCH RESOURCES

Adoption Search - Support

Mary Iwanek
Dept. Child, Youth, Family Srvcs.
PO Box 2620
Wellington, New Zealand
mary.iwanek001@Wcyf.govt.nz

JosieHendry
POBo 38681
Howick, Auckland
New Zealand

Margaret Humphreys/Child Migrant
   Trust
28-A Musters Rd.
West Bridgford, Nottingham NG2 7PL
United Kingdom

Kees Sprengers
N.Z. Adoption Educ. & Healing
PO Box 11466
Wellington, New Zealand
kees@adoptionrefonn.org.nz

Genealogy

New Zealand Founders Society
Box 2457
New Zealand

New Zealand Society
of Genealogists
Box 8795
Auckland 3
New Zealand

New Zealand Family History Society
Box 130301
Armagh Christchurch
New Zealand

Armorial and Genealogical Institute
of New Zealand
Box 13 - 301
Armagh Christchurch
New Zealand

KinQuest's Reunion Report, April 1993: "New Zealand's 'Open Records' Experience Reveals That Extraordinary Measures Are Not Necessary to Protect [Birth]parents and Adoptees From Each Other ... In 1985, the New Zealand Parliament opened previously closed adoption records to adult adoptees and their birthparents. The new law permitted any adult adoptee to apply to the Department for a copy of the adoptee's original birth certificate and any identifying information in the files. Similarly, parents of surrendered children age 20 or older were newly permitted to apply to the Department for the adopted name of their child. If the department found a parent 'veto' on file, identifying information about that parent would not be disclosed to the searching adoptee. In the absence of veto on file, the birth certificate and identifying information would be forwarded to a 'counselor' who, after a mandatory meeting with the adoptee, was permitted to disclose the identifying information to the parent. After several years of experience, counselors began to draw certain conclusions about the effectiveness of the law, particularly regarding the mandatory counseling provision, the 'veto' provision, and the 'adoptee consent' provision. In response to their conclusions, the laws were updated to reflect the newly collected data."

Dear AmFOR:... "Thanks for your letter. It sounds very familiar to me what you are going through. I am glad that we have passed that hurdle. However, once records are open, it is just the beginning. I discovered there are always more things to do, like working for adoption change altogether (doing away with it altogether would be lovely). Then there is the whole issue of new birth technology and surrogacy to tackle. We are just starting that, as well as trying to stop intercountry adoption, etc., etc., etc. So brace yourself. Then there is all the search and reunion support to do. Like you, I believe this should be free of charge and our support groups do just that. There are a few sharks who are starting to cash in on this. I am sorry that I won't be able to meet, but perhaps another time. I can't see myself extending my travels to Palm Springs. Thanks for the offer of accommodation. I will be meeting with Sharon Kaplan at her agency and will visit Jean Paton for a few days prior to Chicago . . . Best wishes, MARY I., Petone, New Zealand."

Nicaragua

Direccion General del Registro
Ministerio de Justicia
Managua, Nicaragua

Although church registers date from the 1500s, vital registration in Nicaragua did not begin until 1867.

Niger

Directeur de l'Etat Civil et de la Population
Ministere de l'Interieur
B.P. 622
Niamey, Niger

Registration began in 1933 for French citizens and expanded in 1950 to include everyone within 15 miles of the registration centers.

Nigeria

State Ministry of Health
Old Secretaria
Ikeja, Lagos, Nigeria

Lagos, Nigeria

Records begin in 1867 for Lagos Island, and expand in 1901 to include Ebute, Metta, and the island of Iddo. By 1903 records include all of Southern Nigeria. The Laws of 1918 and 1979 have helped, but the registration is still not complete.

Niue

Births and Deaths:

Registrar General's Office
Department of Administration
PO Box 67
Alofi, Niue

Marriages and Divorces:

Registrar of Marriages
Department of Justice
Alofi, Niue

Requests may be sent to a New Zealand Consulate. Requests sent directly to Niue must be paid in New Zealand currency. Records are on file from 1845.

The National Archives of Niue also has records. Contact them at PO Box 77, Alofi, Niue; Tel. (011)(683)4019; FAX (011)(683)4010.

Northern Marina Islands

Vital Statistics Office
Division of Public Health
PO Box 500409
Saipan, Northern Mariana Islands 96950
(670) 236-8717

or, Flokerregister
Local Population Register
(Town), Norway

Birth and death records are available from 1945, marriage records from 1954. Some records are at the Hawaii State Bureau of Vital Statistics. Money orders or cashiers checks should be payable to CNMI Treasury.

Norway

Pastor
Lutheran Church
(Town), Norway

Records begin in the 1600s. Divorces are kept by the County Commissioner or local court. The Lutheran pastor in each town holds all vital records. Norway uses a national personal identification numbering system administered by the Central Population Register Central Bureau of Statistics (PO Box 8131 Dep. 0033 Oslo 1, Norway). This computerized office maintains vital records on all persons in Norway as of November 1, 1960, or later. These records are not available to the public.

SEARCH RESOURCE
Norwegian Emigration Center
Bergjelandsgate 30
N-4012 Stavenger
Norway

The Norwegian Emigration Center, established to develop contact among Norwegians around the world, is a nonprofit government-sponsored organization that does research for a fee. It has an excellent collection of "Bygdeboker", local history books which tell about farms and people living from 1500-1900, microfilms of church records, national census and emigrant registers from ports of Oslo (Kristiana), Bergen, Trondheim, and Kristiansand. When making a search request, include as much information as you know about your ancestor—name, date of birth and place, date of emigration and place, etc. The Center charges a nominal fee. They prefer money orders. Response is usually within one to two months.

Oman

Director General of Health Affairs, Ministry of Health
¡PO Box 803, PC 112, Muscat, Oman

The Omani Heritage Library (PO Box 668, Muscat, Oman) can also be of assistance.

Pakistan

Registry of Birth and Deaths tion
(Municipality), Pakistan
7 Civil Center, Near GPO
Islamabad, Pakistan

or, NADRA (new system established in Y-2000)
State Bank of Pakistan Building
Shahrah-e-Janhuriat G-5/2
Islamabad, Pakistan

Before 1948 Pakistan was part of India; pre-1947 records will be Indian. In 1948, most Karachi records were burned.

Palau

Chief Clerk of Supreme Courts
PO Box 2248
Koror, Palau 96940
(011)(680) 488-2461, FAX (011)(680) 488-1597

The Court has records from November 12, 1952. Some records are at the Hawaii State Bureau of Vital Statistics (see "Hawaii"). Personal checks not accepted.

Panama

(see also U.S. Possessions: Panama Canal Zone)

Direccion General del Registro Civil
Betania, La Gloria, Calle 1 No. 195
A.P. 5281
Panama 5, Republic of Panama

(5-7) 207-8053
www.tribunal-electoral.gob.pa/resistro-civil/index.html

Church registers date from the 1500s; modern vital registration began in 1917. The birth registration is considered to be complete. Make money orders payable to Tesoro Nacional. Registro Civil requires two International Postal Reply Coupons, available at your local post office.

The Family History Library of The Church of Jesus Christ of Latter-day Saints in Salt Lake City, Utah has microfilmed original and published records of Panama. For further details on their holdings, please consult your nearest Family History Center.

Papua New Guinea

Registrar General's Office
PO Box 470
Waigani. N.C.D. 131. Papua New Guinea
(675) 327-1732

Divorces to:

Registrar of the Court
National Court of Justice
Port Moresby, Papua New Guinea

Vital registration began in British New Guinea in 1892; but with a limited registration organization, registration of vital records is very incomplete.

Information is also available from The National Archives and Public Records Service of Papua New Guinea, PO Box 1089, Boroki, National Capital District, Papua New Guinea; Tel. (011)(675) 254-4332; FAX (011)(675) 254-4648.

Paraguay

Director
Oficina de Registro del Estado Civil de las Personas
Ministerio de Justicia y Trabajo
Hen-cra 875
Asuncion, Paraguay

Church registers date from the 1500s; registration began September 26, 1880.

> *Los Angeles Times*, 3/21/93 . . . For 18 months, my wife Elizabeth and I had gathered reams of documents, discussed our lives with a social worker and waited anxiously. Bleary-eyed after taking the overnight flight from Miami to Asuncion, Paraguay, we stood in the doorway of our small hotel room waiting for a local lawyer to appear with an 8-month-old baby—our adopted son, Daniel...
> We now took a close, frightening look at Daniel. He resembled not so much a baby as a rag doll. Under layers of clothes and swaddling we found a tiny, pale body. Massive brown eyes blankly, rarely blinking. A bald spot spread across the back of his head. Above his forehead, where cranial bones had not yet formed, a quarter-sized piece of flesh sagged, indicating dehydration of his brain tissue. We lay our son carefully on the bed and realized he could not move. With great effort, Daniel managed to roll his head from side to side. He remained eerily silent—no gurgles, no coos, nothing.
>
> Cases such as ours are not unusual. International adoptions have increased greatly over the past few decades. A decline in the number of domestic infants available for adoption—both black and white—has fueled this trend. These days, virtually all domestic adoptions of healthy white babies are for those who can afford private lawyers rather than public adoption agencies, and usually cost at least $20,000. International adoption, with costs usually ranging from $5,000 to $12,000 proves appealing to prospective parents willing to raise a child of a different race or ethnic background.
>
> International adoptions overwhelmingly involve children of poverty who often have undisclosed health problems. These ailments, such as malnutrition, ear infections and intestinal viruses, usually vanish with proper nutrition and medical care ... A child's current physical condition typically poses fewer problems to adopters than the lack of medical histories for the child and his or her parents . . .Adopters often do not know if their child is prone to a particular genetic condition or susceptible to certain disease ..."

253

Peru

Registro Civil
(Town), Peru

Direccion General de Registro Civil
Institute Nacional de Estadistica e Informatica
Presidencia del Consejo de Ministros
Av. 28 de Julio 1056
Lima 1, Peru
(011)(51)(14) 334-223, FAX (011)(51)(14)333-159

Cost for a Birth, Marriage, or Death Certificate.......................... S 6.00

Civil registration began in 1852, and modern vital registration in Peru began in 1936. Adoptions, legitimizations, and recognition of illegitimate children are recorded in the birth registers. Divorces are recorded in the marriage registers.

Summary of "Street Stories", *CBS* Telecast with Ed Bradley, 7/9/92 ... "In the United States, there is one baby for every 20 couples wishing to adopt.

In Peru, there are 60,000 'orphans' due to civil war and poverty.

It is not unusual for agency and baby broker attorney fees to total $30,000—of which the [birth]mother is paid $300 (in the example cited in the program).

Private adoptions account for 90 of Peruvian adoptions by Americans, facilitated by American agencies and Peruvian lawyers."

Los Angeles Times: Padre Jose—Priest Founds New Family Unit for Children of Peru's Poverty ...
Lurin, Peru—Padre Jose, otherwise known as Father Joe Walijewski of La Crosse, WI, is a celibate priest and happy father to 55 children.

Thanks to Pope John Paul II, who saluted Walijewski's three decades in the barrios of Latin America with a $50,000 gift. Walijewski presides over a family of orphans from the wreckage of Peru's wars and social upheavals.

He cares for his family with love and humor ... For the last three years, Walijeski has been at work on another dream: turning unwanted orphans into a community and teaching them to be leaders capable of changing their country ... Most are orphans; a few are abandoned. One girl was sexually abused by her father and sent out as a child prostitute.

"She always looked down," Walijewski said. 'She wouldn't look you in the face. Today, she is proud of herself and comfortable'... Under the law, parents may reclaim children years after abandoning them, and this discourages adoption, the priest said ... He said he hopes that the children, imbued with a commitment to help others as they were helped, will devote themselves to rural development in Peru when they reach age 18 and set off on their own lives. He envisions young people from the home going back to the highlands, where warfare drove so many thousands to Lima, to revitalize the countryside ... Always ready with an apt aphorism, he said: 'If you give someone a fish, you give a meal. But if you teach children how to fish, you feed them for their whole life' ... Peru is the birthplace of liberation theology, the controversial doctrine of social involvement by the church, in some cases using Marxist theory to explain the causes of poverty ... He said what is needed is a 'government that is really interested in its people.'

"The best thing you can give in life is yourself," he said.

254

Philippines

Civil Registrar General
National Statistics Office
Archives Management Section
PO Box 779 - Stai Mesa
Manilla. Phillipines

or to the:
Local Civil Registrar
Municipal Building
(Town), Philippines

(011)(63)(61-3645 to 54)   www.census.gov.ph/data/civilreg/index.htm

Vital registration began in 1898—although church registers begin much earlier—and is now centrally administered by the Civil Registrar. Birth, marriage, divorce, and death records from 1945 are on file at the central office. Earlier records are on file with the local civil registrars.

The National Library and Archives has microfilmed original and published vital records and church registers of the Philippines. Contact them at T.M. Kalaw Street, Manila; Tel. (Oil) (63) (2) 491-114.

The Family History Library of The Church of Jesus Christ of Latter-day Saints in Salt Lake City, Utah has microfilmed original and published records of The Philippines. For further details, please consult your nearest Family History Center.

GOVERNMENT AUTHORITY IN CHARGE OF ADOPTIONS
Sylvia P. Montes
Ministry of Social Services and Development
389 San Rafael St., Sampaloc, Metro Manila
Philippines
(632)741-0785

Adoption in the Philippines is regarded as one of the best means to restore the family life of deprived children. Adoptions most commonly occur within the extended family; the concept of foreign, unrelated adoption is of relatively recent origin and still evolving.

> *Los Angeles Times*, 2/10/91: "For a New Father, Philippine Adoption is Ordeal by Jet Lag . . . New York—I left New York at noon on Monday, alone. I returned from the Philippines 77-1/2 dizzying hours later—with my new 10-month-old daughter . . . When my wife, Donna, and I decided to adopt a second child two years ago, we assumed the process would be the same as it was for our son, Alexander. We would fill out the paperwork and someone would escort the baby to New York.
>
> But the rules had changed. Our adoption agency. Wide Horizons for Children in Waltham, Mass., said the government in the Philippines wanted parents to pick up their children. They spoke of the enriching experience of seeing your child's homeland and meeting the caretakers in the orphanage ... We turned to foreign adoption because we couldn't afford an estimated $15,000 to $20,000 for a domestic adoption. Wide Horizons charged according to a family's ability to pay ... Her mother was not married and could not afford a child."
>
> *The Desert Sun*, 5/11/93: "Separated at Birth, Twins Reunite After 16 Years . . . Ventura—When Amy O'Lena awoke after giving birth in the Philippines 16 years ago, she thought she had just delivered a girl, whom she named Mary Joy. Nobody ever told her she had actually given birth to identical twins.
>
> Only recently was O'Lena, now living in Ventura (CA), told by a sister that the other daughter had been taken from her. This weekend, Mary Ann Lopez of the Philippines was reunited with twin Mary Joy O'Lena at Los Angeles International Airport.
>
> 'It's a miracle,' said their mom. "I did not know about her at all, and all of a sudden there was another.' Mary Joy said she had always had an eerie feeling—reportedly shared by many separated twins—of the other's existence. 'It was sort of strange at first, but I've got to get used to it,' she said. 'It kind of just filled up this empty spot. I had a sense there was something missing. I'm at peace now."

Mary Ann said she was told at age 7 that she had a sister and mother who lived elsewhere. 'I feel really happy over here because what I really love is here,' she said. When Amy O'Lena gave birth at 14, her family secretly gave one of the twins—Mary Ann—to the doctor and his wife. Amy kept the other baby, married, had a son and daughter and moved to Ventura."

Dear AmFOR: . . . "'Stolen Childhood,' Discovery Channel documentary about children in Subic Bay, Philippines prostitutes: There was a segment about agents trying to get the women to give up babies and another about kidnapping 10-1/2 year olds.

There are several U.S. military mass kidnappings. The biggest were the re-kidnap of Nazi Lebensborn kids and Operation Babylift. Studied silence from law enforcement suggests similar activity. It's worth a look . . . Sincerely, EUGENE AUSTIN, Tilden, NE."

Dear AmFOR:... "The name of your organization came to me as a reference from Carol Gastavsan, of the Adoptive Parents for Open Records Inc., as an agency that might be able to help me. She spoke highly of you, and your skills as a search consultant. As you can probably guess, I am in search of a natural parent, my father Elliott Stuart Kanter ... I was born on April 15, 1965 on dark Air Base in the Philippines. My father was an employee of the State Department officially, but my family also knew that he worked for the C.I.A. in communications. Later that same year in Laos, my mother Binnie, died at the age of twenty-four. I was five months old at the time, and my father sent me and my tow and a half year old sister to live with my maternal grandparents (the Rosenbergs) until he could sort everything out. He was twenty-three years old when all this happened, and I imagine quite confused and distraught. I know very little about what happened during this time, but I do know that in July of 1967, he consented to me and my sister's adoption to my mother's parents. I realize that due to his past involvement with the C.I.A. that finding him might be very difficult. I have contacted both the State Department and the personnel office for the C.I.A. in Washington in request for any information they might be able to provide ... If you believe you can be any assistance, or know of any agencies that may be able to help me please feel free to contact me day or night. . . Sincerely yours, RODGER R."

Dear AmFOR:... "I am an American, looking for my father. It was all told to me by my Mom, Marina Maningo, a Filipino national, that my father was a U.S. serviceman, George Mitchell, serving on the U.S.S. Enterprise around 1971-1972, at Subic Naval Base in the Philippines. Like other fatherless Amerasians in Philippines, I have gone through life with many unanswered questions. Despite of her sad love life, my mom has never loved any other man ... I feel a little bit empty for not ever seeing my father in my life. It is not about what my father owes me but rather a simple wish of a girl wanting to see her father. I hope you can help me ... Sincerely yours, MICHELLE M., Fountain Valley, CA."

Poland

Urzad Stanu Cywilnego
[Civil Registration Office]
(Town), Poland

Help Is also available from the National Archives:
Naczelnik Wydziahu Wspolpracy z Zagranica
Archiwow Pantswowych
ul. Diuga 6
Skrytka Pocztowa 1005
00-950 Warsaw, Poland

There is no central office for vital records in Poland. To obtain copies of birth, marriage, and death certificates, write to the Civil Registration District Office (Urzad Stanu Cywilnego) in the town where the event occurred. Vital records are on file from 1809. Current vital registration is considered to be complete. Many older vital records are on deposit at the National Archives.

The Family History Library of The Church of Jesus Christ of Latter-day Saints in Salt Lake City, Utah has microfilmed original and published records of Poland. For further details on their holdings, please consult your nearest Family History Center.

SEARCH RESOURCES

Government Authority in Charge of Adoption	U.S. Visa Issuing Post	Polish Genealogy Society of California
Stoleczny Osrodek Metki i Dziecka	AmEmbassy Warsaw c/o AmCon Gen	PO Box 713
Warszawa, Poland	APO NY 09757	Midway CA 92655-0714
ul. Czamieckiego 10	Tel. 283041-9	USA

ADOPTION LAW SUMMARY

Two kinds of adoptions exist:

1. Adoption by Proxy. The adopters engage a legal representative in Poland to select a child. The appropriate Embassy conducts an investigation as to appropriate whether the child qualifies as an orphan under the 1-600 Petition. After completion of Polish legal requirements by legal representative and issuance of a valid Polish passport, the embassy will, upon request, issue the orphan visa.

2. Selection of a child by the adoptive parents. After selecting a child in Poland, the parents initiate a background investigation by the Embassy. Legal adoptions under Polish law have to be completed. The actual Visa is issued by the INS office in Vienna, Austria. All Polish adoptions are handled through the Mother and Child Centers, located in Warsaw and the capital cities of each province in Poland.

The Economist, "Boom in the Baby Trade", 1/16/88, v. 306 n. 2, page 44; Abstract 1: "This is a description of the international boom in the baby trade, with a focus on Romania and Poland. In both countries it is hard currency that gets the babies out. In Romania the whole process can take up to a year. Even when there had been a presumed agreed-upon original price, middlemen—lawyers and 'contacts' in Bucharest—charge an additional $100-$200 for every extra piece of paper which has to be signed. And there are many papers: birth certificates, police registration, health and emigration papers. After paying for bribes and travel, a couple adopting a baby can face a total bill of up to $6,000. Conditions in Poland are better for would-be adopters. Orphanages there are also bursting at the seams as economic shortages make it hard to bring up children."

Quest: The Newsletter of KinQuest, Inc., 6/92: "Baby Market Thriving in Poland . . . The New York Times recently reported that traffic in Poland's blond blue-eyed babies is booming. Evidence can be found in a striking rise in the number of residence visas and passports granted to Polish infants and toddlers.

Polish officials report that many of the adoptions are legal but that the black market is growing. Young, unwed mothers are pressed to sign away their rights to their children by maternity home staff members, as well as attorneys involved in the adoptions. These homes and attorneys then receive up to tens of thousands of dollars from eager adoptive couples.

Some of the cases are linked directly to the Roman Catholic Church. Reporting on the church connection, Nie, a weekly journal, chronicled the story of one young woman who surrendered her child to an American couple after being pressed to do so by nuns caring for her in a church home for single mothers. The young mother reported that the Mother Superior routinely received up to $25,000 for boy children and $15,000 for girl children . . . While young women are being pressured to surrender their children to the church, prospective adoptive parents are pressured to make increasingly large payments to the Church. In one particular case, a Western couple spent more than $30,000 in a seven-month adoption process on flights to Poland, lawyer's fees and a 'donation' to a local priest. The "donation," which was near $10,000 disappointed the priest, who reportedly asked: "Is that all?"

Portugal

Los Registros, Civiles
(Town), Portugal

Vital records are on file from 1911. Some local registrars have records from 1832; most older records have been transferred to the District Archives.

The Direccao-Geral dos Registos e do Notariado (Ministry of Justice, Av. Almirante Reis 101, 197 Lisboa Codex, Portugal) directs the work of the local registrars.

ADOPTION LAW SUMMARY

The age limit of adoptive parents is a minimum of 25 years and a maximum of 55 years. An adoptive couple must have been married at least five years; single adopters must be at least 35 years old. The adoption agency will maintain contact with the adopters and the child. Portuguese law does not prohibit adoption by foreigners, but in practice it is not easy since waiting lists for adopters exist and Portuguese citizens are preferred. Portugal has a formal court adoption and a simple adoption. The simple adoption does not qualify a child for an orphan visa under the United States immigration laws. These must be notarized, verified, and authenticated by the Portuguese Consul.

SEARCH RESOURCES

Government Authority in Charge of Adoptions, Lisbon:
Ministerio da Justica
Direccao-Geral dos Service Tutelares de Menores
Praca do Comercio
1100 Lisboa
Portugal

Adoption Agencies:
Insituto de Familia e Accao Social
Largo do Rato
Lisbon, Portugal

The Insituto has about 200 small agencies in Portugal and is under the Ministry of Social Affairs.

Qatar

For certificates from 1959:

Registrar of Births
Ministry of Public Health
PO Box 9374
Doha, Qatar

For other requests:

Age Estimation Committee
Ministry of Public Health
Qatar

Birth records are available from 1959. Marriages are records by the denomination performing the wedding. It is the standard practice to petition the Age Estimation Committee to determine a person's age.

Romania

Civil Registration Office
(Town), Romania

Vital records are on file from 1865 and in many areas begin much earlier. Following is a chronological record of changes in Romania's adoption laws and practices:

The Economist. "Boom in the Baby Trade", 01/16/88 v. 306 n., 2, p. 44; Abstract 1: This is a description of the international boom in the baby trade, with a focus on Romania and Poland. In both countries it is hard currency that gets the babies out. In Romania the whole process can take up to a year. The delay is the result of overbearing bureaucracy and corruption. Even when there had been a presumed agreed-upon original price, Romanian middlemen—lawyers and 'contacts' in Bucharest—charge an additional $100-$200 for every extra piece of paper which has to be signed. And there are many papers: birth certificates, police registration, health and emigration papers. After paying for bribes and travel, a couple adopting a Romanian baby can face a total bill of $6,000 or more. Israelis, French, Italian and Belgian couples have been in the Romanian baby market since the early 1980s. In order to boost his country's birth rate, Mr. Ceausescu has banned all birth control and abortion, so young women are increasingly abandoning un-wanted children in orphanages. Even babies that are wanted by parents have a hard time in Romania, where it is often impossible to obtain milk, nappies and soap.

Will these poor "orphans" ever be able to return to their home country and search for information about their birth families, their heritage and their culture? Can anyone be sure that these children really are 'orphans' knowing now what we do about life in Romania under the dictatorship?

Citizen: 7/7/90 "2 Romanian Orphans Granted Visas ... Two Romanian orphans whose Canadian visas were delayed because they didn't know the difference between apples and pears have been given visas after all... Their visa application was delayed last week by Canadian authorities when they were called 'socially retarded' in an examination by a Romanian doctor ... Dr. Giles Fortin, director of immigration health for Health and Welfare Canada, said social deprivation 'makes sense for a child who has been in an orphanage for two or three years, but that by itself is not a reason for turning down the admission of someone to Canada.'"

Los Angeles Times: 7/24/90 "Wives of Beatles Lead a Crusade to Save Orphans . . . Charity: An all-star album featuring George Harrison, Ringo Starr and a relief fund aims to ease plight of abandoned children in Romania . . . many were abandoned, a large number of them with AIDS.

Harrison said that estimates of the total number of orphans range from 150,000 to 400,000 and that the conditions she saw in the orphanages were appalling. Through private donations the Appeal has already raised nearly $2 million in England, all of which, Harrison said, goes directly to the Romanian effort."

The Press-Enterprise: 1/28/91 "Romanian Baby Comes Home to Corona... The Crawfords' robust brown-eyed, brown-haired son, born Cosmin Constantin, comes from a close-knit family who simply cannot afford to keep him. He was tested for infectious diseases before leaving his country, and will be tested again shortly. Alexander's Romanian family has placed another son, 18-month-old Michael, with a Chi-cago-area family and the Crawfords plan to keep in touch . . . The Crawfords will have spent about $14,000 to adopt their new son."

Los Angeles Times, 2/7/91 "Controls Are Set Up to Halt Baby Trade . . . Previously, adoptions were supervised by district courts. But the disclosure of the baby-trade abuses in the foreign press prompted the government to set up the new regulatory body."

(AP): 4/5/91 "Romania Halts Adoptions ... The number of couples travelling to Romania to adopt chil-dren has been rising, and there are widespread reports of Westerners going to poor rural areas where parents exchange their children for cash. In some villages, poor parents speak of selling children 'by the pound."

Los Angeles Times, 5/23/91 page A-3: "Red Tape Unwrapped for Adopted Romanian Baby . . . Shirley Suffern, who thought she could complete the adoption and return home with her baby over a two-week Easter break, wound up spending nearly eight weeks in Romania. Only after Rep. Eiton Gallegly (R-Simi Valley) called Sununu did the red tape peel away ... Alyssa, the seventh child of a poor family, had been abandoned to the care of a state hospital... After completing the adoption procedures in Romanian courts and following INS directions for immigration, Shirley Suffern said she went with the baby's natural mother to take Alyssa from the hospital. 'She cried and cried when she saw how the babies were kept,' Suffern said of the natural mother. 'Alyssa was sick' . . . INS policy does not allow a baby with living parents to be taken to the United States after adoption."

USA Today: 6/20/91 "New Scrutiny Entangles U.S. Families ... 'The idea of having a baby and fattening it up like a pig (to sell) is just repugnant' ... She and dozens of other foreigners are caught in the backlash of Romania's adopt-a-baby boom. The country suspended institutional adoptions, and is modifying its laws, after allegations of black-market child trafficking surfaced.

Often, officials say, the child's birth certificate bears the names of two parents. U.S. law says that means the child is not really abandoned, required for entering the USA. Gene McNary, Immigration and Naturalization Service (INS) commissioner, says investigators have found cases of Romanian mothers who thought they were only 'loaning' their children to foreigners, expecting to get them back in 10 or 15 years to work in the fields. He also said the service has found cases of poor Romanian parents hawking their children for a 'going rate' of $1,800.

Adds assistant INS Commissioner John Schroeder: 'It's one thing to go over, adopt a child and put him through Georgetown (University). But what about the creep doing kiddie porn, or the millionaire with a son who needs a kidney? One of our jobs is to prevent abuses like this'. . . The April 14 airing of a CBS 60 Minutes segment on baby-selling in Romania... Reporter Leslie Stahl interviewed middlemen brokering baby sales, witnessed one couple trying to sell their child for $500 so they could by a VCR, and was offered two children—one for $7,500 ... Ceausescu, in an effort to boost Romania's population, banned birth control and abortion. As a result, thousands of unwanted children, many of them handicapped, were abandoned at ghastly state-run orphanages. Today, about 6,000 children remain in institutions.

'The system has been careening out of control,' says Jerry Tinker, staff aide to the Senate Judiciary subcommittee on immigration and refugees. 'There's no internationally accepted definition of abandoned children, or who is an orphan.'"

PEOPLE magazine: 8/12/91 "Homecoming ... A picture wasn't enough for this Indiana couple: They wanted the real child ... Adriana was living in an orphanage called Bucharest One in Romania's capital. Despite having been in Bucharest One almost from birth, Adriana was not an orphan. This meant that a second adoption committee had to be persuaded that their parents had truly abandoned her. According to the birthmother, her husband hadn't wanted a child and had beaten her when she refused to get an abortion. When Adriana was born handicapped, the father threatened to starve the child, so her mother turned her over to the orphanage. Since open allegations of the father's conduct might have jeopardized the mother's safety, an intermediary informed the committee secretly. The mother's only stipulations were that Adriana be adopted by a responsible religious family. Finally adoption officials relented. On May 23 Greti walked into the orphanage, and a worker handed her new daughter."

Los Angeles Time, 2/12/92 pageA5: "Romania's Experience Spurs Adoption Treaty . . . Washington— 'Boom in Overseas Adoption,' 'Baby Scam Flourishing,' 'Romania Targets Baby Trade.'"

Russia

Russian-American Genealogical Archival Service (RAGAS)
PO Box 236
Glen Echo, Maryland 20812
USA
(202) 501-5206

Bureau of Acts of Civil Status (ZAGS)
(Town), Russia

By an agreement between the United States National Archives Volunteer Association and the Archives of Russia Society, RAGAS receives and processes requests for vital records in some of the former Soviet republics. Although at this time RAGAS is able to deal mainly with Russia, Belarus, and Ukraine. There is a $2.00 shipping fee per document. The service also is available at an hourly rate. (See "Russia" for application forms.)

The Family History Library of The Church of Jesus Christ of Latter-day Saints in Salt Lake City, Utah has microfilmed published records of Russia. For further details on their holdings, please consult your nearest Family History Center.

For photocopies of the labor camp records of Jews persecuted under Stalin, the basic rate is $12.00/hour plus $1.00/page for copies. To place an order or make inquiries write: Urbana Technologies, 2011 Silver Ct. E, Urbana, IL 61801, USA.

DOCUMENTS OF CIVIL STATUS (In Russian, Acts of Civil Status) include registration of birth, death, conclusion and dissolution of marriage, adoption, the establishment of paternity and changes of name, patronymic, and surname. The law connects the beginning, modifications, or cessation of substantive legal relations with the registration of a document of civil status.

In cities and ration centers, changes of civil status were registered by the city or ration bureaus of civil registry (ZAGS) under the local Soviets and in rural localities and urban-type settlements, by rural or settlement Soviets. The registrations were done upon the application of the interested persons. In some cases, the permission of an appropriate agency is required.

Mandatory time limits have been established by the law for the registration of some civil status documents: births—no later than two months after the birth of the child.

RUSSIA HALTS ALL ADOPTIONS TO U.S..

by Megan K. Stack, in Moscow, for *Los Angeles Times* (4-16-10)

Russia has frozen all adoptions to the United States, the Foreign Ministry announced Thursday as national outrage simmered over a towheaded 7-year-old boy sent alone on a plane back to Moscow by his adoptive mother...Russia is pressing the United States to sign an agreement that would more carefully screen would-be parents and monitor the families after their return to the United States, Foreign Ministry officials have said.

"Russia believes that only an agreement which will contain effective tools for Russian and U.S. officials to monitor the living conditions of adopted Russian children will ensure that recent tragedies in the United States will not be repeated," Foreign Ministry spokesman Andrei Nesterenko said at a briefing Thursday.

U.S. officials denied that adoptions had been suspended... Russia has halted the work of World Assn. for Children and Parents, the adoption agency that paired the child with the Tennessee mother. Ever since the child turned up waiflike in a Moscow airport last week with nothing to explain himself but a letter from his adoptive mother calling him "mentally unstable," anger has boiled in Russia.

President Dmitry Medvedev told ABC News that rejecting the child was "a monstrous deed, not only immoral but also against the law." The boy is in a Moscow hospital, where doctors reportedly have found nothing aberrant in his condition. Just seven months after adopting the boy, 33-year-old nurse Torry Hansen wrote that he was violent, unstable and "psychopathic," and that she had been misled by the Russian orphanage workers who had vouched for his mental health. It is not yet clear whether Hansen will face charges... The boy known as Artyom has become something of a cause celebre in Moscow, with multiple Russian families stepping forward and offering to adopt him.

Last year, 1,586 Russian children were adopted by Americans, a number topped only by adoptions from China and Ethiopia, according to State Department figures. More than a dozen Russian children have been killed by their adoptive American parents since 1996. With each death, public outrage has swelled among Russians --

o In 2006, a woman in Manassas, VA, was sentenced to 25 years in prison after being convicted of fatally beating a 2-year old girl adopted from Siberia;

o In 2008, a Tooele, Utah, woman was sentenced to 15 years after pleading guilty to killing a Russian infant;

o In March, 2010, prosecutors in Pennsylvania met with Russian diplomats to discuss how to handle the case Of a couple accused of killing their adopted Russian son.

The Burbank private investigator who asked not be named turned to property and utility records to hunt for Baklanoffs, Bakhlanovs, Bakhlanoffs, Baklanovs and Baklys. He stuck pay dirt with the last name .. "Look at the Sept. 2 issue of Time magazine," page 52. "There's a picture of a cousin, 'Oleg,' she said. "An accompanying story identifies Oleg Baklanov as a member of the 'Gang of 8,' the so-called State Committee for the State of Emergency that led last month's unsuccessful coup against Soviet President Mikhail S. Gorbachev . . . Braun said he has prepared a detailed family tree that lists 31 Bakly family members. It has already been dispatched to the Moscow policeman."

Rainbow House International, 6/92: Adoption Program Guidelines Out-of-State Families ... We are a licensed child placement agency in New Mexico as well as a charitable, non-profit corporation. We are involved in assistance to children throughout the world, which includes the placement of children for adoption ... The children from Russia and other Eastern European countries are generally age 18 months and older. Some delays in development may be expected as the majority will have been institutionalized. One parent should be prepared to travel to process the U.S. Visa and escort the child home. Families should expect that children referred will often times have alcoholism listed in the family history. Other common diagnoses in family histories include depression, immorality and 'oligophrenia."

Los Angeles Times, 12/9/92, page A3: "From Russia With Love—Children . . . Families: The former Soviet republic has become a foreign hot spot for Americans seeking to adopt... Morgan Bates, founder and executive director of Children of Light, a Mill Valley, California-based group that helps arrange foreign adoptions, said that 'until February of this year there had probably been only 60 adoptions from Russia."

Adoptions from Russia began in June, 1991, and in recent months, 'there have probably been 60 per month,' she said. Bates, whose organization finds Russian children for nine licensed adoption agencies throughout the country, describes the situation as a 'mild frenzy'.

'The word is starting to get out, and people want to get in before it becomes another Romania,' she said . .. Bates returned with a picture of Katya, whose unwed mother had decided to give her up for adoption . . . Since May, Children of Light has arranged at least 35 adoptions nationwide, averaging four to six adoptions a month. And there is no shortage of children. Officials estimate that in Russia alone there are between 30,000 and 400,000 children living in orphanages."

Child Welfare, March-April, 1989: "Care of Children Brought Up at Boarding-Type Institutions in the U.S.S.R ... In the Union of Soviet Socialist Republics, people have always paid special attention to children. In the very first days of Soviet power, an integral system of public education was set up. Pre-school institutions were the first component. The single-labor polytechnical school of two grades (the first grade was five years and the second was four years)—free and secular schools with instruction in the mother tongue—were established for children of school age.

At that time the list of the residential childrens' institutions for orphans included children's homes of various types (children's towns, colonies, and communes) that were committed to preparing the children for socially useful labor. The number of children without homes began to drop; necessary conditions for elimination of homelessness were created by the mid-1930s .. . New children's homes and redemption and placing centers for children were set up and priority given to organizing a supply of children's institutions. A search through address bureaus for parents who had lost their children and the return of children to their families were arranged during the war years (1941-1945) and in the first postwar years... At the insistence of the Soviet Children's Fund, the government is now preparing to carry out a broad social experiment involving the setting up of children's homes for family education and upbringing. Two forms of such education are to be tested: first, children's towns with families consisting of 10-12 persons, and second, houses, cottages and multiple room flats for families with many children who would adopt orphans ..."

Rwanda

Direcion Generale des Affaires Politiques et Administratives
Ministere de l'Interieur et du Development Communal
BP446
Kigali, Rwanda

Vital registration began May 4, 1895.

> *Los Angeles Times*, 8/7/95: IN RWANDA, ORPHANED BROTHERS REUNITE . . . Africa: Loss of family in ethnic chaos darkens their gleeful meeting . . . Kigali, Rwanda—Finally, Sylvestre and Alexis could smile, whoop and jump with joy on the tear-soaked hardpan of Rwanda. Once again, they had each other. And that will have to do. At ages 13 and 10, these brothers are what remains of a family. For 18 months, they had not even this. Two of Rwanda's 100,000 lost, damaged children, they drifted separately through Central Africa's ghoulish chaos. Their nightmare can only be imagined. Or perhaps not. Maybe it is beyond the comprehension of a sane imagination to be young and endure such madness. But last week, the boys were reunited by International Red Cross relief workers in Rwanda.

St. Kitts / Nevis

Registrar General's Office
Health Department
PO Box 236
Basseterre, St. Kitts-Nevis
(869) 465-2521

The Registrar has records from St Christopher from January 1, 1859, and Nevis from August 1, 1869.

St. Lucia

Registrar General
Registry Department
Castries, St. Lucia
(758) 452-1257

The Registrar has records from January 1, 1869. Current registration is considered to be complete.

St. Vincent and the Grenadines

Registrar General's Office
Registry Department
Courthouse
Kingstown, St. Vincent and the Grenadines
(784) 457-1424

Records are available from July 1, 1874.

Samoa - Western

(See also "U.S. Possessions: American Samoa")

Registrar General
Justice Department
P.O. Box 49
Apia, Samoa
(011)(685) 22-671

Registration began in the mid-1800s. The Registrar of the Supreme Court is required to send copies of all divorces to the Registrar General.

SEARCH RESOURCES - ADOPTION ATTORNEYS
Bob Barlow
PO Box 1161
Apia, Western Samoa
David Fong
Box 210
Apia, Western Samoa

San Marino

Parish Priest
(Parish), San Marino
Vital records are available from the Roman Catholic parish churches in San Marino.

Sao Tome and Principe

Departamento do Registo Civil
Ministerio de Jusitica e Funcao Publica
C.P. 4
Sao Tome, Sao Tome and Principe

Sao Tome and Principe were under Portuguese control until independence in 1975. Vital registration is complete.

Saudi Arabia

Agncy of Civil Status
Ministry of the Interior
PO Box 11134
Riyadh, Kingdom of Saudi Arabia

Registration is considered complete.

SEARCH RESOURCE
Dharan International Genealogical Society
c/o Aramco
Box 5868
Dharan, Saudi Arabia

Dear AmFOR:. . . "My father was an Arabian Diplomat who was sent back to his country before I was born. My mother came to Buffalo, NY to give birth to me (for reasons unknown). I was born January 13, 1962, but was placed in foster care until November 1963. My adoptive parents were told that the reason it took so long for me to be adopted was because they had to locate my father in his homeland.

Your address was provided to me by the National Adoption Information Clearinghouse as a resource. Any information about your organization that will aide me in my quest would be greatly appreciated. Thank you for your assistance . . . Sincerely, Linda M., Hamburg, NY."

Senegal

Division de l'Etat Civil
Direction de la Statistique
Ministere des Finances et des Affaires
Economiques
B.P. 116
Dakar, Senegal

Vital registration of births and deaths began in 1916 for most French citizens; modem vital registration in Senegal began in 1961. Currently, the registration is not considered to be complete.

Serbia

Civil Registration Office
(Town), Serbia

Vital records are on file from 1946.

Seychelles

Chief Civil Status Officer
Division of Immigration and Civil Status
PO Box 430
Mahe, Seychelles

The Civil Status Office has records from 1902 to the present. For records from 1794 to 1902, contact the National Archives, PO Box 720, La Bastille, Mahe, Seychelles.

Seychelles is one of the few countries in Sub-Saharan Africa where the registration of births and deaths is considered to be complete.

The Family History Library of The Church of Jesus Christ of Latter-day Saints in Salt Lake City, Utah has microfilmed original and published records of Seychelles and Africa. For further details, please consult your nearest Family History Center.

Sierra Leone

Office of Chief Registrar
Births and Deaths Office
Ministry of Health
3 Wilberforce St.
Freetown, Sierra Leone

Registration began as early as 1801 in Freetown and Granville. Currently, the registration is considered to be incomplete.

The Family History Library of The Church of Jesus Christ of Latter-day Saints in Salt Lake City, Utah has microfilmed original and published records of Sierra Leone and Africa. For further details on their holdings, please consult your nearest Family History Center.

Singapore

Registry of Births and Deaths
10 Kallang Road, ICA Building
Singapore 208718
(011) (65) 6391-6100

Registrar of Marriages
7 Canning Rise
Singapore 208718
(011) (65) 6336-9987

Divorce Records:

Registrar
Supreme Court
St. Andrew's Court
Singapore 208718

Singapore has birth and death records from 1872, marriage records from 1875, and divorce records from 1937. Muslim marriage records are not filed with the Registrar but are kept by their religious leaders.

The Singapore Archives also has records. Contact them at 17-18 Lewin Terrace, Fort Canning, Singapore 0167; Tel. (011)(65)338-3954 or 337-7314.

The Family History Library of The Church of Jesus Christ of Latter-day Saints in Salt Lake City, Utah has microfilmed original and published records of Singapore. For further details on their holdings, please consult your nearest Family History Center.

Slovakia

Ministry of the Interior
Department of Archives
Krizkova 7
811 04 Braislava, Slovakia

Slovakia, formerly part of Czechoslovakia, became independent in January, 1993. The Archives charges an hourly fee of U.S. $15.00 for a search. Church records are available in the Czech Republic and Slovakia from 1785. Modern civil registration began in 1919.

Registration began in 1900 for the foreign population and expanded to the entire nation in 1927.

Slovenia

Civil Registration Office
(Town), Slovenia

Vital records are on file from 1946. Records before that were kept by the local churches.

Solomon Islands

Birth and Death Records:

Regsitrar General
PO Box 404
Honiara, Solomon Islands

Marriage and Divorce Records:

Ministry of Police and Justice
Magistrates Division
Honiara, Solomon Islands

Current vital registration is considered to be 75 percent complete. Information is also available from the Solomon Islands National Archives, Ministry of Home Affairs, PO Box 781, Honiara, Solomon Islands; Tel. (011)(677) 21-399; FAX (011)(677)21-397.

Somalia

There is currently no organized vital registration program in Somalia.

Orange County Register, 1/3/93: "Bush Visits Orphanage at Baidoa . . . Ruth Sinai (AP)—
The president smiled, waved and held out his hand to some of the children lined up in the orphanage courtyard to greet him.

The orphanage's crushing burden mirrors the burden of Baidoa itself, the place to which all roads lead in a region devastated by war, drought and famine, a place where 100 people a day were dying of starvation and disease."

South Africa

Registration Office
Department of Home Affairs
PrivateBagX114
Pretoria, 0001, Republic of South Africa
(011)(27)(123) 148-911   www.dha.gov.za/

The Registration Office has records from 1924. The Director-General of Internal Affairs can, at his discretion, approve or refuse to issue a certificate. A computer printout of the certificate will be issued unless you request an 'unabridged' certificate.

The Family History Library of The Church of Jesus Christ of Latter-day Saints in Salt Lake City, Utah has microfilmed original and published records of South Africa. For further details on their holdings, please consult your nearest Family History Center.

SEARCH RESOURCE
Genealogy Society of South Africa
Box 4839
Capetown
South Africa

Spain

Registro Civil
(Town), Spain

Registro Civil Unico
Calle Pradillo 66
Madrid 28002, Spain

or, Municipal Court (Juzgado Municipal)
(Town), Spain

Records are on file from 1870 and in some areas much earlier. The Direccion General de los Registros y de Notariado (Ministerio de Justicia, San Bernardo 62, 28071 Madrid, Spain) directs the work of the local registrars.

SEARCH RESOURCE
Institute Int. de Genealogie y Heraldica
APDO de Coreos 12079
Madrid
Spain

Sri Lanka

Registrar General of Marriages, Births and Deaths
Ministry of Home Affairs
340, R.A. De Mel Mawatha
Colombo 3, Sri Lanka

Registration began in the Dutch period and by 1867 included the entire population. Marriages are kept separately by religion. Muslims keep separate divorce records. Kandyan divorces are kept by District Registrars, and all others are kept by the District Courts. Each person obtains a national Identity card at age 18. Records are prepared at the local level and are held by the District Registrars and the Registrar General.

Sudan

Registrar, Central Bureau of Statistics
PO Box 700
Khartoum, Sudan

Vital registration only began recently and is not uniform throughout the country. The Sudan became independent in 1956.

Suriname

Registrar General
Central Bureau of Civil Registration
Ministry of Interior Affairs
Coppenamelaan 177
Paramaribo, Suriname

The Registrar is computerizing the vital records concentrating on the Marowjine, Brokopondo, and Sipaliwini districts.

Swaziland

Registrar General
Ministry of Justice
PO Box 460
Moabane, Swaziland

Registration began in 1900 for the foreign population and expanded to the entire nation in 1927.

Sweden

Records 1895-1991:
Lutheran Church Pastor, Pastorsambete
(Town), Sweden

Records after July 1, 1991:
Lokala Scattemyndighetan (Local Tax Office)
(Town), Sweden

While there is no central office for vital records, a national personal identification number has been assigned to every person living in Sweden since January 1, 1947. These numbers are administered by the National Tax Board, Department for Civil Registration and Elections, Ministry of Finance, S-17194 Solna, Sweden. The local pastor serves as the registrar of this system and of the national census. To obtain copies of birth, marriage, and death certificates, write to the pastor of the local congregation. Church registers are on file from the 1600s.

SEARCH RESOURCES

The Emigrant Institute
Box 201
S-351 04 VAXJO
Sweden

Emigrant Register of Vermland
Box 331
S-651-05 Karlstad
Sweden

Genealogiska Fomingen
Box 2029
S-103 11 Stockholm
Sweden

Landsarkivet I Hamostad
Box 161
S-592 01 Hamostad
Sweden

Landsarkivett I Osterund
Postfack 161
S-831 01 Osterund
Sweden

Landarskivet I Uppsala
Box 135
S-751 04 Uppsale
Sweden

Landsarkivet I Vadstena
Box 126
50592 Oovdstena
Sweden

Landsarkivet Visby
Box 142 S-621 00 VISBY
Sweden

Landarskivet Gotenberg
Box 3009 S-40 10 Goteberg
Sweden

Switzerland

Zivilstandsamt

(Town), Switzerland

Records date from January 1, 1876. The Office Federal de l'Etat Civil (Department of Justice, Bundesgasse 32, CH-3003 beme, Switzerland, directs the work of the local registers.

SEARCH RESOURCES

Family Research for Americans of
   Swiss Descent is offered free by:
Swiss National Tourist Office
608 Fifth Ave.
New York, NY 10020
USA

Schweizerische Gesellscahft
Feuer Familienforschung
Engelgasse65
CH 4000 Basel Schweiz
Switzerland

Societe Suisse
d'Etudes Genealogiques
Schweizerische Landsbibliotek
CH-3003 Bern Schweiz
Switzerland

Schweizerische Heraldische
Gesellschaft
Niderhofenrain31
CH-8702 Zollikan
Schweiz
Switzerland

Genealogische
Gesellschaft Zeurich
H Peyer Eichoizstrasse 19
CH-8706 Feldmelen
Schweiz
Switzerland

Geborener Deutscher, Autumn 1991: "SEARCH JOURNAL BY NANCY THOMAS ... I gave a child up for adoption in 1958— in Geneva, Switzerland. I am an American, but my parents took me to Europe to have the baby. Things were different in 1958. There was a terrible stigma attached to an illegitimate child. I named the baby Kathy Jane. I had a choice of giving her up to an American couple or a Swiss couple. I chose American parents. I had to sign the adoption papers at the American Embassy in Geneva.

I wrote to the adoption agency when Kathy was 2 years old and asked for information about her. They would only tell me that her new parents kept the name Kathy . ..

One day I pulled out the paperwork the Embassy has sent us and re-read everything ... Near the bottom of the page it said the birth was registered in Register of Births, Office of Etat Civil, Geneva (Vol. __, Page __, No. _)... All I can figure out is that someone got my letter that didn't read English, but saw the page and volume numbers and they sent back a birth certificate with her new name: Kathryn Anne Walstrom ... I called person-to-person to E.A. Walstrom asking for Kathryn. Her mother answered the phone and said, 'No, Kathy, isn't here, she's my daughter. I'll give you her phone number.' We all started to cry, my husband and son—Kathy's father and her brother . . . 'Were you born in Geneva, Switzerland on June 3, 1958?' (She said, 'Yes.') 'Does the name Kathy Jane Neuweiler sound familiar to you?' (She said, 'Yes, very familiar.')... In November, 1990, my husband and I flew to Hawaii to meet our daughter, her husband and our grandchildren. Everything went real well"

Syria

Director	General Director
General Directorate of Civil Registration	Bureau of Vital Statistics
Ministry of Interior Affairs	(Town), Syria
Fardos Street	
Damascus, Syria	

Registration began in 1923.

Tajikistan

Russian-American Genealogical Archival Service (RAGAS)	Chief, Registration Directorate
PO Box 236	Ministry of Justice
Glen Echo, Maryland 20812	1 Karabayeva Street
USA	73043 Douchanbe, Tajikistan
(202)501-5206	

By an agreement between the United States National Archives Volunteer Association and the Archives of Russia Society, RAGAS receives and processes requests for vital records in some of the former Soviet republics. Although at this time RAGAS is able to deal mainly with Russia, Belarus, and Ukraine they might be able to help you with your inquiries regarding Tajikstan. There is a shipping fee per document. The service also is available at an hourly rate. (See "Russia" for application forms.)

Tanzania

Registrar General
Ministry of Justice
Office of the Administrator General
PO Box 9183
Da E Salaam, Tanzania
(011)(255)(51)28-811

Registration began in 1917 for Europeans; it expanded to Asians in 1923 and to the major towns in 1966. The Registrar General has birth and death records from 1917, marriage and divorce records from 1921.

Thailand

Director
Administrative and Civil Registration Division
Department of Local Administration
Ministry of Interior
Nakhon Sawan Road
Bangkok 10300, Thailand

or, Nai Amphur
(District of Registration), Thailand

Registration began in 1909. In 1956 family registration was also required, and in 1982 a computerized national identification card system was implemented to centralize date on all individuals.

Togo

Division des Affaires Politiques et Administratives
Etat Civil Central
Commune de Lome, Togo

Vital registration in Togo began in 1923 in the larger urban areas; it was not expanded to the entire nation until 1962. Current registration is not considered to be complete.

The Family History Library of The Church of Jesus Christ of Latter-day Saints in Salt Lake City, Utah has microfilmed records of Togo and Africa. For further details on their holdings, please consult your nearest Family History Center.

Tonga

Registrar General
Registrar of the Supreme Court
Justice Department
PO Box 11
Nuku'aloto, Tonga
(011) (676) 23 599

The Registrar General has birth and death records from 1867, marriage records from 1892, and divorce records from 1905. Current vital registration is considered to be 95 percent complete for births and 90 percent complete for deaths.

The Family History Library of The Church of Jesus Christ of Latter-day Saints in Salt Lake City, Utah has microfilmed records of Tonga. For further details, please consult your nearest Family History Center.

Trinidad and Tobago

Registrar General's Office
Ministry of Legal Affairs
Registration House
72-74 South Quay
Port of Spain, Trinidad and Tobago
(*68) 624-1660

The Registrar General has records for Trinidad from January 1, 1848, and for Tobago from January 30, 1868. Trinidad and Tobago were united in 1889. Current registration is considered to be complete. The local churches also have their own records.

The Family History Library of The Church of Jesus Christ of Latter-day Saints in Salt Lake City, Utah has microfilmed records of Trinidad and the Caribbean. For further details, please consult your nearest Family History Center.

Tunisia

Registrar
Centres d'Etat Civil
(Town), Tunisia
Registration began in 1958.

Turkey

General Directorate of Population and Citizenship Affairs   or. Nutus Mudurluga
Ministry of Internal Affairs   (Town), Turkey
T.C. Icisleri Bakanligi
Nufus ve Vatandaslik Isleri Gn. Md.
Bakanliklar
Ankara, Turkey

Turkey was founded in 1923. Over 98 percent of the people are Sunni Muslim. Efforts have been made to expand vital registration, but currently it is not considered to be comprehensive.

Turkmenistan

Russian-American Genealogical Archival Service (RAGAS)
PO Box 236
Glen Echo, Maryland 20812
USA
(202)501-5206

or. Bureau of Registration of Acts of Civil Status
(Town), Turkmenistan

By an agreement between the United States National Archives Volunteer Association and the Archives of Russia Society, RAGAS receives and processes requests for vital records in some of the former Soviet republics. Although at this time RAGAS is able to deal mainly with Russia, Belarus, and Ukraine they might be able to help you with your inquiries regarding Turkmenistan. There is a $2.00 shipping fee per document. The service also is available at an hourly rate. (See "Russia" for application forms.)

Turks and Caicos Islands

Registrar General's Office
Post Office Building
Front Street
Grand Turk, Turks and Caicos
British West Indies
(649) 946-2800.

The Registrar General has records from January 2, 1863. Current registration is considered to be more than 90 percent complete. The local churches also have their own records.

The Family History Library of The Church of Jesus Christ of Latter-day Saints in Salt Lake City, Utah has microfilmed records of Turks and Caicos and the Caribbean. For further details on their holdings, please consult your nearest Family History Center.

Tuvalu

Registrar General, Medical Division
Office of Chief Ministry
Vaiaku, Funafuti, Tuvalu

You can also find information at the National Archives and Library of Tuvalu, PO Box 67, Fanafuti, Tuvalu;

Tel. (011)(688) 711; FAX (011)(688) 819.

Uganda

Registrar General of Births and Deaths
PO Box 7183
Kenya, Uganda

Registration began in 1905 for Europeans, in 1915 for Asians, and in 1973 for the rest of the population.

Ukraine

Russian-American Genealogical Archival Service (RAGAS)
PO Box 236
Glen Echo, Maryland 20812
USA
(202)501-5206

or. Registry of Vital Statistics
Reyestratsiyakriv
4 Romadianskoho Stanu (RAHS)
(Town), Ukraine

By an agreement between the United States National Archives Volunteer Association and the Archives of Russia Society, RAGAS receives and processes requests for vital records in some of the former Soviet republics - mainly Russia, Belarus, and Ukraine. There is a $2.00 shipping fee per document. (See "Russia" for application forms.)

United Arab Emirates

Birth or Death Certificates Section
Central Preventative Medicine Directorate
Ministry of Health
Abu Dhabi, United Arab Emirates

Includes 7 states: Abu Dhabi, Dubai, Ash Sharigah (Sharjeh), Ajman, Um Al-Quiwain, Ras Al-Khaimah, and Fujairah.

United Kingdom - England and Wales

General Registration Offices
PO Box 2
Southport
Merseyside PRB 2JD, England, UK
)011) (44) 845-603-7788
www.gro.gov.uk

ADOPTION RECORDS:

Adoptions Section
Room C208, General Register Office
Trafalgar Road
Southport, PR8 2HH, England, UK

The General Register Office has records from July 1, 1837. If your request is urgent, there is an additional £ 14.50 fee.

The Family History Library of The Church of Jesus Christ of Latter-day Saints in Salt Lake City, Utah has microfilmed records of the United Kingdom For further details on their holdings, please consult your nearest Family History Center.

SEARCH RESOURCES

Adoption Search-Support

Margaret Humphreys/Child Migrant Trust
28-A Musters Rd.
West Bridgford, Nottingham NG2 7PL
United Kingdom

Ariel Bruce
6 Regent Square
London, England WC1 H8H
United Kingdom

Natural Parents Network
11 Green Lane, Garden Suburb
Odam, Lancs, England OL8 3AY
United Kingdom

Mothers Apart from their Children
(MATCW)
London England
Birmingham England WC1N3XX
United Kingdom

Natural Parents Network
3 Ashdown Drive' Mosley Common
Manchester, England M28 1BR
United Kingdom

WarBabes
15 Plough Ave, South Woodgate
Birmingham England 332 3TQ
United Kingdom

There are more than 8,000,000 adoptees living in Britain, according to the National Organization for Counselling Adoptees and Parents (NORCAP). The adoptees' computerized mailing list home page is on: http://psy.ucsd.edu/-jhartung/adoptees.html (Alt.adoption FAQ is at: http://www.webcom.com/-kmc/adoption/faqs.html). For cooperative U.K./USA search help, contact: Pam Martin (ISC), 25433 Via Estudio, Laguna Niguel, CA 92677, USA and Ann Caffari, NORCAP, 112 Church Rd., Wheatley, Oxforsdshire, England 0X33 1LU; enquiries@norcap.org.

UNITED KINGDOM - ENGLAND

Ancient Monuments Society
St. Andrew-by-the-Wardrobe
Queen Victoria St.
London, England EC4V 5Df
United Kingdom

Association of Genealogists
2 Buckhill Rd.
Walton on Thomas
Surrey England

Assoc. of Teachers of Family History
56 Marlborough Rd
Slough England SL3 7H1
United Kingdom

Bath Heraldic Society
9 Newlands Rd.
Kesham Bristol England
United Kingdom

Bedfordshire Family History Society
4 The Glen, Kempstone
Bedford England MK42 7EL
United Kingdom

Berkshire Family History Society
20 Stanhope Rd., Reading
Berks England RG2 7H 1
United Kingdom

Birmingham & Midland Society
31 Seven Star Rd, Solihull
Westmidlands England D43 3U 1
United Kingdom

Bristol & Avon Family History Society
13 The Homsbeams, Frenchoy
Bristol England BS4 3HY
United Kingdom

British Association of Cemeteries
of Southeast Asis
76-1/2 Chartfield Ave.
London England SW15 6HQ
United Kingdom

Buckinghamshire Family History
Society
18 Rudd's Lane, Haddenham
Aylesbury Bucks England
United Kingdom

Cambridgeshire Family History Society
18 CourtlandAve.
Cambridge England CB 1 4AT
United Kingdom

Catholic Record Society
United Kingdom
24 Lennox Gardens, Flat 5
United Kingdom

Channel Islands Family History Society
5 Gordon Avenue
Bromborough
Wirral England M22 4BU
United Kingdom

Cleveland Family History Society
1 Oxgang Close
Red Car England TS10 4NR
United Kingdom

Cornwall Family History Society
Glendoral Lodge
Lusty Glaze Rd.
Newguay England TR7 3A2
United Kingdom

Cumbria Family History Society
32 Granada Rd.
Denton
Manchester England M34 2LJ
England
United Kingdom

Derbyshire Family History Society
15 Elmhurst Rd.
Forest Town.
Mansfield Notts England
United Kingdom

Devon Family History Society
63 Old Laria Rd.
Laria
Plymouth Devon England PL3 3BL
United Kingdom

Devon & Cornwall Record Society
7 The Close
Exeter
Devon England DE5 3DW
United Kingdom

Doncaster Family History Society
65 Kingsgate
Doncaster
Southyorks England DN1 3JY
United Kingdom

English Catholic Ancestors
Hill House West
Crookham Village
NR Andershot
Hants England GUI 3 OSS
United Kingdom

Essex Family History Society
67 Balgores Lane
Gildea Park
Romford
Essex England RM2 5JX
United Kingdom

Essex Archeological Society
11 Plume Ave
Malden
Essex England CM96LB
United Kingdom

Federation of Family History Societies
96 Beaumont St.
Milchouse
Plymouth, England PL2 3AQ
United Kingdom

Folkstone Family History Society
22 Church Rd
Cheriton
Folkstone Kent England
United Kingdom

Gloucestershire Family History Society
18 East Court Rd.
Glouster England GL1 BL6
United Kingdom

Guild of One-Name Studies
15 Cavendish Gardens
Craibrook Ilford
Essex England IG1 3EA
United Kingdom

Hampshire Genealogical Society
36 Carmarthen Ave.
East Cosham
Portsmouth Hants England
United Kingdom

Harlein Society
Arder House
Hill Lane
Godolming Surrey England
United Kingdom

Heraldry Society
28 Museum St.
London England WC1 A1 LH
United Kingdom

Herefordshire Family History Society
255 Whitecross Rd.
Hereford England HR4 OLT
United Kingdom

Herefordshire Family History Society
155 JessopRd.
Setevenage
Herefordshire Emgland

Institute of Heraldic & Genealogical Studies
Northgate
Vantebury Kent England CT1 1BA
United Kingdom
United Kingdom

Jewish History Society of England
33 Seymour Pl. London W1 England
United Kingdom

Kent Family History Society
17 Abbots' Place
Canterbury
Kent England
United Kingdom

North West Kent Family History
Society
39 Nightingale Rd.
Petts Woods
Orpington Kent England
United Kingdom

Leicestershire Family History Circle
25 Homecroft Dr.
Packinton
Leicestership England
United Kingdom

University of Leicester Genealogical
Society
Student Union
Mayor's Walk
Leicester England LE1 7RH
United Kingdom

Lincolnshire Family History Society
34 Beacon Heights
Newark Notts England
United Kingdom

Liverpool Family History Society
11 Lisburn Lane
Tuebrook
Liverpool England
United Kingdom

East of London Family History Soc
32 Whitehom Gardens
Hornchurch Essex England
United Kingdom

Macclesfield Heraldic Society
2 Orchard Close
Chealde Hulme
Greater Manchester England
United Kingdom

Isle of Man Family History Society
5 Willow TerraceDelapre
Souglas I 0 M EnglandNorthhampton
United Kingdom

Manchester & Mancashire Family
History Society
32 Boumlea Ave.
Burnage
Manchester England M 19 1EF
United Kingdom

North Middlesex Family History Society
15 Milton Rd.
Walthamstow
London England E 17 4SP
United Kingdom

Central Middlesex Family History Society
4 Addiscombe Close
Kenton
Middlesex England HA3 8JS
United Kingdom

West Middlesex Family History Society
92 Avondale Rd
Staines
Middlesex England TW18 3HF
United Kingdom

The Names Society
7 AragonAve.
Thames Ditton
Surrey England
United Kingdom

Natural Parents Network
10 Alendale Crescent
Garforth, Leeds
Yorkshire, England LS25 1 DH
United Kingdom

Linda Savell
Norcap
112 Church Road
Wheatley, Oxfordshire
England OX33 1LU
United Kingdom

Norfolk & Norwich Genealogical
Society
13 West Parade
Norwich England NR2 3DN
United Kingdom

Northampton Family History Society
56 Loucster Crescent
England NN4 9PR
United Kingdom

Northumberland & Durham Family
History Society
33 South Road
Brunton Park
Newcastle-Upon-Tyne
England NE3 5TR
United Kingdom

Nottinghamshire Family Hist. Society
35 Kingwood Rd.
West Bridford
Nottingham England
United Kingdom

Oxfordshire Family History Society
Speedwell
North Moreton
Oxon England 0X11 9B6
United Kingdom

Petersborough & District Family
History Society
106 London Rd.
Petersborough
Cambs England
United Kingdom

Post Office HQ Genealogical Society
27 Hayely Bell Garden
Bishops Stortford
Herts England CM23 3HA
United Kingdom

Rossendale Society for Genealogy &
Heraldy
10 Westminster Ave
Royalton Oldham
Lanes England
United Kingdom

Sheffield & District Family Hist. Soc.
58 Stumperlowe Crescent Rd.
Sheffield England SIO 3PR
United Kingdom

Shropshire Family History Society
Portway
Windsor Lane
Bosmere Heath
Shrewsbury England SY4 3LR
United Kingdom

Society of Genealogists
37 Harrington Gardens
London England SW7 4JX
United Kingdom

Somerset & Dorset Family History
Society
Brunlands Sherbourne
Dorset England DT9 4BL
United Kingdom

Spaldings Gentlemen's Society
The Museum
Broad street
1118 Lincs England
United Kingdom

Suffolk Genealogical Society
2 Uplands Rd.
Carlton Colville
East Suffolk England
United Kingdom

Surrey East Family History Society
Court Farm Lodge
1 Eastway
Surrey England
United Kingdom

Surrey West Family History Society
5 St. Catherine's Rd.
Frimley Green
Surrey England GU 16 6PY
United Kingdom

Sussex Family History
44 The Green
Southwick
Sussex England BN4 4FR
United Kingdom

Wetham Forest Family History Society
55 Mersey Ave
London England E 17 5LA
United Kingdom

Wiltshire Family History Society
17 Faircroft
Clough England SL2 1 HJ
United Kingdom

Woolwich & District Family History
Society
106 Oakhampton Crescent
Kent England 01C IDA
United Kingdom

York Family History Society
67 Moongage
York England Y02 4HP
United Kingdom

Yorkshire Archaeological Society
Family History & Population Studies
109 Kitson Himm Rd.
Mirfield
Yorks England WF14 90S
United Kingdom

East Yorkshire Family History Society
9 Stepney Grove
Scarborough
North Yorkshire Y012 5FD
United Kingdom

UNITED KINGDOM - WALES
Clwyd Family History Society
17 Percy Lane
Lanfair DC
Ruthin Clwyd North Wales

Gwyned Family History Society
6 Nant Y Mount
Penthosgarnedd
Bangor Gwyned North Wales
United Kingdom

Powys Family History Society
34 Glebelands Rd.
Knutsford Cheshire England
United Kingdom

Dyfed Family History Society
175 Penybank Rd.
Penybank Ammanford
Dyfed North Wales
United Kingdom

Gwent Family History Society
17 Craig Park Lane
Malpas Newport
Gwent South Wales
United Kingdom

Glamorgan Family History Society
c/o Howard Llewellyn
Llamshen Fack Farm House
Heol Erwin Rhiwbina
Cardiff South Wales
Unlted KIngdom

The Saginaw News, 11/20/90: "British War Babies Allowed to Trace U.S. Fathers . . . Washington—A U.S. District Court settlement announced Monday will allow British children of U.S. servicemen from World War II to get information about their fathers from the Department of Defense and the National Archives. The agreement reversed a long-standing federal policy of withholding such information to protect serviceman's privacy. Up to 100,000 British sons and daughters of U.S. GIs who had been stationed in England during World War II could be affected by the settlement. The action also opens the way for unknown numbers of children fathered by U.S. servicemen in Vietnam and other countries to trace their fathers and possibly be reunited or have their fathers' names included on their birth certificates ... The Britons had cited the Freedom of Information Act in seeking the information."

Shirley McGlade, who is now 45 and has a son, was able to locate her father in 1986. She had been told as a child that he was killed on D-Day. Her reunion with her father in March 1987 and publicity that followed persuaded McGlade to form War Babes to help other people in similar situations.

Former serviceman Martienus Van Lith, 67, of Yakima, WA wrote that he was located by his daughter, Pauline Wendy Marsden, in 1987 after she spent two years searching for him. 'There is no reason why the government should withhold addresses from children of servicemen,' he wrote. 'I would be very angry if I knew that the reason my daughter could not find me was because the government would not release my address to her.'"

The LOG of Orphan Voyage, Cedaredge, CO, Winter 1971-2: "From Child Adoption, England, edited by Margaret Komitzer (1968)... In recent years many of our members have been coming to the view that the law in Scotland, which enables any adopted person over the age of 17 to obtain from the Registrar General for Scotland the information necessary to identify his own parentage, should be followed in England and Wales."

Perth Sunday Times, 3/22/92: "CLUE FROM PHOTO ALBUM LEADS TO MOTHER-DAUGHTER REUNION . . . London—A 53-year-old Perth mother of three who was adopted when she was nine months old has been reunited with the English mother she never knew.

Mrs. Brenda Strahan of Second Avenue, Mt. Lawley, was adopted during World War II and grew up in Northern Ireland with her new parents before migrating to Australia 25 years ago .. . She knew that she had been born in Dewsbury, West Yorkshire so she contacted the town's register office for details and found her mother's name was Isabelle Robinson and an address. Mrs. Strahan's cousin, Mrs. Marjorie Booth of Staincliffe, recognized the family history and contacted the newspaper with details of her mother, now Mrs. Isabelle Autry, and her extended family . . . Mrs. Autry was pressured into having Brenda adopted ... 'I kept her with me for about nine months and didn't want to let her go.'"

WOMAN Magazine (London), 5/31/93: "Simon's Come Back!... In England, adopted children now have the right to trace their real parents. But when mother and child meet, it isn't always easy, as this remarkable story proves . . .

Jennifer's Story ... I married at 17, after a desperately unhappy childhood. But the marriage was a disaster. At 19 and pregnant, I went back home. I'd been sexually abused by my stepfather since the age of 14—though my mother never knew—and when I finally said no to his advances he threw me and my baby out. Two weeks later I had a nervous breakdown. I was admitted to a mental hospital and Simon, who was seven months old, was put into care. I didn't want to give him up. I loved him deeply, but I felt helpless and agreed.

Simon's Story . . . My adopted parents believed that they couldn't have kids. But shortly after they adopted me my half-brother was born, followed by my half-sister. My parents said they loved us all equally and I'm sure they did, but kids who've been adopted often find that difficult to accept. At first I didn't want to think too much about my real mum. People hinted that she was schizophrenic and lived in a slum ... I'm still angry that I was taken away from her. I'm so glad I found (my birthmother). She's beautiful and I love her."

United Kingdom - Northern Ireland

See also Ireland, Republic of

General Register Office
Department of Health and Social Services
49-55 Chichester St.
Belfast BT1 4HL, Northern Ireland
United Kingdom

The General Register Office has birth and death records from January 1,1864, and marriage records from April 1,1854. Write Attn: Adoption Section for Adoption Registry. Your local Family History Library of The Church of Jesus Christ of Latter-day Saints in Salt Lake City, Utah has microfilmed records of Northern Ireland.

SEARCH RESOURCES

Genealogy

McKenna Clan
Kilrudden Clogher
County Tyronne, Northern Ireland
United Kingdom

N. Ireland Family History Society
Queen's University Teacher Center
Upper Crescent
Belfast Northern Ireland BT7 INT
United Kingdom

Ulster Genealogical and Historical Guild
66 Balmoral Ave., Belfast
Northern Ireland BT9 6NY
United Kingdom

Irish Genealogical Association
162-A Kingsway
Dunmurray Belfast
Northern Ireland BT17 9AD
United Kingdom

Glens of Antrim Historical Society
Lennalry House, Comlough
Ballymena County Antrim
Northern Ireland
United Kingdom

Kelso Family
The Manse, Huntley Rd.
Bambridge, County Down
Northern Ireland BT25 3B5
United Kingdom

Suzanna Byrne
The Old Vicarage
Stationsstraat 66
3580 Neerpelt
Northern Ireland

United Kingdom - Scotland

General Register Office for Scotland
3 West Register Street
Edinburgh EH1 3YT, Scotland
United Kingdom
(011) (44) 1313340380   (11)(44)31-314-4400
www.gro.scotland.gov.uk

The General Register Office has records from governmental registers from January 1,1855. In addition, they hold many old parish registers dating back to 1553. These are indexed. The Office has divorce records from May 1, 1984. Divorces before that date are noted on the Registrar's copy of the marriage certificate. Include the estimated airmail postage with your fee. International Postal Reply Coupons are not accepted.

The Family History Library of The Church of Jesus Christ of Latter-day Saints in Salt Lake City, Utah has microfilmed records of Scotland. For further details on their holdings, please consult your nearest Family History Center.

"BIRTH LINK" REGISTER

The following people may choose to register on BIRTH LINK:

- Any person born or adopted in Scotland (or where there is a close Scottish connection).
- Any birth parent who wishes to make contact with the child they placed for adoption.
- Any birth relative who wishes to make contact with the adopted person.

For information and registration form, write to BIRTH LINK, Family Care, 21 Castle Street, Edinburgh, Scotland, EH2 3DN, Tel. 031-225-6441

USEFUL ADDRESSES

General Register Office for Scotland
Adoption Unit
New Register House
Edinburgh Scotland EH1 3YT
United Kingdom
031-314-4443

Scottish Records Office
General Register House
Edinburgh Scotland EH 1 3YY
United Kingdom
031-556-6585, ext. 2114

General Register Office
Adopted Children Register
Smedley Hydro. Trafalgar Rd.
Birkdale, Southport, England PR8 2HH
United Kingdom

ADOPTION SEARCHES

Genealogy

KenBryson
PO Box 337
Kalkaska, MI 49646
U.S.A.
Tuy Valley Family History Society
11 Turfbes Rd
Forfer Scotland DD8 3LT
United Kingdom

Scottish Tartan Society
Museum of Scottish Tartans
Comrie Perkshire Scotland
United Kingdom

Aberdeen/NE Scotland Family History
31 Bloomfield Place
Aberdeen Scotland AB1 5A6
United Kingdom

Barnardos Scottish Adoption
Advice Service
16 Sandyford Place
Glasgow Scotland G3 7NB
United Kingdom
041-339-0772

Scots Ancestry Research Society
20 York Place
Edinborough Scotland EH 3PY
United Kingdom

Highland Family History Society
76 Findhorn Place
Edinborough Scotland DD8 DL5
United Kingdom

Clan Lindsay
16 Dalziel Dr.
Glasgow Scotland G41
United Kingdom

Scottish Record Society
Scottish History Dept.
University of Glasgow
Glasgow Scotland G 12 8QG
United Kingdom

Adoption Registry

Family Care & LINK Adoption Register
21 Castle Street
Endinborough Scotland EH2 3DN
031-255-6441

The International Scene: "The End of the Beginning ... by Rev. Dr. John Cameron. The following is excerpted from an address by Dr. Cameron, of the Campaign for Adoption Reform in Europe ("CARE"), given to the NORCAP A.G.M ... On the 25th day of May 1989, at its Annual General Assembly, the Church of Scotland, which until recently ran the largest adoption agency in the country, declared unanimously its support for the campaign to have natural parents given the absolute right to non-identifying information about the progress and well-being of the children they relinquished for adoption. This was an historic moment, since it was the first time such an agency has accepted that natural parents had any rights whatsoever. In addition, the Church of Scotland gave its blessing to 'BIRTH LINK,' the process used by Family Care in Scotland to facilitate the reunion between natural parents and their lost children. The debate carried live on both the BBC Scotland and STV, and part of it will be incorporated into the 4-program series 'Someone Else's Child,' which is being produced by STV for the network screening in the spring of 1990 ... It was first a major public success for CARE, the Campaign for Adoption Reform in Europe. But no one should be deluded as to the magnitude of the task which remains. We live in a country where authority, from the most petty official in an obscure local authority office to the Prime Minister and her great officers of state, have a perfect mania for secrecy. In addition, our whole legal system is biased in favor of property rights, which are seen as paramount and have the same aura as was once ascribed to the laws of the Medes and the Persians. Those who have had the experience of trying to help adopted children trace their natural parents on both sides of the border since 1975, such as NORCAP's own representative in the north, Charlotte Edwards, comments again and again on how deliberately obstructive Scottish officials are in comparison to their English counterparts ... Already in England, the information natural mothers require can be obtained with the help of private search agencies ... The main opposition in this country tends to come from the Catholic Church, but their counterparts in Europe are gradually coming to the conclusion that closed adoption actually promotes abortion. This fact has been widely researched and seems to me beyond dispute. If the Catholic Church comes to accept this, I think closed adoption is finished. If this happened, and the mistakes of the past were rectified, I believe it would be a major contribution to the sum of human happiness ... Now let us have your view! ... REV. DR. JOHN CAMERON, CAMPAIGN FOR ADOPTION REFORM IN EUROPE, St. Stephan's Manse, 33 Camperdown St, Broughty Ferry, Dundee, DD5 3AA, Scotland."

[Copied to AmFOR and excerpted June 5, 1989] ... "Dear Dr. McWhinnie: ... My name is Cecile Comeau from Quebec. I hope that you remember me. I telephoned you from Canada last April. I had been referred to you by Pierre Julien, Director of Mouvement Retrouvailles of Province of Quebec. He informed you that I am a member of our Political and Juridicial Committee. This one will have to make recommendations to our 'Mouvement' on the actions to be taken for changing the unacceptable attitude of Government of Quebec towards birthparents and children who are searching in this Province of Canada ... We, members of Mouvement Retrouvailles of Quebec,are very touched to know that you are interested in our fight. We thank you very much for your help and kindness towards us; you are a great Lady! Be sure, dear Madam, that your respect of humane dignity and your very noble heart conquered our hurt hearts. We love you ... CECILE COMEAU, POLITICAL/JURIDICAL COMMITTEE, MOUVEMENT RETROUVAILLES, Quebec, Canada."

Uruguay

Direccion General del Registro del Estado Civil
Ministerio de Educacion y Culture
Av. Uruguay 753
11.100 Montevideo, Uruguay

Registration began July 1, 1879.

Uzbekistan

Russian-American Genealogical Archival Service (RAGAS)
PO Box 236
Glen Echo, Maryland 20812
USA
(202)501-5206

or, Civil Registration Office (ZAGS)
(Town). Uzbekistan

By an agreement between the United States National Archives Volunteer Association and the Archives of Russia Society, RAGAS receives and processes requests for vital records in some of the former Soviet republics. Although at this time RAGAS is able to deal mainly with Russia, Belarus, and Ukraine they might be able to help you with your inquiries regarding Uzbekistan. There is a shipping fee per document. The service also is available at an hourly rate. (See "Russia" for application forms.)

Vanuatu

Registrar General
Civil Registration Office
Ministry of Home Affairs
Private Mail Bag 9050
Port Vila, Vanuatu

Vital registration was not formally introduced to Vanuatu until 1975, and so the Registrar General's Office has initiated a program to retroactively register each birth and marriage.

The National Archives of Vanuatu also has information. Write to PO Box 184, Port Vila, Vanuatu; Tel. (011)(678) 22-498; FAX (011)(678)23-142.

Venezuela

Direccion de Registro y Notaria
Ministerio de Justicia
Torre Norte, Centre Simon Bolivar, Piso 20
Caracas, Venezuela

or, Jefe Civil (Chief Civil Authority)
(District and Town), Venezuela

Registration began in 1873.

Vietnam

Registrar
Police Station
(Town), Vietnam

Vietnam has a personal identity card, family registration, and a vital registration system. The family register is the basic document and is registered at the police station.

SEARCH RESOURCES

To locate separated Vietnamese families, worldwide:

The International Committee
of the Red Cross
431 18th St., NW
Washington, DC 20006, USA

Red Cross Overseas Assoc.
PO Box 7406
Benjamin Franklin Sta.
Washington, DC 20044-7406, USA

Vietnam Reunion Planning
Committee
PO Box 2880
Eugene, OR 97402, USA
reunion@holtintl.org

Support group for young Americans whose fathers died in Vietnam War:

Sons & Daughters in Touch
Founder: Tony Cordero
Los Angeles, CA, USA
(213)833-9571

To locate families of orphans in U.S. from Vietnam in 1975 Operation Babylift:

Holt International Children's Service Eugene, Oregon (one of the relief agencies that ran Vietnam orphanages and organized a 2-week 'Motherland Tour' for Vietnamese orphans in U.S. to return to see their country of origin and inquire about surviving birth relatives).

Los Angeles Times, 6/30/91, Front Page: "Amerasian: Odds Are Against Soldiers' Children ... Vietnam's Lingering Casualties . . . Amerasians, subjected to discrimination and hate in their homeland, come to America searching for better futures and answers to their pasts.

When she speaks, her words are Vietnamese . . . 'My mother told me to come and find my father,' she says. 'She says that finding my father will mean that I will have a better future. Then Thu-Ha pauses, looking down. Her father is a Black American, just a story from the war. Her mother is Vietnamese. The mosaic of cultures shows on Thu-Ha's face and in her walk. She says her father was a engineer. 'I'm afraid to find him,' she says, more softly now. 'I think he might have a family and not want me.'... Thu-Ha says she will search for her father nonetheless—because it is her mother's will. There is hope, she says. She knows her father's name. It is John. Nothing else.

Mary Payne Nguyen, at the end of a very long week, sighs loudly, making a face. She has heard this too many times before. She is coordinator of Amerasian services at St. Anselm's Immigrant and Refugee Community Center in Garden Grove, one of 48 so-called cluster sites across the nation where volunteers and near-volunteers work against time and odds to acculturate the often unwanted offspring of an unpopular war. The Amerasians—30,000, maybe more-are casualties of America's national ambivalence about Vietnam.

Never in the history of American warfare has our nation undertaken such a mammoth effort to own up to fathering so many. But the effort took 13 years ... Since the Amerasian Homecoming Act took effect in March, 1988, more than 12,000 Amerasians have entered the United States from Vietnam, three times as many as had arrived since the fall of Saigon in 1975. The State Department estimates as many as 20,000 more—accompanied by some 60,000 Vietnamese family members—will arrive by the end of next year.

'I remember when I was pregnant, people would half smile and laugh,' says Tho Nguyen, who arrived in San Bernardino with her two daughters—the older, Amerasian, and the other Vietnamese—in January of last year. 'Then when I have the baby, they say some bad things because I have an American baby'... But even Mary Nguyen, who is married to a Vietnamese man and has 'adopted' 12 Amerasians, says that loving these young people takes work.

Loc admits to stealing other American flags before.

'I take them to throw them away,' he says. 'I want to [expletive] the American people. They are very stupid'. . . Tai Tran, 22, says he doesn't remember a thing about the first 10 years of his life. He never knew his parents . . . 'One day when I guess I was about 12 years old, my adopted mother pointed out a woman on the street,' Tai says. 'She said that that was my real mother... Hundreds of veterans and other men who spent time in Vietnam have asked the government and the American Red Cross for help in finding the Amerasian children who share their genes. Very few searches produces a match.

The vast majority of potential fathers, however, never ask.

'I have one friend from Texas who was in my unit,' says Benjamin Romero, vice president of the Vietnam Veterans of America chapter in Denver. 'And when he left Vietnam, his Vietnamese girlfriend was three months pregnant. He tried to get her out, but the military and the U.S. Consulate there told him to forget about it, that it wasn't his problem.

'He lost track of her and he has no idea if the baby was ever even born. He's married now and his wife doesn't know about it ... Reps. Robert J. Mrazek (D-N.Y.) and Tom Ridge (R-PA) co-sponsored the American Homecoming Act, which removed any quotas on Amerasian immigration to the United States.

The legislation sailed through Congress in December, 1987, its genesis a tellingly feel-good American tale ... It is unlikely that anyone will be held accountable for Thu-Ha's paper marriage charade. Fraud in the Orderly Departure Program, officials in government and voluntary agencies concede, is almost built-in. Estimates are that 10 to 30 of the family applications involve some degree of lying."

Los Angeles Times, 7/7/91: "He Looks Like Me: Two Amerasians Seek Their Dad—And Their Missing Heritage ... We call them Amerasians; 'half-breeds' say the Vietnamese ... 'I didn't want to find him right away,' Trang Nguyen says. 'I wanted to learn English, to study. I wanted to be something, so he could be proud of me. But then I couldn't wait'... 'My mother, my grandmother would tell me, 'Look in the mirror and you will see your father," Trang says, her smile growing wide.

She searched for her father, a man who left her mother in Saigon before she was even born, and found him—on the first try ... George went to the Yorba Linda Public Library and flipped through the telephone directory for Boise, ID, where Trang's mother had remembered her boyfriend had lived. But that was 1968. The Boise phone book listed two men with Trang's father's name. George dialed the correct number on the first attempt. Rarer yet, this man, an Air Force veteran, did not mind being found. In February, he drove from Boise, where he lives with his girlfriend, to meet his daughter for the first time. He has never married. Trang is his only child.

Like so many Amerasians, Trang Nguyen suggests that her search for her father was indistinguishable from the search for herself. She wants nothing more from him than an acknowledgment of a bond ... He fingers the photographs taken in Vietnam. There is a 2-year-old Bang, his Vietnamese mother, his American dad. All wear smiles."

Yemen

Registrar General
Ministry of Justice and AWQAF
PO Box 5030
Maalla, Aden, Yemen

Vital registration is not considered to be comprehensive.

Yugoslavia

(After 1991, see Bosnia-Herzegovina)

ADOPTION LAW SUMMARY

Paragraphs in a letter from the American Consul of February, 1980, explain that:

1. A foreigner must, if he wishes to adopt a Yugoslav child, contact the Center for Social Works (Centar za socijalni rad) at the local community government (Opstina). There are four or five of these opstina in Belgrade, and each has its own procedures and regulations.

2. Once the Center for Social Works of the Opstina is satisfied, the application is sent to the Center for Protection of Infants and Children mentioned above. This Center makes the final decision on whether the adoption should be put into effect.

AUTHORITY IN CHARGE OF ADOPTIONS (UNTIL 1991)
Center for Protection of Infants and Children
Zvecanska 7
11000 Belgrade
Yugoslavia

For further details, you may write directly to the center above. Contact a local International Institute to translate a letter for you.

Los Angeles Times, 2/23/91: "Yugoslavs Agree to Consider Splitting Nation:... Sarajevo. Yugoslavia— In this mountain resort where an act of violence led to the birth of Yugoslavia, leaders of the crisis-ridden federation agreed Friday to consider ways to grant the 72-year-old state a peaceful and dignified death .

Among the panel's tasks will be defining a legal procedure for secession by the republics. a position that appears to acknowledge determined moves toward independence already under way in the affluent northern republics of Slovenia and Croatia.

Journal Of Family Law, 1987-88: "Yugoslavia: Adoption---Legislation and Practice . . . The Family Relations Act of the Socialist Republic of Croatia defines with great precision the kinds of adoption, prerequisites and procedures for its achievement. the rights and duties arising from it, and its termination.

According to the Act, there are two kinds of adoption: incomplete adoption and adoption with the full effect of parenthood . . . The guardianship agency responsible for adoption must check all the circumstances envisaged by the Act to make sure that the adoption is really beneficial to the child. The question whether adoption enhances the welfare of the child has to be determined by professional social workers ...

Incomplete Adoption: In the incomplete adoption procedure the child's natural parents must give their explicit consent. The consent of the natural parent is not required, however, if he or she has been deprived of parental rights or legal capacity as a result of incapacity to make a judgment, or if he or she has not taken care of the child. Further, adoption may be established even without the consent of a parent who has for more than one year neglected the child and refuses to give consent without any justifiable reason. The consent of the child who is to be adopted is essential if he or she has attained the age of ten years. When only one spouse wants to adopt a child, the consent of the other spouse is required. Proceedings are conducted by the local social welfare authorities. Neither religious nor humanitarian organizations have any rights whatsoever regarding adoption. The public is barred from the proceedings . . . Inheritance matters and the choice of the adoptee's surname may be freely regulated by agreement... The Yugoslav legal system has abandoned the contractual concept of adoption, and court jurisdiction is not provided. Final rulings are forwarded to the registrar for entry in the register of births ... Incomplete adoption does not result in the termination of the adopted child's rights and duties towards his or her natural parents and relations—for example, the obligation to maintain them, or the right to inherit the estate of the natural parents or relations. No kinship relationship between adopted child and adoptive parent is established by adoption . . .

Full Adoption: The second form of adoption was introduced in the legal system of Yugoslavia and the Socialist Republic of Croatia by the enactment of laws in 1974. This form of adoption is called 'adoption with the full effect of parenthood'. . . only a child aged up to five years whose parents have died, or are unknown or have been deprived of parental rights, may be adopted with the full effect of parenthood ... Generally, only spouses may adopt, though an individual may if he or she is the stepfather or stepmother

The Act provides for the secrecy of data, in that the adopters are entered in the register of birth as the child's parents ... the secrecy of adoption is not justifiable ... the legal system does not provide for the possibility of adoption by agreement between adopters and parents. This prevents trade in the personal status of children."

Los Angeles Times, 2/8/92: Mother's War for Children—A California Woman Fights for Return of Youngsters Spirited to Serbia by Ex-Husband . . . Belgrade, Yugoslavia—Five Yugoslav courts have upheld Shayna Gluck Lazarevich's right to custody of her two kidnaped children, but the mounting pile of legal victories is small comfort to the distraught California mother.

More than two years after Sasha and Andre Lazarevich were spirited to rural Serbia by their father, they remain hostages in a country indifferent to its own laws and international pressure ... In September, 1989, after Gluck had moved from Downey to Santa Cruz, Lazarevich picked up the children at her apartment for what was supposed to be a weekend outing. Instead, Lazarevich, who had an extensive criminal record unbeknown to his ex-wife, took them to Yugoslavia and has defied repeated American and Yugoslav orders to return them to their mother. Gluck, who recently reverted to using her maiden name, has spent most of the last two years plodding through the labyrinthine Yugoslav system. All five court decisions have been in her favor. But against a background of disintegrating federal order and the Serb-Croat civil war, Lazarevich kept up a series of nuisance suits to delay enforcement of court orders.

Update—The Supreme Court of Serbia last year upheld federal decisions to recognize Gluck's right to take the children back to California. But the Yugoslav Ministry of Justice refused to enforce the decision as long as Lazarevich's lawsuit alleging that Gluck was an unfit mother was still making its way through lower courts ... 'I was awarded custody, and he was convicted of kidnapping, but he gets to keep the kids!' said a disbelieving Gluck ... Yugoslav law allows children above the age of 10 to decide for themselves which parent they prefer to live with after a divorce. Sasha, who will be 10 in September, has not been allowed to see her mother alone since she was kidnapped, and Gluck fears she is being exposed to intense pressure to stay with her father . . . But the rules of diplomacy appear to dictate against calling in a political debt. Asked whether Washington might cash in on its perceive bargaining clout with Serbia by asking for a gesture of goodwill in the Lazarevich case, U.S. Consul General Robert Tynes replied, 'Diplomats wouldn't do it that way.'"

Zaire

Etat Zairois
Ministere d l'Administration du Territoire
Kinshasa, Zaire

Registration began in 1958.

Zambia

Registrar General
Department of National Registration, Passport and Citizenship
Kundalila House
PO Box 32311
Losaka, Zambia

Registration is not considered to be complete.

Zimbabwe

Registrar General of Zimbabwe
Central Registry
Ministry of Home Affairs
Bag 7734
Causeway, Harare, Zimbabwe

Registration is not considered to be complete.

Index

abducted, missing children
  Argentina, 175
  abduction of 30,000, (Preface)
  outside U.S., child rescue, 173
Adam Walsh Child Resource Center, 15
address, forwarding, 1
address search, 1
adoptees' foreign searches, 171
Adoptees' Liberty Movement Assn (ALMA), 47
Adoption, incomplete, 172
Adoption Laws At A Glance (chart), 26
  International, (See alphabetical country listings)
  U.S., (See also alphabetical state listings)
adoption searches
  adoption files, locating, 30
  black market, 16
  computer searches for adoptees, parents, 37-42
  cost of adoptions, (see Preface)
  disclosure laws and procedures, 26
  international adoptions, citizenship, 172
  letter request - questions to ask court/agency, 35
  non-identifying information, 29
  petitions, (Preface)
  questions for adoptee, parents to ask, 35
  sealed records, states, 26, 29
  search and support groups
    code key to U.S. listings, 47
    directory by alphabetical state/country, 48-286
  unauthorized disclosure, penalties for, 29
Adoptive Parents for Open Records (APFOR), 27
Afghanistan, 174
Air Force records, (See Military records)
Air National Guard records, (See Military Records)
Alabama, 48
Alaska, 49
Albania, 174
Algeria, 174
Amber Foundation, 15
amended birth certificate, (See birth certificate)
American Adoption Congress (AAC), 47, 171
American Samoa, 164
Americans for Open Records (AmFOR) (see Preface)
Angola, 174
ANI, (See Telephone Records)
anti-stalking laws, (California), 1
Antigua and Barbuda, 174
Argentina, 175
Arizona, 50
Arkansas, 52
Armenia, 176
Army records, (See Military Records)
Austin, "Mean Gene," 16
Australia
  Australian Capital Territory, 177
  New South Wales, 177

  Northern Territory, 178
  Queensland, 179
  South Australia, 180
  Tasmania, 182
  Victoria, 183
  Western Territory, 184
Austria, 185
authorized persons (for records access), 1
Azerbaijan, 186
B-CAM., (See Telephone Records)
Baby selling
  Brazil, 192
  Poland, 257
  Romania, 259
background check, 10
Bahamas, 186
Bahrain, 187
Bangladesh, 187
bank records, 9
baptismal records, 7
Barbados, 187
Belarus, 188
Belgium, 188
Belize, 189
Benin, 189
Bermuda, 189
Bhutan, 190
birth certificate, 6-7
  amended/falsified for adoption, 7
birth date, search by, 4
Birth index, 2
black market adoptions, 16
Bolivia, 190
Bosnia and Herzegovina, 190
Botswana, 191
Boystown National Hotline, 17
Brazil, 192
Brunei, 193
Bulgaria, 196
Bureau of Indian Affairs, 22 (See also
  Native American Adoptee Searches)
Burkina Faso, 194
Burundi, 194
California, 54
Cambodia, 194
Cameroon, 194
Canada
  Alberta, 195
  British Columbia, 196
  Manitoba, 198
  New Brunswick, 199
  Newfoundland, 200
  Northwest Territories, 201
  Nova Scotia, 201
  Ontario, 203

Prince Edward Islands, 206
Quebec, 207
Saskatchewan, 209
Yukon, 210
Canadian Mounted Police
Royal National Clearinghouse, 173
Cape Verde, 210
capitalist civil status documents. (See Vital records)
categories of records. (see opposite page 1)
Cayman Islands, 210
Census
European, 170
records in National Archives, 21
U.S., 2, 23
Central Africa Republic, 211
Chad, 211
Child Quest International, 173
Child Support, 25
Children
military, (See Military Records)
runaways (See Missing Children; Runaways)
searching for minor children (via ISRR), 5
Chile, 211
China, 211
Hong Kong, 212
Macau, 212
Mongolia, 212
Taiwan, 213
Church
congregational directory, 1
The Church of Jesus Christ of Latter-Day Saints,
2, 20, 27, 149, 178
Genealogy Library, (See Family History Center)
classmates, former, search, 25
Classmates.com, 29
CNA, (See Telephone records)
Coast Guard Records,(See Military Records)
Colombia, 214
Colorado, 61
Common names, searching, 10
Comoros, 214
Computer
child snatches by, 17
data bases, 37
search engines, 37
searches (adoption, genealogy, military, etc.), 43
Concerned United Birthparents (CUB), 47, 171
Confidential Intermediary System, 36
confidentiality, privacy, secrecy (definitions of), 37
Congo, 214
Connecticut, (see Preface), 64
Consular Services, 171
Cost of searching, 13
Costa Rica, 215
County Records 2, 6, 7
court order (for adoption information access), 26, 29
Court Records, 3
Credit Bureaus, 8, 9
Croatis, 215
cross-referencing birth/adoptive name. (see Birth Index)

CUB, (see Concerned United Birthparents)
Cuba, 215
Cyprus, 215
Czech Republic, 215
Death Index, (See Social Security)
deceased military. (see Military Records)
Delaware, 67
denied information or records, what to do, 12
Denmark, 216
Department of Motor Vehicles (DM V), 2
driver address verification, 2
Driver's License Compact, 2
drivers' licenses, 2
ID cards, DMV, 2
Directories
as obvious starting point (telephone), 1
Directory of Compilers, Genealogists' Address Book, 20
of International search resources, by country, 169
of U.S. search resources, alphabetical by state, 47
Directory Assistance Operators, Telephone, 1, 3
District of Columbia, 68
Djibouti, 216
DNA Testing, 28
Dominica, 216
Dominican Republic, 217
donor offspring/parent searches, 28
e-mail addresses helpful for search, 46
Ecuador, 217
Egypt, 217
El Salvador, 217
England. (See United Kingdom: England and Wales)
Equatorial Guinea, 218
Eritrea, 218
Estonia, 218
Ethiopia, 219
Facebook.com, 2
Family History Center, 20, 149, 170., (See also
alphabetical country listings: Church: The Church of
Jesus Christ of Latter-day Saints)
family tree, 19
Federal Bureau of Investigation (FBI), 1
(see also NCIC)
federal employee, search for, 12
Federal Parent Locator System, 3
fee waiver, 40
fees, search, 5
Fiji, 219
Finland, 219
first name search, 4
Florida, 71
Foess, Mary Louise, 176
forced abortions, China, 213
forced adoptions, Germany, 226
forwarding address, on obtaining, 1
foster care records access, 30
France, 220
Freedom of Information Act (FOIA)
federal, 4
state, 4
Gabon, 221

Gambia, 221
genealogy search, 19
Genocide
    Argentina, 175
    Armenia, 176
    Germany (Holocaust), 222, 225, 226
Georgia (country of), 221
Georgia (state of), 74
Germany, 222
    regions of, 222
Ghana, 227
Gibraltar, 227
Greece, 227
Grenada, 228
Guam, 164
Guatemala, 228
Guinea, 229
Guinea-Bissau, 229
Guyana, 229
Hague Convention
    on Abduction, Adoption, 173
    reciprocal countries, 173
    U.S. policy, 1 (also page 1 footnote: Pfund Memo)
Hague, The, 173
Haiti, 229
Hawaii, 76
heir search, 26
    heir search business, 25
heritage, 24
Honduras, 230
hospital birth certificate, 6
    index or statistical card, 30
    request with known names or "Baby Girl/Boy," 6
Hungary, 230
Iceland, 231
Idaho, 78
identification of recovered children, 17
Illinois, 81
Immigration and Naturalization Service (INS)
    Immigration records, 23
    Naturalization records 23
index card (hospital), 30 (see also hospital birth certificate)
India, 232
Indian Affairs, Bureau of 23, 28. (See also Native
        American adoptee searches)
Indian, Canadian (adoptees)
    Aborigines, 198
    Broken Trails, 198
Indian research, 23, 28
    Mexico, 28
Indiana, 84
Indonesia, 232
infocide, 1
International Message Bank, 170
International searching
    directory of search resources, alphabetically by country, 169
    "how-to," 170
    Red Cross (and other search international organizations), 170
International Social Services (ISS), 171
International Soundex Registry (ISRR), 5

International Soundex Reunion Registry (ISRR), 5
Interpol, 173
investigators, private, 5
Iowa, 87
Iran, 232
Iraq, 233
Ireland, (Republic of), 233
    (see also United Kingdom: Northern Ireland)
Israel, 234
Italy, 234
Ivory Coast, 236
Jamaica, 236
Japan, 236
Jordan, 237
Kansas, 89
Kazakhstan, 237
Kentucky, 91
Kenya, 237
Kiribati, 238
Korea
    North Korea, 238
    South Korea, 238
Kuwait, 239
Kyrgyzstan, 240
Laos, 240
last name (surname) search, 4
Latvia, 240
Lebanon, 240
Lesotho, 241
Liberia, 241
libraries, public, 1
Libya, 241
Liechtenstein, 241
Lithuania, 242
Litigation Index, 2
Lost Friends, 1
Louisiana, 93
lost loves search, 19
Luxembourg, 242
Macedonia, 242
Madagascar 243
mail carriers, 1
Maine, 95
Malawi, 243
Malaysia, 243
Maldives, 243
Mali, 243
Malta, 244
Marianas Islands, 167
Marianas, Trust Territory of, 167
Marina Islands, Northern, 251
Marine Corps Records   (See Military Records)
Marshall Islands, 244
Maryland, 97
Massachusetts, 99
Mauritania, 244
Mauritius, 244
media access to records, 12
Medic Alert (ISRR emergency search), 4

289

Mexico, 245
Michigan, 102
microfilmed genealogy records, (see Family History Center)
Micronesia, Federated States of, 246
Military Records, 10-11
    Air Force, 11
    Air National Guard, 11
    all branches, 11
    Army, 11
    Army National Guard, 11
    Coast Guard, 11
    Civil War soldiers, 12
    Deceased Military, 12
    Marine Corps, 11
    Military Search by computer, 43
    Navy, 11
    Overseas Brats (children of military families), 171
    Prisoners of War, 12
    Veterans, 12
Minnesota, 105
Missing children, 15
    international, 173
    U.S., 15
Missing persons, 15
Mississippi, 107
Missouri, 108
Moldava, 246
Monaco, 247
Montana, 111
Montenegro, 247
Montserrat, 247
Mormon, (See Church: The Church of Jesus Christ of
    Latter-day Saints)
    Family History Centers, 20
Morocco, 247
Mozambique, 247
Myanmar, 248
MySpace.com, 1
Namibia, 248
names searches, (see With or Without A Name)
National Archives, 2, 21
National Center for Missing and Exploited Children, 15
National Council For Adoption (NCFA), 37
Native American Adoptee Searches, 23, 28
Nauru, 248
Navy Records, (See Military Records)
Nebraska, 113
Nepal, 248
Netherlands, The, 248
Network, Worldwide Search, 5
Nevada, 115
New Hampshire, 117
New Jersey, 118
New Mexico, 120
New York, 122
New Zealand, 249
Nicaragua, 250
Niger, 250
Nigeria, 250
Niue, 251

no name search (see With Or Without A Name)
Non-Custodial Parents (resources for), 34
Non-identifying information (adoption), 29
    Questions for Adoptees, Parents to Ask,
North Carolina, 126
North Dakota, 128
Northern Marina Islands, 251
Norway, 251
Ohio 129
Oklahoma, 131
Oman, 252
open adoption records in the U.S., 26
    in New Zealand, 249
    in Scotland, 279
Opening Records Worldwide, 173
Operation Babylift, 282
Oregon, 133
Overseas Brats (children of Military families), 171,
    (See also Military Records)
Pakistan, 252
Palau, 252
Panama (Republic of), 252
Panama Canal Zone, 165
Papua New Guinea, 253
Paraguay, 253
Passport Services, 12
    for obtaining original birth certificate, 30,
Pennsylvania, 135
Peru, 254
Petition to Adopt, and Final Decree of Adoption, 29
Philippines, 255
physicians' records, obtaining, 10
Poland, 256
police reports, obtaining, 12
Portugal, 258
Prisoners of War (See Military Rcords)
Privacy Act, 42
Private Adoption Agency, 42
prisoner locator, 3
property, unclaimed, 25
Puerto Rico, 165
Qatar, 258
R-CAM, (See Telephone records)
Real Estate Index, 2
Records Types, Selecting, (see chart opposite Page 1)
Red Cross, 170
registries, reunion - private (see by-state listings)
registries, reunion - state operated, 30,
reunions, adoptee-parent, 27
Rhode Island, 138
right to know, 27
Rights of the Child, United Nations,
Romania, 259
runaways (and other missing children), 15
Russia, 261
Rwanda, 263
Salvation Army (Locator Services), 9,
Samoa-Western, 264
San Marino, 264

Sao Tome and Principe, 264
Saudi Arabia, 264
school yearbooks, 4
Scotland (See United Kingdom: Scotland)
sealed records, 26
Search and support groups, code key to listings, 47
Search business, how to start your own 13, 26
SearchGateway.com, 1, 37
search organizationss, private,
    adoption search friendly, (see alphabetical state and
    country listings)
secrecy, confidentiality, privacy, (definitions), 37
semi-public records, 13
Senegal, 265
Serbia, 265
Seychelles, 265
Sierra Leone, 266
Singapore, 266
Slovakia, 266
Slovenia, 267
Social Security
    Social Security Death Index, 4
    Social Security Locator Service (discontinued), 4
    Social Security numbers, 2
Social Services (DSS, Human/Family Services). 3,
    (see also alphabetical country and state listings)
    International, 171
    as Confidential Intermediary, 36
Solomon Islands, 267
Somalia, 267
South Africa, 267
South Carolina, 139
South Dakota, 141
Spain, 268
Sri Lanka, 268
St. Christopher/Nevis, 263
St. Lucia, 263
St. Vincent and the Grenadines, 263
state records, 3
State-by-state listings, (Searching the USA), 47- 161
Sudan, 268
Suriname, 268
surrogacy, 28
Swaziland, 268
Sweden, 269
Switzerland, 269
Syria, 270
Tajikistan, 270
Tanzania, 271
Telephone records, 3
Tennessee, 142
Texas, 145
Thailand, 271
Togo, 271
Tonga, 271
Trinidad and Tobago, 272
Tunisia, 272
Turkey, 272
Turkmenistan, 273
Turks and Caicos Islands, 273

Tuvalu, 273
Uganda, 273
Ukraine, 274
United Arab Emirates, 274
United Kingdom
    England and Wales, 274
    Northern Ireland, 279
    Scotland, 279
Uniform Custody/Parental Kidnap Prevention Act, 16
United Nations Right of the Child Project, 173
United States, Searching the
    directory of resources, alphabetically by
        US possessions and territories, 163
    directory of resources, alphabetically by state, 47
Uruguay, 281
Utah, 148
utility companies (records), 9
Uzbekistan, 281
Vanuatu, 282
Venezuela, 282
Vermont, 150
Vietnam, 282
Vilardi, Emma May and Anthony, 5
Virgin Islands
    St. Croix, 166
    St. Thomas, St. John, 166
Virginia, 152
Vital Records, 24 (See also alphabetical country
    and state listings for central offices of Vital Records
    in capitalist countries, 170
    in socialist countries, 170
Voter Registration (as public records), 3
Wales, (See United Kingdom: England and Wales)
War Babes (England), 274
War Babes Down Under (South Australia), 180
War offspring
    Germany, 224
    Vietnam, 283
Washington (state of), 154
Washington, DC, (See District of Columbia)
websites helpful for search, 24, 37-38
West Virginia, 157
WhitePages.com, 1, 37
Wisconsin, 159
Worldwide Search Network, The, 7
Wyoming, 101
Yemen, 294
Zaire, 286
Zambia, 286
Zimbabwe, 286

ADDENDUM

STATE INVESTIGATOR LICENSING BOARDS
including the 50 States, District of Columbia and Puerto Rico

ALABAMA- There is no state licensing for private investigation agencies in the state of Alabama. You do need a state business license. <http://www.ador.state.al.us/> Check your local county/city rules. Related State Law

ALASKA- At this time there is no P.I. Licensing requirements in Alaska. There is a Process Server Lic. Requirement through Alaska DPS. The only License a P.I. needs in Alaska is a State Business Lic.. Per Fairbanks City Licensing Law

ARIZONA- Dept. of Public Safety, Licensing, Box 6638, Phoenix AZ 85005.Phone:(602) 223-2361
Web Site: http://www.dps.state.az.us/

ARKANSAS- Arkansas Department of Private Investigators and Private Security Agencies
#1 State Police Plaza Dr. Little Rock, Arkansas 72209 Phone (501) 618-8600 Fax: (501) 618-8621
Web Site:http://www.asp.state.ar.us/pl/pl.html; State Law: http://www.azleg.state.az.us/ars/32/title32.htm

CALIFORNIA- Department Of Consumer Affairs, Licensing Division, Bureau of Security and Investigative Services
400 "R" Street, Suite 3040, Sacramento, CA 95814-6200 Phone:(800) 952-5210   (916) 445-1254
Web Site:http://www.dca.ca.gov/bsis/ ; State Law: http://www.dca.ca.gov/bsis/piact.htm

COLORADO- There is no statewide control over a Detective business, nor any bonding requirements.

CONNECTICUT- Dept of Public Safety, Division of State Police,294 Colony St, Meriden CT 06450 Phone (860) 685-8470
Web Site: http://www.state.ct.us/dps/SLFU/PrivateDetectivesHome.htm

DELAWARE- Detective Licensing, Delaware State Police, P. O. Box 430, Dover, DE 19903, (302) 736-5900.
Web Site:http://www.state.de.us/dsp/

DISTRICT OFCOLUMBIA- Security Officers Mgmt Branch, Metro Police, Security Unit 2000, 14th St. NW, Washington, DC 20009. (202) 939-8722; Website: http://mpdc.dc.gov/main.shtm

FLORIDA- Department of Agriculture & Consumer Services, Div of Licensing, Box 6687, Tallahassee FL 32314;
(850) 487-0482; Web Site:http://licgweb.doacs.state.fl.us; Check License: http://licgweb.dos.state.fl.us/access/individual.html
Handbook: http://licgweb.doacs.state.fl.us/investigations/index.html; State Law: http://tinyurl.com/3d935

GEORGIA- State Board of Private Detective and Security Agencies, 237 Coliseum Drive, Macon GA 31217; (478) 207-1460
Web Site: http://www.sos.state.ga.us/plb/detective/default.htm

HAWAII- Department of Commerce & Consumer Affairs, DCCA-PVL, P.O. Box 3469 Honolulu, HI 96801, (808) 586-2701
Email: detective@dcca.hawaii.gov; Website: http://www.hawaii.gov/dcca/pvl/areas_private_detective.html
State Law: http://www.hawaii.gov/dcca/hrs/index.html

IDAHO- There is no Licensing Regulatory Agency in the state of Idaho.

ILLINOIS- Illinois Department of Professional Regulation, 320 West Washington St, 3rd Fl, Springfield, IL 62786;
(217)785-0800; Website: http://www.ildpr.com/WHO/dtct.asp; State Law: http://tinyurl.com/4ls6l

INDIANA- Indiana Professional Licensing Agency, (Att: Private Detectives Licensing Board), 302 W. Washington Street, Rm E034; Indianapolis, Indiana 46204; Staff Phone Number: (317) 234-3040 Staff email: pla11@pla.state.in.us
Website: http://www.in.gov/pla/bandc/detective/ State Law: http://www.in.gov/legislative/ic/code/title25/ar30/

IOWA- Administrative Services Div., Iowa Dept of Public Safety, Wallace State Office Bldg, Des Moines, IA 50319.;
(515) 281-3211; State Law: http://www.state.ia.us/government/dps/iowacode/cd9780a.htm

KANSAS- Bureau of Investigation, 1620 SW Tyler, Topeka KS 66612, Phone (785) 296-8200
Email link: http://www.accesskansas.org/kbi/email.shtml: Website: http://www.accesskansas.org/kbi/

KENTUCKY- Kentucky Board of Licensure for Private Investigators, Box 1360, Frankfort KY 40601; (502) 564-3296 ext. 239
Email: Lisa.Shelley@ky.gov; Website: http://occupations.ky.gov/privateinvestigators/
Kentucky Private Investigative License Law: http://24.145.211.47/kpia/legislation.htm

LOUISIANA- Board of Private Investigators Examiners 2051 Silverside Dr, Ste 190, Baton Rouge, LA 70808; (225) 763-3556
Web site: http://www.lsbpie.com Email: lsbpie@intersurf.com

MAINE- Dept of Public Safety, Licensing & Inspection Unit, 164 State House Station, Augusta, ME 04333, (207) 624-8775
Website: http://www.state.me.us/dps/

MARYLAND- Maryland State Police, PI Licensing Division, 7751 Washington Blvd., Jessup MD 20794, (410) 799-0191;
(800) 525-5555; Website: http://www.mdsp.maryland.gov/mdsp/default.asp

MASSACHUSETTS- Massachusetts State Police, Special Licensing Unit, 20 Somerset St., Boston, MA 02108,(617)727-6128,
Website: http://www.mass.gov/msp/massachu.htm State Private Investigator Law;
http://www.mass.gov/legis/laws/mgl/147-22.htm

MICHIGAN- Private Security and Investigator Unit,7150 Harris Drive, Lansing, MI 48913 Phone (517) 322-1966
Department of Consumer & Industry Services, Licensing Division--Private Detectives, Box 30018, Lansing MI 48909
Phone:(517) 241-5645; (517) 373-9808; Website: http://www.michigan.gov/cis/0,1607,7-154-10557_12992_21297---,00.html

MINNESOTA- Board of Private Detective & Protective Agent Services, 1430 Maryland Avenue East, St. Paul MN 55106;
(651)793-2666; Website: http://www.dps.state.mn.us/pdb/ Email: mn.pdb@state.mn.us;
State Private Investigator Licensing Law: http://www.revisor.leg.state.mn.us/arule/7506/

MISSISSIPPI- None

MISSOURI- None

MONTANA- Board of Private Security Officers & Investigators, 301 South Park, Rm 430 , Box 200513, Helena MT 59620;
(406) 841-2300; Website: http://www.discoveringmontana.com/dli/bsd/license/bsd_boards/psp_board/board_page.asp

NEBRASKA- Secretary of State, Ste 2300 State Capitol, Lincoln, NE 68509. (402) 471-2554.
Web Site: http://www.sos.state.ne.us/Privatedetectives/pd.htm:
State Law: http://www.sos.state.ne.us/Privatedetectives/pdregs.htm

NEVADA- Private Investigator's Licensing Board, 100 N. Carson Street, Carson City, NV 89701-4717, (775) 687-3223
Website: http://ag.state.nv.us/faqs/workingaspi.htm; State Law: http://www.leg.state.nv.us/NAC/NAC-648.html

NEW HAMPSHIRE- State Police, Div of Licenses & Permits, 10 Hazen Drive, Rm 106, Concord NH 03305 (603) 271-3575
Website: http://www.nh.gov/safety/nhsp/pluda.html

NEW JERSEY- State Police, Dept of Law & Public Safety, Private Detective Unit, PO Box 7068, W. Trenton, NJ 08688-0068.
(609) 882-2000; Website: http://www.state.nj.us/lps/njsp/about/srb.html#pdu
Rules: http://www.state.nj.us/lps/njsp/about/pdet_rules.html

NEW MEXICO- Private Investigator & Polygraph Board, 2550 Cerrillos Rd, P.O. Box 25101, Santa Fe, NM 87504-5101;
(505) 476-4650; Website: http://www.rld.state.nm.us/b&c/pipolygraph/index.htm

NEW YORK- New York State Department of State, Division of Licensing Services, 84 Holland Ave, Albany, NY 12208-3490
E-mail: licensing@dos.state.ny.us ; (518) 474-4429; Web Site: http://appsext5.dos.state.ny.us/lcns_public/chk_load

NORTH CAROLINA- North Carolina Dept of Justice, Private Protective Services,1631 Midtown Pl, Ste 104, Raleigh, NC
27609; (919) 716-6400; Web Site: http://www.ncdoj.com/law_enforcement/cle_pps.jsp
State Private Investigator Law: http://tinyurl.com/3jvqy

NORTH DAKOTA- North Dakota Private Investigation & Security Board, 513 Bismarck Expressway, Ste 5. Bismarck, ND 58504; (701) 222-3063; Email: ndpisb@midco.net:; Website: http://www.state.nd.us/pisb/ ; Licensing Law: http://www.state.nd.us/pisb/elig.html

OHIO- Ohio Dept of Commerce, Division of Professional Licensing, 77 South High Street, 20th Floor, Columbus, OH 43215-6133, (614) 466-4100, (614) 466-4130; Email: REPLD@com.state.oh.us Website: http://www.com.state.oh.us/odoc/real/pisgmain.htm

OKLAHOMA- Council on Law enforcement Education & Training, PO Box 11476, Oklahoma City, OK 73136 Phone (405) 425-2775; Website: http://www.cleet.state.ok.us/Private_Security.htm State Law: http://oklegal.onenet.net/oklegal-cgi/get_statute?98/Title.59/59-1750.1.html

OREGON- Board of Investigators, 445 State Office Bldg, 800 NE Oregon St #33, Portland OR 97232; (503) 731-4359; Email: pi.board@state.or.us; Website: http://www.obi.state.or.us/ ; Laws And Rules: http://www.obi.state.or.us/LawsandRules/LandR.htm

PENNSYLVANIA- No state licensing--done on the county by county level.

PUERTO RICO- Police, GPO Box 70166, San Juan, PR 00936. (809) 781-0227

RHODE ISLAND- Licensed by each city and town by state law.

SOUTH CAROLINA- South Carolina Law Enforcement Div , PO Box 21398, Columbia, SC 29221-1398; (803) 896-7014 Website: http://www.sled.state.sc.us/default.htm: State Law: http://www.lpitr.state.sc.us/bil95-96/507.htm

SOUTH DAKOTA- No state license required. Some cities and towns require a license.

TENNESSEE- Private Protective Services Div., Dept of Commerce & Insurance, 500 James Robertson Pkwy, Nashville, TN 37243-1158. (615) 741-6382; Email: donna.hancock@state.tn.us Website: http://www.state.tn.us/commerce/boards/pi/index.html

TEXAS- Texas Commission On Private Security, 4616 Howard Lane #140, Austin, Texas 78728; 512-238-5858 Board of Private Investigators & Private Security Agencies, P. O. Box 13509, Capitol Station, Austin, TX Website: http://hera.tcps.state.tx.us/ ; Law: http://www.tcps.state.tx.us/pi.aspx

UTAH- Dept of Public Safety, Bureau of Criminal Identification, 3888 West 5400 South, Box 148280, Salt Lake City, UT 84114-8280; 801-965-4445 Website: http://www.bci.utah.gov/BailPI/PIHome.html State Law: http://www.le.state.ut.us/~code/TITLE53/53_09.htm

VERMONT- Board of Private Investigative & Armed Security Services, Office of Professional Regulation, 109 State St., Montpelier, VT 05609-1101; (802) 828-2837. Email: pskinner@sec.state.vt.us Website: http://vtprofessionals.org/opr1/investigators/ Law: http://www.leg.state.vt.us/statutes/fullchapter.cfm?Title=26&Chapter=059

VIRGINIA- Department of Criminal Justice Services, Private Security Section, Box 10110, Richmond VA 2324; (804) 786-4700 Website: http://www.dcjs.virginia.gov/privatesecurity/index.cfm

WASHINGTON- Department of Licensing , Master License Service , PO Box 9034, Olympia, WA 98507-9034 Web site: http://www.dol.wa.gov/ppu/pifront.htm Email: Security@dol.wa.gov State law requirements: http://www.dol.wa.gov/ppu/pireqmnt.htm

WEST VIRGINIA- Secretary of State, Private Investigator Licensing Division, Secretary of State Bldg. 1, Ste 157-K 1900 Kanawha Blvd. East, Charleston, WV 25305-0770; (304) 558-6000; Email: licensing@wvsos.com Website: http://www.wvsos.com/licensing/piguard/main.htm

WISCONSIN- Department of Regulation and Licensing, PO Box 8935 Madison, WI 53708-8935; (608) 266-5511; Website: http://www.drl.state.wi.us/Regulation/

CPSIA information can be obtained at www.ICGtesting.com
Printed in the USA
LVOW031201290212

270877LV00002B/4/P

461 S1 FM 8756
07/02/12 33529 MC

9 780806 355153

NCR

7-12